Researching Online FOR DUMMIES® 2ND EDITION

by Reva Basch and Mary Ellen Bates

IDG Books Worldwide, Inc.
An International Data Group Company

Foster City, CA ◆ Chicago, IL ◆ Indianapolis, IN ◆ New York, NY

Researching Online For Dummies® 2nd Edition

Published by
IDG Books Worldwide, Inc.
An International Data Group Company
919 E. Hillsdale Blvd.
Suite 400
Foster City, CA 94404
www.idgbooks.com (IDG Books Worldwide Web site)
www.dummies.com (Dummies Press Web site)

Library of Congress Catalog Card No.: 99-69375

ISBN: 0-7645-0546-7

Printed in the United States of America

10 9 8 7 6 5 4 3 2 1

2B/RQ/QS/QQ/IN

Distributed in the United States by IDG Books Worldwide, Inc.

Distributed by CDG Books Canada Inc. for Canada; by Transworld Publishers Limited in the United Kingdom; by IDG Norge Books for Norway; by IDG Sweden Books for Sweden; by IDG Books Australia Publishing Corporation Pty. Ltd. for Australia and New Zealand; by TransQuest Publishers Pte Ltd. for Singapore, Malaysia, Thailand, Indonesia, and Hong Kong; by Gotop Information Inc. for Taiwan; by ICG Muse, Inc. for Japan; by Intersoft for South Africa; by Eyrolles for France; by International Thomson Publishing for Germany, Austria and Switzerland; by Distribuidora Cuspide for Argentina; by LR International for Brazil; by Galileo Libros for Chile; by Ediciones ZETA S.C.R. Ltda. for Peru; by WS Computer Publishing Corporation, Inc., for the Philippines; by Contemporanea de Ediciones for Venezuela; by Express Computer Distributors for the Caribbean and West Indies; by Micronesia Media Distributor, Inc. for Micronesia; by Chips Computadoras S.A. de C.V. for Mexico; by Editorial Norma de Panama S.A. for Panama; by American Bookshops for Finland.

For general information on IDG Books Worldwide's books in the U.S., please call our Consumer Customer Service department at 800-762-2974. For reseller information, including discounts and premium sales, please call our Reseller Customer Service department at 800-434-3422.

For information on where to purchase IDG Books Worldwide's books outside the U.S., please contact our International Sales department at 317-596-5530 or fax 317-572-4002.

For consumer information on foreign language translations, please contact our Customer Service department at 1-800-434-3422, fax 317-572-4002, or e-mail rights@idgbooks.com.

For information on licensing foreign or domestic rights, please phone +1-650-653-7098.

For sales inquiries and special prices for bulk quantities, please contact our Sales department at 800-762-2974 or write to the address above.

For information on using IDG Books Worldwide's books in the classroom or for ordering examination copies, please contact our Educational Sales department at 800-434-2086 or fax 317-572-4005.

For press review copies, author interviews, or other publicity information, please contact our Public Relations department at 650-653-7000 or fax 650-653-7500.

For authorization to photocopy items for corporate, personal, or educational use, please contact Copyright Clearance Center, 222 Rosewood Drive, Danvers, MA 01923, or fax 978-750-4470.

About the Authors

Reva Basch is a writer, editor, and consultant to the online industry. She operated her own online research business for more than 10 years. Before that, she was vice president and director of research at Information on Demand, a pioneering independent research company in Berkeley, California. She is a frequent speaker on online-related topics and has keynoted at conferences in the U.S. and throughout the world. She writes the *Reva's (W)rap* column for *Online* magazine and contributes to several other publications, including *EContent, Searcher* and *Information Today.* She has written three other books, including *Secrets of the Super Net Searchers* (1996), and *Secrets of the Super Searchers* (1993). Reva is executive editor of the Super Searchers book series published by Information Today, Inc. and has edited and contributed chapters, introductions, and interviews to several other books about the Internet and information retrieval.

Reva was the subject of a profile in *WIRED* magazine, which called her "the ultimate intelligent agent." She is a past president of the Association of Independent Information Professionals. She has a degree in English Literature, *summa cum laude,* from the University of Pennsylvania, and a Masters degree in Library Science from the University of California at Berkeley. She began her career as a corporate librarian, and has been online since the mid-1970s. She logs off occasionally to eat, sleep, and perform other essential functions. She is an active participant in The WELL, one of the earliest online communities, and has hosted several conferences there. She lives on the rugged northern California coast with her husband, Jerry Shifman, their three differently-specied children, Abbie, Flash, and Tigray; and a 6,300-watt generator for when the power goes out but the work must go on.

Mary Ellen Bates is an online researcher and writer. She runs Bates Information Services, providing custom research for business professionals and corporate librarians. Before starting her business in 1992, she worked in corporate and legal libraries for nearly 15 years. Mary Ellen is a frequent speaker on the information industry throughout the U.S. and abroad. She contributes the *Bates' Back Page* column to *EContent* magazine, is the contributing editor of *Information Advisor,* and a regular contributor to other information industry publications. She is the author of *The Online Deskbook* (Information Today, 1996), and *Super Searchers Do Business: the Online Secrets of Top Business Researchers* (Information Today, 1999).

She is a past president of the Association of Independent Information Professionals and an active member of the Special Libraries Association. She has a degree in Philosophy from the University of California, Santa Barbara and a Masters degree in Library and Information Science from the University of California, Berkeley. She has been an online researcher for more than 20 years, spends more time online than off, and still has keypunch cards around the house. She lives in Washington, D.C. with her companion and her dog and is a long-distance runner when she's not online.

ABOUT IDG BOOKS WORLDWIDE

Welcome to the world of IDG Books Worldwide.

IDG Books Worldwide, Inc., is a subsidiary of International Data Group, the world's largest publisher of computer-related information and the leading global provider of information services on information technology. IDG was founded more than 30 years ago by Patrick J. McGovern and now employs more than 9,000 people worldwide. IDG publishes more than 290 computer publications in over 75 countries. More than 90 million people read one or more IDG publications each month.

Launched in 1990, IDG Books Worldwide is today the #1 publisher of best-selling computer books in the United States. We are proud to have received eight awards from the Computer Press Association in recognition of editorial excellence and three from Computer Currents' First Annual Readers' Choice Awards. Our best-selling ...*For Dummies*® series has more than 50 million copies in print with translations in 31 languages. IDG Books Worldwide, through a joint venture with IDG's Hi-Tech Beijing, became the first U.S. publisher to publish a computer book in the People's Republic of China. In record time, IDG Books Worldwide has become the first choice for millions of readers around the world who want to learn how to better manage their businesses.

Our mission is simple: Every one of our books is designed to bring extra value and skill-building instructions to the reader. Our books are written by experts who understand and care about our readers. The knowledge base of our editorial staff comes from years of experience in publishing, education, and journalism — experience we use to produce books to carry us into the new millennium. In short, we care about books, so we attract the best people. We devote special attention to details such as audience, interior design, use of icons, and illustrations. And because we use an efficient process of authoring, editing, and desktop publishing our books electronically, we can spend more time ensuring superior content and less time on the technicalities of making books.

You can count on our commitment to deliver high-quality books at competitive prices on topics you want to read about. At IDG Books Worldwide, we continue in the IDG tradition of delivering quality for more than 30 years. You'll find no better book on a subject than one from IDG Books Worldwide.

John Kilcullen
Chairman and CEO
IDG Books Worldwide, Inc.

Eighth Annual Computer Press Awards ≥1992

Ninth Annual Computer Press Awards ≥1993

Tenth Annual Computer Press Awards ≥1994

Eleventh Annual Computer Press Awards ≥1995

Acknowledgments and Dedication

This is where I get to play out my Academy Awards fantasy, thanking everyone who's helped me in any way with this book. The list is a long one, and I can't possibly single out every person who inspired me or provided practical or emotional support. But I must acknowledge Barbara Bernstein and the late Sue Rugge, who first hired me as a freelance researcher, taught me how to do it right, and got me started on my own career as an independent information professional. Thanks, too, to my colleagues in the Association of Independent Information Professionals, who add to my store of knowledge on a daily basis, and especially to Mary Ellen Bates, who made collaboration on this book a joy. My friends and neighbors Janet Hubbard, Rich Kuehn, and Dean Schuler went far beyond my expectations in sharing their favorite online starting points, and my colleague Susan Detwiler contributed valuable advice on medical and healthcare resources. Thanks to all of them, and to my WELL pals who reacted with alacrity, wit, and their usual stunning expertise to my repeated requests for reality-checking that usually began with the phrase, "Would it make sense to say . . . ?" Most of all, I thank Jerry Shifman for the grace with which he shouldered the household and relationship responsibilities yet once more while I worked, glassy-eyed, on completing this project. I owe you big time, Jer — and I dedicate this book to you, with my love and gratitude.

— Reva Basch

For starters, I owe many thanks to Reva for trusting me to update her work. I know how hard it is to let someone else tweak one's words. I hope I've been gentle. By my count, this is the fifth book we've collaborated on in some way, and I have to say they've all been fun. Many thanks to Alex Kramer, who kept me to my running schedule and reminded me that it *is* possible to run a business and still have a life. Even more thanks to my wonderful parents, Flo and Pete Bates, who are enthusiastic and unflagging supporters of everything I undertake, and to my siblings, Amy, Sarah and Russ. And most of all, thanks to Dave and Lucy, both of whom put up with my virtual departure from home while this edition of the book was being written. I'm back now and you can look forward to longer walks and home-cooked meals for a change. Thanks for waiting.

— Mary Ellen Bates

Publisher's Acknowledgments

We're proud of this book; please register your comments through our IDG Books Worldwide Online Registration Form located at http://my2cents.dummies.com.

Some of the people who helped bring this book to market include the following:

Acquisitions, Editorial, and Media Development

Project Editor: Nate Holdread

   (Previous Edition: Bill Helling)

Acquisitions Editor: Laura Moss

Copy Editors: Kim Darosett, Christine Berman, Jeremy Zucker

Technical Editor: Andrew W. Wing

Media Development Editor: Megan Decraene

Associate Permissions Editor: Carmen Krikorian

Media Development Coordinator: Eddie Kominowski

Editorial Manager: Leah P. Cameron

Media Development Manager: Heather Heath Dismore

Editorial Assistant: Beth Parlon

Production

Project Coordinator: Maridee V. Ennis

Layout and Graphics: Joe Bucki, Brian Drumm, Tracy K. Oliver, Jill Piscitelli, Anna Rohrer, Brent Savage, Jacque Schneider, Brian Torwelle, Dan Whetstine, Erin Zeltner

Proofreaders: Laura Albert, Corey Bowen, Vickie Broyles, John Greenough, Marianne Santy, Toni Settle, Ethel Winslow

Indexer: Sharon Duffy

Special Help

   Publication Services, Teresa Artman

General and Administrative

IDG Books Worldwide, Inc.: John Kilcullen, CEO

IDG Books Technology Publishing Group: Richard Swadley, Senior Vice President and Publisher; Walter Bruce III, Vice President and Associate Publisher; Joseph Wikert, Associate Publisher; Mary Bednarek, Branded Product Development Director; Mary Corder, Editorial Director; Barry Pruett, Publishing Manager; Michelle Baxter, Publishing Manager

IDG Books Consumer Publishing Group: Roland Elgey, Senior Vice President and Publisher; Kathleen A. Welton, Vice President and Publisher; Kevin Thornton, Acquisitions Manager; Kristin A. Cocks, Editorial Director

IDG Books Internet Publishing Group: Brenda McLaughlin, Senior Vice President and Publisher; Diane Graves Steele, Vice President and Associate Publisher; Sofia Marchant, Online Marketing Manager

IDG Books Production for Dummies Press: Debbie Stailey, Associate Director of Production; Cindy L. Phipps, Manager of Project Coordination, Production Proofreading, and Indexing; Tony Augsburger, Manager of Prepress, Reprints, and Systems; Laura Carpenter, Production Control Manager; Shelley Lea, Supervisor of Graphics and Design; Debbie J. Gates, Production Systems Specialist; Robert Springer, Supervisor of Proofreading; Kathie Schutte, Production Supervisor

Dummies Packaging and Book Design: Patty Page, Manager, Promotions Marketing

◆

The publisher would like to give special thanks to Patrick J. McGovern, without whom this book would not have been possible.

◆

Contents at a Glance

Introduction 1

Part I: Getting Started 9
Chapter 1: The Many Faces of Online 11
Chapter 2: Thinking and Working Like a Researcher................................17

Part II: The Tools of the Trade 41
Chapter 3: The Search Engine Sweepstakes 43
Chapter 4: Using Specialty Search Engines 57
Chapter 5: Subject Catalogs: The Narrow-Down Approach 71
Chapter 6: Playing the Links: Guru Pages and Mega-Sites 81
Chapter 7: Ready Reference: Finding Facts Fast 89
Chapter 8: Visiting Libraries Online 99
Chapter 9: Knock, Knock: Gated Information Services 115
Chapter 10: The Personal Touch 149

Part III: Putting It All Together 167
Chapter 11: Strange New Worlds: Government, Medical, and
  Sci-Tech Research 169
Chapter 12: Strictly Business 193
Chapter 13: Read All About It: News Media and Publications Online 227
Chapter 14: Life Choices..247
Chapter 15: Recreational Research: Hobbies and Interests........................265

The Researching Online For Dummies, 2nd Edition
Internet Directory...D-1

Part IV: The Broader Picture..................................275
Chapter 16: Keeping Up with the Online Jones(es) 277
Chapter 17: The Big Issues: Copyright, Information Use, and Quality 285

Part V: The Part of Tens 299
Chapter 18: Ten Clarifying Questions for Better Research Results 301
Chapter 19: Ten Simple Tune-Ups for Streamlined Searching 309
Chapter 20: Ten Trends to Keep an Eye On 321

Appendix: About the CD 325

Index 335

IDG Books Worldwide End-User License Agreement.....353

Installation Instructions 356

Book Registration Information.....................Back of Book

Cartoons at a Glance

By Rich Tennant

page 275

page 41

page D-1

page 167

page 299

page 9

Fax: 978-546-7747
E-mail: richtennant@the5thwave.com
World Wide Web: www.the5thwave.com

Table of Contents

Introduction *1*

What Librarians Know 1

Searching versus Surfing 2

What Makes a Good Researcher? 2

What We Know About You 3

How This Book Is Organized 3

    Part I: Getting Started 4

    Part II: The Tools of the Trade 4

    Part III: Putting It All Together 4

    Part IV: The Broader Picture 5

    Part V: The Part of Tens 5

Conventions and Icons Used in This Book 5

What's New in the Second Edition 6

One More Thing 7

Part I: Getting Started *9*

Chapter 1: The Many Faces of Online 11

The Online World: Library, Bookstore, or Shopping Mall after an
    Earthquake? 11

The Net beneath the Web 12

    Gopher it! 13

    Telnetting around 14

Gated, Not Open; Fee, Not Free 14

    Probing professional online services 15

    Members-only Web sites 15

The Human Side of the Net 16

Chapter 2: Thinking and Working Like a Researcher 17

Reference-Interviewing Yourself 18

Where Do You Start? 19

    Mental-mapping your online resources 20

    Reality-checking 24

When Bad Things Happen to Good Searchers 25

    Yikes, 42,178 hits! What do I do now? 26

    Waah! How come I didn't get anything? 27

    Why on earth did I get THIS? 27

    Evaluating what you get 28

Boolean (And Other) Basics 29
    Boolean searching...29
    Proximity operators 33
    Field searching..35
    Pluralization, truncation, and wild cards 36
    Case-sensitivity..38
Knowing When You're Done 39
Using What You Find 40

Part II: The Tools of the Trade 41

Chapter 3: The Search Engine Sweepstakes 43
Timeless Tips for Effective Searching 44
What to Consider When Choosing a Search Engine 45
Exploring General Search Engines 46
    AltaVista 46
    Excite..47
    GO Network 48
    HotBot 49
    Northern Light 50
Making Your Mark with Meta-Engines 52
    Inference Find 53
    SavvySearch 53
    The BigHub.com 53
    Ask Jeeves 54
    Invisible Web...54
    Dogpile 54
The Offline Meta Alternatives..55
    Copernic 55
    BullsEye 56
    Sherlock 56
Watching the Web with Search Engine Watch and Showdown................56

Chapter 4: Using Specialty Search Engines 57
The All-in-One Search Page...57
Search.com...58
Beaucoup Search Engines 58
Searching Newsgroups with RemarQ 58
Pinpointing People..60
    Yahoo!-ing friends and family......................................60
    Plugging into Switchboard 62
Some Tips for People-Finding...62
    The problem with e-mail listings 62
    They're not listed — now what?..................................63

Locating Businesses 63
Finding firms with BigBook 64
Getting info from infoUSA 65
Going global with WorldPages 66
Questing for Maps with MapQuest 67
Shopping for Software with Shareware.com and Download.com 69
Finding freebies at Shareware.com 69
Browsing at Download.com 70

Chapter 5: Subject Catalogs: The Narrow-Down Approach **71**
Narrowing Your Search: The Drill-Down Drill 71
Subject Catalogs versus Search Engines 72
Hybrid Subject Catalogs 73
Getting a hole-in-one with Yahoo! 73
AltaVista's views of the Web 75
Excite-ing possibilities 75
GO seek and ye shall find 76
Pure Subject Catalogs 77
World Wide Web Virtual Library 77
Argus Clearinghouse 78
About.com 79

Chapter 6: Playing the Links: Guru Pages and Mega-Sites **81**
Tapping Into the Contributions of Others 82
Guru Pages: Experts, Enthusiasts, and Obsessives 83
Mega-Sites: Stepping through the Gateway 84
The librarian's guide to everything 84
The joys of jurisprudence 85

Chapter 7: Ready Reference: Finding Facts Fast **89**
Reference: Research Light 89
Virtual Reference Collections 90
Internet Public Library 91
The Virtual Reference Desk 92
Research-It! 92
The Yahoo! Reference Collection 94
Becoming a Reference Ace 94
Hitting (A Few of) the Books 94
The World Factbook 95
Encyclopedia Britannica 95
Roget's Thesaurus 96
Random Reference Goodies 96
How Things Work 97
New area code lookup 97
This day in history 97

Chapter 8: Visiting Libraries Online 99

Libraries: Alive and Thriving Online....................................99
Finding Web-based Library Catalogs 100
    Using WebCATS...101
    Thinking locally 102
Looking at the Library of Congress 103
Telnetting to OPACs 104
    Hytelnetting around 105
    A short side trip to Malaysia.................................105
So It's in the Online Catalog; How Do I Get It? 106
    The ins and outs of ILL 107
    Buying instead of borrowing................................107
    Xerox is not a verb: Requesting article photocopies 108
    Document delivery services 108
The Delights of Digital Libraries..110
    SunSITE: The digital library mother lode...............111
    The American Memory Project 112
    Images from the History of Medicine....................113

Chapter 9: Knock, Knock: Gated Information Services 115

Getting Acquainted with Gated Sites....................................116
Sampling Members-Only Web Sites 117
    The New York Times on the Web 118
    The Wall Street Journal Interactive Edition 119
    Ei Village 120
Consumer Goods: America Online and CompuServe...............121
    America Online 122
    CompuServe...124
Calling in the Pros: Going Wide and Deep with Professional
  Online Services 125
    Some prose on the pros of the pros.......................126
    Dealing with database depth 127
The OTHER Online: Dow Jones, Dialog, LEXIS-NEXIS, and More 128
    Beating the averages with Dow Jones Interactive....129
    Shopping at Dialog's supermarket 132
    Learning the ways of LEXIS-NEXIS.........................141
    Getting it wholesale..143
Web Search Engines Turn Pro 145
    Looking up Northern Light....................................145
    Browsing the Electric Library................................146
    Power up with Powerize.......................................146
How Do You Choose?...146
One Final Point 148

Chapter 10: The Personal Touch **149**

The Human Side of the Net 149

Where Do the Experts Hang Out Online? 150

Newsgroups 150

　Browsing newsgroups with Liszt 151

　Finding newsgroups with RemarQ 153

　Reading newsgroup posts 154

　Taking the temperature of a newsgroup 155

　Before you post: The FAQs of life 155

　Aunt Netty-Quette's priceless pointers for painless posting 156

Mailing Lists 157

　Locating lists with Liszt 158

　Tile.net and the List of Lists 159

　Netiquette revisited 160

　Dealing with info- and subscription-bots 160

Virtual Villages and Conferencing Systems 161

　Exploring virtual communities on the Web 162

　Finding community online 163

Taking It to E-Mail 163

Caveats and Cautions (Dealing with Human Nature) 164

　From the horse's mouth? 164

　The (low) signal to noise ratio 165

　Flame wars 165

　Overload 166

Part III: Putting It All Together *167*

Chapter 11: Strange New Worlds: Government, Medical, and Sci-Tech Research **169**

We're from the Government, and We're Here to Help You 170

　Mastering the info-maze with FedWorld 171

　Life beyond FedWorld 173

In Sickness and in Health 177

　Tapping the medical literature with Medline 177

　Exploring other medical information sources 179

　Seeking support for medical problems online 181

Mere Technicalities 181

　Knowing where to start 182

　What about patents? 185

　Satisfying your scientific curiosity 189

Chapter 12: Strictly Business **193**

Understanding Business Research 194

Getting a Company Backgrounder 194

　Strategizing a background search 195

　Company directories and packaged reports 196

Tapping company and industry news sources...............................200
Broadening your company background search 201
Planning a Competitive Intelligence Operation.................................202
Using a company's Web site..203
Finding alternatives to the annual report 205
Getting informed analysis 205
Monitoring the news 207
The indirect approach 209
Doing Market Research 210
Surveying sources for market research reports...........................211
Getting more for your money with secondary sources................213
Prospecting for Sales 218
Looking for prospects with CompaniesOnline 219
The Dun's-on-the-Web alternative 219
Investigating Investments 220
Ask EDGAR 221
Taking stock 221
Digging deeper 223
Getting personal 223
How Do You Manage? 224

Chapter 13: Read All About It: News Media and Publications Online **227**

Broadcast News...228
Tuning in to the Big Four: ABC, CBS, NBC, and CNN 229
Viewing some other contendahs: Fox and C-SPAN.....................230
Getting the story worldwide 230
News AND weather and sports 230
Newspapers Online...231
Finding your local paper online...232
Searching newspapers on the Web 233
Going deeper into the archives, part 1 234
I Saw It in the Dentist's Office: Magazines Online 236
Locating magazines online 237
Going deeper into the archives, part 2 239
Staying Current...241
The Daily Brief 242
In-Box Direct..242
NewsPage 243
NewsHound 243
Northern Light Search Alert...243
My Yahoo!..244
Other news channels 244
The 'Zine Scene: New Sources for News and Information 245

Chapter 14: Life Choices 247
   Choosing a College. 247
      Finding college and university directories. 248
      Following professional pointers 248
      What's up, pre-doc?. 250
      Feeling listless? 251
      Lessons learned 251
   Finding a Job. 252
      Job boards 253
      Going to the source 255
   Buying a Car. 255
      Browsing car and consumer magazines 256
      Getting serious. 257
      Asking around 258
      Doing the deal 258
      Lessons learned, continued 259
   Planning a Vacation. 259
      Cruising through newsgroups. 261
      Shipping out 262
      We be jammin'. 262
      Travel is broadening 263
      Lessons learned, continued some more. 263

Chapter 15: Recreational Research: Hobbies and Interests 265
   What's Cooking? 266
   Lights, Camera . . . Research. 267
   Playing the Keyboard 270
      Yahoo!ing it. 270
      Shop 'til you bop 271
      Musical true confessions 272
   Indoor Birding. 273
   Doing It Yourself 274

The Researching Online For Dummies, 2nd Edition
Internet Directory *D-1*

Part IV: The Broader Picture *275*

Chapter 16: Keeping Up with the Online Jones(es) 277
   Help Is in the Mail: Electronic Resources. 278
      Netsurfer Digest. 278
      Net-happenings 279
      NEW-LIST 279
      Seidman's Online Insider 280
      Edupage and NewsScan 280
      The Rapidly Changing Face of Computing 281
      Search Engine Report. 281

Remember Paper? — Print Resources 282
System-specific newsletters 282
Independent publications 283
Human Resources 284

Chapter 17: The Big Issues: Copyright, Information Use, and Quality 285

Getting Right with Copyright 286
Fair use 286
Confusion, copyright, and the Net 287
Copyright and the professional online services 288
Copyright and the Web 288
Using Information Responsibly 290
Hopping along the audit trail 290
YOYOW: You own your own words 291
Thinking about Linking 291
Assessing Information Quality 292
Judging quality and reliability on the Net 293
Establishing expertise 295
Thinking critically 296

Part V: The Part of Tens *299*

Chapter 18: Ten Clarifying Questions for Better Research Results . . .301

What Am I Trying to Accomplish? 302
What Is This Really Worth? 302
What Else Should I Consider? 303
Am I Likely to Find My Answers Online? 304
Is Online the Best Place to Look? 304
What's My Plan? 305
Who's Likely to Know the Answer? 305
What Have I Gathered So Far? 306
What Have I Overlooked? 306
How Do I Know the Information Is Good? 307

Chapter 19: Ten Simple Tune-Ups for Streamlined Searching 309

Change Your Start Page 309
Bookmark Your Favorite Web Pages 311
Fight Link Rot 313
Turn Images Off 314
Have a Cookie 315
Don't Just Sit There 317

Pay Attention 318
Resist Temptation 319
Aggregation, Not Aggravation 319
Share Your Toys..320

Chapter 20: Ten Trends to Keep an Eye On 321

Smarter Search Engines 321
Intelligent Info-Bots..322
Online Everywhere...322
Personal Programming...322
Ultra-Personal Programming 322
Virtual Environments...323
Fatter Pipes 323
Looking Forward to the Past 323
Internet Backlash?..324
A Hiccup in the Continuum...324

Appendix: About the CD 325

System Requirements 325
Using the CD with Microsoft Windows...........................325
Using the CD with a Mac OS..326
What You Get on the CD..327
Research help 327
Research tools 328
Internet tools..329
Utilities...330
Knowing the Difference between Freeware and Shareware 331
Using the Internet Directory Links 332
If You've Got Problems (Of the CD Kind) 333

Index..335

IDG Books Worldwide End-User License Agreement......353

Installation Instructions..356

Book Registration Information ....Back of Book

Introduction

· ·

*W*ay back in the dark ages of the online realm — around 1992 or so — *research* was something associated with scientists in white lab coats, scholars in book-filled libraries, and eager librarians helping the public from behind their reference desks. Thanks to the rise of the Internet, and particularly the Web, research has taken on a different meaning. It's a do-it-yourself project now. Research has acquired an aura of hipness, the same way that computer geeks, with their taped-together eyeglasses and plastic pocket protectors, are now considered cool.

You can be your own researcher. Oh joy. Or can you? On one level, the answer is a definite *yes*. The Net has empowered you, given you the tools you need to find information and make decisions, large and small, about your life. It has eliminated the middleman. It has done away with the need to wait in line, whether at the public library or in voice-mail limbo, until it's *your* turn to have your questions answered. The Net has given you instant research gratification — assuming, that is, that you can actually *find* what you're looking for online. That's where this book comes in.

What Librarians Know

In eliminating the middleman, whether librarian or other research professional, we've cut ourselves off from a lot of valuable expertise. Librarians know how the world of human knowledge is organized, from broad disciplines like humanities and social sciences down to the most minute fact. That means that they know where to start looking for information instead of floundering around in a sea of possibilities. It's like the difference between starting out with your friend's address — or, at the very least, a map of his neighborhood and a description of his house — and meandering through the streets of his town with no idea of where you're going or how to recognize your goal when (and if) you get there.

Librarians also know how to choose keywords and index terms that help focus in on the precise information they're seeking, instead of being overwhelmed by hundreds or even thousands of mostly irrelevant references. If their first strategy doesn't work as expected, they've got more tricks up their sleeves. Lots more. You'll find most of them in this book.

Searching versus Surfing

Searching online isn't the same thing as *surfing*. Surfing merely skims the surface. Searching is a lot more like scuba diving; it goes deep. It can still be fun and exhilarating, but getting the results that you want takes thought, care, and planning. Success depends on more than just how the waves happen to be breaking that day.

We don't promise to turn you into a professional researcher. You probably wouldn't want that, anyway. You have your own life; at least we hope you do. But here's where we're coming from: As trained librarians and professional researchers, we watched the Internet grow up around us. At first we were skeptical. We had our own resources — including some of the industrial-strength online databases that we talk about in this book — that we were accustomed to using. But gradually, the Net lured us in.

As we got to know our way around, we realized that the Internet held pockets of incredibly valuable information that we couldn't get anywhere else, or that would take much longer or cost much more to get through our usual means. We also realized that the Net attracted a lot of junk and that finding the good stuff wasn't always easy. We were seduced by the Net but not so completely that we didn't recognize its shortcomings. We've identified what we call The Four Myths of Online Research:

- ✔ Everything is online.
- ✔ It's all free.
- ✔ You just plug it into your computer and pull it out.
- ✔ It's all there for the taking.

If only that were true. It's just not true that everything worth knowing has made its way to the electronic realm. Not everything online is free, especially if you value the time it takes you to find it. Finding what you need takes a bit more effort — despite the occasional miracle — than keying in a word or two and automagically retrieving the answer. And *using* what you find isn't just a matter of plug and play; you have to think about issues like copyrights, giving credit where it's due, and verifying that the information is accurate, current, and complete.

What Makes a Good Researcher?

You don't need a library science degree, years in academia, or advanced training in some specialized field to be a good researcher. Formal education doesn't hurt, and if you've gotten some research experience in school or on the job, you're ahead of the game. But if we had to choose the single most important characteristic for a successful online searcher, we'd pick *curiosity*. Good researchers love to pursue information for its own sake. The thrill of the chase is almost as important as the goal. Many of our colleagues in the research biz are avid crossword puzzlers, word-game enthusiasts, or mystery novel readers. A couple of them even *write* mysteries in their spare time. Give them a challenge, or a clue, and they're off and running.

Practice doesn't make perfect, but it helps. You're not going to become a top-notch online searcher simply by reading this book. You have to get out there and try it for yourself. It's like on-the-job training — *theory* is worthless until you start using what you've learned. Check out the tools, techniques, and resources we recommend throughout this book. Plug in your own search terms; look for what interests *you.* When you catch yourself thinking, "I wonder if *this* will work . . . ?" or "Wouldn't it be *better* if I . . . ?" you're on your way to thinking like a researcher. The best researchers use both halves of their brains — the left side, which is supposed to be the logical, linear part, and the right side, which is said to embody intuition and creativity. Our goal throughout the following chapters is to show you how to do the same.

What We Know About You

We know you're *not* a Dummy. Not really. You're a regular person and, undoubtedly, an intelligent person, too, because you clearly know that one way to come up to speed and acquire new skills is to listen to folks who know more about the subject than you do. (That's *us*, they said, curtseying modestly.) You're obviously a person of great discernment, too, because you turned to *this* particular book for help.

We're assuming that you've already spent at least a little bit of time online, know how to connect to the Internet, and are familiar with basic concepts such as *Web browsers, linking,* and *search engines* — even if you're not entirely comfortable using them. Ideally, you've spent enough time trying to find information online to have become just a wee bit frustrated with the process and to be wondering, right about the time you picked up this book, whether a better way exists.

There is a better way. There are many better ways. And we're delighted to make your acquaintance.

How This Book Is Organized

If you're interested enough in how *our* minds work to start with Chapter 1 and read your way straight through, we're flattered. This book unfolds in a way that makes sense to us — obviously, or we wouldn't have organized it that way. But it works just as well as a reference book. You can dip into it when, where, and for as long as you like. Although some discussions refer to or build on material covered in earlier sections, each chapter also stands on its own. If you feel that you need to fill in the gaps somewhere along the way, you can always go back and do so. Nobody's keeping track of how you use this book. We know *we're* not, anyway.

We're big on chunky-style around here. You'll find chapter-size chunks, and chunklets of easily digestible information, checklists, and fun factoids within each chapter. The book itself is divided into five mega-chunks: "Getting Started," "The Tools of the Trade," "Putting It All Together," "The Broader Picture," and the mysteriously named "The Part of Tens." You'll also find a directory, printed on yellow paper, full of bite-size descriptions of selected research sites, services, and other useful resources. The URLs (Web addresses) for just about all these sites, and others that may interest you, are on the CD that's packaged with this book. Sound good? Good.

Part I: Getting Started

In this part, we talk about the mental skills and the online resources that successful online researchers should master. There's more to *online* than the Web; even the Internet doesn't encompass it all.

Part II: The Tools of the Trade

This part covers search engines, indexes, quick reference aids, professional online services, and many other types of research tools, including human expertise. We also cover Boolean searching and other power-search tips and techniques.

Part III: Putting It All Together

In this part, you get to see how the online tools and techniques covered in earlier chapters actually work in real-life research situations. You also get an in-depth look at some of the best — and sometimes best-*hidden* — resources in important subject areas such as news, business, technology, and government information. We give you some pointers, too, on how to research your personal interests, pastimes, and concerns.

Part IV: The Broader Picture

Approximately 47 minutes into your career as an online researcher, you'll start bumping up against some major issues: How do I keep up with all this stuff? Can I just go ahead and use what I find any way I want? How do I judge the quality of the information I'm getting? In this part, we tackle the big questions that come *after* "How do I find . . . ?" The answers aren't always clear-cut, but the more time you spend researching online, the more often you'll encounter those questions.

Part V: The Part of Tens

Is it just us, or does "The Part of Tens" sound like something from the Letterman show or a mystical incantation from some interactive multiplayer adventure game? Whether or not you get the same weird associations that we do, this part is where we get to reduce everything we've learned about research — well, maybe not quite *everything* — into bite-size morsels, and you get to graze, nibble, and otherwise eat between meals. Here's the section to turn to if you have a really short attention span or are the kind of person who licks the filling out of the Oreos first. We look at "The Part of Tens" as a supplement to, not a substitute for, other parts of the book — a snack, rather than the main course. But we think you'll find these goodies tasty no matter how or when you consume them.

Conventions and Icons Used in This Book

My eyes glaze over when I see
an icon bearing down on me.

Not really; we English majors *love* symbolism. This book uses just a few simple conventions throughout to call your attention to certain kinds of material. Bear with us; this may be tedious, but it'll be over soon. Read fast:

- ✔ URLs and other online addresses are indicated in a boring typeface like this: www.mypage.com.

- ✔ <u>Hypertext links</u> are <u>underlined</u>, just as they appear in your Web browser. Just don't try clicking them here.

- ✔ New terms are *italicized* the first time they appear. This is a clue that you haven't missed anything but maybe you'd better pay attention *now*.

This icon is for gems of hard-earned understanding and insight that are even more valuable than the usual pearls of wisdom that we so liberally disperse.

This icon signals the nitty-gritty steps involved in using a particular research tool.

This icon lets you know when we're heavily into talking like researchers. You can pick up phrases and sprinkle them into your conversations to impress, amuse, or scare your friends.

This icon indicates advanced research techniques or technical stuff — which we define as something you don't need to know unless you're curious about how it really works.

We expect you to commit the entire book to memory. This icon is for material that will be on the final.

This book comes with a CD at no extra charge. Such a deal. It has some great stuff on it, including free software, Web search guides, and links galore. When we mention something that's on the CD, you see this icon.

If disregarding something we say may produce unfortunate or unexpected results, we'll try to tag it with this icon. If we forget, please don't sue us. One person's problem is another person's challenge, you know? Here's a real-life example coming up right now:

Note: Research sites and services change their appearances all the time, especially on the Web. Sometimes all it takes is a new sponsor or partnership deal. Functionality and content — the way sites work, and the sort of information you can expect to find on them — change more slowly. But everything does change. Some sites may look different when you visit them, so you may not find all the features we describe exactly where we left them. It's the way of the Web. Consider it a challenge. We do.

What's New in the Second Edition

For starters, Reva brought along Mary Ellen to help update the second edition. Don't worry — Mary Ellen is another battled-scarred veteran of online research from way back, and she's almost as friendly as Reva.

Oh, you want to know what else we changed?

- We've updated our discussion of search engines to include the new generation of search tools that cover more of the Web, faster and maybe even better.
- We cover search engine output enhancements that help you more easily review your results and fine-tune your research.
- We describe desktop search engines that free you from some of the drudgery of Web research, and information management tools that let you organize the information you find.
- We include dozens of new sites for specific kinds of research.
- We give you new strategies and resources for keeping up-to-date, and for dealing with important issues like copyright and data quality.
- We move two chapters and the lowdown on Boolean searching from the CD to the hard copy of the book, making it easier for you to use these as research tools.
- We provide a completely revised and easy-to-use Internet Directory of the best Web sites for research and quick information lookups.
- We update Web addresses (URLs) throughout this book to speed you on your way to finding and using information.

One More Thing

Under "What Makes a Good Researcher?" earlier in this intro, we said something about the thrill of the chase. Every searcher we've ever asked has told us that, above all else, research has to be *fun*. You can find out the basics anywhere. But if we can convey what it's like to approach the online world from inside the minds of two virtuoso researchers who truly enjoy their work, we'll consider this book a huge success — for you and us both.

Part I
Getting Started

In this part . . .

*I*n this part, you find out what it takes to become an effective online researcher. Anyone is capable of finding out how to think like a researcher, using one's own unique combination of logic and creativity to track down information in a systematic way.

This part introduces the tools and techniques that are available to you online. You discover how and when to use them, when to think about alternatives, and how to tell when it's time to try a different tactic altogether.

In this part, you find that *online* means more than just the Web and that the Web itself includes many hidden and elusive treasures. We show you how to tap into them and how to uncover new ones on your own.

Chapter 1

The Many Faces of Online

In This Chapter

▶ Scoping out the Net

▶ Investigating fee-based services

▶ Contacting the Net's human resources

Amazing as it may seem, the online world was alive and thriving long before the arrival of the World Wide Web. Yes, the Web has grabbed the spotlight as a glamorous, fun-loving, party animal — every would-be information junkie's dream date. But for all its multimedia glitter and flash, the Web is a newcomer to the online world, and a derivative and ditzy one at that.

Harsh words? Not really. We adore the Web. The Web is fast becoming the preferred route for information publishing of all kinds. But the Web is not synonymous, quite yet, with *online*. The Web is an overlay on a much older, quieter, and less-chaotic environment: the Internet itself. Some of the most useful electronic archives — valuable electronic collections of specialized information — were developed back when personal computers were only a sci-fi writer's dream. See the section, "The Net beneath the Web," later in this chapter, for the when, why, and how of accessing these electronic archives directly.

The Online World: Library, Bookstore, or Shopping Mall after an Earthquake?

Coming up with creative ways to describe the online world could be a full-time job for a wordsmith. For all we know, a roomful of English majors are sitting around somewhere, busily minting metaphors on the subject. Make them stop, please, and tell the one who came up with the term *web surfing* to stand in the corner, right next to the guy who invented *Information Superhighway*. Thanks. We feel better now.

Actually, metaphors can be useful. They help you create a mental map of the territory you're getting into. Someone — one of those English majors, probably — once called the Web "the world's biggest library." If only it were as orderly and logical as a real-world library. Some sections, like the **Library of Congress** site (`lcweb.loc.gov/loc/libserv`), really are library-like. Other parts are far more chaotic.

Some people prefer a bookstore metaphor to describe the online world. A bookstore can be as orderly as a library, or a chaotic jumble of idiosyncratic offerings that reflect the proprietor's taste and opinions. Parts of the online world really are like bookstores. You find neatly organized rows of information at `www.yahoo.com`, and highly selective offerings at *guru pages* and *mega-sites* (see Chapters 5 and 6 for more about these resources).

You might even find the online equivalent of helpful bookstore clerks and fellow browsers. In this chapter, we take a quick glance at the human side of online research — the kinds of information you can get from real, live experts who hang out in various places on the Net. Chapter 10 goes into a lot more detail about how to use these people-resources effectively.

Just to complicate the question of what the online world is really like, dozens of well-organized online services exist behind virtual gates, open to subscribers or registered users only. Each of these sites has something unique to offer information-wise, and its own way of organizing that information and making it available. We do a brisk survey of these sites in this chapter and go into more detail in Chapter 9.

Our favorite metaphor for the online world is "a shopping mall after an earthquake." This implies a worst-case scenario. Go in expecting total chaos, and you'll be pleasantly surprised when you stumble across a section that hasn't been thoroughly trashed and that still bears some semblance of order and rationality.

The Net beneath the Web

Most of the online research that we talk about in this book refers to information you can find on the Web. But if you duck below the glossy surface of the Web, you'll find the raw, unvarnished Net, where it all began — plain text on a blank background, no graphics, just information in its pure, unadulterated form. Although we don't take you down to the Net often, once in a while a Web site will point you to a site that doesn't look anything like the friendly, point-and-click world you just left. Don't panic; you're just experiencing Life Before The Web.

Gopher it!

One of the earliest ways of organizing information on the Net was through something called *Gopher*. Gopher is just a menu-based way of filing and finding information online. It's a lot like the Web but without the fancy multimedia effects. To see what a Gopher (of the non-furry variety, that is) looks like, type **gopher://wiretap.spies.com** into your Web browser.

TIP

Because most Web browsers no longer require you to type **http://** at the beginning of a Web address or URL, we generally don't include it here. However, for some other protocols, like Gopher, a prefix is required. When one's needed, we show it.

Figure 1-1 introduces you to the Internet Wiretap Gopher, a name that makes us think of little rodents in their tunnels with FBI badges and earphones. Lovely format on that Gopher site, isn't it? Don't those folders look organized?

Click the folder labeled Government Docs (US & World), and you go to a list of documents available on this Gopher — everything from the Americans With Disabilities Act to World Constitutions. Next to each item is an icon. The icons that look like pages represent files or documents — destinations in themselves. The folder icons, like directories on your hard drive, contain other files and pointers to other destinations.

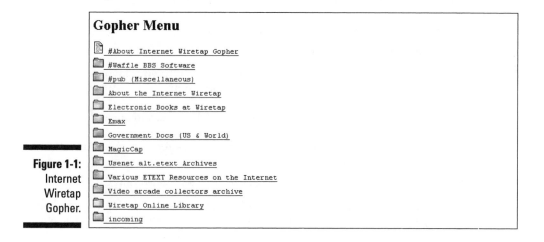

Figure 1-1:
Internet
Wiretap
Gopher.

WARNING

Most Gopher sites were developed years ago, before the Web existed. The people who used to maintain them are now busy putting the same information up on the Web. As a result, many Gophers are stagnant relics containing reams of outdated and no-longer-useful information. Be careful about relying on information from a Gopher site; if it's information that is likely to have been updated in the last year or two, use one of the search engines described in Chapter 3 to see if a more current version is available on the Web.

Why spend any time on Gophers, then? They're still a fast and convenient way to store and retrieve data, particularly lengthy texts and information that doesn't change very often. If you know what you're looking for and have at least a general idea of where to find it, then you can rejoice that Gophers aren't extinct.

Telnetting around

Telnet sounds like some high-tech long-distance phone service, and in a sense it is. Telnet is a means of directly connecting to another computer on the Internet without using a Web browser. The advantage of telnet is that it's fast, but that speed comes at a price: Telnet is text-based — no graphics, no point-and-click, no pretty interface. It's a pre-Web way of getting around the Net, and, well, it shows.

Some libraries use telnet to let you scan their electronic card catalogs. See Chapter 8 to find out more about telnet and library catalogs.

Gated, Not Open; Fee, Not Free

Three of the most enduring misconceptions about online research are

- ✔ The information is all out there on the Net.
- ✔ Everything on the Net is free.
- ✔ All you have to do is type a couple of words into your favorite search engine, *et voilà* — instant, on-target edification.

You mean there's more to research than that? We're afraid so, and here's why:

- ✔ Some online resources are *proprietary* — they require you to use their software to access them.
- ✔ Some make you register first; access is by password only.
- ✔ Some require you to pay a monthly or annual subscription fee, or charge you every time you use the service and/or for each item you retrieve.

We call any online resource that matches one or more of these conditions a *gated* site or service, because the site is set off from the Web at large. Most Web *spiders* (spiders are special software programs used by search engines to crawl around and index the Web) can't climb the walls of a gated site, so whatever information is stored inside the gates is invisible from the outside. To gain access to what's behind the walls, you have to be on the inside yourself.

Gated resources come in two flavors — professional online services and members-only Web sites.

Probing professional online services

The Internet has been around for a long time. But so have dozens of other good-sized computer systems with names like Dialog, LEXIS-NEXIS, and Dow Jones Interactive. These are called *professional* online services. Before you can search most of them, you have to set up an account, and supply a user ID and password or credit card every time you log in to look for information. Professional online services use their own methods of organizing material into giant collections of information called *databases*. They require special protocols that are different from the query languages used by Web search engines to run searches and retrieve information, and they are designed with the professional researcher rather than the one-time visitor in mind.

Professional online services sound like a pain to deal with, don't they? But they have a couple of distinct advantages:

✔ They often contain information you won't find anywhere else online, such as legal cases, conference papers, dissertations, and obscure scholarly journals.

✔ They're masters of *aggregation*. Professional online services collect and make available, under one roof, sources that you would otherwise have to wander the great, wide Web to cover on your own. You can search hundreds, even thousands, of unique and valuable research resources at the same time.

Aggregation means that instead of visiting two-dozen newspaper sites to gather articles on Bruce Springsteen's last tour, you can cover them all, plus hundreds more, with a single search query, if — big IF — you're willing to pay for it. These professional online services don't come cheap. We talk about the costs and about when and whether it makes sense to use them in Chapter 9.

Members-only Web sites

You can find two different kinds of members-only Web sites:

✔ **Sites that just require you to register.** You may have to supply some information about yourself when you first sign up, but after that, you typically just type your name and a password, and you're in. Hundreds of Web sites require registration now, often because advertisers are interested in the data on age, gender, income, occupation, and spending habits that you're sometimes asked to provide.

✔ **Sites that make you register *and* pay a fee.** This may be a subscription fee ranging from a couple of dollars to $20 or more a month, or a charge (often nominal) for every item you view, download, or print. Dozens of Web sites charge for access, from **The Wall Street Journal Interactive Edition** (www.wsj.com) to **Engineering Information Village** (www.ei.org) to the full-text special collection at the **Northern Light** search site (www.northernlight.com).

Whether free or not, gated sites all have one thing in common: A standard search engine won't touch them. You may miss a lot of information if you ignore this sad fact, because gated sites are far too valuable to overlook. Chapter 9 has much more information on gated sites, how to find them, and what they can do for you.

The Human Side of the Net

You probably think that the goal of your research project — the answer to your question — will come from a formal document, such as a product brochure, a company financial statement, a government report, a scholarly journal, or a story from a magazine or newspaper. It could even be a video clip, a sound file, or a piece of software.

But information comes in the form of *conversation,* too. The online world is full of conversation pits, informal gathering places where people chat, tell stories, and express their opinions. Some of these people actually know what they're talking about, and some of them may be willing to share their knowledge with you.

You can find knowledgeable folks hanging out in newsgroups, mailing lists, chat rooms, electronic conferences, and other virtual communities. You can converse with them publicly or go one-on-one in e-mail.

People made the Net what it is today. So going directly to the source sometimes makes sense. Chapter 10 explains how to find, interact with, and get the information you need from other people online.

Chapter 2

Thinking and Working Like a Researcher

In This Chapter

▶ Pinpointing your topic

▶ Getting the lowdown on your resources

▶ Fine-tuning your searches

▶ Managing your results

▶ Putting all the pieces together

*W*hat's your preferred tactic for getting what you want? Do you walk into your boss's office and blurt out that you want a raise? Or do you do some calculations, add a cost-of-living factor, and present her with the facts? If you have a role in a play, do you study your lines and try to get inside the character's head, or do you walk onstage opening night and trust that the universe will channel divine inspiration directly into your brain?

Any good performance takes preparation. For a researcher, half the effort takes place before you even sit down at the computer. If we're paying $15 for each search we run, or $4 for every document we download, we'd better know what we're looking for. We do our thinking *offline* so that when we do go online, we know exactly where we're going and can make maximum use of our time.

You're unlikely to encounter a $15-a-search database in your research travels, but you will do a better job and may even have more fun if you're prepared and focused going in. You'll be more resourceful and less likely to get distracted if you have a clear picture of the goal you're trying to reach and your options for getting there. This chapter presents some techniques for defining your research goal, coming up with a plan for reaching it, and using researchers' tools for focusing and refining your search.

Reference-Interviewing Yourself

Research is more than just coming up with a list of keywords, plugging them into a search engine, and standing back to see what spews out. Librarians and professional researchers routinely do something called a *reference interview.* What they ask themselves, and their clients or patrons, is exactly what you should ask yourself at the beginning of any research quest:

✔ **What are you really looking for? (What, exactly, is your topic?)**

Keywords or phrases, such as *internal combustion engine,* are just a starting point. Do you want a basic description of how an internal combustion engine works or technical information on the kind and quantity of emissions it puts out? Do you want an objective history of internal combustion engines? Examples of how they're used? A reasoned analysis of why they're one of the greatest advances of the 20th century or, contrariwise, the devil's own invention? In other words, what's the *angle* — the aspect of the subject that you really want to know about?

✔ **How else can you describe the topic?**

The English language is rich with synonyms, jargon, and figures of speech. You can usually find more than one way of expressing the same concept: A dip in *employment* is the same as a rise in *unemployment.* If you're looking for statistics on one or the other, consider the mirror image as well.

It works the other way, too: The same word sometimes stands for two totally different concepts. Are you interested in *apple* the fruit or *Apple* the computer company? If the meaning is ambiguous or can possibly be misconstrued, decide how to search for just the concept you want.

✔ **What is the project, or goal, for which you are gathering the information?**

Are you researching for a high school term paper or a doctoral dissertation? Do you want to build a working model of that internal combustion engine, or file for a patent on a new, improved version? Are you just looking to satisfy your curiosity, or gathering information to help you make a major life decision? Your reason for asking the question determines not only where you need to look for the answer — an engineering manual, an encyclopedia, or *Joe's Picture Gallery of Internal Combustion Engines I Have Known and Loved* — but also how much time and effort, and sometimes money, you want to spend.

✔ **Where's the best place to start looking?**

Should you first consult some logical starting points that are not online — such as a phone book, an almanac, or a neighborhood expert? Don't overlook the obvious. You may be tempted to jump online immediately, but maybe you can find an easier way.

✔ **If you could sum up your answer in one ideal article, what would its title be?**

Have some fun: Try to visualize the single, perfect answer to your question — one document that tells you everything you need to know. Then assign a title to that document: "The Internal Combustion Engine: A Detailed History." Or "The Internal Combustion Engine: Environment-Polluting Spawn of Satan." Whatever. Come up with two or three variations on the ideal title that mean essentially the same thing.

The idea behind the ideal-article exercise is to capture the most important concepts and to clarify your goal. Do you notice how the title for the internal combustion engine project immediately suggests some keywords to hang your research on? Not that you're going to hold out for an exact match, but it gives you a yardstick for measuring your results and for evaluating the good and the not-so-good answers.

What if you can't come up with a title at all? That's important information, too. We've heard a saying: "Writing is nature's way of letting you know how sloppy your thinking is." Being unable to put something in writing — or at least in words — is an indication that you don't quite know what you're looking for. "I'll know it when I see it" doesn't cut it in the online research game.

Where Do You Start?

One of the biggest research time-wasters is starting off on the wrong track. You can spend hours pursuing dead ends and wondering why you keep coming up empty-handed. All too often, the problem goes right back to the beginning: You may have made a wrong assumption about how, where, and whether to proceed.

Assumptions may be hazardous to your mental health. For quick relief of nausea, pain, and stress, take one or more of these simple correctives as needed:

✔ There's no such thing as a comprehensive online search.

✔ Information takes different and sometimes unexpected forms.

✔ No single search tool or strategy works throughout the online universe.

✔ Just because it worked last time doesn't mean it will work now.

✔ You can always try something different.

Mental-mapping your online resources

Every search aid and technique covered in this book has its own strengths and weaknesses. This section includes a quick summary of these aids and techniques, their pros and cons, and which chapters contain more information about them.

Search engines

General-purpose search engines — such as **GO** (infoseek.go.com), **Excite** (www.excite.com), **AltaVista** (www.altavista.com), and **HotBot** (www.hotbot.com) — work best when you know — or strongly suspect — that what you're looking for is available on the *open Web*. The open Web refers to sites that don't require registration or charge fees, such as company or personal Web sites, or most sites put up by government agencies, trade associations, clubs, or interest groups. Search engines work well in a variety of situations:

- ✔ Search engines make sense when you're looking for the proverbial needle in a haystack, or when you need to gather a great deal of information on a topic.

- ✔ If you're looking for information in a particular form, such as articles in newspapers or magazines, hold off — unless you find a search engine that specifically lets you search that kind of material. (See Chapter 13 for some examples of this type.)

- ✔ If you're looking for yellow- or white-page-type listings, maps, or software, or if you're looking for what people are saying in online discussion groups, you can probably find a specialized search engine to do the job. (See Chapter 4 for details.)

- ✔ If you're looking for news that happened yesterday or information that's more than a few years old, don't waste your time. Most search engines take a while to update, and the Web as a whole is a bad bet for historical data.

- ✔ Search engines like to chomp on unique, specific, and unambiguous terms. If you're researching a person or company with an unusual name, or if you can include a phrase that's distinctive and meaningful, such as *unidentified flying objects,* that query is a good bet for a search engine.

- ✔ If you're having trouble with terminology or can't pin it down, if you're finding too much out there to sort through, or if you want just a few good references or some general background information on a subject, then a search engine is probably not your best bet.

Check out Chapters 3 and 4 for more about the types of search engines described in this section.

Subject catalogs

We recommend subject catalogs, such as Yahoo!, for two reasons: They're organized (usually by subject, no surprise), and they're *selective*. They don't try to include the entire known universe of Web sites but rather a subset that somebody, often a team of actual human beings, has decided is worthy of inclusion. Here are some helpful hints for deciding when to use — and when *not* to use — subject catalogs:

- Messing around with subject catalogs doesn't make sense unless you're pretty sure that what you're looking for is out there on the Web at large, and that it's fairly current but not brand new.

- The selectivity of subject catalogs makes them *un*suitable for needle-in-the-haystack and no-stone-unturned searches; for all you know, what you're looking for has already been weeded out of the catalog.

- Subject catalogs are great when your interest is general and unfocused or when you just want a sense of what's out there.

- Turn to a subject catalog first when you know that a great deal of information on your topic exists (a topic such as Internet commerce, for example) and when you want to find the sites that are authoritative and devoted exclusively or extensively to the subject.

Check out Chapter 5 for more about subject catalogs.

Guru pages and mega-sites

Guru pages and *mega-sites* are more focused and sometimes more personalized variations on the subject catalog idea. Guru pages are usually assembled by individuals with an interest in a topic. Mega-sites tend to be more official, often the work of a government agency or other institution. Instead of covering the Web from A to Z like a typical subject catalog does, guru pages and mega-sites focus on a single topic or group of related topics. They are often gateways to more information on the topic, rather than the answers themselves.

Guru pages and mega-sites may turn up when you do a search engine or subject catalog search. You may hear about them through word-of-keyboard. An actively maintained guru page or mega-site often points you to new sites and current information that the search engines and catalogs haven't gotten to yet, and to weirder, more specialized, and more esoteric links.

Check out Chapter 6 for more on guru pages and mega-sites.

Library catalogs and archives

An online library catalog contains references to resources that are not on the Web but are physically housed in a particular library. If you're looking for a book or journal article that's already been published in non-electronic form, library catalogs are a good place to start. You can search by title and author, and usually by subject, to get the information you need to compile a bibliography, borrow or order a book, or request photocopies from the institution that carries the original.

Library catalogs can't be beat if you're looking for historical information — not just printed documents but original manuscripts, maps, music scores and recordings, and other special material. They point you to valuable scholarly resources that you won't readily find elsewhere.

Don't look to online library catalogs when what you're seeking is current or fast-changing, or just for fun. These catalogs require concentration and a different sort of approach. And by the time material makes it into a catalog, it's no longer breaking news.

Check out Chapter 8 for more about library catalogs and archives.

Ready reference

Librarians use the term *ready reference* to describe questions that can be answered with a simple fact — a statistic, a date, or a quotation. If you normally turn to a commonly used reference book, such as an encyclopedia, a directory, an atlas, or an almanac, for the answer to your question, consider the Net equivalent — a virtual reference collection or online bookshelf containing the counterparts of those useful and familiar volumes.

Most general-purpose search engines don't dig down in documents where the cold, hard facts are often buried. If you have a quick, fact-based question in mind, seek out a ready reference collection, go to the exact volume you want, and then look up your answer.

Don't take the ready reference approach if your research goal is broad, vague, complex, or multifaceted, or if you're interested in opinion and analysis from several different perspectives. Also, if you're trying to locate a company or person, hold off — specialized sources exist for that kind of research. We talk about some of these sources in Chapter 4. See Chapter 7 for more on ready reference.

Gated Web sites

When does it make sense to pay for information or to seek it out behind a password-protected barrier, as opposed to searching the Net at large?

✔ **When you want scope.** Professional online services, such as Dialog, contain in-depth information, going back many years, on topics ranging from astronomy to zoology, with hundreds of stops in between. Most of the material in these databases originally appeared in print form, in magazines, newspapers, trade publications, or academic journals. You can sometimes find summaries from expensive and hard-to-get sources, such as brokerage-house analyst reports and market research studies.

> ✔ **When you want efficiency.** Professional online services allow you to search anywhere from a dozen to several thousand sources at once, with a single search query. If you don't know or care what publication is likely to cover your topic, a search in one of these online services can save you hours, even days, of effort.

Professional online services are precise and powerful. They allow you to search by author or by standardized keywords, to tailor your output, and to do other research tricks that you can't do on the open Web. But you'll have to master some terse and sometimes puzzling commands, like the ones we describe in Chapter 9, and you'll end up paying anywhere from a few bucks to several hundred dollars for the material you download. You may not want to go this route unless you're willing to spend some money and commit to the training it takes to become proficient at searching.

You can also find some database-type information on consumer online services, such as CompuServe and America Online (AOL). If you're already a member of one of these services, you may want to poke around to see what you can discover there. CompuServe in particular has some useful research databases. In general, though, you can find better, more complete information on the professional online services.

Some Web sites, such as The Wall Street Journal Interactive Edition, require you to sign up before they grant full access to their contents. We call these *members-only* sites. Sometimes members-only sites charge a fee, sometimes not. Signing up is worth doing if you know that you will need this kind of information on a regular or even intermittent basis. The content of members-only sites seldom, if ever, turns up in a general Web search engine search. If a key publication or collection of publications in your area of interest exists on a members-only site, registering and even paying (ouch) to subscribe makes sense. ***Bonus:*** Some members-only sites provide access to experts as well. See Chapter 9 for more on gated Web sites.

Human resources

Finding the right expert online can help you figure out how to tackle a research project, brainstorm alternative approaches, or jumpstart a project that's stalled. But unless you've already established a good working relationship with some invisible buddies in cyberspace, this route should not be your first resort. Net denizens are knowledgeable and generous with their time, but don't think you can use them as a substitute for doing the work yourself. Before you ask for help, make an effort on your own. If you come to a series of dead ends and can honestly say you've run out of ideas, then it's time to call for help.

People are also a good way to track down *soft* news — rumors, *new* news, opinions — news that isn't even news yet and may never be. For more on locating and tapping into human expertise online, see Chapter 10.

Reality-checking

Step back and look at the big picture. Chances are you're not going to subscribe to a professional online service or take the time to master the intricacies of the Library of Congress catalog if you just want to satisfy your curiosity, prove a point, refresh your memory, or bring yourself up to speed on an issue that's been in the news. Real-life, practical concerns — such as planning a trip to Hawaii, looking up the known side-effects of aspirin, or figuring out what movies Kevin Spacey was in before *American Beauty* — call for a Web search or a quick trip to a supersite that you already know, such as the **Internet Movie Database** (us.imdb.com).

See Chapters 14 and 15 for loads of tips on how to research hobbies, personal interests, and life decisions like planning a major vacation, choosing a college, or finding a job.

The bucks start here

Suppose you're researching something that involves investments, key business decisions, legal matters, or even human lives. You can do a Web search to familiarize yourself with the territory or to make sure you're doing a comprehensive search. But you're asking for trouble if you stop with the open Web. Serious research — such as the kind required for a doctoral dissertation, patent application, lawsuit, business acquisition, or medical investigation — calls for heavy-duty resources that you find only in professional online services, library catalogs and archives, and some specialized, members-only sites on the Web. Sometimes you can't avoid using these fee-based services, despite the fact that a sizable investment in time (and fees of anywhere from $9.95 a month to a couple hundred dollars per search) may stand between you and the answer.

Research is a combo plate

In reality, you often use a combination of approaches while researching online. You may start with a subject catalog and move on to a mega-site, and from there, go to an Internet newsgroup where experts on the topic hang out. Or you may run a keyword through a search engine, click a page that turns out to be full of links on the topic, follow a link to a library catalog, and immerse yourself in the virtual stacks.

You may use the Web for current information and use a professional online service to fill in the historical blanks. Or you may gather some experts' names from newsgroups and Web sites, and run a database search to get a list of everything those experts have written.

After a while, researching online becomes a mostly seamless process. You don't even think about it as you glide from one kind of site to another, trying out different tools, tactics, and approaches to your question. You *do* feel a little bump when you move between the open Web and sites where you have to stop and type in a password. You feel an even bigger bump (ooof!) when you decide you need to go from free sites to a site that charges for each search or for every item you look at. But the more you practice thinking like a researcher, the easier that transition becomes.

When Bad Things Happen to Good Searchers

The moment of truth has arrived: You've thought about your research goal and what you really want to accomplish. You've visualized what the perfect answer looks like. You've chosen your search terms and typed them in. Now you just sit back and wait for the answers to pour out, right? Nope. The *pour out* part may be accurate, but the *answers* part is problematic.

Most of the research tools you've been introduced to in this chapter have their own built-in ways of ensuring that you're not overwhelmed with information and that the information you do get is relevant.

Search engines don't work that way — at least not automatically. Whether you use them on the Web or as part of a professional online service, such as Dialog and the others in Chapter 9, search engines are notorious for giving you exactly what you ask for. Sometimes that's way too much to handle. Sometimes it's way too little or way off target. All kinds of things can go wrong, or at least not totally right, during the course of an online search. In the following few sections, we describe what can go wrong and what you can do about it.

If at first you don't succeed. . . .

Before the days of PCs, Reva worked at a research company where the "search room" was a separate office containing an old-fashioned printing terminai as big as a desktop. You'd hear the clacking of the printer head across the paper, and the *ziiiiip* as it moved back to the left side of the page — over and over and over again. Every now and then, there'd be a loud WHOOP! or YEEHAW!! or All RIGHT!!! and one of the searchers would emerge, flushed with triumph and trailing a wide paper streamer as long as the train on a wedding gown.

More often, though, the zipping and clacking noises would go on for an hour, and the person who emerged from the room was quiet and subdued, carrying a stack of folded printouts. She had gotten pretty much what she was looking for, or knew that she'd be able to piece together an answer from the various sources she had checked — or she was resigned to having to go back to her desk and rethink the entire problem from a different angle. Even the pros seldom get it perfect the first time.

A *hit* is researcher jargon for an item retrieved by an online search that matches — or seems to match — the keywords and other conditions you've specified. Your *results list* is made up of *hits*. A hit may be an answer, or part of an answer, or totally useless. Hits retrieved for unforeseen reasons (such as typos), search terms that mean something else in a different context, or mistakes in search logic are called *false hits* or, for reasons buried in the dim past of mainframe computing, *false drops*. Experts call this kind of hit *garbage*. If you want to be elegant, put the accent on the second syllable.

Yikes, 42,178 hits! What do I do now?

What you *don't* do is look at all 42,178 of them. Unless you specify otherwise, most Web search engines use what's called *relevance ranking* when they present you with your results. Relevance ranking means that the best answers — or the ones that the engine *thinks* are best — appear toward the top of your list. If you don't find what you want among the top 50 to 100 items, chances are that it won't appear farther down. Time to try a different search engine or some new search terms.

Most search engines look at the *order* in which you typed your search terms, assuming that you'll put the more important terms first. You may get better, more relevant search results if you put the key ideas and most unusual or unique terms at the beginning of your list of search words.

Some search engines offer *Boolean* searching as an alternative to relevance ranking. For professional online services, such as Dialog and LEXIS-NEXIS, Boolean searching is the default mode. You may do Boolean searches already without even knowing it, as in the follow examples:

✔ When you tell a search engine that you want documents in which ALL your terms appear, or you string terms together with AND — *apples AND oranges* — you're doing a Boolean search.

✔ When you tell a search engine that you want documents in which ANY of your terms appear, or you string terms together by using OR — *apples OR oranges* — you're also doing a Boolean search.

Adding more relevant concepts to your search request and stringing them together with ANDs is one way to cut down on the volume of results. See the "Boolean (and Other) Basics" section, later in this chapter, for more information on techniques for fine-tuning your search.

When you do a Boolean search on a Web search engine, the results may not be relevance-ranked. Don't assume, before checking, that the items at the top of the list are the best ones.

You can also focus your results by using features that automatically restrict your search to certain kinds of information. Dialog, Dow Jones Interactive, and LEXIS-NEXIS all let you limit your results, in advance, to documents published in a particular time period or in specific magazines or newspapers. They often allow you to limit the results by language and sometimes geographic region, too. Most Web search engines also allow some search restrictions. But be careful with date limiting on the Web, because the date often has nothing to do with when the information itself was first published.

Waah! How come I didn't get anything?

A zero-hits scenario isn't always a disaster. If you've invented something and want to patent it, or need to find a unique topic for your dissertation, you may be delighted to discover that nobody has thought of it before. Sometimes, nothing *does* exist on a particular subject. But no results may be bad news, too, and you can do something about it:

- ✔ Double-check your search terms. A typo or misspelling will throw off your results.

- ✔ Think of synonyms for your search term or other ways of expressing the concept you're looking for.

- ✔ Don't over-restrict at the outset to specific dates or sources.

- ✔ Think about whether what you're asking actually has an answer, and an answer that can be found online.

- ✔ Make sure that you're in the right database, or haven't inadvertently told the search engine to check newsgroups or company directories only, for example, when you intended to do a Web-wide search.

Why on earth did I get THIS?

Search engines work in mysterious ways. Some relevance-ranking engines place more emphasis on words that they consider unique, unusual, or distinctive — even if *you* don't think they're the most important concepts in your search. Some engines place more emphasis on the words at the beginning of your search query and less on those at the end. A search engine that assigns more relevance to the terms you enter first gives you different results if you type **height weight children** than if you type **children height weight**. You can deal with these tendencies by:

- ✔ Entering your most important terms first

- ✔ Specifying that the terms *you* consider most important are *mandatory*, meaning that they *must* appear in the results

Other reasons why you may get odd and unexpected results:

- ✔ Your keyword may appear just once, in passing, in a very long document. Chances are that the keyword is irrelevant there, but the search engine doesn't know that. You may find it easy to overlook these fleeting mentions, but the search engine is just doing what it's told.

- ✔ Your keyword may have an entirely different meaning in another context — for example, banking CDs and audio CDs. If you're researching investments and you're turning up music sites, well, we suppose there *could* be a band called *High Yield.* . . .

- ✔ Some Web site promoters engage in a tacky kind of spamming. They load their sites with invisible keywords, such as *sex, Hawaii, sports, money,* and other popular search terms. When you search, you pull up their sites, which may have nothing to do with your topic. Many search engines are now smart enough to detect this invisible spamming, but some sites still slip through.

Don't waste time trying to figure out why you turned up a handful of weird items in a search that otherwise looks okay. Loads of possible explanations exist, and trying to debug the Web is not worth the effort. But if the weird hits outnumber the reasonable ones, heed the signal to rethink your search.

Evaluating what you get

The most tedious and time-consuming part of a search may be paging through your results list. You can speed things up considerably by remembering these three tips:

- ✔ **Reset the display options.** If the search engine you're using offers this option, set it to show the maximum number of hits at once. Paging through 50 or 100 items is much more efficient than clicking the Next 10 button time after time after time. . . .

- ✔ **Don't automatically click every single link that your search engine delivers — not even the ones at the top of the list.** Look at the titles, headlines, or brief descriptions, and follow the ones that sound the most promising.

- ✔ **Use your intuition.** You can knock out many foreign language sites from the get-go (unless, of course, you're fluent in Swedish, Portuguese, or whatever). If you're looking for authoritative sources, you can quickly discount sites that seem to have been put together by kids, jokers, or cranks. You can skip repeated mentions of the same site, and breeze right past other types of sites — such as commercial, promotional, or technical sites — that just aren't a match for the kind of research you're doing.

One of the joys of the Web is that anyone can publish on it. One of the dangers of the Web . . . is that anyone can publish on it. Don't assume that what you've found, no matter how good it looks, is valid — not until you've read what Chapter 17 has to say about information quality and how to assess it.

Boolean (And Other) Basics

In the preceding section, we discuss ways in which good searches can go bad. Experienced researchers have a few tricks up their sleeves that can help keep a search on track or turn an out-of-control or unproductive research project into a success. These tricks have names like *Boolean searching, proximity operators, field searching, wild cards, truncation,* and *case-sensitivity.*

Dialog and the other professional online services (see Chapter 9) offer their own versions of many of these tricks. Web search engines such as AltaVista, GO, HotBot, and Excite do, too — although you sometimes have to hunt for them. Look for pull-down search menus, icons, and labels offering specialized kinds of searches, and for links with names like Advanced Search, Power Search, Search Tips, or Help. Click any of these links for detailed documentation of the tricks that work on that particular search engine and examples of how to use them effectively.

Check the Research Help section on the CD packaged with this book for examples of search engine help pages.

Boolean searching

The odd-sounding word *Boolean* takes its name from George Boole, a 19th-century English mathematician who developed this simple but powerful way to define logical relationships between terms in a search query. The term *Boolean logic* is often used to describe how Boolean searching works.

The three main *Boolean operators* (also called *Boolean connectors*) are familiar English words: AND, OR, and NOT. You can use these operators, individually or in combination, as part of your search statement. Boolean operators make for a more meaningful and focused search, because you're not just stringing words together at random, you're telling the search engine how they relate to each other.

ANDing

Connecting two words with a Boolean AND is sometimes called ANDing them together. AND tells the search engine that both your search terms — or as many terms as you choose to enter and connect with ANDs — *must appear* in any documents retrieved by the search. The terms that you AND usually represent different concepts or angles on a topic that you use to focus and narrow down your search.

If you enter the search query *solar AND eclipse,* the search engine looks for documents containing *both* those words. In Figure 2-1, the shaded portion represents the documents retrieved by this search.

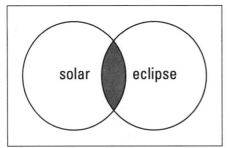

Figure 2-1:
A Boolean
search
with AND.

The AND operator is *restrictive.* It allows you to add more terms to make your search topic as specific as possible. When you search on *solar AND eclipse,* you get fewer hits, and more relevant ones, than if you had searched on either *solar* or *eclipse* individually or told the search engine to look for documents containing either of those words.

If you search a professional online service like Dialog, Dow Jones Interactive, or LEXIS-NEXIS, you can enter the AND operator in your search statement just as we've shown here. Some Web search engines allow you to type the operators as part of your search statement, too; the on-site documentation will tell you if this is the case. Alternatively, look for menu options like `Look for ALL these terms` or the ability to specify mandatory terms — that is, words that *must* appear in any documents retrieved. Both of these features are roughly equivalent to doing a Boolean AND search.

ORing

Connecting two words with a Boolean OR is sometimes called ORing them together. OR tells the search engine that *at least* one of your terms must appear in any documents retrieved by the search. You can enter as many terms as you want in an OR relationship. ORed words are often synonyms or related concepts used to broaden a search.

If you enter the search query *solar OR sun,* the search engine looks for documents containing either of these words, or both of them. In Figure 2-2, the shaded portion represents the documents retrieved by this search. Some of them may intersect — that is, the documents contain both the word *solar* and the word *sun.*

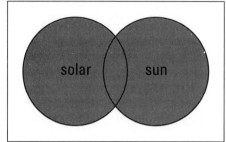

The OR operator is *inclusive.* Notice how much larger the shaded portion is than the AND diagram shown in Figure 2-1? You can OR together as many words in a search statement as you want. If you're interested in lunar eclipses as well as solar ones, you can enter a search query such as *solar OR sun OR lunar OR moon* to increase the retrieval even more. ("How do I get the *eclipse* part in?" you may be asking. See the "A (parenthetical) note" sidebar, later in this chapter, for the answer to that question.)

In Dow Jones Interactive and other professional online services, and in some Web search engines, too, you enter the OR operator in your search statement, just as shown here. On the Web, you may also find menu options, such as `Look for ANY of these terms`, that are more or less equivalent to doing a Boolean OR search.

When you enter multiple words like *total solar eclipse* in a Web search engine without Boolean operators between them, be sure you know how that particular search engine intends to interpret those words. Some search engines only retrieve documents in which the exact phrase *total solar eclipse* appears. The phrase may get you some good stuff, but it will miss a lot, too, including documents that discuss the same topic but that don't happen to use that literal phrase.

Some search engines automatically AND the words together; they look for documents in which the individual words *total AND solar AND eclipse* appear anywhere in the document. You'll get some relevant results, but your search probably won't be as focused as you'd like.

Still other search engines assume an OR relationship between words. Such engines will look for *total OR solar OR eclipse* and bring back documents in which any one of these words (or any two, or all three) appears. That makes for a very broad — and almost always worthless — search.

NOTting

The NOT operator (sometimes expressed as AND NOT or BUT NOT) is used to eliminate certain words from your search request. If you're interested in *dolphins* but not the National Football League team the Miami Dolphins, you might enter a query such as: *dolphin NOT NFL.* The search engine will retrieve items containing the word *dolphin,* but will eliminate any items that also include the word *NFL* anywhere in the document. Figure 2-3 shows how the NOTted-out term takes a bite out of the results. The shaded portion is what you retrieve.

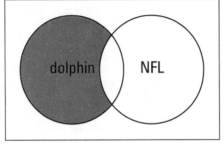

Figure 2-3:
A Boolean
search
with NOT.

Be careful how you use the NOT operator. We hardly ever use it. Why? Because you might inadvertently eliminate good documents along with the poor ones. Suppose you're interested in solar eclipses, and you NOT out the word *lunar* from your search statement: *eclipse NOT lunar.* Now, imagine an article that begins "This article is about solar eclipses. I don't plan to talk about lunar eclipses at all." Of course, that's an awful way to start an article, but you see what happens: Just because the author mentioned the word *lunar,* even in passing, and in a way that makes it clear that you *would* be interested in the article, you won't pick it up, because you told the search engine you're not interested in any references where the word *lunar* appears. In most searches, you can avoid the need to use NOT.

Many Web search engines give you a choice of Boolean versus *natural language* or *plain English* searching. When you go the Boolean route, you sometimes lose the search engine's *relevance ranking* capability; instead of reviewing your search results in the order of their apparent usefulness, you get them by date or by some other sorting mechanism. The best documents may appear at the bottom of the list or somewhere in the middle instead of toward the top. Boolean searching allows you to reduce your results to a more manageable number — but you may have to look at every single item to be sure you see the very best ones.

A (parenthetical) note

Parentheses allow you to use both AND and OR operators as well as NOT (if you insist on using it) in the same search statement. You can make your intentions clear to the search engine by bracketing the terms you want to connect with one Boolean operator or another.

A search phrase like *solar OR lunar AND eclipse* is ambiguous. Are you interested in the word *solar* used in any connection, or anything that mentions both lunar and eclipse, or both? Probably not; chances are you want to tell the search engine to look for anything on solar eclipses or lunar eclipses. You do this by adding parentheses to your search statement, like this:

(solar OR lunar) AND eclipse

You can even include synonyms in your search by saying:

(solar OR sun OR lunar OR moon) AND eclipse

If you're interested in all kinds of eclipses and want to specify some of the scientific terms used to describe various sorts, you might even say:

(solar OR sun OR lunar OR moon) and eclipse and (total OR partial OR annular)

The heavy-duty professional online services such as Dow Jones, LEXIS-NEXIS, and Dialog understand parentheses very well. But not all Web search engines do. Some may not know what to do with two sets of parentheses, like the ones we used in the last example. Before you get too deeply into parentheses, check the online search help file to see how — and whether — that particular search engine handles them.

Proximity operators

Boolean searching is great for increasing or restricting your search results. The AND operator in particular is very useful for narrowing your results by including additional relevant terms and concepts. AND is a fairly blunt instrument, though, compared with a specialized category of connectors called *proximity operators.* In a lengthy document, the AND operator may pick up one of your search terms from the very beginning of the text, and the other from the end; the two terms may not occur in the same context or have any meaningful relationship to each other at all.

Proximity operators allow you to specify

- How close to each other your search terms should appear

- In what order your search terms should appear

Two kinds of proximity operators exist. One kind specifies how many words can intervene between term A and term B. For example, on Dialog, you can say: *total(2n)eclipse.* This tells the search engine to pick up any documents in which the word *total* and the word *eclipse* appear within two words of each other, in any order. This will pick up phrases such as

> total eclipse
>
> total solar eclipse
>
> total lunar eclipse

as well as phrases like

> after the eclipse, total silence reigned
>
> when the eclipse became total. . . .

You may encounter this type of proximity operator on the Web, though it's much more common on the professional online services covered in Chapter 9. If a Web search engine offers a similar proximity option, it may be called something like `Look for all of these words, in any order`.

The other kind of proximity operator lets you tell the search engine that your terms must appear in the same *field* or portion of the document, such as the title. (See the section "Field searching," later in this chapter, for more about document fields.) With this kind of proximity operator, you just tell the search engine that you want the terms to appear somewhere in the same field.

Field-proximity operators are based on the assumption that terms in the same field tend to be conceptually related to each other. If two words occur in the title of a document, for instance, or within the same sentence or paragraph, they're likely to have a meaningful relationship to each other.

You encounter this kind of proximity operator more frequently in professional online services, such as Dialog and the others described in Chapter 9, than you do on the Web, because these services offer highly structured document records with more fields than you tend to find on the Web. See the section "Field searching," later in this chapter, for more details.

Another type of proximity search is *order-dependent proximity*. Sounds like quite a mouthful, doesn't it? Order-dependent proximity just means that for a document to be retrieved, your search terms must occur in the order in which you enter them in your search statement.

Order-dependent operators are useful when you're looking for a well-known term or phrase and don't want to type the entire phrase or aren't sure about intervening words:

> On Dow Jones Interactive, *National Organization adj2 Women* gets you hits on both National Organization *of* Women and National Organization *for* Women.
>
> On Dialog, *jack(w3)box* picks up *Jack In The Box* (search engines usually skip short words like *in* and *the*).

You encounter order-dependent proximity operators on professional online services more frequently than on the Web. When they do show up at a Web search engine site, it's often in the guise of an option called something like `Look for all of these words, in this order.`

Most Web search engines make phrase searching easy — you can select the phrase option from a menu, or enclose your phrase in quotation marks, or just enter it as is. If you enter a multiword search statement such as *solar eclipse* in LEXIS-NEXIS or Dow Jones Interactive, those services automatically *search* for it as a phrase. In Dialog, though, you need to use the *(w)* proximity connector: *solar(w)eclipse*.

Field searching

A *field* is a specific portion of a document, such as the title, publication name, author, or main body of the text. In professional online services, you sometimes find additional fields for keywords and subject terms that have been added to a record. On the Web, you can sometimes search page titles and URLs as fields.

Field searching can make your research results much more precise. Confining your search terms to a specific field — such as the title of a document, or the terms assigned to it by an indexer — helps ensure that those words are the main focus of the document and that they appear in the context you intended. Confining an individual's name to the author field ensures that you pick up articles *by* that person, not articles *about* her.

Field searching on the professional online services

Depending on the database you're searching and the professional online service that it's on, you may have just a few fields to choose from, or several dozen. Field searching on Dow Jones Interactive, for example, looks like this:

Searching for a company name:

> honda.co.

Searching for an author (byline):

> by=nan tucket

Searching for a particular journal (source name):

> sn=wall street journal

Searching for words or phrases in the headline or lead paragraph:

> hlp=boston marathon

Confining your search terms to the headline (or title) may be overly restrictive, because many publications get creative when they title articles. But confining them to the lead paragraph can be useful, especially when searching publications that subscribe to the old journalistic assumption that the who, why, when, where, and how of any event is supposed to be reported in the first paragraph.

You can accomplish these same searches on Dialog or LEXIS-NEXIS by using their corresponding field codes. See the online help files for prefix and suffix searching on Dialog or for segment searching on LEXIS-NEXIS.

Field searching on the open Web

Web search engines don't offer as many field-searching options as professional online services like Dialog, LEXIS-NEXIS, and Dow Jones Interactive. Why not? Documents on the Web tend to be less structured than documents on the professional services. Title and URL are the most common fields defined by search engines on the Web.

On AltaVista and GO, for instance, you can field search like this:

> title:Dummies

> url:msn

On HotBot, you can limit your search to the title field by selecting The Page Title on the Look For pull-down menu.

Click the <u>Search Help</u>, <u>Advanced Search</u>, or <u>Search Tips</u> link to see whether the search engine you're using offers any field-searching options.

Pluralization, truncation, and wild cards

Earlier in this chapter, we use the search topic *total eclipse* to explain how Boolean searching and proximity connectors work. We conveniently glide over the possibility that the word *eclipse* might occur in either singular or plural form. You may have noticed.

Some search engines automatically account for plurals. Unless you tell it otherwise, LEXIS-NEXIS looks for both singular and plural forms of a word: *cat = cats* and *cats = cat.* The Northern Light search engine automatically hunts for both singular and plural forms, too.

Automatic pluralization generally works with regular plurals only. A regular plural is formed by adding an *s* or *es* to the end of a word: *channel/channels; potato/potatoes.* If you want to search for both the singular and plural forms of a word that takes an irregular plural, you usually have to enter both forms:

child/children. And automatic pluralization works only for words the search engine knows. Relatively new words, such as *ecotourist,* may not be automatically pluralized.

Another issue we glide over in the earlier sections is the possibility that the *total* aspect of the *total eclipse* concept might be expressed slightly differently, as the word *totality,* for instance.

One way to account for plurals and word variations in your search statement is to enter all the possibilities you can think of and connect them with Boolean ORs:

> (total OR totality) w/5 (eclipse OR eclipses)

Typing all those variations isn't very efficient, though, and in a more complex search, it can get cumbersome. Fortunately, most professional online services and some Web search engines support *truncation.* Truncation allows you to enter just the first part of the word — enough to capture the meaning — and attach a special character or symbol to the end, called a *wild card.* The wild card tells the search engine to pick up every word that starts with the letters you've specified, no matter how the word ends. In a nutshell: Wild cards are used to represent alternate word endings and plurals.

AltaVista and some other Web search engines use an asterisk (*****) as a wild card. The search term *bank** picks up banks, banking, banker, bankers, bankrupt, bankruptcy — any word that begins with bank.

Dialog uses a question mark (**?**) as a wild card. LEXIS-NEXIS uses an asterisk or an exclamation point (**!**), depending on the situation. Dow Jones Interactive uses a dollar sign (**\$**). All three of these services allow you to limit the number of letters that may appear following your word stem.

For example, if you're searching Dow Jones Interactive for articles on banks, banking, or bankers, but you're not interested in bankrupts, bankruptcy, or bankruptcies, entering the term *bank\$3* filters out much of the noise. The *\$3* tells the Dow Jones Interactive search engine to look for *up to* three additional letters following the root word *bank* and to screen out any words with *more than* three additional letters.

Don't use too short a word stem when you truncate. If you do, you may inadvertently pick up terms that have nothing to do with your research: *cat** picks up not just cat and cats, but also catamaran, catapult, catatonic, catalyst, and fittingly, catastrophe.

Check the documentation at individual search engine sites, or the online help files on the professional online service of your choice. Chapter 9 tells you a lot more about the wild card tricks that Dialog, Dow Jones Interactive, and LEXIS-NEXIS have up their sleeves.

Case-sensitivity

Case-sensitivity refers to whether a search engine recognizes the distinction between upper- and lowercase letters in a search term. Depending on the search engine, *capitalized* words — such as *Chevron* or *Tiger Woods* — or all-capital acronyms — such as *U.N.* or *CIA* — may or may not be recognized as such.

Case-sensitivity can help make your search more precise. If you're using a case-sensitive search engine to look for the name of a person, company, or product — or anything else that's normally capitalized in print — then capitalizing that search term helps target your results: When you're looking for the computer company and not the fruit, *Apple* is better than *apple*.

Search engines handle case-sensitivity in different ways:

- ✔ **Some search engines are 100-percent case-sensitive (or can be instructed to act that way).** They search on the exact form of the word that you enter.

- ✔ **Some search engines are partially case-sensitive.** If you enter the lower-case form of a word such as *apple,* they pick up all forms of the word. But if you enter the uppercase form *Apple,* uppercase is all you'll get in return.

- ✔ **Some search engines are case-insensitive.** They ignore capitalization whether you use it or not. How insensitive.

Among the professional online services, both Dialog and Dow Jones Interactive are case-insensitive. LEXIS-NEXIS is case-sensitive when you want it to be; Chapter 9 describes how to get LEXIS-NEXIS to search for upper- and lowercase word forms according to your precise requirements.

The case-insensitivity of Dialog and Dow Jones Interactive isn't that big a deal, because you can do *field searching* (described earlier in this chapter) to restrict your search terms to companies, personal names, and sometimes even product names.

Web search engines can be very sophisticated when it comes to case-sensitivity. For instance, AltaVista, GO, and HotBot look for both upper- and lowercase occurrences of your search terms as long as you enter them in lowercase only:

> *next* retrieves *next, Next,* and *NeXT*
>
> *aids* retrieves *aids, Aids,* and *AIDS*

But if you include an uppercase letter in your search term, at the beginning of a word or anywhere else, GO, HotBot, and AltaVista look only for terms that match it exactly: *NeXT, Next, AIDS,* and *Aids* retrieve only those exact forms of the words. Lowercase forms such as *next* and *aids* are ignored.

On the other hand, the Northern Light search engine is case-insensitive in the sense that *CAT = Cat = cat* (try telling *that* to a mouse). But the search engine sometimes assigns more weight to the uppercase form of a word, which means that documents containing that form may be ranked differently in the results list.

Moral: If your search term is routinely capitalized or includes uppercase characters, look for a search engine that supports the kind of case-sensitive searching you need.

Knowing When You're Done

If you're doing research at your local public library, your resources may be defined by what lies within those four walls. If you're searching a professional online service, your resources are limited to the number of records it contains. That number may be huge, but it's manageable. The Net, though, is deep, open to everyone, and potentially unlimited. You could conceivably spend your entire life there, trying to track down every last bit of information on a topic. And by the time you get through the process once, it's time to start over and look at all the *new* stuff. What a gruesome possibility.

How you can tell when an online research project is done?

- ✔ You run out of time.
- ✔ You run out of money (if you're searching on a fee-based system).
- ✔ You run out of patience.
- ✔ You find the perfect answer.
- ✔ You reach the point of diminishing returns.

The first three points are self-explanatory. Staying online longer than you have to is a trap entirely too easy to fall into; you waste time, money, *and* patience in pursuit of the perfect answer, whatever that may be. A point comes where you have to hang it up, call it quits, declare it done, and get on with your life. A good rule of thumb is that when you start seeing the same information over and over again, recycled through various Web sites or repeated in different magazines, you've probably reached the end of the research line.

Take a look at the section "Reference-Interviewing Yourself" at the beginning of this chapter. Don't lose sight of what you set out to accomplish, whether the goal is a definition of beta blockers, a map of Philadelphia, or five good articles on the U.S. economy. Found it? Fine; now *stop*.

Using What You Find

Just because you find something online doesn't mean that the information is totally free for the taking. Using information for your own private edification is one thing. Incorporating it into something that you plan to sell, publish, promote, or distribute to others is quite another.

Before you snarf that well-written article for your own report, cop that cool quote for your Web site, or grab that great graphic for your PowerPoint presentation, check out Chapter 17 for the legal lowdown, professional "best practices," and good manners guidelines for using information you find online.

Part II
The Tools of the Trade

The 5th Wave — By Rich Tennant

In this part . . .

*I*n this part, we take a detailed look at search engines, subject catalogs, research databases, newsgroups, and the other resources available to you online.

In each chapter, you find our picks of the best and most interesting research tools around, together with tips on how to use them effectively and examples of the kinds of research to which each one is best suited.

We also give you background and details on Boolean logic, field searching, and other professional research techniques.

Chapter 3

The Search Engine Sweepstakes

● ●

In This Chapter

▶ Building an effective search query

▶ Exploring advanced search engine features

▶ Touring the top general search engines

▶ Shortcutting your search with meta-engines and offline search tools

● ●

*S*earch engines are the media darlings when it comes to researching on the Web. Before you picked up this book, perhaps you thought that's what online research was all about. A good general search engine can be an invaluable research aid, especially when you have unique keywords to feed it, or you're hoping to find everything on a subject, or you haven't been able to find *anything* on your topic through any other means.

We'll be honest with you, though — there's no such thing as brand loyalty when it comes to search engines. Even professional researchers tend to go with the one that produced good results the last time around, and to chuck it away like last month's leftovers — or at least put it aside for a while — if it doesn't continue to deliver.

Web-based search engines operate in ways that even the pros don't understand. Each one uses a different complex mathematical scheme — called an *algorithm* — to retrieve the results it thinks you're interested in. Each one indexes Web sites and Web pages in a different way. No one search engine covers the entire Web.

You can influence the results up to a point, by taking advantage of the powerful features that are sometimes concealed in pull-down menus or behind a button or link innocuously labeled *Help* or *Search Tips*. But you can't predict or totally control the outcome of your search. If one engine doesn't do the job for you, move on.

By all means experiment with the major search engines that we talk about in this chapter. Take a look at the sample help files on the accompanying CD-ROM. Go online and experiment with them. You'll develop your own favorites. Or maybe not.

Most important of all, though, remember that the search engines we talk about in this chapter are just one small part of the online research picture. You have many other resources at your disposal.

Meet the three main types of search engines:

- **General:** Cover — or claim to cover — much of the Web
- **Meta:** Can run the same search through several engines at once
- **Specialized:** Focus on a particular site or kind of research query

We talk about general and meta-engines in this chapter, and about specialized engines in Chapter 4. *Note:* The search engines we talk about here are ones that we tend to come back to because they produce good results. These are just a few of the dozens of search engines in existence. Your mileage may vary, and that's fine with us.

Keep in mind that search engines are in a constant state of flux. They all claim to cover more of the Web, provide the most powerful search options, and present the results most intelligently. Don't get so fond of one search engine that you ignore what the others have to offer.

Timeless Tips for Effective Searching

Regardless of which search engine you use, you can use a few pointers to get you started:

- Keep It Simple to Start (KISS, sort of). The first time you use a search engine, go for the default search mode, whether it's called <u>Quick Search</u> or <u>Simple Search</u> or something equally elementary. Let the search engine do its own thing before you complicate matters with ANDs and ORs, required terms, parentheses, and other advanced options. Before you try something fancy, get a basic grip on how the whole thing works.

- Enter your rarest and most important search terms first. For example, enter **Casablanca movies** instead of **movies Casablanca**.

- Use phrases or proper names whenever possible. Enclose them in quotes if necessary: **"chocolate chip cookies"** or **"Queen Elizabeth"**.

- Use the plus (+) sign to indicate words that *must* appear in each item found.

- Click the <u>Help</u>, <u>Search Tips</u>, <u>Power Searching</u>, or <u>Advanced Search</u> link (just about every search engine has one) to find out more about what the search engine can do.

What to Consider When Choosing a Search Engine

It's boring to write about the mechanics of how search engines actually process your search, and it's even more boring to read about them — until you actually need that information.

At this point, you may want to refer to Chapter 2, which explains the nitty-gritty of such basic research concepts as Boolean logic, proximity operators, case-sensitivity, truncation, and wild cards. Wheee! Understanding at least a little about these features, and knowing how and when to use them, can make the difference between research success and failure.

The following questions should help you evaluate which search engine is right for the job — or whether any one is a clear-cut candidate for first place. Remember that the answers to these questions are usually just a click away, under that button labeled Advanced Turbo Mega Power Searching Help Tips.

- Can you increase the number of results that appear on each page, or specify whether you want to see more, or less, information about each item?

- Does the search engine do *field* searching, which lets you restrict your search terms to the title, summary, first paragraph, or URL? Any of these variables can help focus your results.

- Does the search engine automatically look for plurals, such as *dog* and *dogs,* or let you use a *wild card* to stand in for one or more letters if you want to search for alternate forms of a word (for example, *aviat** = *aviator, aviators, aviation*)?

- Can you specify, by using plus (+) and minus (-) signs, a pull-down menu, Boolean search terms, or some other means, when certain words *must* appear, *could* appear, or should *not* appear in your results?

- Can you search for literal phrases, such as *Your mileage may vary?*

- Can you restrict your results by language, geographic region, or other useful limitations?

- Does the search engine include newsgroups, FAQs (Frequently Asked Questions lists), or specialized sources, such as newswires and business directories, in addition to the Web itself?

- Is the search engine case-sensitive? No, case-sensitivity isn't an allergy that lawyers develop. It has to do with whether a search engine recognizes upper- and lowercase letters. Some even interpret two capitalized words in a row as a proper name, such as *Tiger Woods* or *Apple Computer,* so that you don't get everything that's available on tigers and woods, or apples and — heaven help you — computers.

  ✔ Does the search engine understand plain English queries? Does it present the results as a neat, preformatted answer as well as provide links to the rest of the Web?

  ✔ Does the search engine let you refine your search by looking for new terms within the results you've already retrieved?

Exploring General Search Engines

Every time we fire up a search engine we haven't used in a while, we have to re-familiarize ourselves with the controls. The software mechanics who build these machines are constantly tinkering with them, trying to improve their performance and make them easier to use. Some of the search engine features that we describe here and the screen shots that accompany these descriptions may have changed somewhat by the time you read this. Scuzi. As they say on the Information Superhighway signs, "Temporary inconvenience, permanent improvement."

AltaVista

AltaVista (www.altavista.com) was the first really deep search engine, meaning that it penetrated below the top level of a Web site to pull up references buried one or more levels down. Although it's not the only in-depth player out there anymore, AltaVista is still a good starting point for a comprehensive search. Here are a few reasons why:

  ✔ AltaVista enables you to search Usenet newsgroups as well as the Web.

  ✔ It allows you to search in a couple dozen languages besides English.

  ✔ It lets you look for people and businesses via the Switchboard directory service.

  ✔ It enables you to browse by subject category, as well as run a regular keyword search. If you think this looks like a subject guide (see Chapter 5 for the lowdown on subject guides) rather than a search engine, you're right; many search engines now incorporate both.

You can target your AltaVista search more precisely by limiting it to:

  ✔ The title of a Web page; for example, *title:Dummies*

  ✔ The URL; for example, *url:xerox*

Limiting your search term to the title is a quick-and-dirty tactic for locating pages devoted exclusively to your subject. Downside: The best resources on a topic won't necessarily be labeled this clearly. But it's worth a try — especially if you're overwhelmed with hits and need some way to cut down on the volume.

Limiting your search term to the URL is an even quicker-and-dirtier way to find pages exclusively on your topic. But using the URL alone has an even deeper downside: The domain name may be completely unrelated to your topic. You'd think a URL like `www.goldfish.com` would focus on those low-maintenance pets, but it's actually the Web site for a company called Goldfish Guides that has nothing to do with fish.

Excite

Excite (`www.excite.com`) looks more like a subject catalog than a search engine. Your first view is of a collections of links — shortcuts to news sources, topics ranging from Autos to Travel, shopping sites, and so on.

In addition, Excite offers specialized searching for people, businesses, stock quotes, classified ads, online auctions and other spending opportunities, sports, weather, horoscopes, maps, and more. Click the <u>More . . .</u> link to discover dozens of helpful links to reference books, government information, and other handy resources.

Concept searching with Excite

What about the Excite search engine itself? Excite's main claim to fame is what it calls *concept searching.* Like other search engines, it looks for documents containing the search terms you've supplied. But it takes a giant step beyond that, linking your keywords to its own internal database of synonyms and related concepts, and then searching automatically for those terms and concepts as well. This extra step means that if you enter a keyword such as *teenager,* Excite looks for references to adolescents, youths, and young people, as well. Amazing, isn't it?

After you run your search, Excite suggests additional words that you may want to include and lets you check any that you want to add. Figure 3-1 shows how Excite does that.

Excite not only saves you from having to think of synonyms, but also gives your brain cells a boost when you're having trouble narrowing down your search. If, while browsing your results, you find one or more items very close to what you're looking for, click the <u>Search for more documents like this one</u> link. Excite uses the terms and concepts in that document as a model for your ideal answer, and refines your search accordingly.

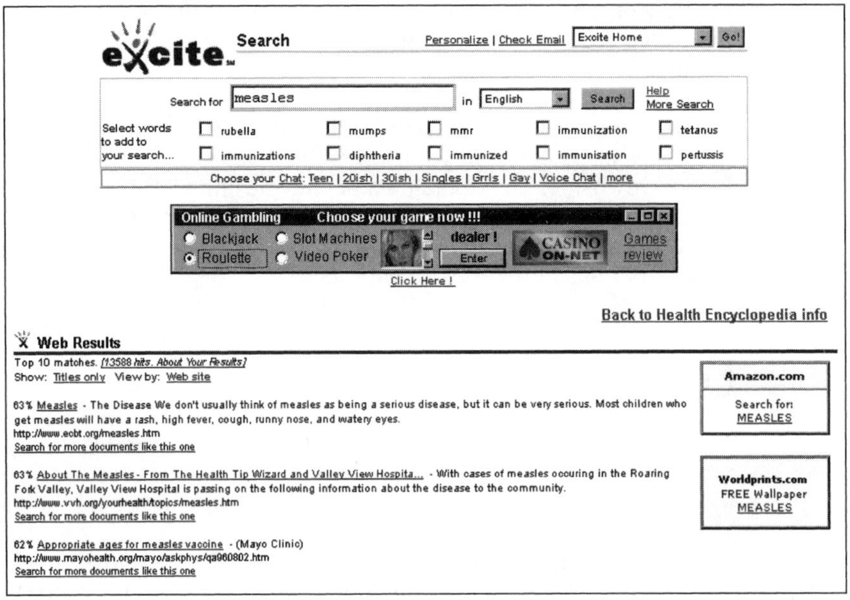

Figure 3-1:
Excite
suggests
additional
words.

In addition to doing some of your thinking for you, Excite makes educated guesses about what kind of information you're looking for. If you search for the phrase *Dallas Cowboys,* Excite provides you with recent football statistics, NFL schedules, and other football-related information.

Excite extras

Click Excite's <u>More Search</u> link to uncover a range of other features:

- ✔ Search the Web, news sources, and international versions of Excite.
- ✔ Specify words or phrases that your results can, must, or must not contain.
- ✔ Tweak your search output to show you more or less description for each item, or to sort results according to the Web sites where they appear.

GO Network

GO — a search engine formerly known as Infoseek (infoseek.go.com) — has always been a solid performer in the search engine sweeps.

- ✔ GO lets you search in ten languages in addition to English.
- ✔ GO covers newsgroups as well as the Web.

✔ If you're looking for news stories or company information, confine your GO search to wire services, industry journals, national newspapers, and other Web-based news sources.

✔ GO offers a subject-catalog alternative, called Topics (see Chapter 5 for more about subject catalogs).

✔ You can refine your GO search, after getting your first round of results, by clicking the Search Only Within These Pages button and entering some additional terms.

GO is smart enough to assume that two or more capitalized words in succession may be a proper name, a company, or another entity, such as United States Postal Service. The good news is that you don't have to put phrases in quotes like you do with some other search engines. The not-so-good news is that if you're looking for two or more capitalized words that you don't want to be searched as a phrase, you have to separate them with commas: for example, *Netscape Navigator, Internet Explorer*.

GO's Site option enables you to pull up all the available pages at a particular Web site. You can then browse to see what the site has to offer or what kinds of folks maintain Web pages there. After doing a site search, you can enter keywords to search for specific information within the site.

Try the following:

> site:well.com
>
> site:mit.edu
>
> site:usps.gov

Using the Site option is sort of like doing exploratory surgery on a Web site. You can see what's really inside a site, as opposed to what its designers choose to reveal with their preplanned links and menus.

HotBot

HotBot (www.hotbot.com) gets our vote for the most colorful search form on the Web. This site uses the type of slick, colorful graphics that its erstwhile sister company, *Wired* magazine, is notorious for. Fortunately, the screen is legible, though you probably don't want to peruse it on a moving bus. Even more fortunate, under its rather whimsical surface, is that HotBot is a lean, mean research machine, particularly if you click the <u>Advanced Search</u> link to bring up its power searching options.

To streamline (and decolorize) your HotBot experience, click the <u>Text-only version</u> link at the bottom of the page.

HotBot enables you to do the following in your search:

- ✔ Easily limit your search by date, geography, and media type (including images, video, and MP3) by using pull-down menus and check boxes.

- ✔ Restrict your search term to the title of a Web page or extend your search to all pages within a site.

- ✔ Specify whether terms must, must not, or should appear in the Web site.

- ✔ Do a follow-up, more-focused search that's limited to the results of your first search.

- ✔ Tailor your search results by specifying how many items you want to browse at once, and whether you want to see full or brief descriptions, or just URLs.

- ✔ Use technology from a company called Direct Hit to see the top ten pages that other people have clicked for searches similar to yours.

In addition to its Web search options, HotBot provides a subject catalog of the best of the Web; see Chapter 5 for more information on using subject catalogs.

Northern Light

Northern Light (www.northernlight.com) is unusual in more ways than name alone. For one thing, it allows you to search not only the Web, but also its special collection of articles from 5,000 magazines, newspapers, books, and other reference sources, most of which are not readily available elsewhere on the open Web. Northern Light is also unusual in that it charges a pay-as-you-go fee, usually in the $1 to $4 range, for individual items from the Special Collection that you may want to read, print, or download in their entirety. These fees are actually pretty reasonable, and they're made more so by Northern Light's money-back guarantee.

To get an alphabetical or subject list of the publications in Northern Light's Special Collection, follow these steps:

1. **Click the __Help Center__ link.**

2. **Click the __Special Collection__ tab at the top of the following page.**

3. **Then click either the subject or alphabetical links.**

4. **Finally, click a subject category or a letter of the alphabet to see specific titles.**

Some sample publications in the trade journal area alone include *Bakery Production and Marketing, Communication World, Graphic Arts Monthly, Journal of Coatings Technology, Machine Design, Oil & Gas Journal, Online, Professional Builder,* and *Robotics World.*

Northern Light attempts to refine and make sense out of your search results by organizing them into Custom Search Folders. It creates these folders on the fly, based on the Web sites and the types of information it turns up. You can either browse a standard, relevance-ranked results list, or click any of the folders on the left side of the screen (as shown in Figure 3-2) to read documents grouped by source or type of site (such as commercial sites or personal home pages), by publication title, by language, or by a particular slant on, or treatment of, your topic.

Northern Light also has an Alert feature that notifies you by e-mail whenever new material is added to the Special Collection or changes are made to Web pages that match your stored search query. See Chapter 13 for more information about this electronic clipping service.

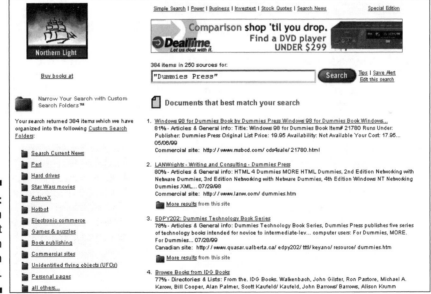

Figure 3-2:
Northern
Light
Custom
Search
Folders.

Peer pleasure

Mary Ellen admits it — she'd often rather read a book recommended by family or friends than one on some professor's Recommended Reading list. She assumes that if her sister Sarah enjoyed a book, she will too. Likewise, you may be more interested in Web sites that lots of other people have clicked on than ones that are ranked most relevant by a search engine.

Several Web search engines factor in a site's relative popularity — as determined by how many other people clicked on that site or by how many other sites link *to* that site — when

calculating what sites to place at the top of your search results list. The **Google** search engine (www.google.com), for example, ranks a site higher if other sites have linked to it. **Alexa** (www.alexa.com), which is software that you install on your computer and access through your browser, tracks the sites that you visit and recommends related sites, based on the browsing patterns of other Alexa users. **Direct Hit** (www.directhit.com), a search engine that sorts results based on Web traffic, also licenses its technology to other search engines such as HotBot.

Making Your Mark with Meta-Engines

A meta-search engine, or *meta-engine,* is an umbrella site: You enter your query just once, and the meta-engine runs it in anywhere from a handful to a couple dozen search engines, more or less simultaneously. You can cover a lot of ground quickly with a meta-engine and save yourself huge amounts of time and effort. Sounds terrific, doesn't it?

The downside of using a meta-engine is that it has a lowest-common-denominator effect on your search. It uses only those features that all the search engines it covers have in common. Not all search engines support features such as phrase searching, Boolean AND/ORs, or wild card searching for word stems and variations. Individual search engines handle details such as capitalization and punctuation differently, too. Meta-engines therefore ignore many of the variations and refinements that you can take advantage of when you go directly to an individual search engine site. Meta-engines do only the most basic kind of search at each one.

Meta-engines also return a limited number of results from each site they search, at least in the first go-round. If you get to see only 10 or 20 hits, you may miss the perfect item that's ranked in 11th or 21st place.

What "lowest common denominator" means for you is a return to the KISS principle: Keep it simple, searcher. That ensures that you don't confuse, or get unexpected results from, any of the search engines involved.

Inference Find

Using **Inference Find** (`www.infind.com`) couldn't be easier: Enter your search term and click the search button. That's it. If you really want to put the pressure on, you can use the MaxTime drop-down list to vary the maximum number of seconds that you want Inference Find to spend on your search. (We can't imagine anyone being in that big a rush; our sympathies to you if your life really is that harried.)

Inference Find goes out to half a dozen of the top search engines, submits your search to each of them, and brings back the hit list from each one. Before presenting the results to you, Inference Find merges them, removes the duplicates (it gets big points from us for that!), and neatly clusters the remaining items according to their main emphasis or the type of site that they came from. Sometimes that's useful, sometimes not.

SavvySearch

SavvySearch (`www.savvysearch.com`) is a meta-engine with a twist. The search form includes check boxes for limiting your search to certain types and categories of information (you can select as many as you want). You can enter multiple words and click a button to indicate whether to search them as a phrase or as separate words. A couple dozen language options for the SavvySearch interface appear at the bottom of the screen.

To customize SavvySearch, click (surprise!) the <u>Customize</u> link. You can select from 100 search engines and sources to search, and in what order. The list includes several daily newspapers, network television sites, travel sites, and so on.

The BigHub.com

The BigHub.com (`www.bighub.com`) takes a different approach — actually, a couple different approaches in a single meta-engine:

- ✔ It enables you to select up to eight of the major search engines and directories.
- ✔ It maintains its own index — at the bottom of the page — to hundreds of specialized databases, guides, and references in particular subject areas. Click any of the categories to choose a specialized search engine — anything from CIA publications (in the Travel category) to market research reports (in the Business category).

Ask Jeeves

Ask Jeeves (www.askjeeves.com) is a meta-engine with a twist. First, it attempts to find the answer to your plain-English question in its own vast collection of Internet resources. Figure 3-3 shows what happens when we ask Jeeves, "Where can I find out about travel to New Zealand?" It displays a list of closely matching questions that it understands. The first question happens to be a good match, and when we click the <u>Ask!</u> link, Jeeves takes us to a fine collection of New Zealand travel sites.

But, as they say on the late-night TV infomercials, "That's not all!" Following the list of questions, Jeeves shows us a list of search engines that it has gone ahead and checked on its own (give that machine a bonus for initiative!), along with the number of hits for each one. We can click the down arrow on the right side of each box to see what else a search engine has turned up. Or we can click the search engine name to go directly to its results list, or click the <u>Ask!</u> link to go straight to the "answer" site displayed in the box.

Invisible Web

What a great name — the **Invisible Web** (www.invisibleweb.com). As we discuss in Chapter 2, the information within most gated Web sites — those that require registration to enter — is invisible to most search engines. Invisible Web is a directory that points you to those gated sites that are likely to contain the information you need.

Keep your Invisible Web search very, very simple. Use a general term that describes what you're looking for — *allergy,* for example, rather than *gluten-free foods.*

Dogpile

We saved the best meta-engine, or at least the best name, for last — **Dogpile** (www.dogpile.com). This puppy runs your search through as many as 18 search engines at once. Its Custom Search feature enables you to choose and prioritize your favorites. You can use the same query in general search engines such as GO and AltaVista, Usenet newsgroup search engines, and even specialized file-finding tools.

Because Dogpile searches so many engines, and each one has its own features, quirks, and limitations, it's best to keep your search query as simple as possible. Be sure to read Dogpile's *Help* section before you get yourself in deep doggy, uh, trouble.

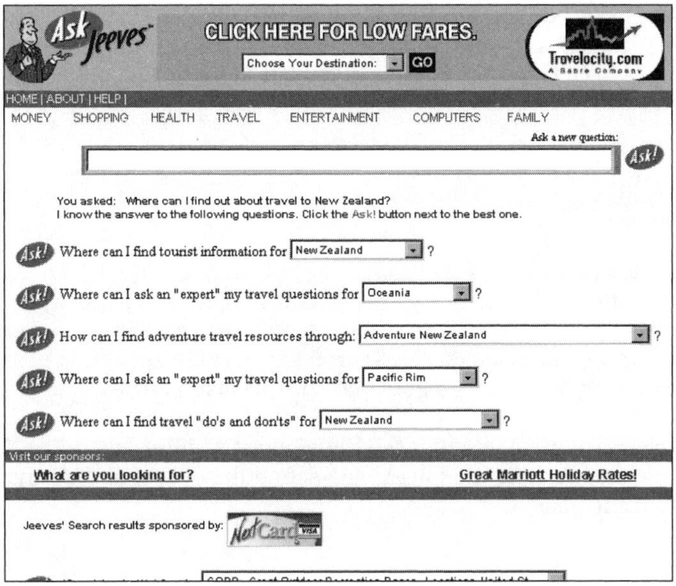

Figure 3-3:
Ask Jeeves
rephrases
our
question.

The Offline Meta Alternatives

One of the drawbacks of meta-engines on the Web is that you must keep your searches v-e-r-y simple. But what if you need to search for an exact phrase, indicate that you want *Apple Computer* but not *apples,* or limit your search to a specialized subject area? A number of offline meta-engine alternatives have sprung up to address those very questions. You load the software on your computer and fire it up when you're ready to search. The meta-engine then goes off to the Web, runs your search terms through the search engines you've selected, and brings back the results. In fact, you can tell some of these packages when you want the search re-run so you can automatically stay current on whatever you're interested in. The advantage of these offline tools is that they're smart enough to use the special features of each search engine, enabling you to construct a more sophisticated search than you could with a Web-based meta-engine.

The bonus CD that comes with this book includes free or trial versions of several offline meta-engines.

Copernic

Copernic offers a free version of its software and two added-value commercial editions. You can download any of these versions from the company's Web site (www.copernic.com). Even the freebie lets you build fairly complex searches, indicating whether you are searching an exact phrase or words that must be capitalized (*Bonds* but not *bonds,* for example). You can download specific Web pages from Copernic's search results to save for later reference. The commercial versions also let you schedule automatic search updates.

BullsEye

You can download **BullsEye** (`www.intelliseek.com/prod/bullseye.htm`) directly from the company's Web site. BullsEye lets you specify words that you want searched as a phrase, limit your search to Web sites added or changed since a specific day, or search for your terms in near proximity to each other (BullsEye gets a gold star for this last feature).

You can save your search and tell BullsEye to monitor any of the Web pages you retrieve, checking the pages on a schedule you set and notifying you whenever the page is changed.

Sherlock

Mac users have it easy. Since Version 8.5 of the Mac operating system, Apple Computer has combined its local "file find" function with an Internet meta–search engine called **Sherlock.** Just select Sherlock from the Apple menu, click the Search Internet tab, and select the Web sites and search engines to search (your choices include AltaVista, Excite, and GO, among others). Then enter your search words, connect to the Net, and see what Sherlock brings Holme. Sherlock 2, available with Mac OS 9, groups similar sources together and retrieves even more on-target results.

Watching the Web with Search Engine Watch and Showdown

Search Engine Watch (`searchenginewatch.com`) and **Search Engine Showdown** (`www.notess.com/search`) are like *Consumer Reports* for truly dedicated Web searchers. These two sites monitor and compare the performances of all the major players you meet in this chapter, and keep you up-to-date on new developments in the field. We devour every edition of the *Search Engine Report,* a free monthly newsletter sent out via e-mail. But then, we get our jollies in some pretty strange ways.

Chapter 4

Using Specialty Search Engines

● ●

In This Chapter

▶ Exploring specialty search engines

▶ Searching online discussion groups

▶ Finding people, companies, maps, and software

● ●

*T*he half-dozen or so search engines whose names you see every time you read an article about the Internet are only a small part of the picture. General and meta-engines, such as the ones described in Chapter 3, are fine when you want to cover the entire Web. But the Swiss Army knife approach isn't always the best one. You may be researching in an area where information is organized in a particular way, such as a phone directory, a shareware catalog, or a collection of maps. You may need to penetrate into sites and special collections that standard Web search tools can't reach. Sometimes you need a tool that's designed to do just one job and to do it well.

How do you find a specialty search engine that'll do that job for you? Luckily, a number of Web sites have taken it upon themselves to catalog and keep track of the expanding population of search engines. Some sites even include a collection of search forms — one for each specialty engine they've identified — so that you can enter your search without leaving the site. Others provide a set of links that let you click and go.

These sites are different from meta-engines. They don't actually take your search and run it through multiple search engines, nor do they process any of your results. These sites simply provide a convenient, one-stop interface to a variety of different search engines — more than any of the meta-engines cover and more than you probably dreamed existed.

The All-in-One Search Page

One of the oldest sites of its type on the Web, the appropriately named **All-in-One Search Page** (www.allonesearch.com) presents a dozen or so broad categories of search engine types, including <u>People</u>, <u>News, Sports & Weather</u>, and <u>Jobs & Career Resources</u>.

Other Interesting Searches, a miscellaneous, catchall category, lists nearly 50 individual search engines, most of which are accompanied by a search form on the All-in-One page itself. Try the FedEx or UPS package tracking service, *Money* magazine's stock quote service, or the Fish Finder directory of fishing information.

Search.com

Search.com (`search.com`) compiles research tools from hundreds of different sites Net-wide. You can search any of a handful of top search engines from Search.com as well. But check out the A-Z List of links to get an idea of what's out there *beyond* the usual suspects: How about the AmeriCom Long Distance Area Decoder? America's Job Bank? The Auto Trader Online Dealer Search? And those are just a few of the *As*!

Beaucoup Search Engines

Beaucoup (`beaucoup.com`) boasts links to more than 2,000 search engines, directories, and indexes. You can browse through a couple dozen broad categories, from the all-purpose to the highly specialized, and then link to the categories that you want to search. Beaucoup provides a terrific summary of hard-to-find resources in education, politics, science, music, art, and *beaucoup* other research areas. Beaucoup means *a lot,* in case you don't speak French.

Searching Newsgroups with RemarQ

Newsgroups — which you may hear Net graybeards refer to as *Usenet* or *netnews* — are a sprawling, global collection of ongoing conversations about everything under, and beyond, the sun. Picture a humongous party with knots of people all talking at once about subjects ranging from medieval armor to microchip technology.

The last time we checked, we found more than 65,000 individual newsgroups, each one devoted to a particular subject. No matter how you look at it, there's a whole lot of schmoozing going on. Those umpteen-thousand groups are organized into several broad categories. Within each category, individual groups are arranged hierarchically, from general discussions down to the ultra-specific. Some categories are several layers deep. The `rec.sport` hierarchy is already one layer beneath the surface. `rec.sport.football` is a layer

below that. You may think we've hit bottom, but no — the `rec.sport`
`.football` **hierarchy goes even lower, to** `rec.sport.football`
`.australian`, `rec.sport.football.canadian`, `rec.sport.football`
`.college`, `rec.sport.football.fantasy`, **and** `rec.sport.football.pro`.

Newsgroups can be an excellent source for fresh and timely news, opinion,
and advice. Chapter 10 tells you more about how to find newsgroups in
certain subject areas and how to act when you get there. Right now, we want
to concentrate on mining that vast conversation pit for specific, focused
information.

The **RemarQ** search engine (`www.remarq.com`) is a fine tool for digging into
newsgroups. It lets you search by newsgroup name; if you want to find that
newsgroup on Canadian football, you can type **Canadian football** in the
search box, click the Forums that Discuss button, and click the <u>Find</u> link. The
first newsgroup in the search results list will undoubtedly be `rec.sport.`
`football.canadian`. At that point, you can click the link to see all recent
postings to the group.

In addition to searching for words that appear in a newsgroup title or
description, RemarQ lets you search through the text of hundreds of thousands of recent newsgroup postings for any mention of your topic. To find
tips on diving in Fiji, we type **Fiji diving** in the search box, click the Messages
that Mention button, and click the <u>Find</u> link. You see the results of our search
in Figure 4-1. It looks like we have plenty of suggestions for the next time we
head to the South Seas.

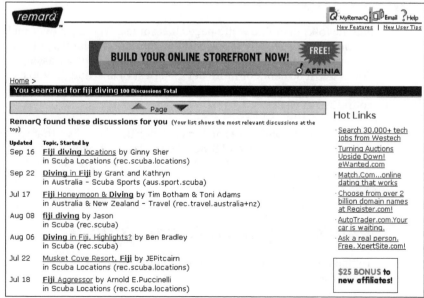

Figure 4-1:
RemarQ
"messages
that
mention"
search
results.

If you already know what newsgroup focuses on your topic, you can drill down through the hierarchy and run your search on that group alone. Drill down? Put down that Black & Decker right now. To drill down in RemarQ, go to the main page, select the broad subject category that describes your subject (say <u>Finance</u>) and then click a subcategory to narrow the focus (say, <u>Taxes</u>). At the bottom of the screen that lists recent discussions, you can type in your search and limit it to the `misc.taxes` newsgroup.

Click the <u>Help</u> link for tips on how to narrow your search. Here are a few pointers to get you started:

✔ If you want to search for a phrase, enclose the words in double quotes ("Boston Marathon").

✔ Put a plus (+) in front of words that *must* appear in the search results (recipes +zucchini).

✔ Put a minus (–) in front of words that *cannot* appear in the search results (python–monty).

As we write this, RemarQ is promising to roll out power search features soon. By the time you read this, you may be able to limit your searches to words in the subject line (a nice way to focus your search), search for postings by a specific author, and limit your search by date. Check out the site and see if a Power Searching option appears on the main search page.

Pinpointing People

Finding folks in online white pages has some advantages over picking up the phone book (especially those pathetic mutilated volumes you find hanging forlornly in some public phone booths). Unlike directory assistance, it doesn't cost 50 cents or more per call. Best of all, though, you can do a nationwide search in just a few seconds — and sometimes pick up e-mail addresses as well.

You run into *people finders* at sites all over the Web. Two that we rely on are Yahoo!'s People Search and Switchboard. infoUSA, which we talk about in the "Locating Businesses" section in this chapter, lets you search for residential phone numbers as well.

Yahoo!-ing friends and family

To find an e-mail address in **Yahoo! People Search** (`people.yahoo.com`), follow these steps:

1. **Enter the name of the person in the search form.**

   If you click the <u>Advanced</u> link, you can select the SmartName feature, which automatically accounts for common variants, such as *Bob* and *Robert.* If you know the domain portion of that person's e-mail address — such as *aol* or *ibm* — you can enter that here, too.

2. **Click the Search button.**

3. **On the results list (if any), scan the names to find the person's e-mail address.**

4. **Write the person and ask for money. Just kidding.**

To find a phone number (in the United States only), follow these steps:

1. **Enter the person's last name and first name (or initial) in the search form shown in Figure 4-2. (Remember that many people prefer to list themselves by first initial.)**

2. **Enter the city and/or state, if you're sure of it. (This helps if the person has a common name.)**

3. **Click the Search button.**

4. **On the results list, scan the names to find the person's phone number.**

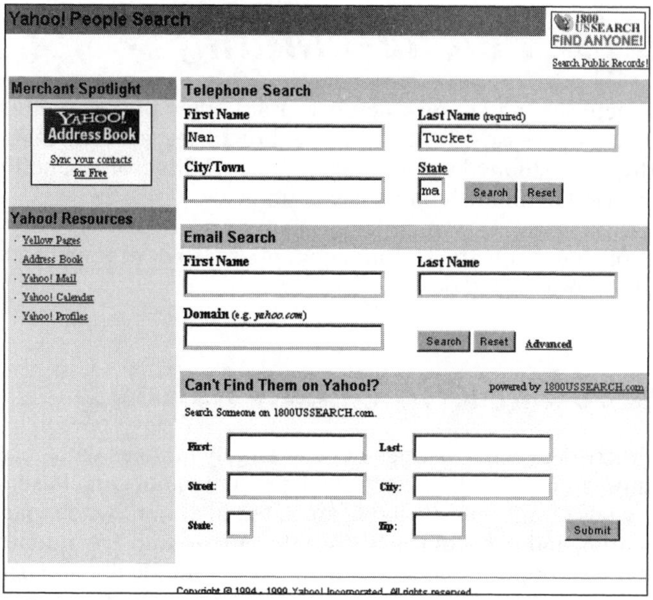

Figure 4-2:
Yahoo!
People
Search.

Plugging into Switchboard

To find an e-mail address in **Switchboard** (www.switchboard.com), follow these steps:

1. Click the <u>Find Email</u> link.

2. Enter the person's last name (if the last name is very common, try entering the person's first name, too, or the first two or three letters of the name).

3. Click <u>Search</u>.

4. Click the person's e-mail address — are you ready for this? — to send him or her mail.

To find a phone number through Switchboard, follow these steps:

1. Click the <u>People Search</u> link.

2. Enter the last name — and city or state, if you want.

3. Click <u>Search</u>.

4. Choose your friend from the resulting list.

Some Tips for People-Finding

Online directories tend to be much better at finding phone numbers than at finding e-mail addresses. That's because directories get their telephone information the old-fashioned way — from published directories and the same databases used by phone companies nationwide.

Many people have unlisted telephone numbers. Most of those listings do *not* appear in the Web-based directories.

The problem with e-mail listings

Online directories' e-mail listings depend largely on folks who volunteer their own listings, and that's still a very small percentage of e-mail users worldwide. Very few of our online friends are listed in either Switchboard or Yahoo! People Search, and some of the listings that we do find are outdated. When you order new phone service, your listing is automatically updated and shows up in the next edition of the phone book — unless you've requested an unlisted number, of course. But no built-in way exists to keep your e-mail listing current — and most people don't have any incentive to do so.

They're not listed — now what?

Here are some tips to keep in mind if you're not having much luck finding a person's listing:

- ✔ If one directory doesn't work for you, try another.

- ✔ Start out with a general search, using the last name and initial, or just the last name. The directory may show an initial, a nickname, or a formal name other than the one you associate with the person.

- ✔ Don't include a city at the outset. The person may have moved but kept the same e-mail address, or even the same phone number.

- ✔ Don't expect online directories to be any more timely than the local phone book.

- ✔ Explore other avenues for finding people online:

  - Do a general Web search to see if the person has a home page.

  - Check student, faculty, and staff directories at colleges and other institutional Web sites. Many college and university sites are listed at `www.clas.ufl.edu/CLAS/american-universities.html`.

  - Check high school and college alumni associations through `dir.yahoo.com/Education/Organizations/Alumnae_i_Associations`.

  - Is she famous, or well-known in her field? Has she written books or published articles? A search in local or national newspapers, scholarly journals, and trade publications, or even online bookstores (such as Amazon.com) may turn up contact information. (You can find out more about these sources in Chapters 9, 11, 12, and 13.)

  - Celebrity listings: Did you go to high school with Courtney Love? Just wanna catch up on old times? Uh-huh. If you seem to have misplaced her e-mail address somewhere along the way, try `dir.yahoo.com/Society_and_Culture/People/Celebrities/Celebrity_Addresses`.

Locating Businesses

Looking up companies can be a tricky business. Is the company listed under *IBM* or *I.B.M.* or *International Business Machines?* Is it *The Gap;* or *Gap, The;* or just plain *Gap?* Good old *Macy's,* or the more formal *R.H. Macy and Company?* Does the subsidiary or division have the same name as the parent company? Are you sure? People-searching has its complexities, too, but at least you don't have to think about who *owns* them.

Business directory searching drives librarians nuts, especially when they're paying a couple of dollars a pop in a commercial database to pull out *wrong* companies along with the right ones. Web directories sometimes charge companies for the privilege of being listed, but they usually don't charge *you* to use them. That's good news, because it means you can afford to experiment if your first attempt doesn't work out.

Finding firms with BigBook

BigBook (www.bigbook.com) enables you to search by company name, or yellow pages–style, by category. It does insist on a city or state, so you can't search for every Ace Hardware in the country. But you can get a list of the 50 or so Ace Hardwares in Chicago. You can also opt for a category search instead, to get *all* the hardware stores in the city, regardless of name.

Category searching

Category searching is tricky at times. Of course you can guess the name under which your business is classified, and maybe you'll hit it right. But if you browse through BigBook's category listing, you won't find hardware stores under <u>Shopping</u>; they're part of the <u>House and Garden</u> category. ***Moral:*** Think creatively, not categorically.

BigBook's <u>Detailed Search</u> mode expands your options in several different ways. You can search by category and name at the same time, though you still have to enter a city or state.

Suppose you want to get addresses of all the banks in area code 415, or all the drug stores in zip code 19102? Key in the category and the code that you want (no need for city or state with zip code searches), and voilà! — your list of possibilities, with links to maps for almost every bank.

What was the name of that great Italian restaurant on Walnut Street in Philly? Can't remember? No problemo: Key **Italian restaurants** into BigBook's category box, enter the street and city, and click the Find It button. BigBook comes back with a list of pasta-bilities. None of 'em sound right? Um, maybe it was on *Locust* Street . . . or possibly *Spruce*. Or. . . .

Where's the nearest. . . ?

BigBook also lets you look for businesses by type or by specific name, within a ½- to 100-mile radius of a certain address or intersection. Click <u>Search By Distance</u>, and then enter the business name or category and the address you're starting from. Use the pull-down menu to specify how far to extend your search, and then click the Find It button.

You can use BigBook's <u>Search By Distance</u> link to help you determine whether an area is already saturated with the kind of business you want to open, or whether a market opportunity exists for you. If you want to open a bookstore but you discover 40 bookstores already operating within 10 miles of your intended location, perhaps you'd better think about opening a different kind of business. Or moving.

Getting info from infoUSA

BigBooks is great if you need to find the nearest Starbucks or all the employment agencies in Seattle. But suppose you have a phone number and need to know what company or person it belongs to, or you want to find all the companies in Florida with *cyber* in their names? Head over to **infoUSA** (www.infousa.com), where you can get the name associated with any publicly listed telephone number, or look up businesses or individuals by name, or companies by category.

Reverse phone number search

Sometimes we get voice mail messages from "Joe at 312-555-1234," asking us to call back. Before we do, we prefer to see if the number is a residential listing for a long-lost cousin, or a business listing for that client we haven't heard from in a while. At the main infoUSA page, click <u>Reverse Lookup by Phone</u> and then type in the phone number in the search box on the next screen. Joe's Fly-by-Nite Roofers? No thank you; we'll let this one slide.

infoUSA's reverse phone lookup does not include unlisted residential phone numbers, nor does it include direct-dial numbers to someone's office phone (unless the number is listed in the white pages of the phone book).

White pages search

infoUSA lets you search for personal and company names and, unlike most other directories, doesn't require that you limit the search to a single city. Say you have a great name for a new business — Monique's Boutique, say — and you want to see if anyone else in your state has already started using it.

Click <u>Search Business Name</u>, and then type in the name or the main part of the name with an asterisk (*) at the end to account for slight variations. To see if someone is already using Monique's Boutique, or Monique Boutique, or Moniques Boutique, type **Monique*** in the Business Name box, select your state, and click <u>Find Businesses</u>. Figure 4-3 shows the results of our search for *Monique** in Texas.

Going global with WorldPages

What if your interests go beyond finding a list of hometown banks, nearby
bookstores, or good restaurants in a U.S. city you're planning to visit?
WorldPages (www.worldpages.com) adds Canada to the mix, to start with.
This business directory site also includes specialized mini-directories of legal,
government, automotive, entertainment, restaurant, and travel resources.

The key to global business research, though, is WorldPages' International
section, which links to company directories in nearly 200 countries. So far,
the resources in some areas are pretty sketchy, but we figure that's because
not all countries are industrialized to the point of using company directories
routinely — let alone putting them on the Web. Factor in the language barriers and problems with displaying different alphabets, and it's amazing that
anyone's figured out a coherent way of getting so much of this stuff online.

WorldPages has made a good start. Just click that International link, select
the country you want to search from the pull-down menu, and then click Find
It. Next up: a list of directories for that country.

From there, you're one short step away from your quest for hotels in
Stockholm or car rentals in Lund. Better make that *two* clicks — you see a
British flag on the upper right to indicate the English-language version of the
site. Ah, there you go. Much better. Unless, of course, your Swedish is a lot
better than ours.

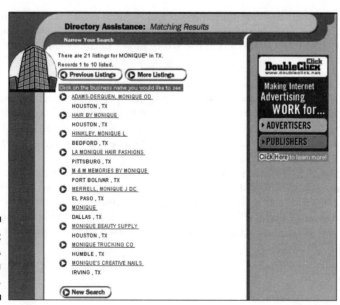

Figure 4-3:
infoUSA
search
results.

Questing for Maps with MapQuest

We love maps. You may have heard the saying, "the map is not the territory." Our attitude is "Okay, but we still love maps." As far as we're concerned, one of the best uses of all that graphical bandwidth enabled by the Web is the ability to display maps online, and even draw them to order.

You can find maps and links to map sites all over the Web, including BigBook and WorldPages, which are discussed in previous sections. But MapQuest specializes in maps, so that's our first stop. At **MapQuest** (www.mapquest.com), you can

- ✔ Browse through an interactive world atlas, zooming in and out from a country-wide view down to a street-level view.

- ✔ Pinpoint an exact address.

- ✔ Get driving instructions (city to city and, for selected urban areas throughout the world, door to door).

- ✔ Locate places of interest, such as restaurants, hotels, museums, theaters, and even ATMs.

- ✔ Create maps that include markers for your friends' addresses and other likely destinations.

- ✔ Print, download, and save your personalized maps.

- ✔ Link from your own Web site to a customized map you've created and saved at MapQuest. (You have to join MapQuest to use this feature, but membership is free.)

- ✔ Plan a trip itinerary with help from the Mobil Travel Guide.

Say you've gotten an invitation to your high school reunion. (If you haven't graduated from high school, use your imagination to visualize that grand event.) Years have passed since you visited your hometown, and a lot has changed — new highways and buildings have gone up, and old landmarks are gone. You think you can still find your way, but wouldn't it help to have a current map?

Point your browser to www.mapquest.com, click <u>Online Maps</u>, and key in the coordinates — an exact address, or the cross streets. Click the Get Map button, and, almost instantly, something like Figure 4-4 appears.

The Map Level panel at the right lets you click in for a closer view of the immediate area, or back up for a picture of the neighborhood. The City view shows your destination in context — what part of town you're headed for.

You're not planning to drive across country for this reunion, but you need some help getting there from the far-flung corner of the city where you're staying the night before. Advance-planner that you are, you click the <u>Directions To</u> link. You enter your starting point in the form that pops up next. MapQuest is smart enough to enter the address that you just used for the destination. Other options on the screen enable you to choose what kind of map you want, or to select written directions instead (Text Only). One more click, and you're on your way, with custom-tailored instructions to print out and take with you — assuming you remember to grab them before you leave.

MapQuest hasn't mapped the entire country, let alone the world, down to street level. Door-to-door directions work only when your journey starts and ends in certain major urban areas. If you can't get door-to-door directions, your fallback is city-to-city.

Want to avoid the interstate, or take the fastest route, even if it involves a few more miles? Click <u>Door-to-Door Options</u> and select Fastest or Shortest. Click any of the listed obstacles — such as toll roads, ferry lanes, or limited-access highways — that you prefer to avoid. Now if only MapQuest could tell you about construction zones and commute-hour traffic backups.

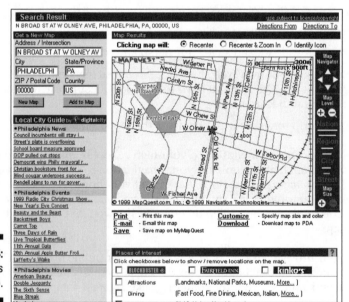

Figure 4-4:
MapQuest's
online map.

Shopping for Software with Shareware.com and Download.com

We used to be wimps when it came to sniffing out neat software utilities on the Net and then figuring out how to get them from *out there* onto our computers. Searching and downloading software is easier with a friendly assist from a helper program such as WS_Archie or Anarchie (check the accompanying CD for some software you can use), but you're still faced with *finding* worthwhile stuff in the first place.

Finding freebies at Shareware.com

Our lives improved — to say nothing of our self-esteem as savvy computer users — the moment we found **Shareware.com** (www.shareware.com). Shareware.com is a catalog of publicly available software found in shareware archives and other distribution sites around the world. You can search it by program name, type of application, hardware platform, or operating system, and by other useful criteria. And you don't need a helper program, just your Web browser, to transfer it to your computer.

Shareware.com offers both shareware and freeware. To make sure that you're clear on the distinction, check out the appendix toward the end of this book.

If you know exactly what you're looking for at Shareware.com, enter the name of the program or file in the Search box, and select your computer type or operating system. Click Search, and Shareware.com displays a list of matches, with descriptions and keywords for each. Another couple of clicks and a copy of the program is en route to your hard drive.

What if you don't have a particular software package in mind, but you know what you want it to do? Or you've heard of a program that you'd like to check out, but you're not quite sure of the spelling? Click Advanced to bring up the form. Then specify your computer type or operating system, and enter descriptive words to help pin down what you're looking for.

The Advanced feature extends your options a gazillion-fold. You can tell Shareware.com to do the following:

- ✔ *Exclude* a certain word — useful when you want to eliminate whole categories, such as games or spreadsheets, from your search.
- ✔ Pay attention to capitalization — Shareware.com is normally case-insensitive.

- ✔ Limit the search to files created after a certain date.

- ✔ Sort by date.

- ✔ Search particular software archives — assuming you know where you want to look.

Browsing at Download.com

Shareware.com's sister site, **Download.com** (www.download.com), differs from Shareware.com in two ways. One, in addition to shareware and freeware, it includes trial versions of commercially available software, plus links that enable you to purchase the complete versions online. Two, it offers an organized catalog of application types ranging from business software to games, utilities, and more. You can click down through a specific category to locate exactly the product you want.

You can also search Download.com by keyword. Type a word or phrase in the search box describing the software you're looking for. Try a search for virus-checking software, for example. Some of the listed packages are free, some are demos of commercially available programs, and some are try-before-you-buy shareware.

For more precise searches, click the Advanced link next to the search box. You can search by category, software author, and title, and limit the results to commercial demos, or to software that's been downloaded frequently or that's new to Download.com.

Don't put that in your mouth; you don't know where it's been! Okay, substitute "on your disk" for "in your mouth." The point's the same: Strange software can sometimes make you sick. Unless you're very, very sure of the source, run every executable file you get from the Net — that means shareware and freeware, Java applets, anything that has the power to write to or modify information on your hard drive — through a virus-checking program before you install it. Shareware.com and Download.com do no virus-screening, and the "reliability guide" they display when you opt to download a file is just a measure of how many successful connections have been made to that software archive or distribution site.

Chapter 5

Subject Catalogs: The Narrow-Down Approach

In This Chapter

▶ Drilling down for precision

▶ Comparing subject catalogs and search engines

▶ Sampling subject catalogs

*R*emember the card catalog? A few still exist out there in library-land. Before libraries went electronic, those wooden cabinets stuffed with 3 x 5 cards occupied a position of honor. And justifiably — they held the key to finding what you wanted, even if you didn't know exactly what you were looking for.

Without a card catalog, you'd have to wander aimlessly up and down the aisles, glancing at the titles on hundreds of book spines until some of them started to look relevant, until you finally found the right shelf and the volume or two that you needed. In a large library, that searching could take hours. With a catalog, though, your fingers — and your mind — do the walking. Good thing libraries still have catalogs, though the cards today are often electronic.

Narrowing Your Search: The Drill-Down Drill

We like the term *drilling down* to describe how you can start out with a very general heading and gradually, by selecting the right subheading and perhaps an even more specific subheading after that, narrow in on precisely the subject you're looking for.

For example, the library subject catalog enables you to start with a broad topic, such as *History,* and then narrow it down by place — *European* — and time — *19th Century* — until you have a manageable number of books on the topic to deal with. You can narrow it down even further, like this:

History

History — European

History — European — 19th Century

History — European — 19th Century — War of 1812

History — European — 19th Century — War of 1812 — Personal Narratives

We're making these headings up, in case any librarians out there are keeping score. But you get the idea: Start broad and then drill down through progressively more specific levels, defining your target as you go. Now, are you going to gasp with surprise when we tell you that online subject catalogs work exactly the same way that offline subject catalogs do? We didn't think so.

You may encounter the terms *channel, subject category, subject guide, subject index,* and *subject catalog* used interchangeably on the Internet. They all refer to pretty much the same thing. We use *subject catalog* in this book.

Subject Catalogs versus Search Engines

Search engines get most of the attention when it comes to researching online. But subject catalogs are just as important, and sometimes even better, and here are a few reasons why:

- ✔ **Subject catalogs are *selective*.** They don't claim to include everything — just the best, most important, or most focused information on a topic. Often, that information is chosen by people who are experts in the field.

- ✔ **Subject catalogs are *more controlled*.** They don't depend on you to choose the right keyword or come up with the optimal search query. Instead, they present a set of logical choices, gateways for you and your questions to flow through.

- ✔ **Subject catalogs are *built by human beings*** who think the way you do — or who understand how most human beings think — whereas search engines are built on a foundation of math, linguistic analysis, and a lot of other abstract constructs.

- ✔ **Subject catalogs *don't contain spam*** — that is, unrelated Web sites with hidden keywords to ensure that they get retrieved, even if you're looking for something entirely unrelated.

When should you use a subject catalog instead of a search engine? No law says that you can't use both, of course, but starting with the subject-catalog approach makes sense in these situations:

- ✔ You don't know quite what you're looking for, but you'll recognize it when you see it.

- ✔ You're looking for general background on a very broad topic, such as American politics.

- ✔ You can express your subject in many different ways; or you can't think of a standard vocabulary term, key phrase, or bit of jargon for a search engine to chew on.

Hybrid Subject Catalogs

Most major search engine sites have recognized the value of the subject-catalog approach and added a subject catalog to their sites. You can still use the search engine to search the entire Web, or confine your search to the subject catalog on the site. We use the term *hybrid* — as opposed to *pure* — to describe subject catalogs that are part of a search engine site and integrated closely with it. We describe several of the biggest ones in the following sections.

Getting a hole-in-one with Yahoo!

Many people think of **Yahoo!** as a search engine, but it's actually a subject catalog, and the first Web-based catalog to attain fame and fortune. That exclamation point isn't just our editorial expression of enthusiasm; it's a trademarked part of the Yahoo! name (although it's not in the URL: www.yahoo.com). Figure 5-1 shows the main Yahoo! search form. But before you type a search term in that box up top, take a closer look at those subject categories below it.

Say for example that your friends have been leaning on you to play golf. You've been resisting — swinging at a little white ball has always struck you as a sure way to ruin a perfectly good walk. But maybe you're getting curious. Rather than ask your friends and betray your budding interest, take your questions to the privacy of Yahoo!. You can type in **golf** and see where it takes you. But maybe you want to explore the whole terrain; get the lay — or the lie (golf joke) — of the land.

Figure 5-1:
Yahoo!
search form
and subject
catalog.

Scanning Yahoo!'s top-level categories, you see that <u>Recreation & Sports</u> is probably a good starting point. Golf, as far as we know, is a sport. <u>Sports</u> is also a link under the main category, so you click that, and come up with an alphabetical list that includes an amazing array of activities: <u>Boomerang</u>, <u>Camel Racing</u>, <u>Dogsledding</u>, <u>Rodeo</u> — oh, and <u>Golf</u>. Try to erase the image of throwing a boomerang while camel racing, click <u>Golf</u>, and review the results.

Yahoo! presents you with a neat three-part summary of golf-related resources:

✔ **The first part consists of sites that the Yahoo! golf pro considers especially timely and relevant.** PGA tour updates, scheduled golf events on the Net (yes, there are such things — real-time golf chat, celebrity golfer interviews, and so on), and a link to Yahoo! discussion areas on golf-related topics.

✔ **The second part includes themes and variations on the subject of golf.** Similar to those subheadings in the library catalog that we talk about earlier in this chapter — history of golf, golf resorts, golf trivia, and so on. It also contains a link to FAQs (Frequently Asked Questions), a valuable research lead.

✔ **The third part is a long list of golf-specific sites.** When we checked, this part contained over 40 sites, and every one of them looked like a hole-in-one.

Compare all these resources to the random assortment of links (no pun intended) that you get if you simply type **golf** into a search engine such as HotBot or AltaVista. Go ahead; try it. We'll wait.

AltaVista's views of the Web

AltaVista (www.altavista.com) is one of the largest of the search engines (see Chapter 3 for details). The AltaVista subject catalog ranges from <u>Arts & Entertainment</u> through <u>Recreation & Travel</u> — that's where we find golf sites, if we want to duplicate the search we describe in the preceding section — to a category called World, which includes non-English-language sites — Icelandic, Afrikaans, Indonesian, even Esperanto.

You may be tempted to just type your keywords in the search box. However, doing so tells AltaVista that you want to search the entire Web, not just the AltaVista catalog. Instead, click the category that generally describes your topic and then either type your search term in the Find This search box or drill down to the specific area that you're interested in (see "Narrowing Your Search: The Drill-Down Drill," earlier in this chapter, for a description of *drilling down*).

Excite-ing possibilities

Excite (www.excite.com) has a reputation as the search engine that knows what you're thinking. Well, not quite, but its concept-based searching and "get me more like this" feature *are* pretty impressive. (See Chapter 3 for more about these Excite features.) Excite's subject catalog isn't as deep or comprehensive as Yahoo!'s, but it does offer a quick route to some of the most commonly researched topics.

Resist the urge to type-'n'-go. Instead of entering a keyword in the search form and letting Excite have its way with you, maintain control by taking the subject-catalog approach.

Say you want to find information on financial aid for college. Click the <u>Education</u> link, and, sure enough, a link to <u>Financial Aid</u> pops up on the next screen. Click once more, and up pops a set of tools, shown in Figure 5-2, for finding scholarships, loans, and other ways of paying for tuition.

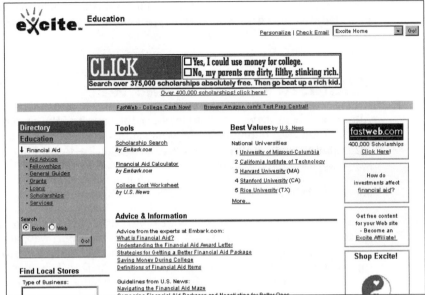

Figure 5-2:
Excite
Financial
Aid search
screen.

GO seek and ye shall find

The **GO Network** (www.go.com) search engine covers both the Web and its version of a subject catalog, called simply Topics. Actually, GO offers two different subject catalogs. When you, er, go to GO's Web site, you see the GO search form and the list of Centers. You can click any of these Centers categories or subcategories to link to discussion groups, sites where you can buy stuff, news sources, tools for posting your resume online, and so on. The Centers all have one thing in common — interactivity. They take you to places where you can talk, shop, find a doctor, or, we suppose, talk shop about finding a doctor.

But if you're looking for in-depth information on a specific research topic, click the Topics tab. Here you find collections of Web sites, organized by subject category and then divided into more specific subcategories. We are both small business owners — that is, owners of small businesses — so we decided to see what kind of information was available on GO to help us run our businesses. We clicked the Topics tab and then the Small business link under Business. At this point, we could click a sub-subcategory like Start-up issues (thank goodness we're both past that stage!), or explore any of the links to small business Web sites listed on the same page.

Pure Subject Catalogs

Yes, pure. Don't laugh. The subject-catalog approach goes back to before the dawn of the Internet, when librarians strode the earth. In that primitive era, subject catalogs were woven out of bark or carved, slowly and painstakingly, in stone.

You don't believe us, do you? Okay: When we talk about a *pure* subject catalog, we mean one that's put together by experts with a focus on finding the very best and most authoritative resources online, no matter how esoteric or deeply buried they may be. Pure subject catalogs don't depend on search engines or need to mesh, as the hybrid catalogs do, with the ever-changing Web at large. They cover academic research topics as well as popular ones, and many have "Heavy-Duty Research Tool" written all over them. The WWW Virtual Library, the Argus Clearinghouse, and About.com are three of our favorite pure subject catalogs.

Scholarly research sites operate at a different, usually far more leisurely, pace than the Web at large. Finding sites that haven't been updated in months, or even years, is not uncommon. Depending on the topic, this may not be a problem; resources in a field such as medieval studies are probably fairly static compared to the rate of change in science and technology. Just be aware that some otherwise excellent subject catalogs aren't all that up-to-date. Remember that they're put together by people — who have *lives* — and not by machines. But some of the sites these catalogs *link to* may, in turn, point to more recent entries.

World Wide Web Virtual Library

The **World Wide Web Virtual Library** (`vlib.org`) — sometimes streamlined to the W3 Virtual Library — is the essence of cool, despite its gawky name. Why? Because it was invented by Tim Berners-Lee, the creator of the Web itself.

Figure 5-3 hints at the range of information that you can find on the Virtual Library's shelves. The catalog pages for individual topics are housed on servers all over the world. Every one is different, but each is maintained by a certified expert in the field. Many pages are written in an easy-to-follow narrative style, with lots of description and personal commentary. It's almost like having a personal guide to the subject.

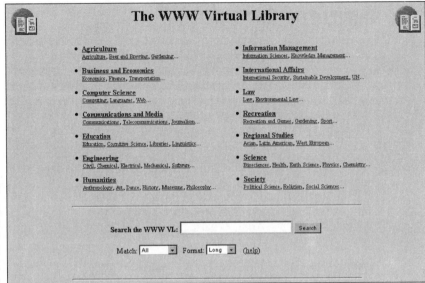

Figure 5-3:
The World
Wide Web
Virtual
Library.

Subject catalogs are a good way to find *mega-sites* and *guru pages* (such as the ones described in Chapter 6) that search engines won't turn up.

Argus Clearinghouse

The **Argus Clearinghouse** (clearinghouse.net) is — are you ready for this? — a subject catalog of subject catalogs. It began as a research project for library school students who were instructed to ferret out indexes, bibliographies, catalogs, and guides-to-the-literature in dozens of academic disciplines, wherever they existed on the Net.

Compared with the hybrid catalogs (see the "Hybrid Subject Catalogs" section, earlier in this chapter), the top-level categories at Argus have a definite scholarly bent. No Automobiles, Games, or Shopping here. Instead, you find groupings such as Arts & Humanities, Business & Employment, Government & Law, and Science & Mathematics.

What's intriguing about the listings on Argus is that each one is rated with one to five check marks, based on the subject catalog's description and evaluation of resources, design, and organizational scheme, and how much information is provided *about* the catalog and its authors.

Yesterday I couldn't even spell engenir, and today I are one

Reva got that line from an engineer. *He* seemed to think it was funny. But hey, why don't we look at the Engineering category as an example of how the W3 Virtual Library works. (Are we smooth or what? Don't answer that.)

The Virtual Library lists more than two dozen subcategories under the general heading of Engineering. They range from specialties, such as <u>Acoustics and Vibrations</u> or <u>Conventional Ceramics</u> at the top, to <u>Wastewater Engineering</u> and <u>Welding Engineering</u> at the bottom.

Under <u>Telecommunications</u>, we notice a subheading — probably because it's the only subheading on this particular list — for <u>Amateur Radio</u>. Back when Reva was a girl geek, she was intrigued by ham radio, but lost her nerve when she discovered she'd have to learn Morse code (she was going to be a doctor, too, before calculus had the same chilling effect). Go ahead, she tells herself; click it.

The W3 Virtual Library comes through: The Amateur Radio page offers more than 50 neatly organized resources — many with descriptions — for hams and wannabe-hams: clubs and organizations, government regulations, frequency guides, packet radio information, amateur satellites and other technologies, and links to sites such as VE2DM's Wonderful World of Amateur Radio (`www.cam.org/~dino/ham.html`). Oh, and tests. *Dit-dit-dit dah-dah-dah dit-dit-dit. . . .*

About.com

About.com (`about.com`) takes the W3 Virtual Library's idea of the expert subject guide and carries it one step further. The company hires real people not only to put together collections of worthwhile resources in their areas of expertise, but also to interact with you and keep you up-to-date through newsletters, e-mail, bulletin-board discussions, and scheduled online chats. These experts are called guides, and their job is to guide you to the premier resources on the Net. About.com distinguishes itself from other pure subject catalogs by including original articles by its guides, as well as a selective catalog to the best of the Net.

We're curious about some of the herbal remedies, such as St. John's Wort, that are supposed to be natural alternatives to prescription drugs. Are they really useful? Can they be harmful instead of helpful to your health? We tried a search engine search, and it pulled up a ton of stuff about herbs and alternative medicine — some of it pretty weird. This strikes us as one research area where an experienced guide could save us a lot of grief.

From About.com's home page, we select the <u>Health/Fitness</u> category, and from the <u>Alternative Medicine</u> submenu, we pick <u>Herbs for Health</u>. We find articles right there on a couple of the hottest herbal remedies, plus links to related subjects such as Chinese herbalism, herb books and manuals, newsletters and 'zines, and sources for herb plants and seeds.

Chapter 6

Playing the Links: Guru Pages and Mega-Sites

. . . .

In This Chapter

▶ Giving something back to the Net

▶ Grooving on guru pages

▶ Making use of mega-sites

. . . .

*T*he Internet has always been a barter economy. Long before anyone dreamed up the phrase *electronic commerce,* people were building useful tools, archives, and collections of information, and offering them up to their fellow Netizens, for free. If you derived value from the Net and were in a position to create something useful in return, you were expected to give something back — not necessarily to the exact person whose tools you'd used, but to the Net at large. A FAQ, or Frequently Asked Questions list (see Chapter 10), is an example of someone — or several someones — giving something back.

What does *giving something back to the Net* have to do with doing research online? That's simple: Much of what people offer up to the Net is useful information on a topic about which they happen to be the resident guru. You know the guy who's a walking encyclopedia of baseball statistics? The woman with her own personal database of every Beatles recording in existence — including the rare, early English imports? The kid who loves stamps, or dinosaurs, or vintage airplanes?

All those folks are on the Web. And they've put up Web sites full of information, and pointers to *more* information that they've ferreted out of the far corners of cyberspace — obsessively, in some cases — just because they love the subject and they want to share their enthusiasm with you. Aren't you lucky?

We're not being sarcastic. You really *are* lucky. You may not want to be cornered by a heavy-breathing philatelist at a party where you can't escape. But if stamp collecting is what you're looking for (and who are we to judge?), finding a good *guru page* puts you one step ahead in the information-gathering game.

In this chapter, we cover both guru pages — those helpful sites put together by dedicated individuals like the ones we just described — and the slightly more formal *mega-sites*.

Tapping Into the Contributions of Others

Institutions such as universities, libraries, government agencies, and businesses sometimes perform a guru-like function similar to that we describe in the previous section. They compile pointers to useful sites for particular kinds of information, or coordinate the Web resources of their entire organization — and sometimes other, related entities, too — and present it in a way that helps ease your way through the bureaucratic maze. We call these concentrations of institutional wisdom *mega-sites* (*mega* meaning large) because they act as gateways to anywhere from a handful to hundreds of other individual sites.

Mega-sites are a form of guru pages, but since a guru is usually a person, we've reserved that term for Web-spun labors of love, and the more formal-sounding *mega-site* for pages put together by some official agency or institution.

What guru pages and mega-sites have in common is *links*. Each one includes — and some consist of nothing but — a compilation of links to *other* sites that someone has checked out and deemed worthy of inclusion. Often, the links are right up front; you see them as soon as you navigate to the site. If they're not obvious, you may have to click around a bit; look for pointer-type phrases such as *Useful Links, Related Sites,* or *Other Blah-Blah Resources* (for *Blah-Blah,* fill in the topic that the site is dedicated to, assuming you're not actually looking at the Ultimate Blah-Blah Page). The real value of such sites lies in their expertly chosen links to new and potentially useful information. Finding a good guru page or mega-site is like having a librarian hand you a ready-made list of books on your topic when you thought you'd have to compile your own from scratch.

And don't forget — it's hard work pulling all those links together, maintaining the list, and replacing or updating links to pages that have moved. If you find a link that's dead, or if you find what looks like a great resource on the topic that the guru page or mega-site hasn't included, here's your chance to give back to the Web. E-mail the owner of the page and let that person know — politely, of course — about the change in a URL or the new site you've found.

Guru Pages: Experts, Enthusiasts, and Obsessives

Here's our guru joke: A guy goes to India on a spiritual quest and climbs a high mountain peak to talk to the guru, reputedly the wisest man in the world. "Guru," he asks, bowing deeply before the ancient, bearded figure in tattered robes, "please tell me the meaning of life."

The wise old man is silent for a minute and then replies, "The meaning of life is . . . fish."

"FISH???" the seeker responds, incredulously. "You're telling me that the meaning of life is FISH?!"

The guru looks at him mildly and says, "You mean it *isn't?*"

The world is full of gurus, very few of whom live on mountaintops and dress in rags. The word originally referred to a spiritual teacher, but now the term *guru* is used more broadly to refer to a genuine expert of any kind — from a competent car mechanic to an awesome Nintendo master to a corporate mentor who knows how to play *that* particular game. Gurus not only *know* but are also willing to share. Fortunately for you, the Net is full of them, too.

You can think of a *guru page* as a highly specialized subject catalog that covers just a small portion of the Web. A guru page doesn't aspire to the encyclopedic reach of the subject catalogs described in Chapter 5. Instead, it focuses on a single topic or theme. See the sidebar "A grab bag of guru pages" for examples of several different guru pages, each very useful in its own way.

Subject catalogs are a good way to find guru pages — a better bet than search engines, which aren't as good at distinguishing the *echt* (German for genuine) from the *ecch* (American for not-that-great). You may also read about guru pages in business and hobby magazines, and hear about them from your friends and fellow stamp — or whatever — collectors.

Bookmark it! When you find a great guru page, add it to your browser's bookmarks or Favorites list as soon as you realize you've struck gold. Don't leave the site without bookmarking it, or you may never find your way back. And, in the spirit of Giving Something Back, share the wealth — tell other interested parties about it, too.

Mega-Sites: Stepping through the Gateway

A mega-site can be a convenient gateway into an unfamiliar subject area or a means to ensure that you don't overlook key resources in a field where you're expected to be well-versed. Many of the starting points that we recommend in later chapters for particular kinds of research — including FedWorld for government information (see Chapter 11), WorldPages for company directories (see Chapter 4), and AJR NewsLink (see Chapter 13), among others — are actually mega-sites as well. Here, we provide just a few examples of mega-sites that you may not otherwise encounter.

How do you find a useful mega-site in your particular field or occupation? Be on the lookout for articles in professional magazines, conference presentations, and continuing-education seminars that spotlight Web-based research aids. If we don't happen to touch on your specialty here, it's a sure bet that your colleagues in the field will call your attention to the resources *they've* uncovered. Listen up when they do.

Subject-oriented Web catalogs like the ones in Chapter 5 can be a good way to locate mega-sites. In Yahoo!, for instance, select your specific subject category and then scan the descriptions of individual sites with an eye out for ones that sound comprehensive. Look for phrases like "Index to . . ." or "Directory of . . .," and telltale words like *Pointers* or *Links*.

The librarian's guide to everything

Librarians and research professionals have been on the Net from the beginning. They created gopher pages (see Chapter 1 for a discussion of gopher-space), constructed online public access catalogs, and have been busy organizing and indexing the Web since the first Web page went online. So it should come as no surprise that librarians and other professional researchers have also built mega-sites to point you to the best of the Web. In this section, we introduce you to three such professionally crafted sites. Check with your friendly neighborhood librarians to see what they've built. You can often find a link on the library's Web site.

> ✔ **Direct Search** (gwis2.circ.gwu.edu/~gprice/direct.htm) is a collection of links to directories, lists, and other resources that most search engines don't capture. Gary Price, the site developer, has organized it

into general topics such as Business/Economics, Government, and Humanities, with detailed subcategories such as lists of lists, salary surveys, databases of nonprofit organizations, and currency converters.

✔ For the best source of information on fill-in-the-blank — you know, general research starting points on topics from A to Z — check out the **Librarians' Index to the Internet** (sunsite.berkeley.edu/InternetIndex). You'll find subject pages for everything from Museums to Law to Seniors. Each subject includes a list of best resources, such as directories, databases, and expert sites; each entry includes a well-written description so you know what to expect when you click the link to that site.

✔ *The New York Times*' **Cybertimes Navigator** is the research starting point for the *Times* newsroom; that's a good recommendation as far as we're concerned. Head over to www.mytimes.com/navigator and select any of the main links — Net Search, Journalism, Reference, Directories, Publications, Politics, New York Region (okay, it *is* The *New York* Times), Commerce, Entertainment, Sports, or Miscellany. *Note:* You may have to register at www.nytimes.com first.

The joys of jurisprudence

FindLaw (www.findlaw.com) is remarkably similar to Yahoo! in format. But instead of spanning the globe, subject-wise, FindLaw spans the legal world with categories such as Federal and State Courts, Cases and Codes, Legal Organizations, Legal Practice Materials, Law Schools, Consultants & Experts, News, and even a collection of e-mail discussion groups and message boards.

Click FindLaw Library for publications on specific legal issues such as the use of the word *free* in advertising, immigration law for employers, and "Estate Tax Problems for the Un-rich and Un-famous." Hey, that's us!

If FindLaw doesn't sate your desire for legal information, head over to the **Social Law Library** (www.socialaw.com), which started off as a resource for Massachusetts attorneys and developed into a one-stop clearinghouse for legal research of all kinds. Click Other Resources for links to the U.S. Supreme Court and Circuit Courts, federal-level rules, regulations and codes, state tax forms, and more. It's enough to make a litigator's little heart go pitty-pat.

And one more bit of legal advice: Our colleague T.R. Halvorson, a practicing attorney and legal researcher, has put together a fine collection of resources for legal research at www.netins.net/showcase/trhalvorson/law/index.html.

A grab bag of guru pages

Finding a guru page is often a matter of good luck, hearsay, or poking around the Web on your own. One of our earliest discoveries was John Makulowich's Awesome Lists. John put the Awesome Lists together to answer a question he was hearing repeatedly: "But what's the Internet good for?"

The **Awesome Lists** 209.8.151.142 are two collections of random-appearing but carefully chosen links to about a hundred URLs that demonstrate the variety of cool sites on the Web. John began his project several years ago. The Web has grown so much that, to keep up, he's had to divide his collection into two lists — A (the truly awesome) and B (the merely awesome). Explore the **Great Outdoor Recreation Pages** at www.gorp.com. Check out the **Earthquake Bulletin** (gldss7.cr.usgs.gov/neis/qed/qed.html) to find out what's shakin'. Or reawaken those formaldehyde-laden memories of biology lab at the **Virtual Frog Dissection Kit** (george.lbl.gov/ITG.hm.pg.docs/dissect/info.html).

We almost hate to tell you this, but the Awesome List has an evil twin, **The Worthless Page List,** at www.nktelco.net/worthless, if you must.

John Skilton's obsessively thorough **Baseball Links** site (www.baseball-links.com) fits the image of a fanatical baseball fan to a glove — or a mitt. This guru page lists two dozen subcategories ranging from Major Leagues to Baseball History, Cards and Collectibles, and the ever-popular Stats & Analysis. Click one, and you're presented with dozens of links — out of more than 6,000, site-wide — to individual baseball-related resources on the subject.

"I get by with a little help from my friends" could be the Official Guru Page Theme Song. The Beatles, living and dead, are commemorated copiously on the Web. One of our favorite sites is Dave Haber's **Internet Beatles Album** (www.getback.org), a site cleverly designed to look like, well, a record album. (You remember records? Vinyl, played on a turntable, broke if you dropped 'em?) Click the album title to get to the main site, which includes links to other people's Beatles pages, more specialized sites, newsletters, song lyrics pages, official fan club pages, Beatles cover — er, tribute — band sites, collector pages, sites devoted to people and themes that are somehow intertwined with the Beatles, plus newsgroups and archives.

Gurus operate in the professional realm as well. Susan Detwiler, a specialist in healthcare and medical industry research, has put together a collection of her favorite, clinically tested sites. To uncover Detwiler's handpicked collection of useful healthcare industry resources, go to www.detwiler.com and click Healthcare Business Links. You find an annotated list of links to groups such as the American Medical Association, specialized sources such as Healthfinder (for reputable consumer-type health information), HospitalWeb, and the National Library of Medicine's PubMed database.

Web rings: Another way around the Web

If you feel like you're going around in circles when you try to find something on the Web, you ain't seen nothin' yet. Thousands of people apparently believe that the quickest way from Point A to Point B on the Web is not a straight line, but a circle — or, to be more precise, a ring. What's a Web ring? A linked collection of anywhere from three to several dozen individual sites, all focused on the same subject or theme. Each site is linked to the one before and the one after it in the chain. You navigate around the ring by clicking links to the next or previous sites. You can also skip links or ask to be taken to a random site in the chain.

What's the advantage of Web rings? Like guru pages and the subject catalogs covered in Chapter 5, Web rings provide a more focused and selective perspective on a topic. But they also have geometry going for them: Web rings, by their very nature, encourage you to stay within the circle. That means that, unless you're seriously directionally impaired, you'll be able to find your way back to your starting point with a minimum of effort.

How do you find a Web ring to match your interests?

✔ **The search engine approach:** Enter your keyword or phrase and the words *ring* or *webring* (sometimes Web ring appears as one word, and sometimes the concept is referred to as simply a *ring*).

✔ **The Yahoo! approach:** Go to **Yahoo!** (www.yahoo.com) and drill down a few layers until you reach the subcategory Computers and Internet: Internet: World Wide Web: Searching the Web: Indices to Web Documents: Rings.

✔ **Beam yourself aboard the Web ring mothership, RingWorld:** Connect directly to www.webring.com (www.webring .org works, too) and either browse the categories for one that interests you or use the search feature to home in on a relevant ring.

Chapter 7

Ready Reference:
Finding Facts Fast

- -

In This Chapter

▶ Reference: Answering questions quickly

▶ Locating virtual reference books

▶ Finding the facts online

▶ Using primary sources

- -

The preceding chapters cover online resources that are a means to an end: search engines, subject catalogs, and guru pages — all are tools to help you find information that you can analyze and add to your understanding of a research topic. But sometimes you just need a quick fact or two to enhance your research and ensure its accuracy — or simply to satisfy your curiosity. That's what *reference* is all about.

Librarians know about the *ready reference* shelf — a section of books that they can reach without getting up from their desks, books that they keep handy because they use them often. You probably have something equivalent in your home or office — *The World Almanac,* a dictionary, an atlas, *Roget's Thesaurus, Bartlett's Familiar Quotations,* or an encyclopedia. You undoubtedly have other favorites, too: shop manuals, engineering handbooks, gardening books, *The Joy of Cooking,* your favorite *For Dummies* guides — they're all ready references, every single one, for somebody.

Reference: Research Light

When you hear the word *research,* you probably think of fairly complex, multi-stage research projects such as:

    ✔ What are the most effective treatments for Alzheimer's disease?

    ✔ Can I get a patent on my invention?

    ✔ Where should I go on vacation and what should I do when I get there?

    ✔ I'm having this persistent problem with Windows 98. . . .

For the answer to such questions, you almost certainly have to check more than one source, analyze and synthesize the information you find, and, most important of all, draw your own conclusions.

Not all questions require that much effort. You can find the answers to 84.7 percent of the questions that arise in the world every day — a statistic we just made up — in a handful of directories, almanacs, compendia, and guides. These are called *reference* questions. They involve very little analysis (except to ask yourself, "Can this statistic possibly be right?"). You have a question, you look it up in the appropriate source, and, assuming you have good karma and the planets are in alignment, you get the answer — almost without having to think about it.

Reference questions look like this:

    ✔ How tall is the Empire State Building?

    ✔ Where is Kenya, exactly, and what form of government does it have?

    ✔ What's the population of Chicago?

    ✔ Who won the 1948 U.S. presidential election, and by how many votes?

    ✔ Does *anal-retentive* have a hyphen?

    ✔ How many holes does it take to fill the Albert Hall?

If you find out the answers to the last two, will you let us know?

Virtual Reference Collections

A good way to familiarize yourself with reference books online is to browse the Net equivalent of that librarian's standby we mentioned at the beginning of this chapter: the ready reference collection. You'll find dozens of collections of electronic resources similar to that handy shelf of well-thumbed volumes with which you and your local librarian are familiar. Some collections are actually maintained by real live librarians. In the next few sections, we check out (no pun intended) a few of our favorite starting points.

Internet Public Library

Figure 7-1 shows the comfy lobby of the **Internet Public Library** (www.ipl
.org/ref). The picture is an *image map,* which means that you can click any
of the labeled portions — such as Education, Associations, or Arts &
Humanities — and go directly to a list of resources in that broad subject area.

Click the Reference link, and you're transported to the general reference sec-
tion and a list of subcategories, including Almanacs, Biographies, Calculation
& Conversion Tools, Census Data & Demographics, Dictionaries,
Encyclopedias, Genealogy, Geography, News, Quotations, and Telephone.

Now click Dictionaries. A list of 35 or so different dictionaries appears, ranging from well-known tomes such as the *Merriam-Webster* dictionary, to a
rhyming dictionary, a dictionary of American Sign Language, a reverse dictionary (for when you know the meaning but can't think of the word), dictionaries of Net-related terms, early English, acronyms, and abbreviations.

One more click, on the dictionary link of your choice, and you have the virtual volume in your hands. Ready, set, go for it: *Thixotropic! Metonymy!
Aphasia!* Or whatever words have *you* scratching your head. For us, the possibilities are boundless.

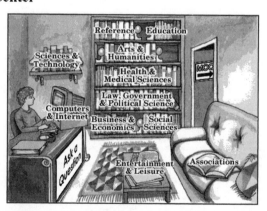

Figure 7-1:
The Internet
Public
Library.

the Internet Public Library

Reference Center

Welcome to the Reference Center. The above picture is an image map of the center. Click on the desk to Ask a Reference Question, or a book to browse a specific section of the Ready Reference Collection. You may also wish to search the collection.

The Virtual Reference Desk

The Virtual Reference Desk (`thorplus.lib.purdue.edu/reference`), a Purdue University Library production, is a no-nonsense listing of reference books in the categories shown in Figure 7-2.

Consistent souls that we are, we click <u>Dictionaries</u> once more. (Actually, the category is <u>Dictionaries, Thesauri, Acronyms, Almanacs</u>, but who's keeping score?) The lineup here includes the old standby, *Merriam-Webster,* some specialized science and technology dictionaries, three acronym-finders, and several English-other language translation dictionaries. Again, one more click on the title of your choice, and a world of definitions awaits you.

Research-It!

Again with the exclamation points. Well, Yahoo! (`www.yahoo.com`) was there first. We're not going to make any jokes about yelling in the library, either.

Our only quibble with **Research-It!** (`www.iTools.com/research-it/research-it.html`) is that, given our earlier distinction between *research* and *reference,* it should be named *Reference-It!* instead. But the site makes up for its lapse in nomenclature with the convenience of direct searching in dozens of individual reference sources. Enter your search term in the appropriate box, click the Look It Up! button, and your answer appears.

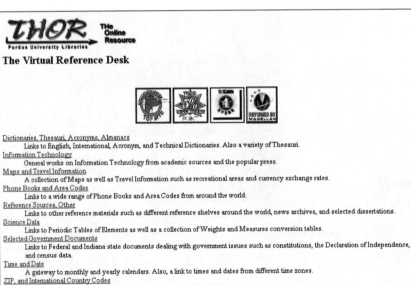

Figure 7-2:
The Virtual Reference Desk.

Figure 7-3 shows the top of the Research-It! reference collection. Besides dictionaries and a thesaurus, your options include

- ✔ Translations
- ✔ Acronyms
- ✔ Biographies
- ✔ Quotations
- ✔ Maps
- ✔ Phone books
- ✔ Currency converters
- ✔ Stock quotes
- ✔ Zip codes
- ✔ Package-tracking services (you won't find *those* on the shelves of your local public library)

Okay, we know we're supposed to be focusing on productivity here, but you know what they say about "all work and no play." Take a minute and scroll down Research-It! to one of our favorite time wasters, the Internet Anagram Server. Reva can rearrange her name to spell *Crab Shave, Brave Cash,* or *Brash Cave.* Mary Ellen's name spells *Bleary Meat Lens* or *A Lab Sent My Reel.* And you? Okay; time's up. Back to *real* ready reference.

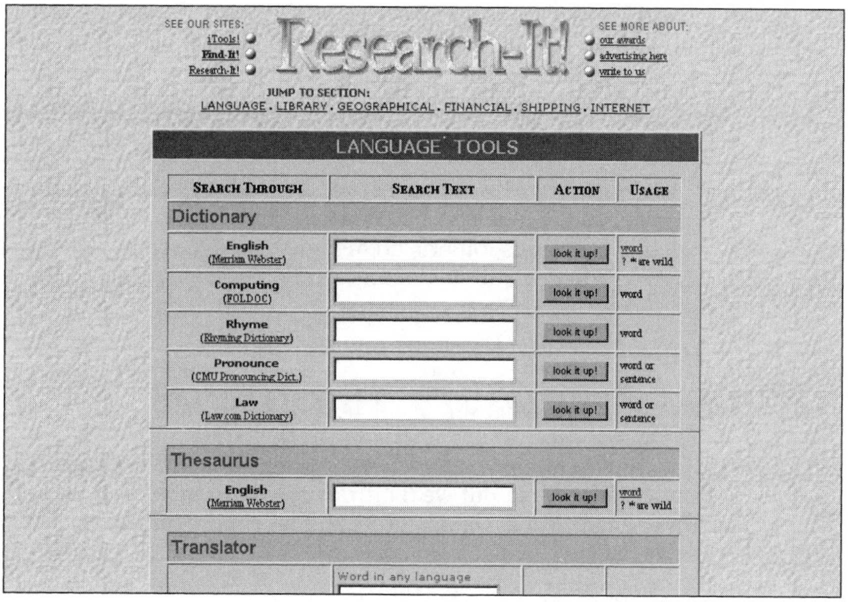

Figure 7-3:
Research-It!.

The Yahoo! Reference Collection

Yahoo! is a great starting point for reference questions as well as for many other kinds of info-quests. For a glimpse of the quick-lookup side of Yahoo!'s personality, go to www.yahoo.com and click Reference. Then click Dictionaries (our current fixation), and Yahoo! presents a breakdown of dictionaries by type: English, foreign language, subject-specialized, and slang. Each of these subcategories links to a list of titles. Pull one from the shelf, so to speak, and you're out on the Web, doin' the definition dance. (The Commercial@ category points you to dictionaries that you can buy in print and on CD-ROM.)

The Slang listing is a great read in itself. Check out the Dictionary of Mountain Bike Slang and find out what a gravity check is.

Becoming a Reference Ace

How can you possibly keep track of the hundreds of reference works available to you online? You can't, but you *can* master the sources you use most often. Follow our tips for becoming a ready-reference ace:

- ✔ **Spend some time poking around in virtual reference collections like the ones in the preceding section.** Get to where you can recognize the titles of some of the books that are shelved there. Develop a sense of the kinds of questions you can reasonably expect these books to answer, even if all you can say is, "Oh yeah; I'm pretty sure I saw a reference site that may cover that."

- ✔ **Get to know both the content and the organization of the books you use the most.** Try them out with different kinds of questions.

- ✔ **Add your favorite online reference tools to your Bookmarks or Favorites list.** If your Web browser allows you to organize your bookmarks in various folders, create one called *Reference*. Before you know it, you'll have your *own* online ready-reference shelf.

Hitting (A Few of) the Books

Obviously, we can't give you a personal introduction to every reference book you might ever need. But we'll introduce you to three that we find handy and return to again and again: an international country almanac, an encyclopedia, and a thesaurus.

The World Factbook

Although they downplay the fact a lot more than they used to, the CIA produces **The World Factbook** (www.odci.gov/cia/publications/factbook/index.html). Yes, *that* CIA — the U.S. Central Intelligence Agency. The CIA has been keeping tabs on countries all over the world, so why not share some of the information with us-the-people? In fact, *The World Factbook* was one of the first published reference books to make its way onto the Net. For each country, it includes detailed data in the following broad categories:

- ✔ Geography
- ✔ People
- ✔ Government
- ✔ Economy
- ✔ Communications
- ✔ Transportation
- ✔ Military
- ✔ Transnational issues (including border disputes and so on)

Each country record includes a color map and flag as well.

To research a particular country, click <u>Countries</u> and then select a country — say, <u>Kenya</u> — from the resulting alphabetical list. Remember the sample reference question earlier in this chapter about Kenya and its form of government? The map at the top of the country description shows you where Kenya is located, and the Geography section that follows gives you the exact coordinates and more. Everything you wanted to know about the Kenyan government — at least the basic facts — is just a scroll away in the section headed <u>Government</u>.

Various editions of *The World Factbook* have been floating around the Net for years. To be sure you're using the most recent version, go to the source — the official CIA <u>World Factbook</u> site.

Encyclopedia Britannica

Remember when encyclopedias were sold door-to-door and were considered a major family investment? Now you can read the entire *Encyclopedia Britannica,* all 32 volumes, on the Web, for free at britannica.com.

WWWebster's

What better tome than that good ol' Merriam-*WEB*ster to test how familiar reference books translate to the Net? You can click the <u>WWWebster Dictionary</u> link at the **Internet Public Library** (`www.ipl.org/ref`) or navigate directly to `www.m-w.com`.

Key in your word, click the Search button, and enlightenment (in the form of a definition, pronunciation, word origins, alternate forms, and all those other lexicographical — look it up — goodies) awaits.

Use the search box at the top of the main **Britannica.com** page if you're impatient to look up a factoid. However, if you just type in your word and click the Find button, you search Web sites, magazine articles, descriptions of in-print books, *and* the encyclopedia. If you want just EB articles, click the <u>More Options</u> link. That takes you to an advanced search page with a drop-down list that lets you limit your search to the *Encyclopedia Britannica* itself.

Roget's Thesaurus

Are you ever at a loss for just the right word? Reach for a thesaurus — or perhaps (we looked these up) a lexicon, glossary, or concordance. *Roget's Thesaurus* — serving up synonyms since 1852 — is on the Net at **Thesaurus.com** (`www.thesaurus.com`). Enter a word in the search box, click <u>OK</u>, and you get a list of brief entries; click the one that most closely describes the meaning you have in mind, and you see a complete list of alternative and related terms.

We bibliophiles (philologists, lexicologists, bibliomaniacs) find thesauri delightful because we love to see all the possible meanings of a single word. Type in the word **drive**, for example, and you see listings for the concepts of success, journey, haste, parsimony ("driving a hard bargain"), compulsion, and so on. The next time you're tempted to use the same old expression, consult Thesaurus.com to find a new turn of phrase.

Random Reference Goodies

Net denizens are nothing if not helpful. Many individuals across the Web create and maintain sites that fall into the reference or quick lookup category. Sometimes these have printed book equivalents; often they do not. But they're all designed to give you an answer — fast.

How Things Work

The no-frills search form for **How Things Work** (Landau1.phys.virginia.edu/Education/Teaching/HowThingsWork/qsearch.html) enables you to search a database of questions and answers about — take a guess — how devices ranging from the very simple to the very complex actually work. We follow the simple directions, and key in **internal combustion engine** — our obsession since, oh, Chapter 2 or so — and get an exceedingly slick and useful summary.

Can't find what you're looking for? Back up a level to Landau1.phys.virginia.edu/Education/Teaching/HowThingsWork and pose your query to the guy who wrote the book. And for a glossier variation on the same theme, take a look at www.howstuffworks.com, by the aptly named Marshall Brain.

New area code lookup

Ever try to return a call to one of those new U.S. area codes, but you have no idea where you're calling? Maybe you've forgotten the new one assigned to *you* or to your nearest-and-dearest? Get thyself to **555-1212.com** (www.555-1212.com), where you can look up the area code for a city or the areas covered by a particular code. Type in an area code or click <u>Area & Country Codes</u> to search by city as well. You can also browse lists of area codes by number and by state — and a list of country codes, too, if you want to reach *way* out and touch someone.

This day in history

We love those "on this date in history" features. When you navigate to **The History Channel** (www.historychannel.com), you automatically see what key event happened on today's date at some point in the past. Click for the full story or select one of the special categories: this day in Wall Street, Automotive, Civil War, or Technology history. Or click <u>This Day in History</u> and then <u>What Else Happened Today?</u> for a complete cross-section of events, including notable birthdays and hit recordings. From the This Day in History page, you can search for a specific event, or use the <u>What Happened on Your Birthday?</u> feature (it doesn't have to be your birthday; we won't tell) to check any date's claim to fame.

Literary lookups: Full-text books online

If you're a lit major or just happen to have a question that a quick lookup in a classic text might answer, check out these literary sites. Some offer full-text search capabilities, too.

The Online Medieval & Classical Library (sunsite.berkeley.edu/OMACL) features Chaucer, Icelandic sagas, and other treasures of early literature. (Hey, if that's your thing, *this* is your site.)

Bulfinch's Mythology (www.webcom.com/ shownet/medea/bulfinch) specializes in the classic tales of Greek and Roman legend.

Bibliomania (www.bibliomania.com) encompasses a history of classic literature from 1607 to the 20th century, with complete HTML versions of titles such as *Little Women,* Freud's *Interpretation of Dreams,* the collected poems of William Blake, and others.

Project Gutenberg (www.gutenberg.net) showcases hundreds of classic novels, poems, plays, epics, and treatises from all eras and cultures. Recent additions include works by Robert Louis Stevenson, P.G. Wodehouse, and Oscar Wilde.

Chapter 8

Visiting Libraries Online

· ·

In This Chapter

▶ Finding and searching online library catalogs

▶ Getting your hands on the documents you need

▶ Discovering digital libraries

· ·

*O*kay, you may be thinking — game's over, and the Net has won. Anything we may possibly want to know is just a few keystrokes away. It's all there, somewhere, online. Real-world libraries may as well close up shop, lock the doors, and stick For Sale signs on the front of their buildings. Thanks for all your efforts; we appreciate your work; and will the last one out please turn out the lights?

Not . . . so . . . fast.

You knew we were going to say that, didn't you? Libraries were on the Internet from the beginning, and despite the rise of do-it-yourself researching, they're not about to leave anytime soon. Libraries are *committed* to online information, and they're continuing to contribute in some very significant ways.

Libraries: Alive and Thriving Online

The *library* metaphor is a natural one for online research. The Internet is loaded with virtual reference shelves, subject catalogs, and libraries of this-and-that. But make no mistake: Right now, we're talking about *real* libraries — actual institutions with brick-and-mortar buildings, bookshelves, print volumes, and flesh-and-blood staffs inside them.

Why are old-fashioned libraries still so important in this increasingly digital world?

✔ **Libraries have more stuff.** You can find material in real-world libraries that you won't even find *pointers* to in a casual online search.

✔ **Libraries have deeper stuff.** No virtual library, no matter how rich, is as complete or deep as even the most modest neighborhood library.

> ✔ **Libraries have stuff that the Net may never have.** No matter how fast the Web is growing, a lot of information — historical, esoteric, highly specialized, and often quite rare — takes a long time to migrate to the Net, if it makes it at all.
>
> ✔ **Libraries put good stuff on the Net.** Libraries are at the forefront of some pretty amazing projects to digitize at least a fraction of their collections — including rare manuscripts, old photographs, and other archival treasures — and make it available to everyone with a modem and a connection to the Net.
>
> ✔ **Libraries have librarians.** Forget that stodgy image of the sour-faced librarian with sensible shoes and her hair in a bun. Librarians have been online since the 1970s — well, the more seasoned ones, anyway. They can help you find information in their own libraries as well as tap into resources around the world. And the word *shhhh* is not in their vocabularies.

Although much of the material housed in real-world libraries isn't directly accessible online, you can browse through online library catalogs to discover what's available. Then you can make arrangements through interlibrary loan, or place a photocopy request or document delivery order (we describe all of these procedures later in this chapter), to get hold of the actual document or a copy of the text. Library catalogs are also useful for answering questions related to authorship, spelling, publication dates, and so on, and for compiling bibliographies or lists of publications by a particular writer or on a certain theme.

Finding Web-based Library Catalogs

Just about any kind of library you can name has a presence on the Web. Some library Web sites are purely informational: They give you the library's physical location, hours, policies, and a reminder to bring quarters for the photocopy machine. It takes serious money to implement a full-fledged interactive Web site with the back-end software and data entry that are required. And libraries, especially public libraries, are chronically strapped for funds. Support your local Friends of the Library. Give generously. End of commercial.

But many library sites do provide a gateway into the collections themselves — not the actual *text* of all the books and periodicals housed there, but a record of what materials the library possesses, searchable by author, title, or subject. The online catalog can be useful to your research in a number of ways:

> ✔ You can search for everything published by a particular author — and verify that she is, in fact, the expert she purports to be.
>
> ✔ You can search for documents by subject and find publications that you didn't know existed.

✔ You can tap into special collections — works donated by a local patron, regional archives, or information about businesses, events, and people with ties to the area served by a particular library.

✔ You can verify author names, book titles, editions, publishers, and dates of publication for research papers and bibliographies.

✔ You can arrange to borrow books or order photocopies of articles.

Using WebCATS

To get a list of library catalogs on the Web, point your browser to WebCATS (www.lights.com/webcats) and then click either Geographical Index or Library-Type Index. Here is what you see next:

✔ The **geographical** track brings up a list of countries, in alphabetical order by continent. Bet you can guess the next step: Click a country to get a list of libraries. Finally, click the name of a library, which should then connect you to the library's Web site and its catalog.

✔ The **library-type** approach brings up this list:

Armed Forces	Law
College and University	Medical
Consortia	Public
Government	Religious
Junior College	Special
K-12 Schools	Unknown

Most of these choices are straightforward. If you're seeking something specific, such as a topic in the medical or legal area, you can head right for that category. A couple of categories, though, take a little more explanation:

- **Consortia** are groups of libraries, usually in the same state or geographic region, that band together for cataloging, book borrowing, and other cooperative efforts. If a consortium has put its joint, or *union,* catalog online, you can cover dozens, even hundreds, of libraries at once. For instance, click the State of Iowa Libraries Online (SILO — don'tcha love it?) link. Then, on the State Library of Iowa page, click SILO and finally click Silo Locator. Key in your search, and the results list shows you which libraries in the consortium carry copies of the publication you're looking for. Click the record number for even more detailed information.

- **Special** libraries, in the United States at least, are usually corporate, government, or institutional collections — in other words, anything *other* than a public, university, or school library. In WebCATS, it's a catchall category that may include what you're looking for.

Panning for gold at Penn

Penn, or the University of Pennsylvania — not to be confused with Penn State — is an excellent research institution that just happens to be Reva's *alma mater.* Ben Franklin himself founded the university more than 250 years ago. Old Ben gets his payback by way of *Franklin,* the name of Penn's online catalog. We're sure he'd be thrilled.

To pay personal homage to Ben, get yourself to the **Penn Library** Web site (www.library.upenn.edu) and click the Franklin link. Your main search options are

- ✔ Author/Title/Subject/Call No.
- ✔ Keyword
- ✔ Guided Keyword
- ✔ Relevance Ranked
- ✔ Course Reserve

A Help button at the top of the Franklin screen leads to detailed help and search hints for each of these options.

In addition, a Set Search Limits option lets you impose certain universal filters or restrictions, such as date or language, on a keyword- or relevance-ranked search.

That Guided Keyword search feature is a powerful one. It offers both Boolean AND, OR, and NOT operators, and *field searching,* which lets you restrict your search terms to certain *fields,* or parts, of a document record. Franklin's fields include author, title, subject, series title, publisher name, conference name, and place of publication, among others. (See Chapter 2 for more about Boolean searching, field searching, and other powerful search aids.)

The Penn catalog is just one of thousands of online library catalogs worldwide. Each one has its own, sometimes unique, search features. To get the most out of a particular library collection, familiarize yourself with how its online catalog works. Try looking up a particular author, or a subject that you're researching or that currently interests you. Try out any special features offered by the catalog, such as Penn's Guided Keyword option. See whether relevance ranking or any other display options are useful for your purposes. As with any other research tool, the better you know a particular library catalog's capabilities, the more it can do for you.

Online catalogs cover more than just books. You can also search for specific journal names (though not specific articles) and discover how far back the library's collection extends and which branch libraries subscribe. At some libraries, you may have to select, and then search, a separate periodicals catalog. At others, you just select journal titles or serials — or a similar term — as a search option, or even easier, opt for a title search and then key in the name of the periodical.

Thinking locally

If your research plan involves finding resources that you may want to borrow or photocopy on your own, start locally, with the nearest university library. If you know — or can easily guess — the address of the university's home page, you can sometimes shortcut the search for its online library catalog. A Library link is usually visible from the main university page. From there, the catalog is just a click or two away.

Sometimes local sources give you more than you bargained for. The **Indiana University/Purdue University of Indianapolis Library** (`www-lib.iupui.edu`) offers IndyCat (click the IndyCat link) and IUCAT (click the Search link), which, between them, cover materials in all Indiana University Libraries. And that's not all. Click Library Catalogs for links to the Indianapolis Marion County Public Library, the Indiana State Library, and other university libraries in Indiana.

Looking at the Library of Congress

The **Library of Congress**, the U.S. national library, is reputed to carry a copy of every book published in the country. It doesn't really. But it does contain more than 17 million books, including foreign publications, plus something like 100 million other items, such as maps, manuscripts, multimedia, and much, much more. If what you're looking for isn't listed at LC — as librarians fondly refer to it — well . . . are you sure you didn't *imagine* it?

LC offers lots to see; if you want to wander around the virtual halls, head over to `lcweb.loc.gov`. But right now, we're heading straight for the catalog, so point your browser to `catalog.loc.gov`.

Figure 8-1 shows the main search screen for the Library of Congress catalog. If you're looking for books by a specific author, if you know the title of the book and need to confirm the author, or if you want to see all the books about a subject such as *Wine and Wine Making,* use the Subj-Name-Title-Call# search option. If you have a more complicated search in mind, such as a search for an exact phrase or for books on a particular topic written by a certain author, choose the Guided Keyword search. Command Keyword is for searchers who know how to use LC's index codes; this option is not for the faint of heart. And finally, the Keyword search lets you type in several words, any of which can appear in the catalog records.

The Library of Congress catalog on the Web represents our tax dollars at work, fellow Americans. It's one use of those bucks that neither of us can argue with.

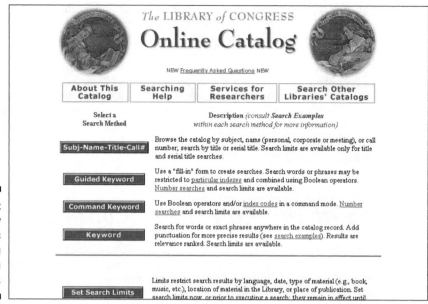

Telnetting to OPACs

Lovely phrase, isn't it? Rolls trippingly off the tongue . . . telnetting to OPACs on a summer's day. Oh, you want to know what it *means?* Okay, here goes:

- ✔ **OPAC is librarian jargon for *Online Public Access Catalog.*** If you've checked out the Library of Congress, Indiana University, Penn, or any of the other library sites we mention in this chapter, you've already visited an OPAC without even knowing it. That was easy, wasn't it?

- ✔ ***Telnet* is a means of connecting to another computer on the Internet.** Telnet is a text-based protocol that predates the Web.

Libraries all over the world have put their catalogs — the electronic equivalents of the old 3-x-5 card catalogs — online. Some are directly searchable on the Web. But not all of them. You can access some library catalogs only via telnet. And some you can access through the Web as well as via telnet. Telnet can be faster, if you know how to use it and can stand the sometimes funky and awkward interface.

The telnet protocol uses a software application called a *telnet client.* You probably have a telnet client on your computer; it comes with both Macs and Windows machines and is often included in the software package that you get when you sign up with an Internet Service Provider, or ISP. If you can't find a telnet client on your computer, you can download one from www.shareware.com that works with your computer platform or operating system.

Most Web browsers are designed to work with a telnet client. If you click a link to a library catalog (or another Internet site) that requires telnet for access, your telnet client fires up and takes you to the spot. Internet Explorer seems to know how to find our telnet clients automatically. We had to configure Netscape Navigator, though, by choosing Edit⇨Preferences and, under Navigator, selecting Applications and then pointing Navigator to the path and filename for the telnet program on our computers.

Hytelnetting around

Many major library sites, especially university libraries, offer telnet access to other sites besides their own. Look for a link labeled <u>Other Library Catalogs</u> or <u>Internet Resources</u>, or something similar; or a link labeled <u>Hytelnet</u>. Hytelnet is a directory of telnet-accessible libraries and other information resources worldwide that some libraries have incorporated into their own sites. It allows you to search sites by geographic region (and sometimes by type of library) and click and go directly to the library of your choice without having to type in its address.

You can also access **Hytelnet** directly at `www.lights.com/hytelnet/` and — ignoring the distressing message at the bottom about the service closing down — click <u>Library Catalogues, arranged geographically</u> or click <u>Search</u> to locate them by name, type, or subject.

Not all telnet sites expect outside visitors. They're set up for use primarily by the campus community or the library's main constituency, whoever that may be. You're not doing anything illegal if you drop in; it's just that they don't always make it easy to enter, disconnect cleanly, or adjust the default display mode so that you can read the text on the screen. Telnetting to OPACs can be challenging, but who ever said travel to exotic lands was easy? At least you won't pick up intestinal parasites this way.

A short side trip to Malaysia

How far can telnet take you? We're going to find out. From the Hytelnet site in the preceding section (`www.lights.com/hytelnet`), we click <u>Library Catalogues, arranged geographically</u>. On the next screen, we see these links:

- ✔ The Americas
- ✔ Europe/Middle East
- ✔ Asia/Pacific/South Africa

We pick Door Number Three and are presented with an alphabetical list of exotic destinations, ranging from Australia to Thailand. We click Malaysia, a place neither of us has been to, in virtual *or* real life.

Next up: A list of half a dozen OPAC destinations. We click Universiti Sains Malaysia, because it sounds so very far away. After we click this link, we get a brief set of basic directions:

- **A link to the telnet address.** Here, it's lib.usm.my.

- **The logon ID that we need to key in.** In this case, it's opac (remember this).

- **The type of OPAC software used.** This one says HOMEGROWN OR UNKNOWN; doesn't that sound just fraught with intrigue? (You can probably ignore this information.)

- **The command used to exit the system.** It's a good idea to remember this, too.

We click the lib.usm.my link. Our telnet software comes to life and spins into action. Whee.

We can see telnet connecting to the faraway OPAC. It asks for our login. We type **opac**, and then we're prompted for our terminal type. After selecting VT100-compatible, we see the welcome screen. Because we've come all this way, we have to actually try *using* this thing. We do a title search and whaddaya know — 20 *For Dummies* books! Hmmm, if we're going to borrow from a library, we can probably find one a little closer to home.

Assuming that you know a library's telnet address to begin with, you can bypass Hytelnet by firing up your telnet program and typing in the address directly. On NCSA telnet for the Mac, you press the Apple or Command key (⌘ or ⌘) and then type your destination in the Host/Session Name box. In Microsoft telnet for Windows 98, you choose Connect➪Remote System, and then key in **lib.usm.my** or wherever you want to go today. From here on, everything's exactly the same as connecting via Hytelnet.

So It's in the Online Catalog; How Do I Get It?

A library catalog is like a restaurant menu. It's educational, but it's no substitute for the real thing. When you're hungry, you want a hamburger, or maybe a Caesar salad, not just a description of one.

So, how do you actually get hold of items that you've located in an online catalog? It depends, first, on whether you're looking for a book, or for an article from a magazine. Unless they're in a library where you have direct borrowing privileges, books (and some other materials, such as audio recordings) are subject to a policy called *interlibrary loan,* or *ILL.*

The ins and outs of ILL

Interlibrary loan is a process where your librarian acts as your agent, requesting a book on your behalf. In fact, librarians can sometimes shortcut your online catalog search by checking to see whether any library — anywhere in the region, state, or country — has the book you want. You're responsible for returning what you've borrowed, in good shape, on or before the date it's due. Some materials, especially reference books and rare or expensive volumes, don't circulate at all. Beyond that, libraries have different policies regarding interlibrary loan; check with yours to see what other conditions apply.

ILL operates most smoothly if you're affiliated with a university or college, or can deal with the main branch of your local public library. If you work for a company, your corporate library or information center can often handle your ILL requests. Libraries may be part of a borrowing consortium or have informal lending policies in place.

Buying instead of borrowing

You can use an online catalog to verify information about a book that's out of print (librarians use the term *OOP*) or not widely available. You may want to buy a copy, not just borrow one. Supplying a complete and accurate description helps a bookseller more easily locate what you want.

The Web is home to hundreds of bookstores, many of which specialize in certain types of books or provide added-value services, such as searching for rare and out-of-print books. One of the best known, **Amazon.com** (www.amazon.com), does an okay job of locating out-of-print titles. But our favorite starting-URL for hunting elusive volumes is www.powells.com. That address takes you to the online home of **Powell's,** an amazing, multilevel bookstore in Portland, Oregon. Powell's catalog is a record of the bookstore's inventory, showing both new and used books that are actually on the shelves (or were there recently). Of course, you can order on the spot. Don't overlook your local independent bookstore, though, for special orders and other custom services. Allez-OOP!

Xerox is not a verb: Requesting article photocopies

Back issues of magazines, scholarly journals, and other periodical-type publications rarely leave the library — partly because if they're lost, they're very hard to replace. If you want to look through 1940s issues of *Life* magazine, say, you may be able to make special arrangements to borrow those issues, but chances are you have to visit the library to see them.

But suppose you have a particular article in mind, and you know the author or title, and the issue in which it appeared. That's a different story:

- ✔ If the article is fairly recent, you may be able to get a copy from the publisher, either in print or from its Web site.

- ✔ Professional online services (see Chapter 9) include the complete text of articles, sometimes going back many years, from thousands of magazines, newspapers, and scholarly and professional journals. You can get a list of such publications from the online service itself or from individual database producers. The single best guide to what's available in these professional online venues is a comprehensive directory called *Fulltext Sources Online.* Your library may have a copy at the reference desk, or you can check `www.infotoday.com/fso/default.htm` for details.

If neither of these alternatives works for you, it's time to turn to some not-exactly-cutting-edge technology — the good old photocopy machine. You can

- ✔ Make a photocopy at your library, assuming it has the periodical you want.

- ✔ Ask your librarian to submit a *photoduplication request* to another library.

- ✔ Pay a commercial document retrieval service to find and make a copy for you.

Document delivery services

That's right. Some businesses — actually lots of them — are totally dedicated to finding, ferreting out, and photocopying articles on request. You pay for the service, of course — anywhere from a few dollars for something that's easily locatable, to $25, $50, or more, for an item that takes an extraordinary effort to locate. A significant chunk of this sum goes to cover copyright fees that the document supplier must pay on your behalf. (See Chapter 17 for more about copyright issues.)

Ordering a document can be as simple as picking up the phone: "One article to go, please; no anchovies." But the online approach works, too.

UnCover

UnCover (uncweb.carl.org) lets you search its database and place credit card orders; you receive the articles by fax. Setting up an account is hassle-free and nearly instantaneous, and the rates are reasonable, too. Some items are even available within the hour.

Click the Search UnCover link to locate an article by writer, title, journal name, or subject, or to browse a particular journal by issue.

After you find the article you want, click it to see whether UnCover can supply it via fax. If so, you can order it on the spot. First, though, you have to fill in a Profile form and furnish that all-important credit card information. Oh, and your fax number, too, of course.

. . . and beyond UnCover

The downside to UnCover is its limited article selection. Because of copyright and licensing considerations, not everything in its database is actually available for ordering. You may have to pay a bit more and wait a while longer for service from an operation such as **FYI** (fyi.co.la.ca.us), **Information Express** (www.ieonline.com), or **InFocus Research Service** (www.infocus-research.com), which actually sends representatives out to libraries worldwide. For an extra fee, services like these will extend the quest to trade associations, conference organizers, and, if necessary, the authors themselves.

Hundreds of document delivery businesses exist worldwide. Some specialize in material from certain regions of the world, others in particular kinds of information. For leads to additional document delivery businesses or to get an idea of what's available, go to the Web site of the **Association of Independent Information Professionals** at www.aiip.org. Click the Membership Directory link and then use your browser's "Find on this page" function (in both Netscape Navigator and Internet Explorer, it's on the Edit menu; or you can simply press Ctrl+F) to search for the phrase *document delivery.*

The Delights of Digital Libraries

Various projects are underway to digitize classic works and put them on the Net. (See the sidebar at the end of Chapter 7 for pointers to some of these projects.) Researchers use electronic editions — sometimes called *e-texts* — to locate information quickly, discover recurring themes, analyze patterns, and commit various other unspeakable scholarly acts. Some people just get a perverse thrill out of reading *Alice in Wonderland* on a monitor.

You won't find a single, universally accepted definition of what constitutes a *digital library.* The term has been floating around for years. Most people would agree that e-texts — like the ones at Project Gutenberg and Bibliomania, which we mention in Chapter 7 — are part of the concept, however it's defined. But plain-text versions of familiar literary and historical works are ho-hum compared with some of the digital library initiatives that have emerged on the Net. Rare and unique artifacts — including historical photographs, maps, hand-written letters, original manuscripts, and other image-based material — are showing up online.

It used to be that the only way you could examine such material firsthand was to travel to the library or archive that housed the collection and make special arrangements for access. You generally had to present acceptable academic credentials in advance; a mere undergraduate degree wouldn't do. You were strip-searched at the door, and your pens and other sharp objects were confiscated until your departure. You were issued a gray smock to wear for the duration, and a blunt pencil for note-taking. Okay, we're exaggerating, but only slightly.

Digital libraries take many forms, but they have one thing in common: They bring one-of-a-kind treasures and curiosities within everybody's virtual grasp. They're a boon for researchers who need primary source documents — such as photographs, sketches, maps, and manuscripts — to help fill in the gaps. The multimedia sound and video clips available at some digital library sites are icing on the cake. Imagine being able to describe, in your own words, how Franklin D. Roosevelt or Winston Churchill spoke, and the gestures they used. Yes, you may have seen old film footage on TV, but a digital library enables you to view and analyze the clips to your heart's content.

In this section, we introduce you to just three of the many digital libraries on the Net. One digital library is a comprehensive starting point, as well as a fascinating destination in itself; another is what librarians call a "special collection," concentrating on American history from colonial days to the present; the third illustrates the value of the Web in presenting photographs, drawings, and other graphical material.

SunSITE: The digital library mother lode

As Berkeley partisans, we may be a wee bit prejudiced, but we're convinced that the **University of California's Digital Library SunSITE** (`sunsite.berkeley.edu`) is the best place to start — and perhaps even end — your digital library explorations. It's an umbrella site (despite the Sun) that not only covers several outstanding collections of its own, but also offers a set of research tools, pointers to other archival sites on the Net, and resources for exploring and building digital libraries.

Click the Collections link for an inkling of what SunSITE has in store. Two of our favorites are the Emma Goldman Papers, an archive of documents related to the early 20th century anarchist's life, and the Jack London Collection, which, among other things, includes some, er, revealing photographs of the author of *Call of the Wild*.

Speaking of which, remember what we said in the preceding section about having to submit to strip-searches (well, security checks, anyway) before being admitted to a research archive? Reva was thinking of her own experience, years ago, at the entrance to UC Berkeley's own Bancroft Library, a treasury of California and western history. Highlights from the Bancroft collection are now online at SunSITE; click Collections and then click Pictorial Highlights from UC Berkeley Archival Collections. Figure 8-2 gives a preview of what the Bancroft Library digital collection has in store. You're on your way. And you get to keep your writing implements, too.

 Berkeley Digital Library SunSITE · · · · · · · · · Home · · · · · · Search · · · · · · Index

Pictorial Highlights From UC Berkeley Archival Collections

The Bancroft Library of the University of California, Berkeley is blessed with rich text and image collections. The images below are but a very small sampling of some of the Bancroft image collections. For more images and information, see Archival Finding Aids and California Heritage here on the Digital Library SunSITE. Or use the Digital Library SunSITE Image Finder to locate selected images both here and at other collections such as the Library of Congress and the Smithsonian Institution. Please note that clicking on an image below will bring up a larger version.

Salmon fishing on Deer Creek [Ishi], May, 1914.
Photographer/Artist: Unknown
Original:Photoprint
Collection: C. Hart Merriam Collection.

Grandfather and grandson.
Photographer/Artist: Lange, Dorothea
Original: Photoprint
Collection: War Relocation Authority records.

Migrant family of Mexicans on the road with car trouble, February, 1936.
Photographer/Artist: Lange, Dorothea
Original: Photoprint
Collection: Farm Security Administration records.

Figure 8-2:
Highlights
from the
Bancroft
Library
archives.

The American Memory Project

Figure 8-3 shows the main page of the Library of Congress **American Memory Project** (`lcweb2.loc.gov/ammem`). You can go directly to any of the special exhibits; just click the <u>Collection Finder</u> link and then drill down to the topic and subtopic that interest you. Once inside, you can walk through an exhibit from the beginning, or visit a particular portion of what we intuitively picture as the exhibition hall. (Finding your way around is easier if you think of a digital library as an actual place; the most successful ones are designed to encourage that.) Within the exhibit, you can read explanations, examine manuscripts, look at vintage photographs and illustrations, and listen to sound clips and view movies of famous speeches and other historic events.

You can also do a keyword search to discover whether the American Memory archives contain anything on a specific topic. Click the <u>Search</u> link on the main page to get to the screen that lets you search for words or phrases, limit your search to specific types of documents, or restrict your search to certain collections.

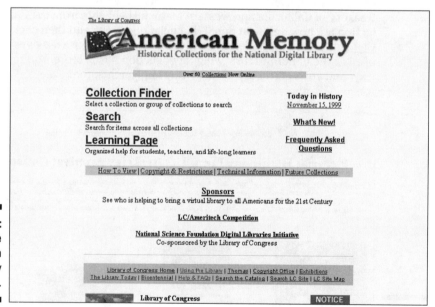

Figure 8-3:
The
American
Memory
Project.

If you click <u>Limit Search to: Photos & Prints</u>, you can then enter keywords to find specific images, or browse a list of collections with descriptions for each one. American Memory starts with the ABCs — architecture, baseball cards, and California folk music — and goes on to list more than 30 other graphical collections, including portraits of the presidents and first ladies from the 18th century on, pictures from the women's suffrage movement, and historical photos of Washington, D.C. And that's just the beginning. Check out the early movies, audio clips, panoramic maps, and historical manuscripts, too.

To see the complete contents of the American Memory archive, click the <u>Search</u> link and then scroll down past the search box to the list of all collections, alphabetized by keyword.

Images from the History of Medicine

A digital archive can be extremely specialized. For example, the **National Library of Medicine's Images from the History of Medicine** (www.ihm.nlm.nih.gov) has assembled an amazing collection featuring nearly 60,000 portraits, photographs, drawings, caricatures, cartoons, and other forms of graphic art relating to the history of medical practice and its role in society. You can browse the collection by subject or search by keyword.

A Browse Database search on *surgery,* for example, also turns up subject headings for surgery and art, military surgery, minor surgery, operative surgery, urogenital surgery (we'll pass), and surgical assistants. Each category contains at least one, and often several, images. Clicking a category produces basic information about the size and medium of the original illustration(s), and a thumbnail (hmmmm . . . we think we'll leave that one alone) sketch for each one. You can click the thumbnail to see a larger version of the image.

Chapter 9

Knock, Knock: Gated Information Services

In This Chapter

▶ Why gated Web sites are (sometimes) worth it

▶ Using America Online for research

▶ Exploring the *other* online

▶ The time-versus-money tradeoff

*M*uch as we hate that term *surfing the Net,* we have to admit that the Internet does feel like an ocean. It's deep, it's dangerous, and it's teeming with life — some very *strange* life forms, in fact. We do love riding those waves.

But sometimes we'd just as soon swim in a pool, a more controlled environment with some rules and boundaries. It may not be as exciting as the Net at large, but the water's warm, smooth, and clear all the way to the bottom. Someone takes care of it, too, adjusting the chemicals, skimming off debris, making sure it stays clean, and blowing the whistle when the kids at the diving board start getting rowdy.

Here's the analogy, and thanks for hanging in this far: If the Net is the sea, then the information sites and services that we talk about in this chapter are pools — some of them individual swimming spots, some of them very deep and wide, all of them neatly maintained.

Another metaphor we use (Oh no! Not another metaphor!) is *gated* sites, to distinguish these special, more controlled resources from the open Web (see Chapter 1 for a quick summary of gated sites). Why *gated?*

▶ **Gates are usually locked.** You need a key, or a combination, to get in. (Picture one of those parking lot barriers that lifts up when you feed in your ticket. Are we the only ones who hurry through thinking "Aaack! Automobile guillotine!"?)

> ✔ **Gates restrict access.** Most standard Web search tools are barred from entering and indexing these sites; the information in gated sites is invisible from the outside.

And it's good information, too — information you won't find duplicated anywhere on the open Web, *or* information that's organized so conveniently, or retrievable with such precise search tools, that you may actually be willing to spend the money to get it from a gated site rather than hunt for it on the Web at large.

Getting Acquainted with Gated Sites

All gated sites have one thing in common: You have to register before you can access the information they contain.

Beyond that, they vary considerably:

> ✔ Some gated sites are free; others charge a subscription fee, or a fee for every item you view, download, or print.
>
> ✔ Some look and act just like ordinary Web sites. Others are actually proprietary online services with highly specialized search languages and unique collections of documents, databases, and other resources.

Gated sites come in three flavors: members-only sites, consumer online services, and professional online services. The distinction among the three has to do with what the service is like after you get inside — the type and quality of information it contains and the search tools you're given to work with.

Overall, our gated-site classification looks like this:

> ✔ **Members-only sites:**
>
>   • Registration required, or registration plus a fee (per document, per search, per month, or some combination)
>
>   • Access to a single source or to a focused collection of information sources
>
> ✔ **Consumer online services:**
>
>   • Registration plus a monthly fee
>
>   • Require proprietary software
>
>   • Access to members-only discussion areas as well as the open Web

✔ **Professional online services:**

- Registration plus a monthly and/or yearly fee, plus additional per-document or per-search charges

- Wide variety of information sources

- Heavy-duty tools that let you build complex searches

The Web is a dynamic critter, and the boundaries between members-only sites, regular Web search engines, and professional online services are constantly blurring and changing. In the section "Web Search Engines Turn Pro," later in this chapter, we cover a few of the hybrid sites that span two or more of these categories.

Sampling Members-Only Web Sites

Members-only Web sites run the gamut. Many are indistinguishable — after you're through the gate — from sites that you find on the open Web. If it weren't for the extra step of registering and signing in, you wouldn't know the difference. Some gated sites, such as **Consumer Reports** (www.consumer-reports.com), provide even unregistered guests with useful information, reserving only the most detailed reports and value-added services for their paying customers. In effect, you can wander through the grounds of the estate and enjoy the gardens and landscaping, even peek in the windows if you want, but you have to buy a ticket for admission to the mansion itself. Other gated sites, though, clang down those portals the moment you try to set foot inside. You can navigate to the front door of the **PDR.net** site (www.pdr.net), but you can't look up anything in the *Physicians' Desk Reference* without supplying a user name and password. And you can't get either of those without proving that you're a practicing physician. Clang!

We've selected just three of the thousands of gated Web sites that exist to give you an idea of the different forms gated sites can take:

✔ **The New York Times on the Web** is easily recognizable as an online version of the printed publication of the same name.

✔ **The Wall Street Journal Interactive Edition** goes far beyond the publication on which it's based, encompassing other periodicals published by the same firm that produces the *Journal,* plus value-added services for investors, and access to a rich and varied collection of online databases.

✔ **Ei Village** goes even further by not only including published information, but also providing access to human experts, colleagues, and other specialists who may be able to help.

The pros and cons of cookies

Web sites that require registration often do so to capture demographic data (usually through a questionnaire that you're expected to complete) that the site owner can use to lure advertising support. But registration can work to your advantage, too. The site owner can keep track of your preferences and the parts of the site you use most heavily, and can direct you to new content in your areas of interest.

Customizing your interaction with a site is what the sometimes-controversial *cookies* technology is about. Cookies are software applications installed by the site owner that can track your movement through the site and record the clicks and choices you make. Cookies are used to set placeholders and preferences so that, on subsequent visits, you can go directly to the portion of the site that interests you or to the point where you left off last time. Cookies are also used to record information, such as your password, so that you don't have to supply it every time you log on.

Some security risks are associated with cookies, as with any situation in which you allow a program access to your computer. Privacy is also a concern. You may prefer to set your Web browser so that it notifies you whenever a cookie is about to be transmitted, and lets you reject the cookie if you want to. Problem is, cookies are so pervasive that such notification can be a constant pain. Call us naive, but we've found cookies to be more helpful than not. Your mileage, as always, may vary.

For more information about cookies, check the mouth-filling and nutritious **Cookie Central** (www.cookiecentral.com), which attempts to be an objective and up-to-date voice in the cookie debate.

The New York Times on the Web

Prefer to read your daily newspaper online? **The New York Times on the Web** (www.nytimes.com) is only one example — a high-profile one, for sure — of the kind of thoughtful reporting and in-depth coverage of national and international issues that a general Web search won't turn up. You can read today's headlines, of course. You can also call up a year's worth of background articles — the news behind the news.

Suppose you want to read what Katie Hafner, a writer who focuses on technology and the Internet, has written about Bill Gates. Start by clicking the Archives link on the front page of the *Times* site. Then enter the search query **Hafner and Gates** in the search form that appears next and click Search. (For help in formulating — or interpreting — that search request, click Search Tips or see Chapter 2 in this very book.) You find a handful of articles on your topic and can click to read any or all of them. Note that some recent articles are free, but you must pay $2.50 each for older items you want to read in full.

If your research project can benefit from the detailed perspective you get from this kind of online journalism, remember to visit the *Times* and other newspapers on the Web. (Chapter 13 provides more information on researching with online news sources.) Bookmark the sites you want to visit regularly. (See Chapter 19 for more about bookmarking as a technique for effective research.) Many newspaper sites, both national and small-town, require registration, which effectively cuts them off from the search engine spiders that crawl around the Web, looking for new content to index.

The *Times* site's internal search engine lets you look for specific information in today's paper, or check back issues of selected sections, such as Books, Living, Automobiles, Real Estate, and Travel. Or, you can read the way you do at the breakfast table, thumbing your way through from front-page news to sports, business, and opinion.

The *Times* on the Web adds new and updated stories throughout the day, so you can read what's happened *since* the dead-tree version went out.

The Wall Street Journal Interactive Edition

Business researchers, corporate CEOs and managers, stock analysts, and investors all regard *The Wall Street Journal* as the most complete and authoritative U.S. source of timely business and investment information. The daily edition of the *Journal* includes business news, in-depth profiles of companies and people, stock quotes, and other investment data covering both domestic and international markets. The Web edition of the *Journal,* **The Wall Street Journal Interactive Edition** (www.wsj.com), is equally comprehensive.

Not surprisingly, all this information comes with a price tag attached. The Interactive Journal requires not only that you register, but also that you pay an annual or monthly fee, which is actually pretty reasonable: $5.95 a month or $59 a year, or even less if you subscribe to the print edition, too.

The *Journal*'s Interactive Edition (shown in Figure 9-1) includes the newspaper itself, as well as electronic editions of two other publications: *Barron's* and *SmartMoney.* Subscribers also get access to detailed company profiles and to the Dow Jones Publication Library (see the section, "Beating the averages with Dow Jones Interactive," later in this chapter, for more about the Publication Library). *The Wall Street Journal* is an indispensable resource for business research. See Chapter 12 for why that's so, and for some examples of how to use the Interactive Edition and the other resources provided at this site for your real-life business research needs.

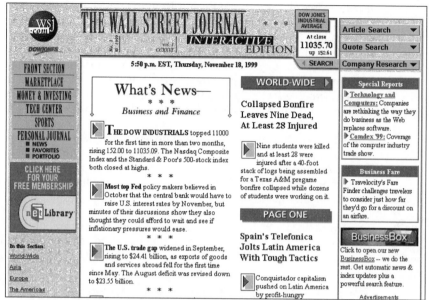

Figure 9-1:
The Wall
Street
Journal
Interactive
Edition.

As a subscriber to The Wall Street Journal Interactive Edition, you have the option of setting up a Personal Journal to get customized information on the companies, industries, and stocks you want to follow. You can supply key words and phrases, or the names of companies and industries, to capture the news stories that interest you most. You can also select the *Wall Street Journal* columns and other regular features that you want to see. You can create up to five portfolios to help you organize and track your investments. After you've configured your Personal Journal edition, just click Personal Journal whenever you visit the site to enter your own private info-domain. Gates within gates, it sounds like.

Ei Village

A pride of pocket-protectors, a gaggle of geeks, and an entire town full of badly dressed people wearing glasses held together with tape. *Tweeeet!* Stereotype alert! But the founders of **Engineering Information Village** (www.ei.org) are committed to bringing engineers and other techno-types together in a virtual environment that answers all their information needs.

Subscribers enter the Village through a link marked Residents' Entry. You couldn't ask for a clearer indication that this is a gated site. The village is made up of several neighborhoods — one for engineers in general, one for computing professionals, one for folks in the pulp and paper industry, and one for oil and gas industry specialists. Ei Village is expensive; it's set up for multiple users within corporations and other institutions, and costs way more than our allowances cover. When we need engineering and technology information, we generally start with one of the databases described in Chapter 11. Ei Village residents have access to some of this information from inside the gates of the site. After you're enrolled, you can also sign up for technology news updates to stay current in your areas of interest; discussion groups for networking and information-sharing with colleagues; and document delivery services to provide copies of journal articles, conference proceedings, and other material you may need to track down. Ei even provides formal research assistance with features such as Ask a Librarian and Ask a Senior Engineer.

Ei Village is an interesting mix. It offers premium databases such as Compendex, a guide to engineering literature published since 1970. But it also features links to Web sites and other resources that you can navigate to, for free, on your own. Part of what Villagers pay for is the convenience of having all these related resources available in one spot. Another membership benefit is the chance to hang out and exchange information with colleagues who speak the same language. We talk more about that community aspect in Chapter 10.

Consumer Goods: America Online and CompuServe

If we were writing this book three or four years ago, we would have given equal time — and quite a lot of it — to the then-big guns of consumer online services: CompuServe, Prodigy, America Online (AOL), and The Microsoft Network (MSN). Each of these services still exists, but Prodigy seems to be turning into an Internet access provider rather than a destination in itself, and MSN still hasn't figured out what it wants to be.

AOL and CompuServe (which AOL acquired a while back) provide both Internet access and a range of members-only features to millions of subscribers. Both charge a fee, and both require special software for full access to the service.

CompuServe and AOL are worlds in themselves. If you doubt that, talk to a long-time CompuServe forum member or a denizen of AOL chat rooms. Finding your way around these services takes a while, let alone trying to locate the precise information you're hoping to find. Given that so much information is out there on the open Web, why even consider signing up?

✓ **To ease into the Web.** If you're new to the online realm, these services are like training wheels when you're first learning to ride a bike. They give you a selected set of resources to begin with and a kinder, gentler introduction to the wider world of the Net. Contacting a customer support person on these services (and maybe even getting a response) is much easier than it is on the Web at large.

✓ **To get into the online community.** These services are *communities* as well as providers of content and access to the Web. You can participate in forums and discussion groups, and tap into software libraries and other member-generated archives. If you enjoy the conversation enough to stick around, it makes sense to start your research there, too, in an environment that's friendly and familiar.

What do CompuServe and AOL have to offer, research-wise, and what does it take to connect? We take a very quick look at these services in the next few sections. For more detailed information — and even more important, a sense of whether one is a comfortable fit for you — take advantage of each service's free trial membership offer.

America Online

If you've had any online experience at all, chances are good you had it on **America Online.** AOL claims to be the largest and fastest-growing online service in existence and is particularly hospitable to novices. Not only that, AOL is almost impossible to avoid — if you subscribe to a computer-related publication, you've probably received at least one introductory offer from AOL, complete with a diskette or CD-ROM good for up to 50 hours of free use. Thanks to AOL, we never have to buy blank diskettes again. We're set, too, with a lifetime supply of shiny, high-tech coasters and Frisbees for very small dogs.

If AOL's massive marketing mechanism has somehow managed to overlook you, you can download the proprietary software and get the scoop on joining at www.aol.com. AOL currently charges $21.95 per month for unlimited usage, less if you provide your own Internet access or sign up for one of the light- to moderate-usage plans.

Finding your way on AOL

America Online gained popularity right around the same time as the Web. Many people — close to 20 million, if you believe AOL's publicity — are still loyal to AOL despite the growing domination of the Web. That customer loyalty may have more to do with AOL's infamous chat room activity than with the quest for enlightenment. But if you poke around AOL, you can find some useful research tools — many of which lead you right back out to the Web.

Poke around is the key phrase there. AOL's information resources are widely scattered across the service's special-interest channels. You can use AOL's Find command to search for a particular publication by name or to search for a type of resource, such as an almanac. If you already know that AOL has what you want, you can use the Keyword shortcut to go directly there.

Most of the in-depth information sources you find through AOL are actually sites on the open Web. The benefit of using AOL to get there is that AOL makes finding and navigating those sites easy.

Channel surfing on AOL

AOL offers a broad subject approach, too, letting you drill down through any of a dozen or so channels until you find what you want. Here are some channels that we've found useful as research starting points:

- ✔ The **Research & Learn** channel (we prefer its previous name, *Reference Desk,* but nobody asked us) includes atlases, country reports, links to Web-based encyclopedias, and resources in other areas such as history, science, health, and business. Click <u>More Subjects</u> and then click <u>Business Research</u> to access the following:

  - Recent company press releases from Reuters, the Associated Press, PR Newswire, and Business Wire

  - International country profiles and updates from the Economist Intelligence Unit

  - A link to Hoover's Company Directory on the Web

  - Searchable archives of *Inc.* magazine, *Home Office Computing,* and *Business Week*

  - Links to patent and trademark information on the Web

  - D&B@AOL — access to Dun & Bradstreet company profiles, financial information, and credit reports (many of these services cost extra)

- ✔ The **Computing** channel includes information from and about a selection of high-tech companies, arranged alphabetically by company name. You also find links here to computer-related publications, most of them on the Web.

- ✔ The **News** channel brings you current news headlines, as well as stories from today's *The New York Times* and the most recent Sunday *Times Magazine,* plus back issues of selected sections. You can get the most recent issues of a number of newsmagazines, too, many with searchable archives. The News channel's own Newsstand consists of links to a variety of publication sites on the Web.

✔ The **Personal Finance** channel has a lot of information for stock-market groupies and would-be investors. It features recent market quotes and business headlines up front, but the real gold is in the <u>Investment Research</u> section. There, you find historical stock quotes, earnings estimates, financial statements, and company filings with the SEC (Securities and Exchange Commission), which regulates the affairs of publicly traded U.S. companies. The Personal Finance channel offers some references for beginning investors, too — a dictionary of Wall Street terms, lessons in the basics of investing, and information on specific subjects, such as 401(k) retirement plans.

The Personal Finance section was catapulted into stardom — no joke — by the arrival of the Motley Fool, an investment forum hosted by a couple of guys who can make a bear market seem like fun. If you're at all interested in investments, check out Fooldom and what it has to offer. Even if you keep your money under your mattress, The Motley Fool is a great example of an online resource that manages to be both informative and entertaining. The keyword *fool* takes you directly there. Chapter 12 tells you more about the Fool and other investment resources.

CompuServe

CompuServe's traditional strength lies in its hundreds of Forums — discussion groups on subjects ranging from accounting to weather. Many of these groups have, over the years, developed into close-knit, supportive communities as well as founts of information on their respective topics. Clustered around those special-interest areas are pertinent publications, news stories, archives, and tools. In the personal finance area, for instance, you're likely to find newsletters, headlines relating to specialized investment instruments or techniques, advice columns and feature articles, freeware or shareware accounting and portfolio-tracking software that you can download, and, of course, those ongoing discussions about every aspect of personal finance you might imagine.

CompuServe contains a couple of very useful hidden resources — IQuest InfoCenter and the Dow Jones Publications Library. IQuest is a gateway service to a broad selection of databases covering business, news, medicine, science, and technology drawn from the extensive Dialog collection described in the "Shopping at Dialog's supermarket" section, later in this chapter, as well as from other online sources. IQuest uses a simplified search form to streamline your research. You pay per search for some databases (anywhere from $1 to $25), and you pay again for any articles that you view. It sounds expensive, but it's a bargain if you need only occasional access to Dialog's vast collection of information. The Dow Jones Publications Library, described in the "Beating the averages with Dow Jones Interactive" section, later on, gives you access to a wide variety of business, professional, and trade periodicals. Searching is free; you pay $2.95 for every article that you view on the screen or download.

A full membership to CompuServe currently costs $24.95 a month for unlimited usage, or $9.95 for up to five hours, with additional hours at $2.95. To access the service, you need CompuServe's proprietary software, which you can download from its Web site (www.compuserve.com) or order there, at no charge, on floppies or CD-ROM.

Beware of hourly and premium service charges when you're shopping for an online information service. It's easy to lose track of the ticking meter, and you can pile up a hefty bill before you know it.

Calling in the Pros: Going Wide and Deep with Professional Online Services

We learned to search by using professional online services such as Dialog, LEXIS-NEXIS, and Dow Jones. This was way before the advent of the Web, and even before the graphical, point-and-click environment that's made millionaires of Messrs. Jobs and Gates. Monitors were monochrome, and mice were unheard of (except in the rodent-based form). We had to trudge 20 miles to school, in the snow, uphill in both directions. Instead of clicking icons, we had to type — and know how to interpret — strange command strings such as ss s1 and s4; t/3,k/1-5,12,22.

Dow Jones News/Retrieval, as it was then called, used the notorious *dot-dot* language, where you had to remember to type two periods before ..just ..about ..any ..command.

LEXIS-NEXIS gave smooshed-up and totally non-intuitive names to its databases. You were expected to remember these and type them in perfectly each time: BUSWK, FORTUN, FINPST (um, we'd like to buy a vowel . . .).

After you connected to Dialog, you found yourself in a Zen-like environment: a totally blank screen with a question mark in the upper-left corner. *Now what?*

But y'know what? All these aggravating quirks were worth it. The early command-line database services were fast and powerful. Besides, they built character — they made us feel like gods for having mastered them.

All of these services are easier to use now that you can search them on the Web with point-and-click ease. But they're still complex; figuring out how to use them effectively takes time and practice.

The other downside to the professional online services, besides their built-in quirks, is *cost.* If you're used to browsing Web documents and downloading or printing them at will, beware — you're in a different environment now. You may not be paying by the hour or by the search, the way we did in the old days; but you're almost certain to be charged for each document you ask to see in full, or in any format other than the brief default display.

Some prose on the pros of the pros

These industrial-strength database services have several advantages over all the other online research tools that we cover in this book:

- ✔ **The information is often unique.** Sources include the complete text of legal cases, investment analyst reports, and market research studies, as well as detailed summaries of conference papers, master's and doctoral dissertations, international scholarly journal articles, and more. Unlike the Web, the professional online services have long memories and maintain archives of documents going back many years. *Result:* If you can't find it on the Web, or if a piece is missing, you may well find it in a professional online service.

- ✔ **You can cover dozens, even hundreds, of individual publications and other information sources with a single search request.** You don't have to visit individual publication sites — many of which are closed to general Web search engines, remember — and run your search in each one, because professional online services *aggregate* thousands of such resources under one roof. *Result:* It's the time-versus-money tradeoff — you may spend more money to get the answer, but you're saving yourself a lot of time.

- ✔ **The search engines are extremely powerful and sophisticated.** They understand not only phrase searching and Boolean ANDs, ORs, and NOTs, but also relative adjacency — finding words near, or within so many words of, each other. They also support truncation; some even enable you to specify how many more letters to look for following the word root you've supplied. *Result:* More precise searching and more relevant answers. (See Chapter 2 for more complete descriptions of all of these search features.)

- ✔ **The information is highly processed, down to the level of individual records or documents.** *Processed* may not be what you want in *cheese,* say, but in databases, it's a good thing. Processing a database record enables you to search by author or to look for words in specific parts of a document, such as the publication name or article title. Some databases include keyword and concept indexes so that you can search by subject, using a standard vocabulary, and find what you want even if your keyword doesn't occur in the text of the article itself. *Result:* More flexible searching and a better chance of finding information you may otherwise miss.

> ✔ **The information is often more reliable than on the Web at large.**
> Much of the information in professional database services originally
> appeared in a printed publication, so it has been edited and fact-
> checked. *Result:* Though you can't believe everything you read in print,
> either, at least you know that somebody's taken responsibility for what
> you're pulling up. You have a basic quality filter in place.

Dealing with database depth

We've been talking about *professional online services* and *database services*
more or less interchangeably. You've probably gathered by now that both
terms refer to a much more complex research environment than single-publi-
cation sites such as The New York Times on the Web, and even the channels
of information you navigate through in a service such as CompuServe or
America Online.

Each of the services we're dealing with here can lay claim to housing at least
as much information — *useable* information, anyway — as the entire Web. The
head of Dialog claimed at the end of 1999 that its total information content —
6 billion pages of text and 3 million images — was greater than the Web's. A
big part of what makes all that information useable is the database structure
into which it's organized.

The information pyramid

The most basic unit of a database is an individual *record*. A journal article is a
record. So is a patent, or a company directory listing, a legal case, or a profile
of a chemical substance. A *database* — sometimes called a *file* — is a collection of individual *records*. A database may include records from a single publication only, or from a group of publications. In some professional online
services, related databases may be grouped together into a larger database,
or *group file*.

Before your eyes roll up into your head, just wait: We're telling you this for a
reason. The databases you select, and the level at which you select them, has
a lot to do with the success of your search. Too narrow, and you may get
nothing because you've selected the wrong database. Too broad, and you
may get more information than you can deal with.

Picture a pyramid, with the answer you're looking for — the ideal document —
at the top, as shown in Figure 9-2.

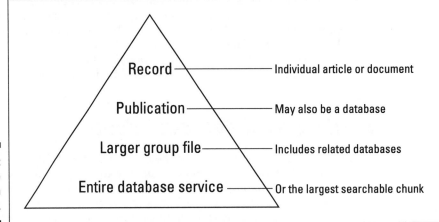

Figure 9-2:
The
information
pyramid.

The pyramid (top to bottom):

Record — Individual article or document

Publication — May also be a database

Larger group file — Includes related databases

Entire database service — Or the largest searchable chunk

Climbing up and down the pyramid

To find that ideal document, you can

- ✔ Try to guess what publication it may have appeared in. In some online services, each publication is a separate database. In others, you have to move down to the next layer to pluck the one you want from a larger selection.

- ✔ Select a category or type of publication that makes sense, such as major newspapers, computer magazines, medical literature, patents, or conference papers.

- ✔ Select an even broader category, such as News, Magazines, or Trade Journals.

- ✔ Opt to search the entire system, or as much of it as you can search at once.

Different kinds of databases have different structures, even within the same online service. Searching patents and company directories together, for example, can produce weird and unexpected results. For that reason, some services block you from searching dissimilar databases at the same time. Trust us; it's for your own good.

The OTHER Online: Dow Jones, Dialog, LEXIS-NEXIS, and More

In this section, we give you the briefest introduction, though it may not look that brief, to the *other* online — the research services that were around way before the Web, and that grew up independent of the Internet itself. Our mission here is to convey why these services are important and what they can do for you. If you still opt not to use any of them, at least you know what you're missing.

Searching a professional online service is usually a three-step process. The order may vary, but the basic idea is the same:

1. **Pick your sources — the exact publication or group of publications that you want to search.**

2. **Type in your search query.**

3. **Determine the format — short, medium, or long — in which to review the answers.**

Before you opt to review your search results in *any* format, make sure that you know the costs, if any, for doing so.

Beating the averages with Dow Jones Interactive

Dow Jones Interactive (djinteractive.com) started out, as its name implies, as part of the Dow Jones family of Dow Jones Industrial Average fame, and the publishers of *The Wall Street Journal.* But in 1999, Dow Jones Interactive spun off and formed a joint venture with Reuters Business Briefing to form a new company called Factiva. At some point (maybe by the time you read this), the Dow Jones Interactive content will merge with the Reuters content and be rebranded as Factiva. Until then, it's still DJI — a great source for business-oriented information online.

What'll it cost ya? Sixty-nine dollars a year. It's the most searcher-friendly pricing plan offered by any of the professional online services. You can search and browse headlines and lead sentences for free, but you pay $2.95 for every article you view, download, or print. Some articles also offer enhanced display options — text plus graphics (such as tables or graphs) for an additional $2, or a PDF (Adobe Portable Document Format) file with the exact image of the article as it appeared in print, for an additional $4. For an overview of what DJI has to offer, go to the Ask Dow Jones page (askdj.dowjones.com) and then click the <u>About Dow Jones Interactive</u> link.

DJI gives you not only *The Wall Street Journal* but also a cluster of other information services, including today's top news stories, in-depth company and market research reports, historical stock quotes, links to other highly rated Web sites, and CustomClips, an automatic update service for topics you want to follow.

DataBasics

Each of the professional online services in this section contains hundreds of individual databases. Some of them are highly specialized, with unique fields and features that drive even professional researchers back to Reading The Fabulous Manual. Yes, it *can* get that extreme. Searcher folklore is full of tips, tricks, and shortcuts that you won't really appreciate until you've been driven to distraction by the system's — or an individual database's — quirks. In the meantime, we highly recommend two coping strategies:

- ✔ Take any formal system training — online, or even in person — that's offered.

- ✔ Buy (unless it's free, of course) and *read* at least the basic system manual, plus detailed documentation for the databases or parts of the service that you plan to use the most.

The heart of DJI, though, is the Publications Library, a collection of more than 6,000 newspapers, magazines, trade journals, and specialized business periodicals. You can find everything from *The Wall Street Journal* to newspapers such as the *Los Angeles Times, The Washington Post,* and some smaller city papers as well. You can also find a bulging magazine rack stocked with familiar periodicals such as *Esquire, Country Living,* and *Smithsonian,* plus an array of more erudite titles, such as *American Behavioral Scientist, Institutional Investor, American Druggist,* and the *Journal of International Affairs.*

Dow Jones offers two detailed search guides at the publicly accessible portion of its Web site. Go to askdj.dowjones.com, scroll down to the Quick Links pull-down menu, and select Tools for Becoming an Expert Searcher.

You can run your DJI search in a single publication, a generic category (such as Top 50 U.S. Newspapers), or a focused industry or regional grouping. Click the <u>Revise Publications</u> link to change or add to your selection of sources.

Try the following methods to explore the range of sources that DJI offers:

- ✔ Click any category link to get a list of the publications included.

- ✔ Click an individual publication title and then click the <u>View Publication Details</u> link to see how far back it's carried, how frequently it's published and updated online, and the date of the most recent issue available through DJI.

- ✔ To see the titles of all publications in the library, click the <u>Title</u> link and then pick a letter, from A to Z.

Figure 9-3 shows the default Dow Jones Interactive search form, which is called Search by Words. To search — assuming you've already signed up for the service and surrendered your billing information — you need to do the following:

1. **Log on to DJI (**djinteractive.com**) and click the <u>Publications Library</u> link.**

2. **Enter your keywords or phrases and use Boolean ANDs, ORs, and NOTs, if you want, between them.**

   You can also use search tools such as NEAR*n* (the first search word within so many words of the second search term), truncation, and field limits. (See Chapter 1 for more about these power search tools.)

3. **Select the sources you want to search, by group or individual title(s).**

   Your default group files are Major News and Business Publications, Top 50 U.S. newspapers, and Wires: Press Release Wires. You can customize your selection by clicking <u>Revise Publications</u> and adding publications grouped by industry, by type or region, or by title.

4. **Click the Run Search button.**

5. **Click any headline to read the full article.**

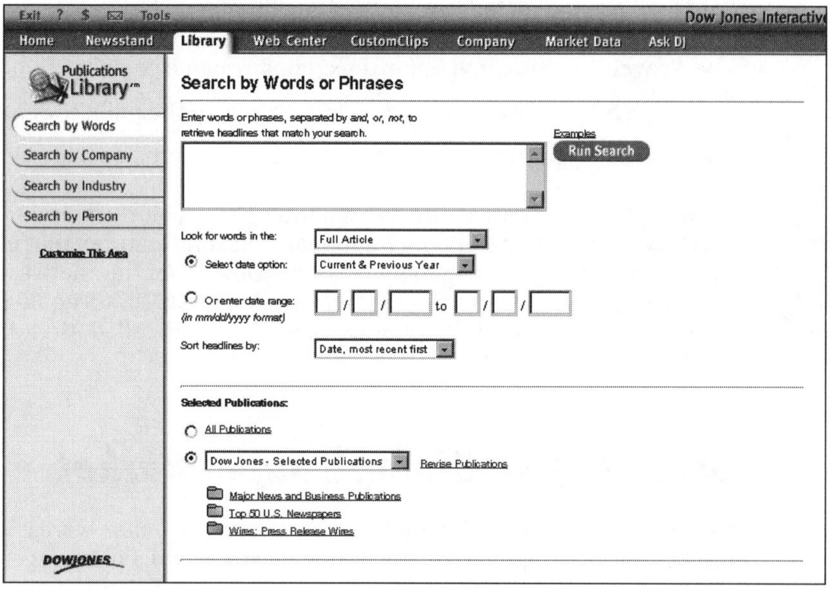

Figure 9-3:
Dow Jones
Interactive
search form.

The pull-down menus on the search form allow you to do the following:

✓ **Increase the precision of your search by limiting your entire search to the headline, headline and lead paragraph, or lead paragraph only.** This is based on the old journalistic adage (widely ignored in the New Journalism) that the *who, where, what, when, why,* and *how* of the story are supposed to be wrapped up in the first paragraph. On the other hand, you can go for broke — or maximum information retrieval, anyway — by looking for your terms in the *full article,* anywhere they may appear.

✔ **Restrict your results to articles published this year or last, or between certain dates, or on a specific date.** If you're looking for a particular article, or for very recent information, or for coverage published when a story was first breaking, this is the way to go.

✔ **Sort the results by relevance or — if you want to see the most recent articles first — by date.**

Click the <u>Examples</u> link in the search form to reveal some powerful and only semi-documented Dow Jones Interactive features. Besides the standard Boolean AND/OR/NOT operators, you find a bunch of handy *proximity* or *adjacency* connectors, which allow you to specify how close to each other, and in what order, you want your search terms to appear, as well as how to truncate or limit a search term to a specific data field. Chapter 2 tells you more about all these features and how to use them.

Dow Jones Interactive offers several other search options in addition to *Search by Words.* These options are listed to the left of the search form in Figure 9-4. Each of these options allows you to select specific publications, limit by date, and include any other terms that may be pertinent:

✔ **Search by company:** Enter the company name or ticker symbol.

✔ **Search by industry:** Select an industry from the pull-down menu.

✔ **Search by person:** Look for articles by or about a specific individual.

Want to stay up-to-date on a research topic? The major professional online services in this chapter all offer automatic alerting features that enable you to monitor topics on an ongoing basis. On Dow Jones Interactive, click the CustomClips tab at the top of any screen. The LEXIS-NEXIS equivalent is *Eclipse,* as in e-lectronic clipping service. Dialog's is called Alert, fittingly enough.

Shopping at Dialog's supermarket

Searchers have likened **Dialog** to a supermarket of online wares. It's a fish market, a wine shop, a bakery, a hardware store, and a baby vegetable boutique — all under a single capacious roof. You want imported olives? No problem. Paper towels? They're on Aisle 4.

Dialog doesn't hold an exclusive on business information, general magazines, and news; you can find much of the same information at the other gated sites and services we visit in this chapter. But Dialog is a convenient place to shop, especially if you're hungry for scholarly or technical medical, aerospace, nuclear energy, chemistry education, history, or engineering research, — in fields —. You never know when you may get a craving for biotechnology patents or rubber chemistry. We know it hits *us* at the oddest times.

Aisles of files

Dialog identifies its individual databases in a straightforward way: It numbers them. The numbering is arbitrary, but easy to look up and not that hard to remember. Well, not all 600 or so of them, but the ones you use most often.

The key to understanding a Dialog database lies in its *Bluesheet,* a two- to eight-page detailed guide to what the database contains, how far back it goes, and all the different ways you can search it. The Bluesheets (which really are blue) are online at library.dialog.com. You can read them, even without subscribing to Dialog, if you want to satisfy your curiosity about what kinds of databases you'll find there, or if you're suffering from insomnia.

Dialog databases are highly structured. Each one has its own searchable fields. Some use special codes and index terms to make searching even more precise.

In ABI/Inform (File 15) — a database of business, management, and marketing information — you can search for a specific slant or type of article. For example, after typing **b15** to begin your search in File 15 on Dialog (www.dialogweb.com), you enter the following in the search form:

s cc=9110

s stands for <u>Select</u>, the basic Dialog search command. Unlike Dow Jones or LEXIS-NEXIS, you have to tell Dialog every time you give it some terms to search on.

cc stands for <u>Classification Code</u>, which ABI/Inform uses to define broad concepts such as management function, industry and market, or type of article.

cc=9110 tells Dialog to look for articles in the ABI/Inform database that focus on a specific company.

Enter **s cc=9130** for theory.

Enter **s cc=9140** for statistical data.

You can also use the made-up word *manycompanies* to limit your search to articles that survey, well, many companies in the same industry or involved in whatever topic the article is discussing.

In Dun's Market Identifiers (File 516), a company directory, you can look for firms with a certain number of employees or annual sales above a certain amount:

s EM=300 finds companies with 300 or more employees.

s SA=50M:100M finds companies with annual sales in the $50- to $100-million range.

In Medline (Files 154 and 155), which covers medical literature and related fields, you can use a Limit command to restrict your results to human subjects, or English language records, or both at once. The following example means *limit* the results of *set 12* — see the next section, "What's that hissing sound?" for an explanation of Dialog *sets* and how to use them — to articles that deal with *human* subjects and that are written in *English:*

L12/human, eng

You can also link subject headings from the Medline index of terms to specific subheadings that closely define the topic: For example, you can enter the following search statement to locate drug therapies (DT) that are specifically associated with the treatment of arteriosclerosis:

s arteriosclerosis (L) DT

Or you can look for surgical methods (SU) of dealing with arteriosclerosis like this:

s arteriosclerosis (L) SU

In Claims/U.S. Patents (File 340), you can search by inventor (the person who discovered it) or patent assignee (the person — or, more likely, the company — that gets the money from manufacturing or licensing it):

s IV=Berlekamp searches for an inventor named Berlekamp.

s PA=Kodak searches for the patent assignee, Kodak.

Actually, personal- and company-name searching on Dialog involves more than just entering what you assume is the correct name and specifying the appropriate field. Using the Expand command is a good idea because it shows you the various permutations of the name, with and without middle initials, and so on. You can pick the right one(s) from the Expand list and use it (or them) in your search.

Unlike Dow Jones or LEXIS-NEXIS, Dialog databases are independent creations with little if any integration among them. The codes that you use in one database may not appear in another. Some databases contain duplicate material. Searching a single publication is harder on Dialog, because many of its databases cover multiple sources. Be sure to consult the Bluesheet (database guide) before searching an unfamiliar file.

What's that hissing sound?

One of Dialog's unique strengths is the ability to create a separate set of results for every search term you enter, and to combine those sets any way you want. Each of the simple searches that we use as examples in the last section results in a single *set.*

If you're doing a more complex search, or if you want to see how many documents are available for each of the concepts you're searching, we recommend using a variation on the Dialog <u>Select</u> command called *Select Steps.* To use Select Steps, you just use *ss* instead of the single *s* to introduce a search request. *ss* gives you a separate set of results for each term in your search.

For example, if you're doing a search on *cats* and *mice,* you may enter

s cats and mice

You get a single set of documents, all of which mention both cats and mice. But when you start reviewing your results, you realize that you forgot to include the synonym *felines* in your search. Meeeeoooowww. You may be missing some important information. You can get around the problem in various ways, but the most elegant way is to avoid it in the first place by using *ss* in place of *s* to introduce your search request:

ss cats and mice

> set 1: cats
>
> set 2: mice
>
> set 3: cats and mice

ss felines

> set 4: felines

ss s1 or s4

> set 5: cats or felines

ss s5 and s2

> set 6: cats or felines, and mice

If you were running an actual search, Dialog would also show you how many hits it found for each of your terms. If you're on the right track, an OR command increases the retrieval, because you're including more terms; an AND command reduces the retrieval, because you're imposing added restrictions. Chapter 2 has more information on using ANDs and ORs.

Stepping through a Dialog search

The standard drill for searching Dialog goes like this:

1. **Point your browser to** www.dialogweb.com **and log in.**

2. **Select your database(s).**

   You can string file numbers together or select a broad category, such as Papers, to search many files at once.

3. **Enter your search strategy.**

   Remember that you can combine set numbers with ANDs, ORs, or NOTs to broaden or narrow the results.

4. **Review interim results in one of Dialog's brief formats.**

5. **When you're satisfied that you're on target, print or download your results.**

Special search features on Dialog

Dialog's search engine is based on essentially the same constellation of Boolean operators and proximity connectors that Dow Jones and LEXIS-NEXIS use. But each of those services offers its own refinements and specialized ways of handling certain features. Dialog is no different; here are just a few of its distinguishing characteristics:

- ✔ **The Link operator (L),** which we used in the Medline example (see the section "Aisles of files," earlier in this chapter), tells Dialog that your two terms must occur in the same *descriptor*. A descriptor is a standardized indexing term used throughout a particular database and assigned to documents dealing with a particular topic — such as *arteriosclerosis*. Usually, you link a subject heading with a subheading, such as *drug therapy* in the Medline example. You probably won't use the Link operator very often, but when you do, you'll be glad it exists.

- ✔ **The Field operator (F)** tells Dialog that both your terms must occur in the same part of the database record, for example in the title, or in an *abstract* or summary of the document. For more about field searching, see Chapter 2.

- ✔ **The question mark (?)** is used for both internal *wild cards* and end-of-word *truncation*.

   A *?* in the middle of a word is a wild card. For example, **wom?n** picks up *woman* and *women* (there you have it: the secret for picking up women) as well as the new-agey *womyn*.

   A *?* at the end of a word can be tuned to pick up just one additional letter at most, or no more than a specific number of letters, or an unlimited number. Here are a few examples:

   - **dog???** picks up anywhere from zero to three additional letters following the root word *dog*. You get *dog, dogs,* and *dogged,* plus anything else that starts with *dog* and contains up to three additional letters.

   - **dog?** with a single *?* picks up everything in the world (and *don't* they?) from *dog* and *dogs* to *dogged, dogcatcher, dogfight, doghouse, dogleg, dogwood, dogmatic,* and *doggone*.

   - **dog? ?** — that's a space between the first and the second *?* — gets just *one* more letter, max: *dog, dogs* — and *doge,* a Venetian nobleman. Won't *he* be surprised!

✔ **Target** is Dialog's supplement to the Boolean search mode described earlier in this chapter and in Chapter 2. *Target* searches and delivers results in order of their supposed relevance. You just key in your search words and indicate with an asterisk (*) which ones *must* appear. Type **target** when you're online on Dialog to get a brief summary of commands.

Target works best when you want just a few key articles on a subject. You can use it in combination with a Boolean search. Say you've run a search, gotten more hits than you can use, and can't figure out how to narrow them down. Entering *target s4* (assuming set 4 is the last set of your Boolean search) re-ranks them in relevance (you hope) order and presents you with Dialog's top 50 picks.

Output options

Record Format: Dialog is big on numbers. It numbers its databases, and it also numbers its various formats for printing, displaying, and downloading database records. Fortunately, you don't have to memorize format numbers, because the search results page includes a pull-down menu for the commonly requested formats in plain English. Formats give you different amounts of information about the document, as follows:

✔ Some formats are very short and are intended just to show you whether you're on the right track in the course of a search. (Typically, that's Format 6 or 8, and it's traditionally, although not always, free. The equivalent is the *free* format on the pull-down menu.)

✔ Other formats give you basic information, such as author, title, publication name, and date (Format 3 or the *medium* format).

✔ Still others give you a brief summary or abstract (often Format 4 or 7 — though it varies a lot — or the *long* format).

✔ Yet other formats give you the whole shebang — complete text, all the numbers, coding and index terms, whatever's in the record (usually Format 5 or 9, or the *full* format).

You can also roll your own — format your own format, in effect. Dialog's UDF (User-Defined Format) feature enables you to specify the fields or document sections that you want to see:

t/au,ti/1-5 tells Dialog to *type* just the *author names* and *article titles* for records *1 through 5* in the current set.

UDF documents don't always save you money; if you specify a field that's otherwise available only in one of the higher-priced numbered formats, you're likely to pay that price — even if all you've ordered is one field.

Dialog's pricing is based on which databases you search, the type of commands you use, how many documents you print or download, and the format in which you retrieve them.

In any given database, a brief citation costs less than an abstract, and an abstract costs less than the full text (abstracts aren't available in all files).

If you display a document while searching and order it later in the session, you pay for it twice. That's why we suggest that you keep your display format brief and order the complete item only if you're sure you want it. It's not like the Web, where you can browse and read to your heart's content!

Sorting: Dialog normally presents your search results in date order, most recent first. You can override this order by specifying how you want the results to appear:

> **sort s3/all/au,py** tells Dialog to *sort all the documents in set 3* by *author,* and for each author, by publication *year.*

Rank: The Rank command lets you determine the most common (highly ranked) terms or concepts in a set of search results — without having to know what any of them are to begin with.

> ✔ You can use *Rank* after running a patent search to find out what companies hold the most patents in the area you're researching.
>
> ✔ You can use it in a search of the medical or engineering literature to identify prominent experts who've written a lot on the subject.
>
> ✔ You can search a company directory by geographic location to find out what kinds of businesses exist, or search by type of business and rank them by city.

The basic Rank syntax is easy: **rank pa** ranks the most recent set of search results by *patent assignee.* Substitute *au* for *author* or *cy* for *city,* and you're on your way — no longer a Rank amateur.

Rank is free in most databases, but in some, including patent files, you may be charged from 2 cents to 10 cents a record. That doesn't sound like much, but when you're ranking 5,000 records, the cost does add up.

Report: The Report feature lets you extract certain fields from database records and rearrange them into tables. Report is available only for databases where it makes sense to use it, such as company directories.

> **report s5/co,cy,st,te/1-50** produces a tabular report with the headings *Company, City, State,* and *Telephone Number* across the top, and the information you've requested, for the first *50* records in *set 5,* arranged in columns.

Want the top ten companies by sales? Or an alphabetical listing? Do a Sort on your final answer-set and then run Report on the sorted set.

Other dialects of Dialog

Dialog offers several connection options: You can search **Dialog on the Web** (www.dialogweb.com). You can connect to the Dialog service by using DialogLink, Dialog's proprietary software. You can telnet to dialog.com from elsewhere on the Net. You can use one of the options described in the following section, if you want preformatted search screens that do some of the heavy lifting for you.

One advantage of Dialog on the Web is that you can poke around and read the copious help files, online Bluesheets, and other documentation, without having to pay a cent. It's like driving down a long and gently winding road until the enter-your-password gate clangs down.

Although the Web's pointing-and-clicking makes it easy to get around, we sometimes prefer to roll up our sleeves and telnet to the pre-Web version of Dialog, known as **DialogClassic** (telnet dialog.com). You get the same data, and you use the same commands, as Dialog on the Web, but telnetting offers a couple of advantages that we long-time searchers like:

 ✔ System responses are faster because you're using the telnet protocol — a continuous direct link to Dialog — rather than the Web.

 ✔ You can log your entire search session (capture and save it to a file on your computer) and scroll back to review what you've done.

See Chapter 8 for more about telnet.

Dialog also offers something called **DialogClassic** on the Web (www.dialogclassic.com), which can be useful if you don't want to use the Dialog Web interface but don't have access to telnet or prefer not to use it. It strikes us as the worst of both worlds: No helpful menus or free documentation, and you still have to cope with the World-Wide-Wait.

Easy answers

If you're impressed but a little daunted by the power and depth of the Dialog service, one of the following may help:

DialogWeb offers a **Guided Search** option that enables you to search the Dialog system without knowing any Dialog commands at all. Click the Guided Search link, select your databases, and then fill in the appropriate forms to define and focus your search.

DialogSelect Open Access (openaccess.dialog.com) offers Web access — independent of DialogWeb — to selected Dialog databases. DialogSelect provides easy-to-use predefined search forms with fill-in-the-blank boxes.

DialogSelect greatly streamlines the search process, although you're still ahead of the game if you understand how the Dialog service is structured and how Boolean logic works. (**Hint:** We discuss Boolean basics in Chapter 2.) DialogSelect offers 11 *channels* broken out by general subject, such as Business, Medical, News, Reference, and Technology.

The *Open Access* part means that you don't have to set up an account with Dialog or pay monthly or yearly fees (see the next section, "At the checkout counter," for more about these fees). Instead, you can simply do a search, browse the results, and select the items you want. Dialog doesn't ask for your credit card number until you're ready to read items in full. (What, you thought it would never ask?) The per-document charge is higher than what Dialog subscribers would pay, but you're not charged an annual fee or monthly minimum — it's strictly pay-as-you-go.

At the checkout counter

The moment of truth has arrived: How much is this load of groceries — or maybe just a bag of organic tomatoes — going to cost me?

Dialog pricing has four main components:

- ✔ **Yearly membership fee:** $144, plus an initial set-up fee of $295 when you establish your account.
- ✔ **DialUnit charges:** How hard the system has to work to process each command.
- ✔ **Hit charges:** How many records you print, display, or download, and in what format(s).
- ✔ **Monthly minimum:** If your monthly charges from DialUnits and hit charges are less than $75, you'll still be charged $75, the monthly minimum.

The price of a DialUnit varies from file to file, and ranges from $1 to $30. Exactly what fraction of a DialUnit you'll incur for any given search or individual search command is impossible to say, because DialUnits are based on how busy the system is and how much *thinking* it takes to execute each command.

Record charges also vary from one database to another. Some formats, such as title-only, are usually free. A full record typically goes for $1 to $3, though government-subsidized databases are often less, and some business, financial, and specialized technical files can run considerably more. You can find all the gory details at `products.dialog.com/products/dialog/dial_pricing.html`.

We know that those DialUnits sound scary — they *are,* compared with the open Web, and with services such as Dow Jones Interactive that don't charge a search fee at all. In reality, though, most Dialog searches don't incur more than a DialUnit or two, from start to finish.

Learning the ways of LEXIS-NEXIS

As the name implies, the **LEXIS-NEXIS** service has two sides. The part that sounds like a luxury automobile (that's a sore point — a trademark infringement suit was actually filed over the similarity with *Lexus*) encompasses case law, U.S. and international governmental statutes, federal and state agency regulations, plus secondary material, such as bar journals, law reviews, and other lawyerly fare.

We'll be honest with you: Legal research is a science unto itself. If you're deeply involved in the law, you're probably already acquainted with Lexis or its chief competitor, **Westlaw** (www.westlaw.com). If you're *not* involved in the law, we're not going to teach you here. We're not looking for a lawsuit, ourselves. If you need legal research, it's best to contact an attorney or a qualified research professional, or buckle down and let LEXIS-NEXIS train you.

The other half of the service, Nexis, focuses on global news, politics and economics, company directories, financial filings, and other kinds of business, management, and marketing information. Nexis is particularly strong in full-text newspapers and general interest magazines, business and trade journals, international country and economic data, and market research reports. As with Dow Jones Interactive and Dialog, you can cover dozens of publications at once with a single search query.

Going online with LEXIS-NEXIS

For access to the full LEXIS-NEXIS service, you have to contract with the company and negotiate a payment plan (either pay-as-you-go, or a customized flat-fee subscription that is generally in the thousands-of-dollars-per-year range). Pay-as-you-go may be your best option if you only use the service occasionally, but if you use it regularly, a flat-fee contract will probably save you money. You can use L-N's own imaginatively named Research Software, or navigate to www.lexis-nexis.com/ln.universe/ and search LEXIS-NEXIS Universe, its counterpart on the Web. Your contract may or may not include access to certain premium and specialized sources.

Low-volume users — that's us, and most likely you — often sign up for LEXIS-NEXIS's transaction-based fee schedule, which means that you pay either for every search you do or for every minute you're online. A group file consisting of several publications costs more to search than a single publication within that group file. The bigger the database, roughly speaking, the greater the cost per search or per minute. And the bottom line for that per-search pricing is that mistakes, even typos, can be expensivo.

We prefer Universe for its ease of use and handy access to help files and other useful documentation. We especially like the way it makes sense of L-N's erstwhile-confusing hierarchy of libraries, group files, and individual publications. Click Search, followed by a category such as News, Government, or Legal; then click the appropriate subcategory within one of these groups. Each type of search uses a customized, fill-in-the-blanks search form. You can enter a simple search or, if you know how, take advantage of some of the special L-N search features that we describe in the following section. Universe also delivers special, preformatted reports on businesses called Company Dossiers.

The Universe Advanced Search mode lets you select your own sources from the LEXIS-NEXIS hierarchy and enter a free-form search without any additional prompts.

LEXIS-NEXIS special searching features

LEXIS-NEXIS is a complex research service with dozens of specialized features. Like the other professional online services in this chapter, it utilizes the ol' Boolean AND/OR/NOT operators and many of the other power-searching capabilities covered in Chapter 2. But LEXIS-NEXIS is unique in many ways. A full-fledged tutorial could take a whole book (and *does* — you can buy it from LEXIS-NEXIS). Here are highlights of some of its special features:

- **Automatic pluralization:** LEXIS-NEXIS looks for both singular and plural forms of words, as long as the plural is formed by adding *s* or *es*.

- **Equivalents:** LEXIS-NEXIS automatically looks for both U.S. and British spellings of common words such as *program(me)* and *colo(u)r*.

- **Truncation:** LEXIS-NEXIS uses two different *wild card* symbols. The exclamation point (!) stands for any number of letters at the end of a word root. The asterisk (*) stands for a single character anywhere in a word (except at the beginning). Here are a few examples:

    - **wom*n** looks for both *woman* and *women*.

    - You can use more than one wild card symbol: **r**t** retrieves *root, rust, rent,* and *rapt* — though we can't imagine why you'd want to.

  You use asterisks at the *end* of a word to retrieve up to and including that many additional characters in the word: **bank*** retrieves *bank, banks, banker, bankers,* and *banking,* but not *bankrupt, bankruptcy,* or *bankruptcies*.

- **Case sensitivity:** LEXIS-NEXIS enables you to search for uppercase letters anywhere in a word, for all-uppercase, or for lowercase-only forms.

    - **caps (Apple)** retrieves references to Apple computers, or the company, or people named Apple, or any occurrence of the word *apple* that happens to come at the beginning of a sentence.

    - **allcaps (era)** retrieves references to the Equal Rights Amendment, and anything else with the same acronym, but not to uses of the word *era* as a measure of geological or historical time.

    - **nocaps (era)** does the opposite.

✔ **atleast*n*:** Your search term(s) must occur *at least* so many times in a document in order for it to be retrieved, which is a slick way of avoiding material in which your term is mentioned, but only in passing. If you specify a high value for *n,* you generally limit your retrieval to long documents. If you're looking for a good *short* article and not a whole treatise on the subject, try setting your atleast value in the 6–10 range: **atleast8 (kodak).**

Dow Jones Interactive offers an *atleast* feature, too.

✔ **Focus:** Enables you to look for occurrences of a new keyword within the set of documents you've already retrieved. Focus is a good way to zero in on the good bits buried in a steaming pile of not particularly glorious-looking articles.

✔ **More Like This:** Allows you to tag a particularly juicy-looking document and tell LEXIS-NEXIS to *get me more like this one.* Depending on your payment plan, you may get dinged for an additional search fee.

Other LEXIS-NEXIS access options

In the last few years, LEXIS-NEXIS has spawned a confusing variety of products, both Web-based and proprietary, aimed at various target markets — accountants, advertising, media, sales, marketing professionals, political consultants, pizza delivery persons, who knows. If you feel a bit daunted by the number and variety of sources and commands we describe in the preceding sections, don't worry. You may not *need* all that. If your main interest is business research, or you work for a government agency, a law firm, or an academic institution, just click the appropriate block on the LEXIS-NEXIS home page (www.lexis-nexis.com) and survey the choices available to you. Or simply click the Contact us link and fill in the form. You'll end up speaking to an account specialist who can recommend a service option suited to your needs.

LEXIS-NEXIS also offers a service called reQUESTer that lets you purchase a day pass to LEXIS-NEXIS with a credit card, even if you're not a current subscriber. Depending on the files you want to search, you pay from $29 to $69 for an all-day excursion or $129 for a week-long pass. No additional document charges, no per-search fees. It may sound like a lot of money, but if you're faced with a heavy-duty research project where you know LEXIS-NEXIS can help, you'll definitely get your money's worth.

Getting it wholesale

For the most part, the three professional online services we've described in the preceding sections don't actually own the contents of the databases they provide. They license the material from wholesalers who either produce the information themselves, or negotiate the electronic rights to the information from individual publishers or authors.

Discount databases

Many of the databases carried by LEXIS-NEXIS and the other online services described in this chapter are also available through university libraries to affiliated students, faculty, and staff, and sometimes to members of the community on a walk-in basis. You may have to show up at the library and sign up to use a public terminal. If you're interested in exploring these resources but not ready to commit to a particular online service, check out the free-access angle through your nearest institution of higher learning. Even if the library charges you to use the online service, you almost always pay less than if you subscribe to the service yourself because the institution has negotiated a cheaper rate.

Several of these database wholesalers also offer direct access to their files, independent of Dialog, Dow Jones, and LEXIS-NEXIS. You subscribe to these databases directly, search them from a members-only Web site, and download or print the articles you want.

Three of the major article wholesalers are

- ✔ **ProQuest Direct** (`www.bellhowell.infolearning.com/proquest`): Offers summaries of articles from about 8,000 publications, as well as the complete text of many titles and, for some, article images complete with the original layout and illustrations that appeared in print.

- ✔ **Insite 2** (`www.insite2pro.gale.com`): Offers a good collection of general and consumer-type publications as well as health, business, and marketing publications — the majority of which are available in full text — and directory listings for close to 200,000 companies.

- ✔ **Responsive Database Services** (`www.rdsinc.com/suite`): The smallest of these three, with about 1,300 publications, but also the producer of TableBase, a useful database for researchers who need "just the data, Ma'am" that we describe in Chapter 12.

These all sound like great resources for the serious researcher, don't they? So, what's the catch? Cost. You can't subscribe to any of these wholesalers' databases for less than several thousand dollars. They're geared toward libraries, businesses, and other institutions with a number of users to offset their high subscription costs. Ask around; a local university or public library is likely to offer at least one of these wholesaler databases on-site.

Web Search Engines Turn Pro

At the beginning of this chapter, we divided the gated Web into three general categories — members-only sites such as The New York Times on the Web, consumer online services such as AOL, and professional online services such as Dow Jones. However, some gated information services don't fit neatly into any of these three groups. In the following sections, we look at three of these hybrid services. All of them offer some of the same high-value information as the professional online services we describe earlier in this chapter.

Looking up Northern Light

Northern Light (www.northernlight.com) is one of the largest Web search engines, but with a twist. Northern Light searches not only the Web, but also its Special Collection, which includes some of the same databases and publications you find in the professional online services described earlier in this chapter. You can search Northern Light's collection of articles, broadcast transcripts, and Investext reports (see Chapter 12 for a discussion of Investext) by using the same technique you use to search the rest of the Web. Type in a few terms that describe your concept and let Northern Light sort the results with the most relevant materials at the beginning of the list.

You can search the Web and NL's Special Collection at no charge, but you have to set up an account and supply your credit card number in order to purchase the full text of any Special Collection items. Most articles are modestly priced, and Northern Light tells you the cost before your credit card is charged. Plus, it offers a money-back guarantee!

NL makes reviewing your search results easier by filtering items into Custom Search folders that it creates, on the fly, depending on the subject of your search and the kinds of information retrieved. Instead of scrolling through the relevance-ranked list, you can browse through folders according to what they tell you about the results they contain: If you do a search on Alzheimer's disease, for instance, you may get folders labeled Medical Sites, Psychological Disorders, and Nursing Homes, among others.

You can also set up a free Alert service, in which you specify the topic or topics you want to monitor, and Northern Light sends you an e-mail notice whenever it finds relevant new content on the Web or articles in the Special Collection.

Browsing the Electric Library

The **Electric Library** (www.elibrary.com) provides access to books, magazine and newspaper articles, maps, pictures, broadcast transcripts, and more. You can search by using Boolean logic (see Chapter 2 for more on Boolean searching) or natural language — just type in a few keywords that describe what you're looking for. Search results are listed by type of document — newspaper articles, book sections, and so on. You can browse the headlines and bibliographic citations (author, title, publication name) for each item, and change the display ranking from relevance to date order. When you decide that you want to see the complete text of one or more items, you're prompted for your user ID. Subscriptions to Electric Library cost less than $10 a month (or $60 a year), with no limit on the number of items you can read or download — one of the best bargains, for access to a wide range of general interest publications on the Web.

Electric Library's Advanced Search feature lets you search by publication, author, date, and title words. You can set up a free *eLibrary Tracker* to monitor the database for new items that match your specified keywords, and e-mail you the headlines. You need not be a subscriber to use the eLibrary Tracker; however, if you want to actually *read* any of those items, you have to pony up that monthly subscription fee.

Power up with Powerize

Building on the assumption that sometimes there *is* such a thing as a free lunch, **Powerize** (www.powerize.com) gives away some articles, press releases, and company profiles at no charge. Other items cost a few dollars. Unlike most other online services, Powerize always lets you read the first paragraph or so without pulling out your credit card; for some kinds of research, the first paragraph may be all you need.

Powerize includes articles and other items from around 10,000 sources, of which about a quarter can be viewed for free, and three-fourths are pay-per-view. In addition to newspaper, newsletter, and magazine articles, Powerize offers stock quotes, U.S. company directory listings, and links to Web-based business directories from more than a hundred countries.

How Do You Choose?

As you may have gathered by now, a lot of overlap exists, content-wise, among online services. LEXIS-NEXIS, Dow Jones Interactive, and Dialog offer many of the same publication sources and database compilations. And some of the newer players offer some of the same sources with more affordable pay-as-you-go options. So how do you know which service is right for you?

It's mostly a matter of

- ✔ Power
- ✔ Preference
- ✔ Price
- ✔ Availability

Most professional researchers favor the online service they learned first; typically, they have one *home* system and several supplementary ones that they use for unique sources and features they can't get elsewhere.

We recommend that you

- ✔ **Check out the pricing options for the service that appeals to you most.** If you're an individual, as opposed to a big corporation, and you anticipate only using the service occasionally and can't justify much out-of-pocket expense, it may be out of the running on economic grounds alone.

- ✔ **Check out the contents.** What does it have that you really want, and that you can't find (as far back, as complete, as fully searchable) on the open Web or elsewhere?

- ✔ **Check out the look and feel.** Sign up for an introductory trial. Sit in on a class, if the service offers one. Submit yourself to an online or disk-based tutorial. Take the system for a test drive any way you can. Are you comfortable with the steering? How's the air conditioner? What kind of gas mileage do you think you're getting? Does it accelerate on the hills? Handle well around curves? Do you like the view? Hey! Watch out for that tree!

Our own preferences? Oh dear. We both grew up with Dialog, and can search it in our sleep — and on occasion, have. It's fast, and flexible, and we can do just about anything with it that we want to. Dialog is the only alternative, as far as we're concerned, for non-business searching (medicine, patents, science, and technology) and for databases that rely on codes and indexes for precision. It's pricey, but we sometimes don't have a choice.

On the other hand, Dow Jones Interactive has a pricing model that you can't beat — $69 a year for access and then a flat $2.95 per article. And DJI is number one when it comes to general business and financial research. We like its interface, the ability to mix and match sources so you can search just the most relevant publications, and its date-sorting *and* relevance-ranking capabilities.

Our friends at LEXIS-NEXIS know how we feel: The system is fast, and Universe, the Web interface, makes it easier to select the right files and carry out an effective search. But the pricing is still not user-friendly, particularly for small-time searchers. If you do elect to sign up with LEXIS-NEXIS, opt for the hourly pricing plan as opposed to the per-search alternative. The latter charges you for every search you do, even when you've made a mistake and just want to start over. Sloppy typists pay the price! Our opinion: For legal researchers, LEXIS-NEXIS is a must. For other types of inquiries, you can usually find the same information elsewhere.

Chapter 2 tells you how to think like a researcher: figuring out what you need, coming up with synonyms, broadening or narrowing your search results. You need that context to successfully tackle any of the industrial-strength gated services covered in this chapter. It helps to read and reread that chapter.

One Final Point

The key thing to realize about members-only Web sites and online services, whether or not they charge a fee, is that you have to know about them before you can take advantage of them. You won't just stumble across the information they contain, or even find out that they exist, in a standard search engine search. The extra effort of bookmarking a great gated Web site, or signing up and becoming proficient with a full-featured professional online service, is worth it — especially if you're serious about mastering the research game. Bottom line: Remember that these services exist and ask yourself whether your research project can use the added boost.

Chapter 10

The Personal Touch

In This Chapter

▶ Finding out where the experts hang out online

▶ Getting around in newsgroups, mailing lists, and other virtual venues

▶ Asking for information: the do's and don'ts

Maybe you've heard the joke: There are two kinds of people in the world — those who divide the world into two kinds of people, and those who don't. As analytical types, we've divided the world of online research into two kinds: *publication* and *people*. *Publication* includes most of the resources covered elsewhere in this book: Web sites, databases, virtual reference shelves, library catalogs, and indexes. But how do *people* figure into research? Think about how you find the answers to your questions in real life: Sometimes you look at a book or visit your local library. But aren't you just as likely to pick up the phone and call an expert — a doctor, accountant, travel agent, or somebody who knows a lot about the subject — or ask friends for their opinions?

The Human Side of the Net

The online world does opinion really, really well — everyone has an opinion on everything. It's also an incredible source for fresh, fast, deep, and detailed information about subjects that haven't yet made it into print. People online are usually willing to help, if only because it gives them a chance to show off how much they know. The human side of the Net is where you find firsthand reports, original data that never made it into print, controversy, alternative viewpoints, and hot-off-the-presses new developments.

People resources are great when you're looking for hands-on perspectives and personal accounts:

✔ What's it like to skydive?

✔ Do I really want a career as a caterer?

✔ What should I pack for a holiday in New Zealand?

✔ How do I set up a salt-water aquarium?

✔ How do I solve a particular problem with Excel?

✔ Are herbal remedies for weight control effective?

✔ Can someone recommend a good management consultant?

Where Do the Experts Hang Out Online?

You can find knowledgeable and opinionated folks everywhere you go online. Depending on your perspective, you can carve up the territory in different ways, and the borders between neighborhoods aren't always clear. But the way we look at it, the Net has four main venues for conversation:

✔ Newsgroups

✔ Electronic mailing lists

✔ Virtual villages and conferencing systems

✔ E-mail

Just like neighborhoods in your own town or city, each of these online hangouts has its own geography, flavor, and population, complete with local heroes, unsavory characters, and yep, village idiots. Each one has its own value for research, too, individually or in combination with other techniques.

For leads to *official* experts — people who are willing to lend their expertise, sometimes for a fee — check out **Kitty Bennett's Sources and Experts** listing (sunsite.unc.edu/slanews/internet/experts.html).

Newsgroups

Don't let the name fool you. Newsgroups have nothing to do with the top-of-the-hour updates you see on TV. In fact, they're about as far as you can get from mainstream media while still staring at a screen. Think about a giant, messy bulletin board — the cork-and-thumbtack kind — where anyone is free to post notices, comments, and comments on *other* people's comments. Someone tries to maintain order, but it's a constant battle against chaos and confusion. Sounds like a really promising place to do research, doesn't it? Actually, it can be if you approach it correctly.

A *newsgroup,* singular, is an ongoing conversation devoted to a particular topic — quantum physics, body-piercing, snowboarding, tropical fish, you name it. Anybody who finds his way there can chime in, whether he's the world's leading expert on the subject, someone who just wants to register an opinion, or an online researcher, like you.

Browsing newsgroups with Liszt

The **Liszt** search engine is a window into the world of newsgroups. It's also a massive directory of mailing lists, which we describe later in this chapter. For a quick flyover, point your Web browser to www.liszt.com/news. You see broad categories that cover the vast majority of newsgroups, and smaller categories covering non-English language and regional interest groups. Click one of the categories — for example, the rec link (short for *recreation*). Figure 10-1 shows the list of subdivisions within the *rec* category. Each of these subdivisions corresponds to an individual newsgroup or collection of related groups.

Notice how some of the newsgroups are listed in **bold** type with a number in parentheses, and some are underlined? The names in bold indicate that the newsgroup is divided into more specific subgroups.

Click one of the bolded newsgroups — skiing, farther down the list, is a good example — to see a list of the subgroups. Figure 10-2 shows the rec.skiing hierarchy.

Deja.com (www.deja.com), the newsgroup search engine formerly known as DejaNews, used to be the star of the show. It has changed its focus and its name, and now Deja.com focuses on building its own discussion groups and collecting users' ratings of everything from biotechnology stocks to car batteries. You can still use Deja.com to locate newsgroups if you want — click the general category you're interested in and then click the Discussions tab for links to related groups.

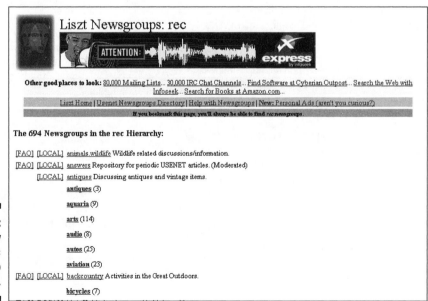

Figure 10-1:
Liszt's view
of the rec
newsgroup
hierarchy.

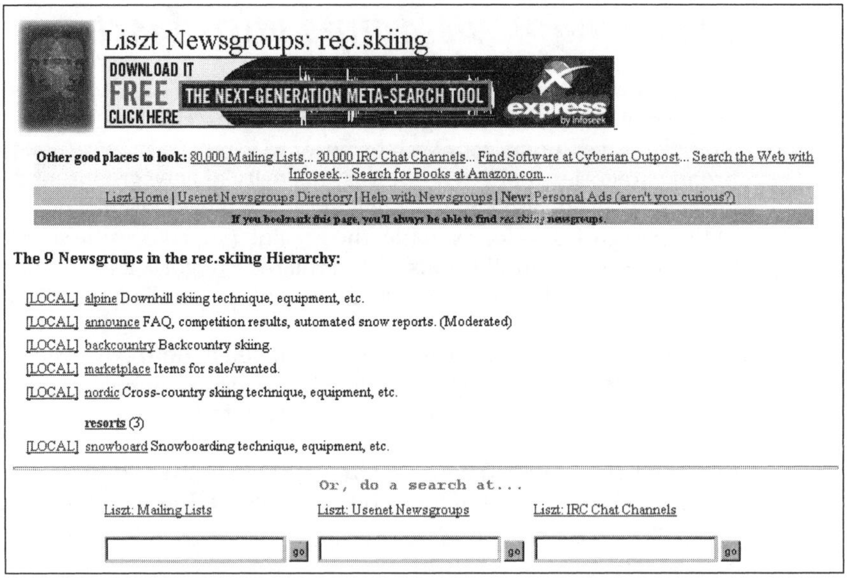

Other good places to look: 80,000 Mailing Lists... 30,000 IRC Chat Channels... Find Software at Cyberian Outpost... Search the Web with Infoseek... Search for Books at Amazon.com...

Liszt Home | Usenet Newsgroups Directory | Help with Newsgroups | New: Personal Ads (aren't you curious?)

If you bookmark this page, you'll always be able to find *rec.skiing* newsgroups.

The 9 Newsgroups in the rec.skiing Hierarchy:

[LOCAL] alpine Downhill skiing technique, equipment, etc.

[LOCAL] announce FAQ, competition results, automated snow reports. (Moderated)

[LOCAL] backcountry Backcountry skiing.

[LOCAL] marketplace Items for sale/wanted.

[LOCAL] nordic Cross-country skiing technique, equipment, etc.

resorts (3)

[LOCAL] snowboard Snowboarding technique, equipment, etc.

Or, do a search at...

| Liszt: Mailing Lists | Liszt: Usenet Newsgroups | Liszt: IRC Chat Channels |

Figure 10-2: The rec.skiing hierarchy.

The basic newsgroup hierarchy

rec — Hobby and recreational topics ranging from antique collecting to motorcycle riding. rec.pets is a fairly tame example of a newsgroup hierarchy; it's further subdivided into discussions on birds, cats, dogs, and reptiles. Check out rec.music, though, for a real taste of how deep and rich newsgroup discussions can be. We found 44 subdivisions when we looked, covering all the bases (and basses) from rec.music.a-cappella to rec.music.hip-hop to rec.music.video.

comp — Anything related to computers, from the mundane to the terminally geeky. You can get down as deep as comp.graphics.rendering.raytracing, if that's your fancy, or stay as straightforward and aboveboard as comp.forsale.

sci — Where the true scientists and science buffs hang out in newsgroups ranging from sci.aeronautics to sci.virtual worlds.

soc — Social and cultural topics, such as politics, religion, and women's issues, as well as international discussions grouped by country, region, religion, or ethnicity.

talk — Think talk show; talk is the online equivalent, full of news reports, rumors, banter, and raging debate on current events and controversial subjects, such as abortion, gun control, and euthanasia.

misc — Just what it sounds like: a miscellaneous collection of discussions on topics such as transportation, writing, survivalism, kids, health, and so on that don't fit anywhere else.

news — Updated information and bulletins about newsgroups and the Net itself. Check out news.announce.newgroups, news.new users.questions, or the elegantly named news.answers.

biz — Business-related topics and announcements. Most biz newsgroups are designed specifically for selling merchandise or for business-related announcements.

`alt` — An alternative hierarchy, much looser than the ones listed earlier and likely to include discussions on just about anything you can imagine. Anyone can start an `alt` group, on any subject. As soon as a certain purple dinosaur hit the scene a few years back, so did an `alt.barney.dinosaur` newsgroup. The Barney-hating contingent countered with `alt.barney.dinosaur.die`, and even more vociferous opponents spawned `alt.barney.dinosaur.die.die` and `alt.barney.dinosaur.die.die.die`. You won't be surprised to learn that the alt groups are almost single-handedly responsible for the steep growth in the total number of newsgroups in the last several years.

A set of `k-12` newsgroups exists for both teachers and kids from kindergarten through 12th grade. You also find a whole slew of international groups operating under their own country-based hierarchies (and native languages), and a collection of newsgroups in just about every U.S. state. A few places, such as Austin, Texas, and the San Francisco Bay area, maintain their own newsgroups independent of state and national hierarchies.

Finding newsgroups with RemarQ

Browsing by topic in Liszt is one way to locate newsgroups in your area of interest. But with thousands of newsgroups out there, some of them buried several levels down, it's not the most efficient way. Luckily, a specialized search engine called **RemarQ** (`www.remarq.com`) offers several more-focused alternatives.

Say you're thinking about starting your own business. Where can you pick up firsthand tips for budding entrepreneurs? Where are people talking about the joys and travails of running a small business? If the thought of running your own business leaves you cold, pick something that interests *you,* such as our skiing example in the last section. Here's how to find newsgroups through RemarQ that match your interests:

1. **Point your Web browser to the RemarQ URL (**`www.remarq.com`**).**

2. **Type a search term in the Find on RemarQ search box, select the Forums That Discuss option, and click the Find button.**

   For example, we typed *entrepreneur* in the search box.

3. **Scan the resulting list of newsgroups, each of which has the search term in its name. At this point, you have two choices:**

   - You can zero in on the newsgroups that sound as though they may be useful (we would go for Entrepreneurs (Moderated) and Entrepreneurs-Business).

   - Or you can just start at the top and go down the list, checking out each newsgroup in turn.

4. **If you want to expand your search to find any newsgroups that have messages containing your search term, type the search term in the Find on RemarQ search box, select the Messages That Mention option, and click the Find button.**

   You see a list of individual messages in each group that mentions the word, which in our case is *entrepreneur*.

5. **Click any promising message headers to check out the information they contain.**

6. **If you find the content useful, click the <u>Watch This Forum</u> link.**

   You then go through the process of signing up for a (free) personalized MyRemarQ page, where you can keep track of the newsgroups that interest you.

Think about alternative ways to express what you want to find. If *entrepreneur* doesn't work for you, try *small business.* You can't predict exactly what words, terms, and phrases people may use to talk about your topic.

Reading newsgroup posts

Whether you find your way to the newsgroup of your dreams through browsing in Liszt or searching on RemarQ, you're still just standing at the doorway. Now it's time to enter and take a look at what's going on inside.

Start from either the Liszt newsgroup directory (www.liszt.com/news) or the RemarQ search results screen (www.remarq.com) with a list of newsgroups that may be useful. Here's what you do to start reading messages:

1. **Click the name of a newsgroup you want to read.**

   This action brings up a list showing the titles of recent posts made to the newsgroup, the dates, and the names of people responsible for the postings.

2. **One more click on the title of an interesting-sounding post, and voilà! You're reading a newsgroup message. Finally.**

Want to post your own message to the newsgroup? Hold on a minute. Take a deep breath and read the next three sections — up to "Mailing Lists" — and maybe even the rest of the chapter, before you start.

Taking the temperature of a newsgroup

A quick scan of newsgroup headers can reveal a lot of information, not only about the subjects under discussion but also about the culture and customs of the group that you're about to join. Does the newsgroup sound like a friendly place, helpful and welcoming to newcomers? Or is the atmosphere more smart-alecky and in-groupy? The less comfortable you feel with the prevailing tone of the group, the more cautious you should be in your quest for information.

Headers can tell you other things about the group, too:

- ✔ **Do you see an abundance of current postings?** If so, the group is probably active and a good place to get current information on your topic.

- ✔ **Do you see a lot of spam?** If the majority of postings are advertisements for get-rich-quick schemes or worse, the group is probably no longer visited by people who actually care about the subject.

- ✔ **Do you see lots of nonsense headers?** The group may have outlived its usefulness as a research tool and deteriorated into a social hangout or a total waste of time.

- ✔ **Do the headers themselves give you a good idea of what people are actually talking about?** If so, it's probably going to be easier to find focused information there.

Before you post: The FAQs of life

If you have a question, chances are someone else, somewhere in the world, has already wondered about the same thing — or something very similar. That's a basic fact of online life; it has two implications you should be aware of:

- ✔ People get irritated when they're asked the same question over and over again.

- ✔ To minimize irritation, many newsgroups have compiled archives of Frequently Asked Questions, or FAQs.

Before you post your burning question, only to be met with a chorus of "Oh no, not *this* again" (or worse), look for a FAQ covering your subject. Trust us: It is worth the effort and may save you from a lot of grief.

To locate FAQs online, you can

- ✔ Look up the newsgroup on **Liszt** (www.liszt.com/news) and check for a [FAQ] link.

> ✔ Try the **Internet FAQ Archives** (`www.faqs.org`). You can search with newsgroup names or subjects and keywords, or browse an alphabetical list.

When hunting for FAQs, keep your keywords general; for example, *skiing* produces better results than *bindings,* even if *ski bindings* is what you're ultimately interested in. After you find a FAQ, scan through it or use your Web browser's find-in-this-document function to locate the specific term you're looking for.

Aunt Netty-Quette's priceless pointers for painless posting

Long-time Net denizens follow a code of conduct — sometimes referred to as *netiquette* — that's designed to preserve the core values of the Net. These values include non-commercialism (which sounds pretty funny in the context of the Web), consideration for one's fellow humans, and concern for the preservation and well-being of the Internet itself. Most experienced newsgroup posters subscribe to the same general values and expect others to do the same. To help you avoid that awful feeling of blushing in front of your monitor — or sobbing, getting angry, or experiencing other strong negative emotions — our alter ego, Aunt Netty-Quette, has put together this handy list of tips:

> ✔ **Do your homework first.** Look for a FAQ to see whether someone has already answered your question.
>
> ✔ **Lurk before you leap.** Each newsgroup has its own culture, customs, and taboos. Read the newsgroup for a while before you even *think* about posting, to get a sense of whether the group is friendly and tolerant, a little high-strung, or a bunch of barbarians to whom a newbie is just fresh meat. Attune yourself to the dominant conversational style: Is the group scholarly and formal, or casually conversational? Do posters use smiley faces and acronyms, such as PMFJI (Pardon Me For Jumping In), or do they frown on such conventions?
>
> ✔ **Avoid commercial messages or shameless self-promotion.** You'll only irritate the people to whom you are trying to sell.
>
> ✔ **If you're tempted to post your question in *all* the newsgroups that sound as though they might be useful, *don't*.** That's called *spamming,* and there's zero tolerance for it on the Net.
>
> ✔ **If in doubt, ask your question privately.** After you've hung out in a newsgroup for a while, you can easily identify the people who know what they're talking about. You may still be hesitant about speaking up in the group; if so, try sending an e-mail message directly to the designated expert.

✔ **Choose a descriptive subject header.** This holds true for both public postings and private e-mail. A subject header such as *Help! Info Needed!!!* conveys nothing but urgency and desperation. Chances are slim that a busy expert is going to stop to see what your message is about, let alone be favorably inclined to help you. You would get better results with a header such as *Accounting software for start-ups?* or *Best cross-country ski bindings?* A clear subject header is as important as a good book title; it draws the reader in.

✔ **Be succinct and considerate in your message.** Use as few words as possible to introduce yourself, convey your question clearly, and indicate where you've already looked for information. Make sure that your request is reasonable — for busy people, time and attention are precious commodities. "Tell me everything you know" will be a lot less productive than "Can you recommend a good book or online starting point where I can find out more?"

✔ **Give something back.** Offer to share your findings with the group, or compile the answers and add them to the FAQ, or supply a link to wherever you plan to post your summary or research results.

Mailing Lists

Online mailing lists are sometimes called *listservs,* a name taken from the software used to manage certain ones. Sometimes they're simply called *lists.* Most people use all three of these terms interchangeably. L-Soft, the company that developed LISTSERV software, takes a dim view of the use of its trademarked name as a generic term for electronic lists. As the makers of Kleenex, Post-Its, and Xerox machines know, they're facing an uphill battle.

Mailing lists are different from newsgroups in several ways:

✔ You have to subscribe to a mailing list in order to participate. You can't just wander in and start reading and posting.

✔ Messages come to you as e-mail. You don't need to go anywhere or use any special software in order to read and respond.

✔ Because subscribing generally means you have an interest in and commitment to a topic, mailing list discussions tend to be more focused.

Mailing lists come in assorted flavors. All are some combination of these types:

✔ **Private versus public:** Some lists are open only to members of a particular association, employees of a given corporation, or qualified practitioners in a certain field, such as computer security or nursing.

Newsgroups in action — a thrilling true-life scenario

A colleague of ours who specializes in international trade research needed to find out whether a market existed for electric food dehydrators in Eastern Europe. This example is typical of the exciting projects that independent professional researchers get to sink their teeth into every day. She posted the question on a couple of newsgroups and, within 20 minutes, had three responses, all of which said that she and her client were thinking irresponsibly and should be investigating the market for *solar* food dehydrators instead. But within 24 hours, allowing time for the European work day to begin and for users in that part of the world to wake up and go online, she had two or three solid leads, one of which led to a business deal for her client.

- ✔ **Moderated versus unmoderated:** Some lists have hosts or administrators who help direct the conversation and keep things running smoothly. Others are freewheeling, with nobody visibly in charge.

- ✔ **Open posting versus edited posting versus read-only:** Some mailing lists allow anyone to post directly to the list. With others, all messages go to the moderator, who screens them for usefulness before posting them to the list. Some lists don't allow posting at all; they're more like electronic newsletters where the publisher or editor talks, and your role is to read only (you can talk back, if you want, in private e-mail).

Many lists that allow posting offer a digest version, too. Instead of seeing all the messages as soon as they're posted to the list, you get a single long message, usually once a day, containing all the postings in the order received. The digest version doesn't significantly cut down on your reading time, and it interferes with your ability to respond to individual posts in a timely way. But some people prefer it because it reduces e-mail clutter.

Locating lists with Liszt

How do you find a mailing list to join? The easiest way, other than by word of mouth, is to use **Liszt** (`www.liszt.com`), a comprehensive searchable directory of — at this point — 90,000 mailing lists worldwide. (You can also use Liszt to locate newsgroups, as we describe in "Browsing newsgroups with Liszt," earlier in this chapter.) From this huge assortment, Liszt has culled about 3,000 lists that it believes to be public, active, and worthwhile. You can do a keyword search on the entire directory or drill down through broad subject categories in the handpicked Liszt Select collection.

The search form lets you enter your search terms and use the pull-down menu to select the All These Words, Any of These Words, or This Exact Phrase option.

Liszt employs a junk filter to strip out as many private lists as it can identify and to show you only the lists that you may be eligible to join. You can set the filter to Lots if you want to retrieve only lists for which Liszt has detailed information. Or you can turn the junk filter off completely if you want to see what all is out there and are prepared to deal with whatever Liszt may dredge up.

Click the Go button, and Liszt displays the following information:

✔ Links to any Liszt Select subject categories that match your search terms

✔ Links to any Liszt Select lists (the actual mailing lists) that match your terms

✔ Links to *all* lists in the Liszt directory that match your terms

From Liszt's list listings — *that's* fun to say — you can click a Liszt Select subject category (assuming you have any matches) at the top of the page to see what lists Liszt has selected. Or you can click the name of a particular Liszt Select list or, below that, the name of a list from the larger Liszt directory, and get a description of its focus, purpose, and membership. Read that description to make sure it's the right group for you and that you qualify for membership. If no description is available, Liszt supplies an e-mail address where you can request more information.

So far we've talked about locating mailing lists through keyword searches. If you prefer to browse by subject category through Liszt's own preselected collection, scroll down past the search form shown in Figure 10-4 to Liszt Select. Click the category you're interested in and then drill down through subcategories until you find lists that sound useful.

Tile.net and the List of Lists

Liszt does a fine job of keeping track of electronic mailing lists. But it's not the only game in town. Sometimes you need to check elsewhere to find exactly the list you want.

Tile.net (www.tile.net) has nothing to do with bathrooms or kitchens; it's a Web site for locating mailing lists — and newsgroups, too — on a particular topic. You can type in a keyword that describes what you're looking for or browse by name, description, or (for mailing lists only) Internet address. Unfortunately, descriptions of individual lists and groups are sometimes missing; the trade-off is that Tile.net is updated frequently, and you can subscribe to mailing lists or go directly to newsgroups right from the Tile.net site.

The List of Lists (`www.catalog.com/vivian/interest-group-search.html`) has an awesome-sounding name and was one of the very first attempts to catalog all the e-mail discussion lists on the Net. Showing its roots in the pre-Web era, the List of Lists offers no hypertext links or other fancy features. What it does offer are well-written descriptions of all the lists it lists. Each word in each description is searchable, so you can easily find lists on your topic. Be careful, though — the List of Lists isn't updated very often, so newer lists may not appear.

Netiquette revisited

Observing the local customs is just as important in mailing lists as it is in newsgroups — perhaps more so, because many mailing-list subscribers are serious-minded or deeply committed to the subject at hand. Some of them may be refugees from the noise and clamor of public newsgroups, and the last thing you want to do is reintroduce the kind of clueless behavior they thought they had left behind.

So, check out Aunt Netty-Quette's advice about how to behave in newsgroups in "Aunt Netty-Quette's priceless pointers for painless posting," earlier in this chapter. Ninety-nine percent of it applies to mailing lists as well.

Dealing with info- and subscription-bots

You can get more information about a mailing list by sending e-mail to the address shown in the description of the list or by using one of the search tools, such as Liszt or Tile.net, that we describe earlier in this chapter. These messages are usually processed by *'bots* (short for robots; the apostrophe is optional), specialized software that sends out information in response to a precisely worded request.

How you word your request depends on the type of software used to administer the list. The description tells you what command to send and the e-mail address to send it to. The info request typically looks something like `info Travel-L`. Sometimes, you can get a help file by sending the single-word message *help* (yes, it sounds pathetic) to the same address. Remember that these messages are read by a dumb piece of software, not a smart human being. If you don't follow the rules, it won't understand what you're asking, so resist the urge to say "please."

Mailing-list subscriptions are handled the same way. The protocol often involves a command such as `subscribe Travel-L myname` in the body of the message. But do go through the robotic info-request routine first. The file you get back in e-mail contains complete instructions for signing up — and signing off. Keep this file forever and ever, or for as long as you subscribe to the list. The file tells you what address to use when you want to post a message to the other members of the list (or to the moderator, if it's that kind of list) and what address to use when you want to reach the list *server,* the bot responsible for the mechanics of subscribing and unsubscribing. The addresses are not the same, and the consequences of mixing them up may be embarrassing and frustrating to you, and annoying to others. Sending a `subscribe` request to all members of the list is not the best way to win friends.

Most mailing lists accept *unsubscribe* requests only from the same e-mail account that you subscribed from.

Virtual Villages and Conferencing Systems

In Chapter 9, we mention online venues — such as The Motley Fool, CompuServe forums, and Ei Village — where people get together to exchange information, assert their opinions, and generally hang out. We call such sites *virtual communities,* a phrase popularized by Reva's friend Howard Rheingold in the early 1990s. Another term for them is *online conferencing systems.*

Virtual communities are organized differently from newsgroups and mailing lists, although some newsgroups and lists have developed a community feeling over the years. Virtual communities are organized in a three-tiered structure:

- ✔ **Virtual communities contain anywhere from a half-dozen to a hundred or more individual *forums*, also referred to as *conferences* or *discussion areas*.** Each forum is devoted to a particular subject or interest. In a mega-conferencing system, you may find a Cooking forum, a forum devoted to Windows-based computers, and an Investment forum, right next door to each other and open to anyone on the system.

- ✔ **Each forum is divided into a number of *topics* or *threads* (America Online calls them *folders*).** Each topic is a separate conversation about some aspect of the forum's overall subject. In a Cooking forum, you may see topics on vegetarian cooking, barbecuing, cookware, Jell-O salads, and what to do with leftovers (putting them in a Jell-O salad has always been our approach).

- ✔ **Each topic consists of a series of *postings*, or messages, from different users.** You can go back to see what others have written (in some communities, topics are preserved for years) or read a current discussion as it unfolds. You can lurk quietly — reading and never posting — or jump in and add your own comments.

The posting style in a virtual community is usually informal and conversational; it's basically just a bunch of people talking online. Communication isn't instantaneous as it is in a chat room — although when a hot discussion is going on, it can feel like a real-time environment. Reva was on a local conferencing system when a fire broke out in a nearby neighborhood; people were falling all over themselves, and each other, in their eagerness to ask questions and supply eyewitness reports.

Virtual communities require a commitment. To get the most out of them information-wise, you have to build and cultivate relationships, and give back as much as you get. They require more effort than just scanning listserv messages when they land in your mailbox or hunting for a newsgroup FAQ. But these communities offer many other benefits — *besides* getting the answers to your questions — if you stick around long term.

Exploring virtual communities on the Web

The most easily accessible communities, especially if you want to browse before you make a commitment, are on the Web. Most of them don't charge a fee but do require you to register for full access.

Check out **Parent Soup** (www.parentsoup.com) for searchable message boards dealing with topics such as prenatal testing, attention-deficit disorder, and parents of only children.

Third Age (www.thirdage.com) is aimed squarely at aging boomers. Not that *we* know anything *at all* about that demographic. Ahem. Third Age forums have names such as Money, News & Politics, Tech, and Travel.

SF Gate (www.sfgate.com) is jointly sponsored by two newspapers, the *San Francisco Chronicle* and *San Francisco Examiner.* Click <u>Conferences</u> on the main page to get to the discussion areas. Participants at SF Gate get to talk back to the newspaper columnists and reporters whose bylines they read every day. Newspaper journalists even host some of the SF Gate forums, which cover subjects such as business, books, current events (of course), movies, health, technology, and the Net itself.

At **The WELL** (www.well.com) (which stands for Whole Earth 'Lectronic Link, believe it or not), discussion topics don't always stay in their neatly marked-off areas. In fact, some topics seem designed to promote anything *but* linear thinking. A topic called Experts on The WELL is a prime example, with people carrying on interwoven conversations about how to build backyard ponds, how a capacitor works, whether recycling really helps the environment, and where to get the best espresso drinks in Berkeley (answer: the French Hotel). You have to sign up and pay a monthly fee before you can fall into The WELL.

Finding community online

How do you find a virtual community where you feel at home? Sometimes it just happens, as it did with Reva when she landed in The WELL in the late 1980s. We both got there via word-of-mouth from people we already knew in real life — Mary Ellen heard about it from Reva, in fact. Friends and colleagues may tell you about the cool places they've discovered, too.

You can survey the range of virtual community life through **Forum One** (`www.forumone.com`). Forum One isn't all-inclusive, but it's a start. After you're there, you can either

✔ Do a keyword search to identify online communities devoted to a subject, and relevant discussion topics *within* those communities.

✔ Drill down through the Recommended Forums listing to get a list of communities only. The "Mega" Forums category lists venues that talk about a variety of topics.

Taking It to E-Mail

When people in a public venue, whether it be a newsgroup, mailing list, or virtual conferencing system, start going at each other too heavily, you hear the plea, "Hey, guys, take it to e-mail." Electronic mail is the best way, short of a phone call or face-to-face meeting, to resolve personal disputes or carry on a conversation that's only of interest to the two participants.

As Aunt Netty-Quette points out earlier in this chapter, e-mail is a graceful way to ask for guidance when you're not sure whether your question is appropriate for the group at large, or when you hesitate to jump in because the pace of conversation is so frenetic or the group seems kind of intimidating. Pick someone who sounds supportive and follow Aunt Netty-Quette's tips, especially the ones about being clear, concise, and considerate of people's time.

E-mail can take your research project to the next level, by putting you in touch with the experts. Start in a public space, such as a newsgroup or mailing list. Do your homework first, whether it's looking for a FAQ or reviewing the archives. Then follow up, selectively, with a politely worded e-mail request. You can get maps, manuscripts, and countless helpful pointers simply by knowing how, when, and whom to ask.

Professional communities on the Web

Some virtual communities center around a specific profession, such as doctors, lawyers, or . . . farmers. Take **Agriculture Online** (www.agriculture.com), for example. Sponsored by a trade magazine, the discussion groups are a window into what modern farming is all about. We click the Talk link at the main Web page to get to discussion groups. Next we click Wildlife (why not?) and fall into discussions about muskrats, moose hunting, and Midwest fur prices. These were separate conversations, we hasten to add. Though we can imagine, sort of, how they might relate.

Farmers are online, big time, talking about crucial concerns such as weather, crop prices, and cattle deals. Other professions — including accountants, human resource specialists, librarians, and researchers — have their own online hangouts as well. Lawyers can subscribe to a private forum called **Law News Network** (www.lawnewsnetwork.com), whereas doctors can participate in **Physicians Online** (www.po.com).

Caveats and Cautions (Dealing with Human Nature)

We say at the beginning of this chapter that *people* research is different from hunting for documents or looking something up in a virtual reference book. You find information and opinions that you can't get anywhere else online. But you also have to deal with some human factors that you don't encounter when you're dealing with books, subject catalogs, or other inanimate research aids.

From the horse's mouth?

There's nothing like getting your information directly from the source. But people have all sorts of motives for helping and all kinds of agendas to promote. People aren't perfect; their memories are faulty, and they may, in all innocence, misrepresent the facts or leave out a crucial bit of data.

Unless you're dealing with the most straightforward, factual questions and answers, don't take what people tell you at face value. Examine their advice, and adjust for possible bias. Try to get a second and even a third opinion ideally from someone who's not involved in your conversation and doesn't have an ax to grind. See Chapter 17 for more about judging the reliability of information.

The (low) signal to noise ratio

Ever try to pull in a baseball broadcast on a funky old radio up in the mountains? Sometimes you have to filter out a lot of static in order to get the score. It's the same way online — lots of noise, relatively little *signal,* or hard information. A newsgroup, mailing list, or online conference can shortcut your information-hunt dramatically if you know where to go and who to ask. If you're in luck and find a FAQ, you're golden. But hanging out online, hoping for enlightenment because the subject headers in a current thread sound promising, isn't always the most efficient way to get research done.

Flame wars

Some people love to be provocative online. Others love to provoke them. Depending on where you hang out (newsgroups are particularly prone to this phenomenon), you'll eventually see a heated argument break out over something. When an online disagreement turns rude or abusive, it's called *flaming.* A full-scale battle is called a *flame war.*

Flame wars can also break out as the result of simple misunderstandings. Online is a low-bandwidth medium. You don't have cues, such as facial expression and tone of voice, to tell you how someone is feeling or to show the intent behind his words. All you have is text on a screen, and words can easily be misinterpreted. That's why some online denizens use smiley faces and other *emoticons* — smiles, frowns, and other facial expressions recreated, roughly, with keyboard characters, for example :-) — to give some context to what they post.

Abide by these three simple rules to avoid getting embroiled in a flame war:

- ✔ Do unto others as you would have them do unto you. (Where have we heard *that* before?)

- ✔ If you must disagree, attack the *argument,* not the *person.* For example, say, "I think your statement (or position, or reasoning) is idiotic," not "I think *you're* an idiot." It does help to think of a slightly less loaded word than *idiotic.* How about *fallacious, untenable,* or *flawed?* (This moment brought to you by *Roget's Thesaurus.*)

- ✔ Don't post anything online that you wouldn't say to the person's face. Remember — you're "talking" to other human beings, even if you can't see them.

If all else fails, log out. That's right: Disconnect from your computer, catch your breath, and take a walk around the block until you calm down. Never post or send an e-mail message while you're angry or tired. Drop that bone, lighten up, give the other person the benefit of the doubt. Move on.

Overload

Flame wars or not, sometimes the online world gets overwhelming. There's just *too* much going on, too many people talking, too many annoyances, too much information to absorb.

When you reach that point — and you will — you can take comfort in knowing that you're not the only one who's ever felt this way. Software solutions abound: You can get spam filters to reduce the amount of junk mail, or bozo filters to silence those whose postings you can't bear to read. You can change your mailing list subscriptions to the digest version. You can set up filters in your e-mail program so that everything personal goes in one box, everything business-related in another, and all your mailing lists in a third, or however you want to set it up. For this, Mary Ellen uses a program called **Eudora Pro** (www.eudora.com), available for both PCs and Macs. Reva recently converted to Microsoft Outlook, which lets you do the same thing. Regard this as an unsolicited testimonial: E-mail filtering changed our lives.

Part III
Putting It All Together

The 5th Wave   By Rich Tennant

©RICHTENNANT

"Ronnie made the body from what he learned in Metal Shop, Sissy and Darlene's Home Ec. class helped them in fixing up the inside, and then all that anti-gravity stuff we picked up off the Web."

In this part . . .

*1*f we were Julia Child and you happened to be someone who had never set foot in a kitchen, we could talk to you all day about chef's knives and wire whisks, reducing a sauce and clarifying a stock — and you still might starve before you figured out how to put a meal together. TV cooking shows are popular for a reason — you learn the tools and the techniques as you go, as part of creating a dish or an entire menu. And after you understand how and when to use them, you're on your way to becoming a competent, intuitive, and even inspired cook.

That's what we're aiming for here. Parts I and II tell you all about search engines, subject catalogs, reference books, digital libraries, database services, newsgroups, mailing lists, and other tools and techniques for researching online. But without a sense of context — how and when to apply them to a particular research project — they're about as useful as a scalpel in the hands of a first-year medical student.

This part is all about context. Whether you've read the earlier chapters or not (don't worry — we're not keeping track), here's where you discover how to apply those online search tools and tactics in a variety of real-life research situations, from tracking business competitors, to wading your way through government bureaucracies, to keeping up with the news, to researching important personal decisions.

Chapter 11

Strange New Worlds: Government, Medical, and Sci-Tech Research

In This Chapter

▶ Coping with government bureaucracies

▶ Making informed decisions about healthcare

▶ Finding and using scientific and technical information

*R*emember that old song, "Bewitched, Bothered and Bewildered"? We're not sure what to do with the *bewitched* part, but bothered and bewildered are we. And you probably are, too — when it comes to dealing with the government, or trying to figure out what to do about your family member's illness or newly diagnosed medical condition, or solving a problem that requires getting hold of information in a highly specialized technical field, such as engineering or computer science.

All of us are at a loss when we're operating in an unfamiliar environment, whether it's a strange country, a bureaucracy, or a scientific discipline where we don't know the rules and can't speak the language. We fall into sort of a trance — maybe *that's* where "bewitched" comes in — and often try ineffective, pointless, and sometimes counterproductive tactics before we give up and collapse into an exhausted, frustrated puddle.

Maybe you think the entire Internet is a foreign country. Trust us, unless you live there, these specialized research areas — we sometimes think of them as the Feds, the Meds, and the Ph.D.s — can be as rocky and inhospitable as the far side of the moon.

We're not promising you any miracles. If we could cut through the morass of government bureaucracy, let alone all that other stuff, somebody would have noticed by now, and we'd be rich, retired, and wreathed in clouds of glory. What we *can* do, and show *you* how to do in this chapter, is gather information effectively from within the esoteric and often confusing realms of government, medicine, science, and technology.

How do you find information in a complex environment when you don't even speak the language? By looking at it through a researcher's eyes.

When you're investigating in an unfamiliar research environment, you need to know three things:

- ✔ Where to start
- ✔ What's available
- ✔ Where to get it

In this chapter, we give you a few starting points, an idea of what you can get from them, and the precise coordinates. Consider it a large-scale map of a foreign capital. When you walk around by yourself, you'll start discovering new neighborhoods, special attractions, and shortcuts of your own.

So pack your bags. Our flight's departing. Don't forget your passport.

We're from the Government, and We're Here to Help You

Getting information from the U.S. federal government may be one of the most frustrating and, at the same time, one of the most rewarding experiences you can live through. And you *will* live through it.

You'd be amazed at the depth and variety of information collected by various agencies and analysts. Through our years as researchers, tackling client projects using whatever combination of phone, online, and library visits necessary to get the answer, we've discovered government analysts whose sole job is to monitor water-pumping windmills, processed tomato products, or imports of wine and roses from Mexico (the last two occupied the same trade category, those romantics!). Some of these guys *lived* for a phone call from a private citizen who was actually interested in their work.

Budget cutbacks happen, and much of that data isn't collected in as much depth as it used to be — or at all. A piece of legislation called the Federal Paperwork Reduction Act resulted in the elimination of many kinds of reports. But savvy federal agencies (and some, you may discover, are a lot smarter and more responsive than others) realized that the then-emerging Web was the answer to at least *some* of their budget- and policy-mandated restrictions: If publishing and distributing reports in print costs too much, why not just put them online?

Mastering the info-maze with FedWorld

FedWorld (www.fedworld.gov) is your gateway to the wide world of U.S. government publications, regulations, and sadistics . . . we mean, statistics. Figure 11-1 shows FedWorld's no-nonsense but option-packed front door. Without preamble — to the Constitution or anything else — it presents you with two search forms, a drop-down menu, and two browsable links, each one an entryway to a particular star cluster within the FedWorld galaxy. Click the category link, or pull down the menu, to discover what each one contains.

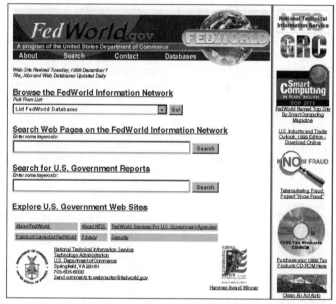

Figure 11-1: FedWorld search options.

Browse the FedWorld Information Network

If you already have some idea of which government agency can help you, start here. You can browse the drop-down list of FedWorld sources and go directly to that agency. Planning a trip abroad? Select the U.S. Customs Service's site and look through the Traveler Information area for tips on what and how much you can bring back. Need more information? The Customs Service has prepared a detailed FAQ (Frequently Asked Questions list). "What gives Customs the right to search me?" you may ask indignantly. The answer: Title 19 of the United States Code, Sections 482, 1467, 1496, 1581, and 1582. Will you please open that *other* suitcase now, ma'am?

FedWorld gives you several access points for forms and other information from the Internal Revenue Service. But we prefer to hit the **IRS** site directly (www.irs.ustreas.gov). *Prefer* may seem an unlikely word to use in the same sentence as *IRS* — but we're telling you, this is one fun Federal site.

We know you don't believe us. But when you visit the IRS site, you tell *us* if it looks like Fear and Loathing personified. And behind the smiling façade, you can find every tax form you'll ever need — and dozens that, if you're lucky, you've never heard of. The site offers explanatory publications ("How to Depreciate Property," "Tax-Exempt Status for Your Organization," "Your Rights as a Taxpayer"), a fax information service, a section endearingly entitled "Tax Regs in Plain English," and links to state forms and other information.

We never thought we'd say it, but we actually look forward to our visits to the IRS site. We're learning to love Big Brother.

Search Web Pages on the FedWorld Information Network

The second option on the main FedWorld page allows you to search the entire FedWorld network and zero in on the federal agency, and often the specific report or document, that can answer your question. (Click the title link <u>Search Web Pages on the FedWorld Information Network</u> for a list of individual sites you can search by using the same form, and for additional search options.)

A few quick searches demonstrate how, by entering a key phrase or concept that interests you, you can quickly identify the agency where you should start your research. FedWorld supports Boolean search logic, as described in Chapter 2, as well as the phrase searching we use in these examples:

- ✔ If you key in *transportation statistics,* you get a reference to the Bureau of Transportation Statistics, plus document titles such as *National Transportation Atlas.*

- ✔ By entering *child welfare,* you get several references, including videos about child support. When you click the titles, you find references to the Department of Health and Human Services, which oversees that area.

- ✔ What about *taxes?* We know the government takes an interest, to put it mildly, in that subject. Sure enough, you find publications on property taxes, sales taxes, income taxes, even a delightful-sounding video titled *What Happened to My Paycheck* produced by our friends at the Internal Revenue Service.

<u>Search Web Pages on the FedWorld Information Network</u> is your best prospect for getting to the information you need quickly when you don't know, or much care, where it's coming from. A FedWorld-wide search like the ones we just ran can be useful as a fog cutter. You may not find the answer online, but you can quickly identify the agency you need to contact.

Search for U.S. Government Reports

The third search option enables you to search the National Technical Information Service (NTIS), the distribution channel for thousands of reports funded in some measure by the federal government. It includes technical reports and documents from the Departments of Defense, Energy, Commerce, and Transportation, as well as agencies such as NASA, various government labs, and private universities and consulting firms. As we write this, the future of NTIS is uncertain; Congress is considering closing the service and encouraging each agency to publish its own reports on the Web. Assuming it survives another round of budget cutbacks, NTIS is a great resource.

The NTIS database, also up on Dialog and other professional online services (see Chapter 9), contains detailed abstracts, or summaries, of research studies in everything from management theory to civil engineering, space medicine, and library science. You can't get the complete text online, just the summaries, but you can order full reports and other documents from NTIS. NTIS is one of the core databases for serious research in science and technology. You can also get to it directly from the NTIS Web site (www.ntis.gov).

FedWorld lets you do a limited but quite powerful search of the NTIS database by using Boolean AND/ORs, phrases, and truncation (see Chapter 2 for more about these features). At the FedWorld site, click the <u>Search for U.S. Government Reports</u> link to get a more detailed search form.

Explore U.S. Government Web Sites

Here you can browse the labyrinth of the federal government structure. You can search government Web sites by keyword or select from lists of commonly requested sources, various gateways to government information, or executive branch agencies. At the bottom of the page, you find a list of links to the Web sites of independent agencies, ranging from the Advisory Council on Historic Preservation to the U.S. Chemical Safety and Hazard Investigation Board and the Peace Corps.

Life beyond FedWorld

FedWorld is fine — more than fine — as far as it goes. But its charter is limited to research, regulation, and other activities that fall under the broad umbrella of the executive branch of government. That includes independent and quasi-official agencies such as NASA, the Environmental Protection Agency, the Federal Reserve System, and the Small Business Administration.

Many of these agencies maintain their own Web sites where you can find additional information — a lot more information than you can get by probing at them through FedWorld. After you know what bureau or department you're looking for, we suggest visiting it directly. FedWorld is just a starting point; many government Web sites are massive dataspheres in themselves. Some, such as the IRS site, even have a distinct and engaging personality of their own.

How do you locate the government Web site you want?

✔ Sometimes you can find a link at FedWorld, or from FedWorld search results.

✔ You can take a quick guess at its URL — www and the agency acronym, followed by .gov, as in www.nasa.gov, gets you there a surprising percentage of the time.

✔ Or you can look it up in Thomas' comprehensive directory, which is part of the Library of Congress Web site (lcweb.loc.gov/global/executive/fed.html). We introduce you to Thomas in the next section.

No doubting Thomas

Keeping an eye on Congress? Your best friend when it comes to insight into the legislative branch of government is named Thomas (see Figure 11-2). The Library of Congress's **Thomas** site (thomas.loc.gov), named in honor of Thomas Jefferson, enables you to track bills as they move through the House and Senate, read and download the text of pending legislation, and monitor roll call votes to help keep your local representatives honest, or at least accountable. Thomas has a sophisticated search engine that allows you to look for particular bills by name, number, subject, sponsor, and numerous other criteria.

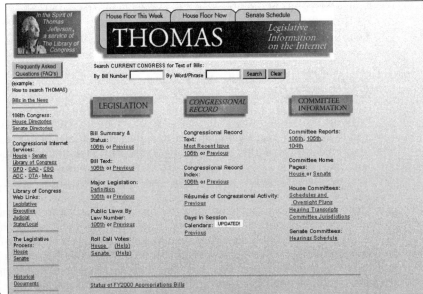

Figure 11-2:
Thomas, your key to U.S. Congressional information.

Thomas features the text of the *Congressional Record* — actual transcripts of senators and representatives doing what we elected them to do, in their own inimitable personal styles. Read these for a while, and you'll understand the saying about how nobody ought to watch how laws or sausages are made.

Thomas also gives you background information, which is great for school reports, on how laws are made and enacted, and the text of great historical documents such as the Constitution and the Declaration of Independence.

Thomas offers an excellent collection of links to other sites for all three branches of government: legislative, executive, and judicial; plus state and local governments and related agencies on the Web. Sausage-making machinery aside, Thomas is worth a bookmark for this set of resources alone. Like FedWorld, it's a gateway to government goodies.

USGovsearch

Northern Light, a combined Web search engine and gated Web site that we describe in Chapters 3 and 9, offers a fee-based search service for government Web sites and NTIS documents. (See the earlier section "Search for U.S. Government Reports" for a description of NTIS.) Point your browser to **USGovsearch** (www.usgovsearch.com) to get a description of the service and to sign up. You can buy a one-day pass for $5, or you can get a monthly or yearly subscription. You can search the NTIS database through USGovsearch; summaries of individual reports cost a couple of dollars each.

Why pay to search the open Web, you may ask. Northern Light's search engine drills down deeper into Web sites than many other search tools do, including FedWorld, which we describe earlier in this chapter. That means you can locate more detailed and specific information. And you can limit your search to just government sites, which produces much more focused results. We tried a search for *child welfare* and turned up experimental child welfare programs sponsored by the U.S. Department Health & Human Services, fact sheets on states' child welfare initiatives, and a mega-site of links for child welfare professionals. This is one time when it makes sense to pay a modest fee to take advantage of the added value of a Web search engine's specialized features.

Stalking statistical sources

People poke fun at the government for endlessly generating statistics. We happen to think that's one of its most useful functions. But of course, we're info-junkies. The central clearinghouse for U.S. government statistics is the **Economic Statistics Briefing Room** (www.whitehouse.gov/fsbr/esbr.html). You can pick up stats in any of these categories:

- Production, Sales, Orders, and Inventories
- Output
- Income, Expenditures, and Wealth
- Employment, Unemployment, and Earnings
- Prices
- Money, Credit, and Interest Rates
- Transportation
- International Statistics

Another good starting point for statistical information is the **U.S. Census Bureau** (www.census.gov). The Bureau not only collects, analyzes, and publishes the familiar age, gender, race, family-size, and housing-type data that you see quoted in newspapers and magazines and on TV, but also offers a broad range of other demographic and economic facts and figures at both the federal and the local level.

The Census Bureau site features data from the current edition of the *Statistical Abstracts of the United States* (www.census.gov/prod/www/ statistical-abstract-us.html). You can download individual sections in Adobe Acrobat (PDF) format, which preserves tables and other special formatting, and print it out or read it by using the free Acrobat reader software. The Census Bureau thoughtfully includes a link to the Adobe site, just in case you don't have a copy of the current version. And we've made sure to put a copy on the accompanying CD.

Stat Abs, as librarians fondly call it, is one of the few reference books we actually still own in print. If you need statistical information frequently, it's worth ordering a copy in print or on CD, because downloading chapters from the Web site can be time-consuming.

Just one more pointer before we leave the fascinating world of statistics. (No, really. Like anything else, statistics *can* be fascinating once you unload your prejudices and spend some time with them. Statistics may lie, but they tell some pretty good stories, too.)

Statistical Resources on the Web
(www.lib.umich.edu/libhome/Documents.center/stats.html) is an awesomely rich, deep resource for statistical information from non-governmental and governmental sources alike, both domestic and international. The categories read like the sections of a good college bookstore, including: Agriculture, Business & Industry, Demographics, Economics, Education, Environment, Health, Housing, Labor, Politics, Science, Sociology, Transpor-tation, and Weather. If you can't find the numbers you're looking for here, you may have to make up your own.

In Sickness and in Health

If you're lucky, your encounters with the medical establishment will be casual ones. Knock on wood, take two aspirin, and call us in the morning.

People flock to the Internet for medical information, sometimes because they can't get it from their own physicians or are hesitant to ask. Often, though, the Net is the route to self-empowerment as a medical consumer: What better time to become an informed citizen than when your health or the health of a family member is at stake?

You can find some good medical advice online. You can also find some advice that's dubious, and worse. Before self-administering any treatment that involves ingesting, injecting, or for that matter, any practice more strange or controversial than a warm bath, check with your own health practitioner. Be especially wary of the credibility of health and medical Web sites. Read the sections in Chapter 17 about how to judge the quality of information you find online. Make sure that you know where the information is coming from, whether it's current, the qualifications of its author(s), and who has reviewed the material. Who's behind the Web site itself? Aside from the banner ads and e-commerce links, is the site trying to push a particular product or service? In other words, does it have an agenda, other than good health, to promote?

Tapping the medical literature with Medline

The U.S. National Library of Medicine is the mothership of the medical info-fleet. NLM is home to **Medline**, a venerable and highly respected database of clinical and experimental medical literature, worldwide, that's been around since 1966. If you're looking for a research paper or an article from a medical journal such as the *New England Journal of Medicine* or the *Journal of the American Medical Association,* Medline is a good first stop. Medline won't deliver the complete text, at least not on the first go-round, but you often get a detailed abstract or summary, and the NLM site tells you how to order a copy of the article.

Medline is available through Dialog and several other professional online services (see Chapter 9 to read about these professional services). But Medline is searchable for free at the NLM Web site (www.nlm.nih.gov). Click the Medline link, and you get your choice of three versions: PubMed, Internet Grateful Med, and a streamlined alternative called Medline*plus*.

Power searching with PubMed

The PubMed approach to Medline allows Boolean AND/OR/NOT search statements, including complex queries such as *multiple sclerosis AND (heat OR humidity)*. You can search by author, journal title, or publication date by using field labels, if you happen to know them, or by selecting fields from the pull-down menu. (Chapter 2 tells you more about Boolean and field searching.) You can limit your results by language, age and gender of subject, type of article, and other factors. PubMed is powerful medicine and just what the doctor ordered — as long as you're comfortable juggling all the options and alternatives it offers.

There's nothing like a Grateful Med search

Grateful Med is much, much milder and won't upset your stomach. It uses pull-down menus and step-by-step forms, like the ones shown in Figure 11-3, to target your search by date, language, and other restrictions. Grateful Med also offers separate searching of several supplementary NLM databases, including AIDS-related ones.

After you do a search, you can click the Full Citation button to read a more complete abstract or description, or click the Related Articles button to pick up references that your initial search may have missed. You can print or download your results and/or order article copies from the NLM's document delivery service, Loansome Doc. The name *Grateful Med* is more than fine with us, but *Loansome Doc* may be pushing it.

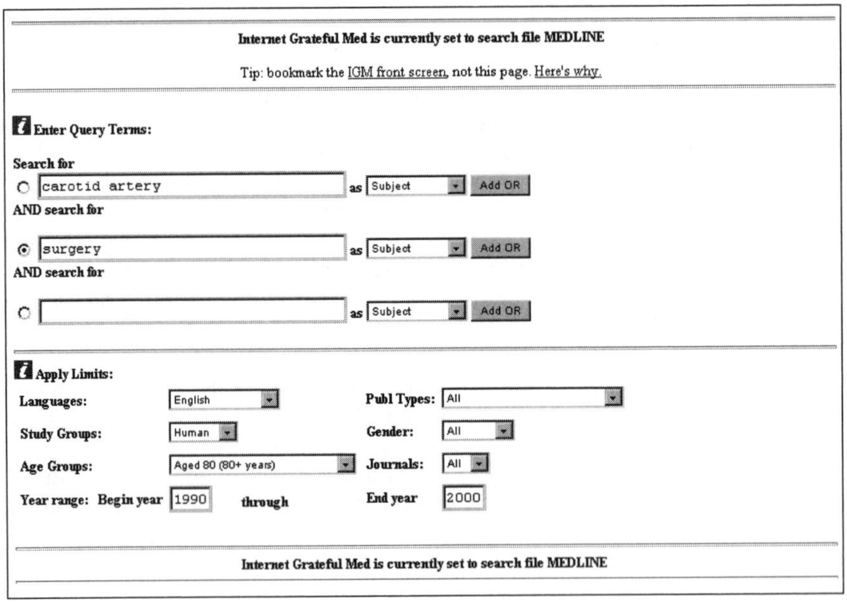

Figure 11-3:
Grateful
Med search
form.

You can improve your search results by adding key words from MeSH, the official *Medical Subject Headings* used in the Medline database. Look at the indexing terms that turn up in the Mesh Headings portion of the best and most relevant items you've retrieved. Do another search that incorporates one or two of those terms in place of the corresponding words you came up with. If you get really serious about this stuff, you can download the MeSH headings list (`www.nlm.nih.gov/mesh/filelist.html`).

One of the slickest uses of Medline's comprehensive database of medical literature is to identify individuals and institutions that specialize in cutting-edge (no pun intended) treatments and procedures. Each article includes not only the author(s) but also the name of the institution with which they're affiliated. You can help your physician locate specialists and treatment centers beyond her local referral network. You can also search for papers published by a particular author — for example, a specialist to whom you or a family member were referred — or for papers published in a specific journal.

Medlineplus

Medline*plus* goes down easily; it takes no searching expertise at all. Medline*plus* consists of authoritative, reliable articles and information on a huge variety of medical and healthcare topics chosen by the staff of the National Library of Medicine itself. You can select your specific topic from an alphabetical list, or select a broader category from a pull-down menu and then select a narrower topic on the resulting page. Or you can do a keyword search by using a friendly search form that's just packed with helpful advice.

Exploring other medical information sources

Medline may be the mothership, but it's not the only ship in the medical sea. It's not that hard to use, especially if you opt for the Medline*plus* approach, but to master the medical literature, having a firm grasp on the terminology helps. Let's face it, Medline was designed for the white lab coat crowd, not the guy in the street (let alone in the sickbed). More important, Medline doesn't give you a whole lot of context for making informed medical decisions. You can gather the facts — or the abstracts that lead to the facts — but where do you go from there, other than directly to your doctor?

Several other medical Web sites do give you more to go on.

CBS Healthwatch

Okay, it sounds like the name of a TV program, but **CBS Healthwatch** (`cbs.medscape.com`) is produced by the same medical professionals who created Medscape (no, not *Netscape*), a highly respected Web site aimed at practicing physicians. You can browse the site and read magazine-style articles on health topics in the news or search for elementary-level, yet detailed information on specific medical topics from A to Z. Or register (it's free) and get access to Medline and other information from the professional medical literature. No need to keep a medical dictionary at your elbow; CBS Healthwatch has a searchable one built in, as well as a handbook of medical tests, and a drug directory that lets you look up pharmaceuticals by name or according to the condition for which they're prescribed.

Galaxy: Medicine

Galaxy is a subject catalog, similar to the ones we describe in Chapter 5, to information resources on the Web. The **Galaxy Medicine** section (galaxy.tradewave.com/galaxy/Medicine.html) allows you to drill down from very broad categories — such as <u>Diseases & Disorders</u>, <u>Health Occupations</u>, <u>Human Biology</u>, <u>Operative Surgery</u>, and <u>Therapeutics</u> (*treatments,* for us lay people) — sometimes through several levels, to the exact topic you want.

The advantage of the drill-down approach is that you don't have to know much medical terminology to find the information you need. If you do have a term to start with, you can enter it in Galaxy's search form and come up with a list of references. Click the <u>search options</u> link for some advanced search features and click the <u>Help</u> link for pointers on constructing an effective search.

The information available through Galaxy includes not only articles from the medical literature drawn from all over the Web, but also pointers to other relevant sites and archives. You can also find cross-references to additional Galaxy categories and subcategories that may be relevant to your search.

Galaxy's top-level Medicine section includes links to dozens of medical schools and centers, organizations, periodicals, newsgroups, and other medical sites on the Web. Click the <u>Merck Manual of Diagnosis and Therapy</u> link to connect with searchable versions of both that authoritative reference and the *Merck Manual of Medical Information — Home Edition.* The home manual on the Web includes extensive sections on heart and blood vessel disorders, infections, eye disorders, and women's health issues. You can get to both of these sites directly at www.merck.com.

More medical pointers

The quest-for-health trend is probably part of the Aging Baby Boomer Syndrome. That huge chunk of the American population is growing older and becoming more concerned about their health, their symptoms, and getting and staying well. Whatever the reason, a massive amount of medical information exists online, for boomers and everyone else.

If you don't find what you're looking for at one of the sites we describe earlier in this chapter, check out some of the following ones:

- **DrKoop.com** — (www.drkoop.com) named for the former U.S. Surgeon General, who has a presence on the site
- **InteliHealth** (www.intelihealth.com) — Johns Hopkins University Health Information
- **HealthGate** (www.healthgate.com)
- **StayHealthy.com** (www.stayhealthy.com)
- **Health A to Z** (www.healthatoz.com)
- **Pharmaceutical Information Network** (www.pharminfo.com), also known as PharmInfoNet — for drug and pharmaceutical news and information

Seeking support for medical problems online

In Chapter 10, we explain how newsgroups and other electronic discussion forums can add a perspective and a depth of understanding that you won't find anywhere else online. That's true no matter what you're researching, and it's especially true when you're talking about illness and disability. What's more personal than your own or a family member's health and well-being?

Participants in newsgroups such as alt.support.mult-sclerosis and alt.support.cancer.prostate find support, commitment, and empathy, 'round the clock, seven days a week. Not only that, the level of information exchanged — much of it more accurate, helpful, and current than what you find in print — is awesome.

If you or a family member could use this kind of support, look for pointers at some of the medical mega-sites mentioned in the last few pages of this chapter, or visit Liszt (www.liszt.com) or RemarQ (www.remarq.com) to search for newsgroups, mailing lists, and other discussion forums on your topic. See Chapter 10 for more on Liszt and RemarQ and how to read and participate in online discussions.

Online support groups can be literal life-savers. But be aware that healthcare horror stories are over-represented on the Net. People are more likely to talk about bad experiences than about treatments that went smoothly.

Mere Technicalities

If it weren't for scientists and engineers, you might not be online at all. That sounds like an obvious statement, but we don't mean it the way you might imagine: The World Wide Web, without which online would be a whole lot harder and far less fun to master, was actually developed by a group of physicists as a way to distribute technical documents and work with them more easily.

Tech-types have been online since the beginning of the Net. Some of the earliest databases on professional online services (such as Dialog) were created by and for the scientific and technical community, 30 or more years ago.

That's all very admirable, you may be thinking, but when does the average person — you, for instance — need sci-tech information?

Suppose you're

- A printer trying to figure out why a certain ink is causing problems
- A clothing manufacturer with a piece of equipment that keeps breaking down
- A golfer with an idea for an improved putter design
- A city public works administrator faced with rust on the concrete walls of the new civic auditorium
- An entrepreneur who wants to set up a fish-farming business
- A do-it-yourselfer who wants to build a second-story addition

What our examples tell you is that even non-scientists occasionally need to wrap their minds around concepts such as thixotropic materials, metal fatigue, patentability, concrete reinforcement, aquaculture, and load calculation.

Knowing where to start

The hardest part of sci-tech research for non-scientists is figuring out where to start. That's where consultants and freelance researchers earn the big bucks (consultants do anyway). They know how to find the information, and you know how to write a check to pay them for their expertise.

Scientists rely heavily on their own personal networks: They don't just *know;* they ask their colleagues on the Net or down the hall. Engineers (Reva has seen this in action) may spend hours mulling over a problem with the guy in the next cube. Then they pull out handbooks, open filing cabinets, look through textbooks that they've had since college — in information-intake mode all this time — before they actively start researching.

Your best resource when you're faced with a technical problem is often someone who's faced the same or a similar problem — a member of your trade or professional organization, a fellow hobbyist, a person in a related field, a vendor, a supplier, or a customer. Failing that, you've got *us.*

Stop a minute and analyze the nature of the problem. It may turn out to be different from what you initially assume, but that's science for you. You have to start somewhere. What category or branch of sci-tech knowledge do you think holds the answer?

Dividing and conquering

Engineers and scientists divide their realms into several broad disciplines. You'll encounter these when you start looking for scientific and technical information online, and it helps to have at least a general sense of where you're headed.

In engineering, you have these areas:

- ✔ **Civil/structural engineering:** Buildings, bridges, dams, and other structures, and the materials (most commonly concrete and steel) used to construct them

- ✔ **Mechanical engineering:** Anything that moves (because it's supposed to), such as gears, levers, engines, vehicles, and machinery

- ✔ **Electrical/electronics/computer engineering:** Wiring, electronic equipment, telephones, black boxes, and other mysterious stuff

Materials science is part of all three engineering disciplines. It refers to the use and properties (quality, strength, durability, and failure) of the concrete, steel, aluminum, rubber, silicon, duct tape, or bubble gum used in structures, machinery, or equipment.

In the sciences, you have these areas:

- ✔ **Life sciences:** Biology (including genetics and biotech), physiology, botany, zoology, and ecology

- ✔ **Hard (or physical) sciences:** Chemistry, physics, mathematics, and specialized fields such as hydrology, metallurgy, and optics

Actually, we classify chemistry with the *very* hard sciences. After we get in above our knees, and that doesn't take long, we call in a colleague who specializes in the field. Learn to recognize, and respect, your limits as well.

Patents are in a class by themselves. They play a role in almost every branch of science and engineering. Obtaining, or failing to obtain, a key patent can make or break a company's or an individual's fortune. We talk about patent research later in this chapter, in the section "What about patents?"

The database approach

When we're doing serious sci-tech research — and, believe it or not, every one of those hypothetical examples at the beginning of this section was something that a client actually asked us to help with — we *don't* go to the Web.

We head straight for a professional database service, usually Dialog, because of its wide range of science and technology databases. Unlike the Web, we can search hundreds of journals, conference papers, and reports at the same time. We can take advantage of the special keywords, concepts, and coding offered by each database to make our search more targeted and precise. If necessary, as it is for certain kinds of research, we can go back not just a couple of years, but decades in the scientific and technical literature.

Visit the **Dialog Library** site (library.dialog.com) and click the Bluesheets link. The Bluesheets are detailed descriptions for individual Dialog databases. Then click Subject and scroll down to the sections listed under Science:

- ✔ Agriculture & Nutrition
- ✔ Chemistry
- ✔ Computer Technology
- ✔ Energy & Environment
- ✔ Medicine & Biosciences
- ✔ Pharmaceuticals
- ✔ Science & Technology

Check out the subdivisions under these topics, too, for an idea of the number and variety of databases you have to choose from. If you really get into this, you can click the names of individual databases to read their complete Bluesheet profiles.

Which database(s) you select (often you need several to get the complete picture) depends on the exact nature of your question. Pay special attention to the File Description, Subject Coverage, Sources, Dates Covered, Update Frequency, Document Types Indexed, and Geographic Coverage, as described in the Bluesheet, to make sure that the database is appropriate for your search. And take a look at the Sample Record to see if it's the *kind* of information, generally speaking, that you're hoping to get. If you're expecting articles, a directory or standards database won't do the job, and vice versa.

Unlike the Web, many professional databases don't include the complete text of the documents they reference. Instead, they provide summaries, or *abstracts.* Some give you less than that: just the author, title, publication name, volume and issue, and date of publication. These *bibliographic* or *abstract-and-index* databases are very useful for certain research projects — compiling a list of articles by a particular author, for instance, or doing a preliminary check to see what's been published on a specific topic. The database producers assume that if you want to see the complete article, you can get it at your local library, or order it from the publisher or database producer or from a document delivery service. See Chapter 8 for more about document delivery.

Because bibliographic and abstract-and-index database records include far fewer words than the complete document text, it's best to keep your search terms broad. Too specific a keyword or search statement may eliminate useful documents. Better yet, check the standard indexing terms used in the database you're searching, either online or in a print thesaurus, and add the appropriate ones to your search statement.

Dialog offers a *Science Portal* and a *Technology Portal* with credit-card entrée to selected Dialog databases through the same Open Access arrangement described in Chapter 9. The portals include links to selected news stories and Web sites covering scientific and technical topics, respectively. For simplified searching of key sci-tech files, you may want to try the portal approach. If so, check out openaccess.dialog.com.

What about patents?

A patent is a document that grants you, the inventor, or the party to whom the patent has been assigned (usually your employer), the rights to manufacture and market an invention. Patents are valuable because the holder of a patent controls the technology it describes, and the rights to that technology can be licensed or sold for massive amounts of money.

To be patentable, a process, design, device, or chemical composition has to be *useful,* which means that it's non-trivial, it's practical, and it works. It also has to be *novel,* meaning it hasn't been done before. That's why you do a patent search — to make sure that nobody's beaten you to it.

But there's more to patent searching than searching patents. If you're checking for *patentability,* you also have to look for *prior art:* anything that may indicate that someone else had the same or a similar idea before you. Engineering journals, conference papers, hobby and popular magazines — they're all grist for a prior art search. That's one reason why those extensive backfiles — documents going back more than just a few years — in databases on Dialog are important.

Patent searching is hard; that's designed into the system. Think about it: A patent is supposed to disclose what's unique about an invention without revealing so much that a competitor can challenge its claims, file a competing patent, or improve significantly on the idea. Patents may hint at possible uses for the invention, but they seldom spell them out.

Patent language is intentionally general and vague. The titles are almost useless. Would you guess that a patent having to do with a *flat planar surface* actually described a table? Patents have to fit into certain broad categories of subject and type, yet they impose no restrictions on the words that may be used to describe the inventions. Those words are where most of the patent-searching action takes place, and where patent attorneys make their living.

Patent litigation and defense (when someone claims that somebody else has infringed on his technology, or attempts to prove that his invention or use of a technology is entirely in the clear) is a big part of the professional patent-searching scene.

The U.S. Patent and Trademark Office

Got a bright idea? In the United States, at least, the **Patent and Trademark Office (PTO)** Web site (www.uspto.gov) is a good first stop. You can find basic information on patents, what they consist of, and how and when to file an application.

If you're located somewhere other than the United States, click the Related Web Sites link and look over the list of Other Intellectual Property Offices, worldwide. For international patent work, the Big Kahuna is the **World Intellectual Property Office (WIPO)** in Geneva, Switzerland (www.wipo.org).

The PTO site offers free searching of U.S. patents from 1976 to the present, both bibliographic and full-text databases. Searching bibliographic databases is faster and sometimes more concise than searching full-text. Full-text may produce more comprehensive results — and includes images in TIFF format. You can perform the following types of searches:

- ✔ **Boolean Search:** Use pull-down menus and look at the results in chronological or relevance-ranked order. But you're limited to two terms per search. (See Chapter 2 for details on Boolean searching.)

- ✔ **Manual or Advanced Search:** Use whatever terms and qualifiers you want. Be sure to click Help to see how the advanced search syntax works.

- ✔ **Patent Number Search:** Use if you're looking for a specific item.

Learning to speak Patentese

Synonyms are the key to successful patent searching. That's why the U.S. PTO's Advanced Search mode, or any option that allows you to enter multiple terms, is your best bet for patent subject searching. The more terms you can think of to describe your idea, the better. Keep them as specific as possible, and avoid using the word *device.* Chemists joke about newbies who use the word *polymer* as a search term; that word appears in zillions of chemical database records and has very little meaning on its own. *Device* is a similar deal — it's the patent-database equivalent of a *whatchamacallit.* You know, a thingy, a doodad. You get the idea.

The PTO site also includes patent classification listings that you can browse and add to your search. A Patent Class is a broad grouping similar to a top-level subject category in a Web catalog such as Yahoo!. Adding a Class number helps narrow your search to the right general field.

For instance, if you want to search for patents on the kind of fork you use to twirl spaghetti — as opposed to forklift trucks, forks in roads, or robotic serpents with forked tongues — you can browse the list of patent classes, locate the word *Cutlery,* and add Class 30, the appropriate class number, to your search. *Bon appétit* — or should we say *buon appetito?*

To add a Class number to your patent by using the PTO's bibliographic database and the Boolean Search form shown in Figure 11-4, follow these steps:

1. **Click the <u>Searchable Databases</u> link on the PTO home page.**

2. **Click the <u>Patent Bibliographic and Abstract Database</u> link on the next page.**

3. **Click the <u>Boolean Search</u> link under Bibliographic Database.**

4. **Enter** fork **in the Term 1 text box, leaving Any Field showing in the Field 1 drop-down list box.**

5. **Enter** 30 **in the Term 2 text box and select Current U.S. Class in the Field 2 drop-down list box.**

6. **Select a year to search (we chose** *All* **because, well, maybe we have a thing for forks).**

7. **Select either Chronologically or By Relevance under Rank Results (we chose By Relevance in case we get a lot of listings; many patent searches require a chronological listing instead).**

8. **Click the Search button.**

When we click the title of one of the top-ranked items, "Eating utensil for pasta" (Patent number 5,697,160), we find this abstract or patent summary:

> "An eating utensil used in cooperation with a fork to eat elongate type pasta in a manner which prevents splattering of pasta sauce onto the user. The utensil is comprised of a handle which carries a bowl which is formed with an upwardly concave center portion. A rim on the outer periphery of the center portion extends in an oval-shaped configuration, and a shield is mounted on one side of the rim. The shield is comprised of an upright wall having a curvature which conforms with the rim curvature. The height of the wall is effective to constrain the pasta and sauce above the bowl and within the shield as the tines of the fork, while being held and twisted by the user, turn and wrap the pasta into a bundle which can then be lifted away from the utensil for eating."

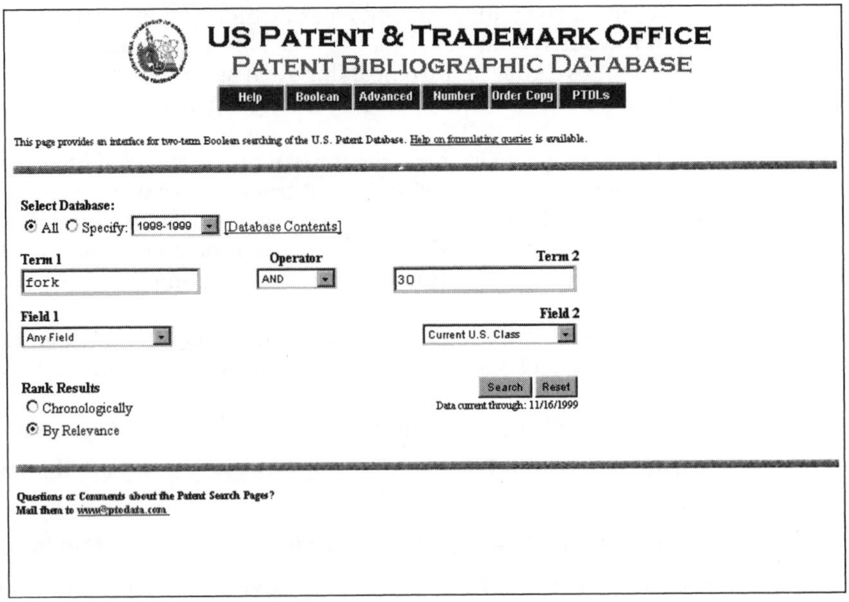

Figure 11-4:
U.S. PTO
patent
search form.

See what we mean by the language used in patents? And notice — the patent isn't even *for* a fork, but for a device intended to be used in conjunction with one.

Big Blue does patents, too

All U.S. patent filings come from the PTO, but the PTO isn't the only source for patent searching on the Web. The **IBM Intellectual Property Network** (www.patents.ibm.com) goes five years farther back in its patent coverage, to 1971, not 1976. IBM offers several search options up front, including the ability to confine your search to various key segments of the patent document, or to search by inventor or assignee or by patent number. You can also do a Boolean keyword search and select fields from a pull-down menu to make your search more precise. (See Chapter 2 for more about Boolean and field searching.) Or choose Advanced Text mode for scads of additional options on a lengthy fill-in-the-blanks search form. The IBM site also covers European patents and patent applications, Japanese patents, and publications from the World Intellectual Property Office. And you thought they just made computers.

If in doubt, refer it out

Professional patent searchers use databases such as Claims/U.S. Patents and Derwent World Patents Index, which are available through Dialog and some other industrial-strength online services. They can make these files jump through flaming hoops and do lots of other tricks that the Web-based patent databases can't do, or can't do as gracefully. Patent searching is as much an art as a science, with a lot to discover as you go along. *We* sure don't know it all.

You don't think making sure that your patent search covers *all* the bases is worth the effort? Well, ask yourself what's at risk if you act without sufficient information. Income? Market share? Your professional or even personal reputation? Forgive us for getting all preachy on you, but if you don't want to take the time to get up to speed yourself, contract with a scientist, a patent attorney, a librarian, or an independent information specialist who knows his or her way around the patent databases. You'll pay for that person's services, but it's a sound investment.

The Association of Independent Information Professionals, an organization of research entrepreneurs, maintains a membership directory on the Web (www.aiip.org). Click the <u>Membership Directory</u> link, and then use your browser's "find on this page" function (it's on the Edit menu in our versions of both Netscape and Internet Explorer) to search for the word *patent.* You may do better if you pick someone whose areas of expertise are in science and technology instead of all over the map.

Do-it-yourself is fine if you're just trying to satisfy your curiosity, wondering if anyone else has glommed onto your own best and brightest ideas. Remember that golf putter example we mention earlier in this chapter? You wouldn't believe how many duffers think they've come up with the ultimate solution. In fact, that's a fun patent search to try on your own. Go back to the PTO site (see "The U.S. Patent and Trademark Office" section, earlier in this chapter) and key in **golf AND putter** as your two terms, setting the date limit to *All.* When we tried it, we got more than 2,000 hits. Do you still think you've got a marketable new idea for a putter? Or are you teed-off that someone's probably thought of it first?

Satisfying your scientific curiosity

Researching a scientific or technical topic is serious business. But just plain curiosity is something else. Early on, teachers discovered that the Web is a great tool for getting kids excited about science. If you don't know much biology but you've got a question mark in your mind that you just can't dislodge, try baking powder and a vigorous scrubbing motion. No, sorry — try the Net.

Even professional scientists sometimes need a boost when they're investigating in fields other than their own. The Web abounds in general science megasites full of pointers to the best resources in various fields and disciplines, as well as science-oriented sites maintained by educational institutions, science museums, broadcast media, and magazines. Some sites are geared to scientists, others to students, and others to just plain folks. Nobody's checking your I.D. or asking for your resume, though, so use whatever sites work for you. If you find a great starting point, bookmark it, whether it's geared toward professionals or toward 12-year-old kids.

In the following sections, we look at a jumping-off point for scientific explorations of all kinds, a sampling of science museums and popular science webzines, the online homes of some respected science journals, and some suggestions for keeping up with the unceasing march of scientific progress.

Exploring science with SciCentral

SciCentral (www.scicentral.com) is a gateway to more than 50,000 online resources in the biological and health sciences, earth and space sciences, engineering, chemistry, and physics. The site also features news stories, and links to government agencies, universities and research institutes, information sources on science policy and ethics, and much more. You can click down through categories to find the specific links you need, or do a keyword search to locate your topic wherever it appears, or scroll through a site index that conveniently outlines the entire content of the SciCentral site.

For quick answers to your burning scientific questions — at least the kind that other people might ask, too — don't overlook two sites that we point you to in Chapter 7: **How Things Work** (Landau1.phys.virginia.edu/Education/Teaching/HowThingsWork) and the uncannily similarly-named **How Stuff Works** (www.howstuffworks.com).

SCOUTing out new science sites

The Scout Report for Science & Engineering (www.scout.cs.wisc.edu/report/sci-eng/current/index.html) is a heavy-duty guide, updated every two weeks, to online resources in the life sciences, physical sciences, and engineering. You can read current and past issues at the Web site; search by keyword and click to go directly to individual sites that cover your topic; or subscribe and get your biweekly updates by e-mail.

Visiting science museums online

Some of the world's best-known science and natural history museums maintain branches on the Web as well. Now you can expand your scientific education without cracking a book or even leaving your chair. Start with these virtual excursions:

- ✔ San Francisco's **Exploratorium** is known for its creative, hands-on exhibits. When you visit the Exploratorium on the Web (www.exploratorium.edu), you can find exhibits on earthquakes, origami, optical illusions, and life on other planets, plus an archive of past exhibits and live Webcast events.

- ✔ At New York's **American Museum of Natural History** (www.amnh.org), you can tour exhibits on butterflies, body art, and giant squids, and poke around the fossil halls and the planetarium. You can also browse articles from the latest issue of *Natural History,* the museum's monthly publication.

> ✔ **The Smithsonian Institution** (www.si.edu) actually comprises more than a dozen museums, most of them on the National Mall in Washington, DC. See video highlights of the National Air and Space Museum and the National Museum of Natural History, or explore links to affiliated research institutions such as the Astrophysical Observatory.

Speaking of space, check out **NASA** at www.nasa.gov for an entrée into space science and NASA's rich web of related resources.

Science TV on your PC

The Discovery Channel and Public Broadcasting's Nova, two popular TV science broadcasts, have online counterparts as well. **Nova Online** (www.pbs.org/wgbh/nova) includes an archive of past programs as well as coverage of ongoing scientific explorations, plus program transcripts and resources for teachers. **Discovery.com** (www.discovery.com, as you might imagine) offers feature stories, games and quizzes, reports from expeditions to the far corners of the earth, and live webcams focused on everything from the sun, to a colony of naked mole rats, to the surf at Daytona Beach. Try finding programming like that on network TV.

Tracking news from the world of science

Maybe you need your *Time, Newsweek,* or *People* magazine fix each week. Reva needs *Science News.* To be perfectly honest, another name appears on the mailing label, but he lets her look at it when he's finished. ***Science News*** has a fine Web site (www.sciencenews.org), as do several other excellent print publications read by scientists and interested nonscientists as well:

> ✔ ***Nature*** (www.nature.com)
>
> ✔ ***New Scientist*** (www.newscientist.com)
>
> ✔ ***Scientific American*** (www.scientificamerican.com)

EurekAlert doesn't have a print equivalent, but it sure is fun to say: EurekAlert! EurekAlert! EurekAlert! "Eureka!" is what scientists are supposed to exclaim when they make a momentous discovery. It means "I have found it." Actually, the story we've heard is that all the great scientific discoveries were preceded not by a cry of "Eureka!" but by some guy in a lab muttering, "Hmmm, *that's* funny. . . ."

Anyway, ***EurekAlert!*** (www.eurekalert.org) is produced by the American Academy for the Advancement of Science (AAAS). Its primary mission is to make sure that science writers and other journalists get the story right. To ensure accuracy, it includes all kinds of auxiliary resources: links to dictionaries and scientific glossaries in various disciplines; pointers to image sources; and links to research sites, organizations, and science publications for professionals and lay people alike. But the heart of the site is its collection of news releases on a wide range of research fronts. Most of these news stories aren't of headline-making stature, like the discovery of life on other planets. But scanning through them periodically gives you a good sense of what real scientists are working on, and how our knowledge of the world — and of worlds beyond our world — is increasing all the time.

Chapter 12

Strictly Business

● ●

In This Chapter

▶ Gathering background information on a company

▶ Researching industries, markets, and products

▶ Identifying and tracking competitors

▶ Finding financial and investment information

● ●

*F*or businesses, information is like oxygen. They inhale it constantly, without even noticing. It's in the air; it's a pervasive part of the environment. Unfortunately, the atmosphere in a few companies is on the stale side. Some organizations still haven't gotten the word that information is a vital part of their operations. They make decisions based on outdated facts and figures, and on assumptions about the marketplace and their competitors that they haven't tested in years. Check the business section of your local paper — you're sure to spot them. Look in the bankruptcy filings, for starters.

After the Web got going, savvy corporations were among the first on board — if only to claim their domain addresses and plant their virtual brochures and business cards in cyberspace. But as the Web began to include real, substantial content along with sites and services geared toward the business community, *information* became a high-profile priority. Now that useful data for making business decisions is just a few keystrokes away, plugged-in business people know that staying informed is an imperative.

In this chapter, we show you how to find and use business directories, financial reports, public company filings with the Securities and Exchange Commission, stock quotes, investment analyst and market research reports, press releases, trade journal articles, and other forms of company, business, and marketing information. The open Web isn't always the most complete or efficient resource for business research, but it's a start. And after you're on the Web, it's much easier to tap into other useful online resources, especially the members-only sites and professional online services we wax rhapsodic about in Chapter 9.

Understanding Business Research

Business research takes on many forms, depending on what you're hoping to accomplish. The main forms that we look at in this chapter, along with an idea of what each one involves, are

- **Company background:** Assemble a profile of a company, its history, and its lines of business. Obtain organizational information including location, top executives, major divisions, and subsidiaries. Get basic or detailed financial statements, and perhaps a credit history and rating as well. Collect news stories and press releases showing quarterly earnings, new products, management changes, and other timely information.

- **Competitive intelligence:** Identify companies competing in a particular industry. Scan analyst reports, market surveys, and trade journal articles to determine the market leaders and to get a sense of their strengths and weaknesses, current and long-term. Read closely to determine their market strategies, their research and development efforts, and their plans for the future.

- **Market studies:** Determine the market for a new product or service by checking to see what's already out there, who's selling it, and how much they're selling. Gather historical data to compare and determine trends. Is the demand for the product going up or down? Look at published market studies and articles in trade journals to identify the major players and their market shares. Scan the consumer, regulatory, and broader business climate to identify opportunities and dangers.

- **Sales prospecting:** Build a list of potential customers by screening them according to location, size, type of business, or other meaningful criteria. Get names, addresses, and phone numbers so that you can contact them.

- **Stocks and investment research:** Gather current and historical quotes for stocks and other investments. Focus on a particular company's stock performance over time and its prospects for the future. Compare notes with other investors. Set up an alerting service to keep tabs on the companies and markets you follow. Manage your investment portfolio online.

- **Management theory and practice:** Figure out new techniques for managing companies, people, and corporate operations. Discover other companies' methods and best practices. Read case studies, surveys, and executive interviews.

Getting a Company Backgrounder

Why gather background information on a company? Perhaps you're thinking about doing business with that company, as a customer, partner, supplier, investor, or even a potential employee, and you want to be sure that it's stable and reputable — in other words, that it's going to *remain* in business and deliver on what it has promised you. A company backgrounder is like a resume, a quick-sketch portrait of the organization.

Company backgrounders are a fundamental part of business research. You may assemble one as part of a larger research project, zeroing in on a particular competitor, or potential client or joint-venture partner, after first surveying the field.

A basic company backgrounder includes the following types of information:

✔ Name, address, and telephone number of the company

✔ Names and titles of its top executives

✔ A general description of the company's products and services

✔ Number of employees

✔ Names and locations of subsidiaries and major divisions

✔ Annual sales and other financial figures

✔ Credit rating and history

✔ News about new product introductions, current earnings, executive appointments, and corporate strategies and goals

Strategizing a background search

The preceding list sounds like a lot of information, doesn't it? Luckily, you can usually find much of it in one place, in an online directory database or at the company's own Web site. It makes sense to start where you think you can get the biggest payoff.

Say you're gathering background information on Eastman Kodak Company. Your first stop is the **Eastman Kodak** site (www.kodak.com). Among all the product news and tips for taking great pictures is an About the Company header. Under this header, you find the organizational lowdown that you're looking for — or as much of it as the company wants to tell you. The site is the company's, after all, and it controls the content.

Clicking the About Kodak link brings up information about the CEO, a history of the company dating from its founding in the late 19th century, an Investor's Center with complete financial information, a searchable collection of press releases, descriptions of individual business units such as the Business Imaging Systems division, and a copy of the most recent company annual report — complete with photos, of course.

The fastest way to locate a company's Web site, if you don't already have the URL, is to guess. For example, `www.vw.com` is a no-brainer for Volkswagen. If you don't find the site in a couple of tries, plug the company name into a search engine, such as AltaVista or Excite, look it up in Yahoo!, or check a company directory site like CompaniesOnline or Hoover's (more about both of these sites in the following section).

If you're planning to explore every byway of a company's Web site, it helps to have a road map. You often find a link to <u>Site Map</u> or <u>Site Index</u> on the main page of the site. The link to the VW site map, for example, is at the top of the page. The site map gives you the layout of all the main content areas within the site. You can print the site map and check off each area after you've gone through it.

To gather background information on a company, you may have to go beyond its own Web site, looking for business directory profiles, credit reports, and opinions from investment analysts, competitors, suppliers, and writers for newsletters and other trade publications. Exploring some of these alternatives is a good idea, even if you did strike gold at the corporate site itself, because they add a different, and often more objective, perspective. A complete backgrounder often involves a three-stage effort:

1. **Start with the most specific, structured sources — the kind where you can look up the business by name and know that you're getting everything there is to get. Company directories and credit reports fall into this category, along with the company's own Web site.**

2. **After that, broaden out to industry information sources that offer a good chance — but not a guarantee — of gaining more insight into the company and its doings.**

3. **Finally, depending on how much information you've gathered and how much more you think that you need to get, extend the search still further, to magazines, newspapers, and other publications that may or may not provide useful information. If you haven't found much at this point, try plugging the company name into a Web-wide search engine.**

Company directories and packaged reports

Company directories are not all alike. Some offer a detailed portrait of the firm, and sometimes links to additional sources of information. Other directories provide just a bare-bones sketch of what the operation is about.

Directories vary in their coverage, too. Some are strong on both public and private companies, while others focus on public companies only. Some are international in scope, while others restrict themselves to the U.S. or another specific country or region. Some have a minimum size cutoff, while others strive to be as comprehensive as possible, seeking out one-person operations as well as Gigundo Megacorp International Inc. and its corporate peers.

Bottom line: You may have to check more than one directory to get the complete picture, or to even *find* the company you're looking for.

Hoovering it up

Hoover's Online (www.hoovers.com) is a great source for background information on a company. Suppose that you're looking for a snapshot of Kodak. Head over to the Hoover's site, type **Kodak** in the search box, and click <u>Go</u>. You get a listing of options, including <u>Capsule</u>, <u>Financials</u>, <u>Profile</u>, and <u>Officers</u>. The last two areas are only available to subscribers, indicated by the keys next to those options. (A subscription is about $15 a month and gains you access to a lot of useful information — a good deal if you research companies regularly.) Below the Hoover's listings are links to several other sources of business information, including Dun & Bradstreet (which we discuss later on).

Click <u>Capsule</u> for a narrative company description, information on key competitors, rankings (Kodak ranks 121st in the Fortune 500), subsidiaries, selected news stories, a company history, and more. Figure 12-1 shows the start of Hoover's Company Capsule on Kodak. You can click <u>Company Profile</u> (if you're a subscriber), <u>Financials</u>, <u>News & Analysis</u>, or <u>Industry</u> to get more detailed information and current news about the company and the industry.

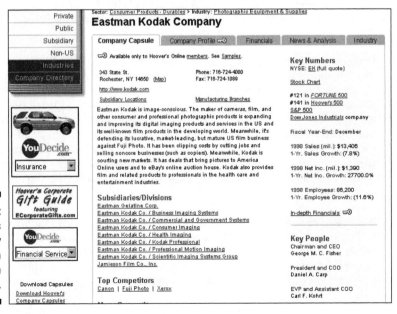

Figure 12-1: Hoover's Company Capsule on Eastman Kodak.

Delving deeper

If you want to dig a little deeper, you have a couple of other options. First, head over to **Vault.com** (`www.vault.com`). This site is primarily for job seekers, so you see message boards, job listings, and other career-related information. But the most valuable information in this vault is its company reports. At the main page, type **Kodak** in the search box and click <u>Go</u>. Vault.com displays a company profile of Kodak. Click the Company Snapshot tab, and get a panoramic shot that even Kodak would be proud of — a lengthy discussion of corporate history and culture, tips on getting hired, and even "uppers" and "downers" of life at Kodak. Vault.com offers even more in-depth reports on 50 or so major companies (alas, not Kodak) and an equal number of law firms. Sign up as a Vault.com member (it's free), and you can download those reports as well.

Your other option is to check out Dun & Bradstreet (D&B), probably the single most comprehensive source of basic company information worldwide. D&B maintains a huge database of business profiles, as well as a variety of more detailed reports, for both public and private firms.

CompaniesOnline, a joint venture of D&B and the Lycos search engine folks, allows you to search for a specific company by name or ticker symbol, or to locate businesses that meet certain criteria. (We say more about criteria-screening in the "Prospecting for Sales" section of this chapter.)

Still pursuing our research on Kodak, we go to `www.companiesonline.com`, type in **Eastman Kodak**, and click <u>Go Get It!</u> What's "it"? In this case, "it" is Kodak's mailing address and phone number, and the URLs for the company and a number of its related sites.

Company name searching is a challenge. Sometimes the official corporate name is different from the name that most people use — *Eastman Kodak* versus just *Kodak*. If you know or can determine the *ticker symbol* (the abbreviation used to identify a public company's stock — the Kodak ticker symbol is EK) or its official name, you're in good shape. Otherwise, be prepared to pull up subsidiaries and branch offices along with the main headquarters location. You can usually identify the main office, which is almost certainly what you want for a background search, if you know where the company is based. And, simple but effective, look for phone number listings that end with a couple of zeros.

When you're searching for company info — in Companies Online, on Yahoo!, or in a search engine like Excite — avoid using words like Corp., Inc., or Co., either abbreviated or spelled out. These words clog up the search and won't help narrow the results. Of course if you're looking for something like The Corporation Company, you may not have a choice.

Dun & Bradstreet also offers you the option of purchasing an in-depth Business Background Report (BBR) from its main Web site (`www.dnb.com`). The BBR includes contact information, sales figures, number of employees, lines of business, and top executive names and titles. But it goes considerably beyond that, including a history of the business, number of shares issued, background on senior management and their experience and education, and a brief description of any special circumstances, such as fires, floods, or major lawsuits, that may have affected the business in a significant way. A typical D&B BBR describes the corporate organization — the parent company, subsidiaries, and branch offices — and provides an assessment of the company's financial condition in very general terms. A BBR costs $20 per report plus tax; D&B accepts credit cards from registered users.

Follow these steps to locate a BBR:

1. **Go to the D&B Web site (**www.dnb.com**).**

2. **Pull down the Access the D&B Database menu and select Order by Credit Card.**

3. **Click the <u>Register</u> link to register at the site, if you haven't done so already. Follow the prompts to complete the registration.**

4. **Click the <u>U.S. Company Reports</u> link.**

5. **Type in the company's address, telephone number, or D&B DUNS number.**

Looking for a non-U.S. company? Check out **WorldPages** (www.worldpages.com) for links to individual business directories worldwide. See Chapter 4 for more about WorldPages.

Public versus private companies

We got lucky with Kodak. The Web site gave us all the background information we wanted, and more. But — confession time — we *knew* that it would. Some companies are a lot more forthcoming than others. Publicly owned firms, such as Kodak, are required by law to divulge certain details about their operations, including financial information, to potential shareholders and government regulatory agencies like the U.S. Securities and Exchange Commission.

Privately owned companies present more of a challenge. Small, family-controlled firms may be the hardest to research because they're not required to divulge financial data or other details of their operations. Small companies — unless they're the latest hot high-tech startup, or involved in a scandal, or newsworthy for some other reason — tend to keep a much lower profile than large, well-known public firms.

Even some public companies, especially in highly competitive industries, are stingy with the details, although bona fide investors can usually get more information than window-shoppers like us.

Tapping company and industry news sources

Business directories are just the foundation of a company background search. They're fine for the basic facts, but, like their printed counterparts, most of them are updated annually at best — and a lot can happen in a year. Not only that, directory listings don't provide much, if any, insight into the company's activities, new product introductions, or changes in strategic direction.

If you're lucky, as we were with Kodak, you may find some of that supplemental information right at the company Web site. Look for a link called Press Releases or Investor Relations or something similar. Even then, however, all you're getting is the company's own perspective, and that's not enough. Organizations are notorious for tooting their own horns while gliding over not-so-wonderful news that may make their shareholders and customers unhappy.

Business Wire (www.businesswire.com) and **PR Newswire** (www.prnewswire.com) are press release distribution services where client companies pay to be listed. Check out these sites if you don't find what you're looking for at the company's own site.

For a complete and accurate company backgrounder, you have to see what the rest of the industry (or people and publications that follow the industry) and the larger business community are saying. The easiest way to tap into that broader perspective is through articles in trade, business, and general news publications.

Start with the links to news stories that Hoover's (see the earlier section "Hoovering it up") thoughtfully provides along with its Company Capsule. From there, you can branch out to other sites and sources.

You can also try the local approach: **American City Business Journals** (www.amcity.com) is a mega-site for the online editions of more than forty local business publications, such as the *Cincinnati Business Courier,* the *Philadelphia Business Journal,* and the *San Francisco Business Times.* City business papers are great sources for in-depth info on companies headquartered or doing business in a particular region. They're also excellent for gathering a variety of local opinions from the business community's perspective. The American City site allows you to search a particular publication, or all of them at once, and to restrict your search to the current issue or to cover an archive of back issues. Figure 12-2 shows the kind of information we found when we ran a search for Kodak in all 41 American City Business Journal publications. See what we mean about getting a variety of perspectives and something besides the company's official line?

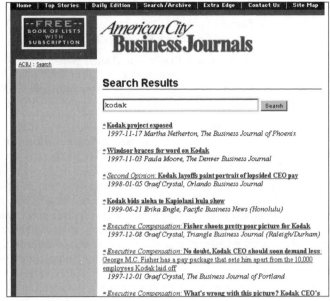

Figure 12-2: American City Business Journals search on Kodak.

Broadening your company background search

You've probably found enough background information to get you started by now, especially if the company you're researching is publicly traded, good-sized, or newsworthy in some way. But suppose all that you want more comprehensive information, or you still haven't filled in the blanks? Chapter 13 is about tracking down information of all kinds in newspapers, magazines, and other periodicals. That chapter describes individual Web sites as well as online services and mega-sites, such as **NewsTracker** (`nt.excite.com`) and the **Electric Library** (`www.elibrary.com`), that cover dozens or even hundreds of publications.

A special business edition of Electric Library (`www.elibrary.com/business`) includes additional information that's not available through the public site. However, the information is priced for companies, not individuals; check it out if you work for an organization that may want access to such a resource.

If you don't feel like turning to Chapter 13 yet, start with some of the key business and news sources in the following list. Some of these sources require you to register before you can use the site, and some charge a fee for subscription:

✔ **U.S. business periodicals: Wall Street Journal Interactive Edition**
(www.wsj.com), *Forbes* (www.forbes.com), *Fortune*
(www.fortune.com), or *Business Week* (www.businessweek.com)

✔ **International business periodicals:** *The Asian Wall Street Journal*
(available through Dow Jones Interactive at djinteractive.com), the
U.K.-based *Economist* (www.economist.com), or *Financial Times*
(www.ft.com)

✔ **National newspapers:** *The New York Times* (www.nytimes.com),
USA Today (www.usatoday.com), *Christian Science Monitor*
(www.csmonitor.com), or your local paper's Web site

Still coming up dry, or barely damp? It may be time for a needle-in-a-haystack
search — the kind where you have no idea where information on your subject may appear, or how far back you may have to dig, but you'll take whatever you can get. If you haven't yet thrown the company name into a
general-purpose search engine, or a meta-engine (such as Inference Find,
Dogpile, or one of the others we describe in Chapter 3), now may be the time.

But your best resource in a worst-case scenario is a comprehensive collection of business, trade, and general-interest magazines that indexes several
years' worth of periodicals, not just several months. You can find such extensive databases on professional online services, such as Dialog, Dow Jones
Interactive, and LEXIS-NEXIS. We say more about these databases, which play
a key role in other kinds of business information-hunting, in the "Planning a
Competitive Intelligence Operation" section that follows, and the "Doing
Market Research" section later in this chapter.

Planning a Competitive Intelligence Operation

What's *competitive intelligence,* anyway, and why is it staring at us like that? If
a company backgrounder is a *portrait,* then a competitive intelligence, or CI,
investigation is a *movie.* A backgrounder shows you what a business *looks*
like; a CI report shows you what it's *doing* and where it's planning to go.

Like a movie, a CI investigation can reveal subplots and motivations. Like a
movie, it's set against a backdrop — not an exotic locale, but a particular
industry. And, like a movie, it features a supporting cast — other competitors, suppliers, customers, and regulatory and environmental issues — that
play a role in determining the main character's fate.

Some corporations have entire departments set up to gather competitive intelligence. The department's responsibility is to monitor other companies in its industry, or companies that manufacture, distribute, or sell similar or complementary products and services. A good CI initiative helps companies anticipate what the competition is doing so that they can react quickly to changing conditions and profit from them — or at least minimize their losses. Suppose that you discover, through a patent filing or a brief mention in a trade magazine, that your chief competitor in the upscale eyewear industry is thinking about introducing a model with windshield wipers so eyeglass-wearers can see better in the rain. You may want to crank up your own product development cycle and get *your* company's Wiper-Specs out on the market first.

A CI initiative is both broader and deeper than a company background investigation. A CI initiative is *broader* because you have to look at the company in the context of the marketplace — other companies, consumers, and outside events and conditions (such as lawsuits or regulatory changes) that could affect its profitability and its strategic direction. A CI initiative is *deeper* because you go beyond the general background data that we gathered in the last section, and hunt for news — new plant construction, partnerships, management changes, patent applications, and so on — that may signal what the competition is up to.

CI reports are *analytical,* not just descriptive like background reports. You have to think like a detective, piecing together the facts, opinions, and analyses that you find, trying to discern meaningful patterns, and drawing conclusions based on the evidence you find.

How you approach a CI investigation depends to a great extent on the type of company that you're researching and what you turn up as you go. For starters, though, we can retrace some of the same ground we covered in our company background search. This time we're going to pay closer attention to some areas that we brushed by last time around.

Using a company's Web site

Your first stop is the Web site of the company that you're researching. We're still interested in Kodak — maybe we're strategic analysts for Fuji Film, or entrepreneurs with our own hot ideas about digital cameras or imaging technology — because it's a global operation with a corner on at least the U.S. film market, but it has some significant weaknesses, too.

This time, we skip past the basic factoids and Kodak moments on the company's Web site, and look for clues in areas such as the following:

✔ **The company annual report:** This document is usually heavy on the horn-tooting, because it's designed to reassure shareholders that all is well with the company and that they should invest even more heavily than they already have. However, publicly traded companies are required to reveal the bad along with the good. You may have to read between the lines and deduct 50 percent for management-speak, but look for the truth in the shareholder report, financials, and management discussion sections. In Kodak's annual report, we zero in on the Year in Review, Letter to Shareholders, and Financial Review. We check key indicators, such as annual sales, comparative stock prices, and earnings per share, comparing the most recent year's figures with those of the year before. We read CEO explanations like this one with a critical eye:

Worldwide sales for 1998 were 8% lower than in 1997, largely due to the transfer of a portion of Kodak's graphics business to a joint venture, Kodak Polychrome Graphics, on December 31, 1997 (see Note 15, Acquisitions and Joint Ventures) and the reclassification of certain promotional expenses by the Company.

Uh-huh. We pay attention to the company's own spin on its new product introductions, acquisitions, joint ventures and partnerships with other firms, new facility construction, and directions for the future. We draw our own conclusions about whether they're expanding or consolidating, on shaky ground or firm footing, and whether the overall trend is up, down, or, as the Magic 8-Ball likes to say, *unclear at this time.*

✔ **Job listings:** Is the company hiring at all? If so, what kinds of positions is it advertising? In what divisions or departments? Can we draw any conclusions from the kinds of listings we find in the marketing and technical areas? Is Kodak beefing up its marketing efforts, for instance, or hiring engineers in advanced digital design areas as well as its core chemical base? Obviously, the more you know about the company and its history and strategic directions, the more meaning you can read into its on-site employment advertising. And don't discount the possibility that it may be in a hiring freeze, and that all those ads may be outdated or strictly to keep up appearances.

✔ **New product announcements, press releases, and company news:** You can draw some conclusions, from the products and services highlighted at a company's site, about what it sees as its main business or its flagship product or line, and where its development and marketing efforts are centered. As long as you're at the site, you may as well tap into the firm's own press releases and flattering news clippings from other sources. You can find routine information, such as quarterly earnings, senior personnel changes, and other matters the company is required to report or doesn't mind your knowing about. You may also find rave reviews, from trade and consumer publications, of some of its products and services. For the real lowdown, though, you have to use other news and business information sources, which we talk about in the following sections.

Finding alternatives to the annual report

Not all companies are as forthcoming as Kodak. Privately held companies —
those that don't issue stock to the public at large — don't have to be, unless
they're part of a heavily-regulated industry such as pharmaceuticals or
public utilities. Private companies are not accountable to shareholders in the
same way that public firms are. Private companies may be required to file
certain types of documents with regulatory agencies, but in general, they're
not required to open their books or reveal the details of their operations
across the board. Some private firms do publish annual reports or post financial statements on their Web sites, but you can't count on it, or on the strict
accuracy of the information you do find there.

Hoover's Online (www.hoovers.com) and **Dun & Bradstreet** are a couple of
options for finding financial data and other leads on a privately owned company's fiscal condition. For more detailed information, go to the D&B site
(www.dnb.com) and spring for one of those Business Background Reports
that we describe in the section, "Company directories and packaged reports,"
earlier in this chapter. Besides the raw numbers, you can gather insight from
the corporate history, the management profiles, and even the description of
the premises the company occupies.

The downside of a D&B report, and most other sources of financial information about private companies, is that the data tends to be self-reported. You
get only what the company itself has volunteered, and the information isn't
always accurate, complete, or timely.

Getting informed analysis

Investment banking and brokerage firms employ teams of analysts who
follow individual companies and industries closely, tracking not just stock
performance, but a constellation of other activities that may affect business
operations, and issuing detailed reports. These reports focus on publicly
traded companies, but also include private firms if they're significant players,
have an interesting approach to the market, or own a promising technology.

Many of these investment reports are available online, both directly on the
Web and through the professional online services.

The Investext Group offers the complete text of company and industry
reports from well-known investment firms, such as Bear Stearns, Morgan
Stanley Dean Witter, Merrill Lynch, Kidder Peabody, PaineWebber, and hundreds of others. The Investext Research Bank on the Web also includes
reports from market research firms and trade associations.

You have several options for tapping into Investext:

✔ **Through the Research Bank Web service** (see the Investext Web site at www.investext.com for details). You can also opt to subscribe and have Investext do the searching for you, but that seems like cheating, doesn't it? Either way, you can download complete reports, including tables, charts, and other illustrations, in Adobe Acrobat (PDF) format.

✔ **Through professional online services, such as Dialog and Dow Jones Interactive,** which give you plain-text versions of complete reports or selected sections. On Dialog, select File 545 and confine your search to the company field. On Dow Jones, click <u>Company & Industry Center</u> to get to Investext Company Reports, and then enter the company ticker symbol and browse the tables of contents of individual reports until you find the complete report, or the sections, you want. Figure 12-3 shows the kind of detailed competitive intelligence you can get from investment reports.

Be sure to study the database Bluesheet before searching Investext on Dialog. Unlike many databases where you go directly to the documents you've retrieved, Investext is designed so that you can browse tables of contents or zero in on the report sections you need by entering qualifying fields and phrases. Why the indirect approach? Complete reports can cost you $100 or more, and you don't always need the whole thing.

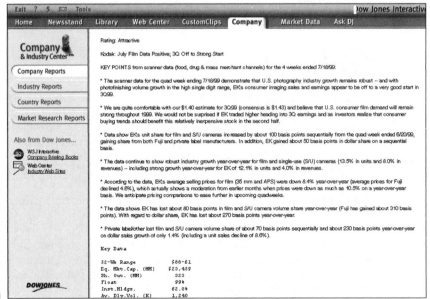

Figure 12-3:
Company report from Investext via Dow Jones Interactive.

Prepackaged market research reports, such as those offered by Investext's MarkIntel division, are a terrific source of competitive intelligence information. In fact, CI and market research are similar in many respects, and often go hand-in-hand. See the "Doing Market Research" section, later in this chapter, for some specific leads on locating these reports.

Monitoring the news

Back in the Company Backgrounder section, we talk about using newspapers, magazines, and business publications to round out and lend some color to the bare-bones facts about a company and its operations. Competitive intelligence-gathering uses all of those sources — newswires, regional business journals, national and city papers, specialized trade periodicals — and more.

Now, you're not just looking for background, but for specific information about a company's current and future directions. You may scan the same headlines as before, but now you focus on news items that someone working on a broad-brush general picture of the company may dismiss as trivial and incidental:

- ✔ Plant openings that indicate expansion or new product lines
- ✔ Management changes that signal either a problem with turnover or a steady new hand on the wheel
- ✔ Contracts and agreements-to-purchase that clue you in on increases in production
- ✔ Licensing agreements, partnerships, and corporate acquisitions that tell you when a company is committing to new ventures and technologies
- ✔ Lawsuits, accusations, and regulatory actions that may spell trouble on the environmental, consumer, or new-product-approval fronts

Local color

For a deep and unvarnished look at how a company is faring, nothing beats the local paper in the town where that company is based. Think about it: among its subscribers are hundreds, even thousands, of employees and family members whose lives are influenced by that firm.

After you have a headquarters address, check one of the newspaper mega-sites in Chapter 13 for newspapers in that city or area. Local papers give you more steady and detailed coverage of the company — especially if it's a major regional employer — than you get anywhere else. You also get information on issues, such as employee policies, internal politics, and concerns about environmental pollution, which the national press tends to overlook.

Don't just take our word for it. Aim your browser at the Rochester, N.Y., *Democrat & Chronicle Digital Edition* (www.rochesterdandc.com), click **Search**, key in Kodak, and check the kinds of stories you pull up.

Or go to the San Jose, California *Mercury-News* site (www.sjmercury.com), and search the archives for articles on Apple Computer, say, or any other Silicon Valley or computer-industry firm.

Calling in the cavalry

Some of the best-informed and most valuable competitive intelligence insights come from articles in specialized industry newsletters and trade publications. Some of these periodicals do have Web sites with searchable archives, but visiting them one by one is tedious and time-consuming. Besides, unless you're in the industry yourself, or have some bizarre personal interest in it, how are you going to know that publications, such as *Chain Store Age, Chemical Marketing Reporter, Restaurants & Institutions,* and *Automotive Parts International,* exist in the first place, let alone anticipate that any one of them may cover the company that you're investigating?

If you're serious about competitive intelligence-gathering, it pays to invest whatever it takes to get up to speed on some of the heavy-duty trade and industry databases on Dialog and the other professional online services described in Chapter 9. These databases cover anywhere from dozens to hundreds of periodicals in industries ranging from aerospace to zymurgy (look it up). They include articles ranging back 5, 10, 15 years, or more, so that you can gather historical data or compare a company's early stages with its present-day situation. And each database features a range of field options and specialized keywords and concepts, so that you can search not only by company name or ticker symbol, but also by specific topics, such as management philosophy, joint ventures, marketing, and new products.

Some of our favorite trade and industry databases are

- ✔ **Dialog:** Business & Industry (File 9) and Gale Group Trade and Industry Database (File 148) cover general business and specific industry publications worldwide, with a focus on companies, products, and markets.

  Gale Group PROMT (File 16) adds facts and figures from market surveys, investment analyst reports, government studies, and more general, business, and trade publications.

  Gale Group Newsletter Database (File 636) offers detailed coverage and insider analysis from industry-specific newsletters.

  Business Dateline (File 635) includes local and regional business journals, newspapers, and magazines.

  Go to Dialog Web's reference site (library.dialogweb.com) and check the Bluesheets (detailed database information) for the lowdown on how to use these resources. You may want to open a Dialog account and take its basic system training.

✔ **LEXIS-NEXIS:** In LEXIS-NEXIS Universe (`www.lexis-nexis.com/ln.universe`), click <u>Search</u>, then <u>Industry News</u>, then type the industry terms in the Subject search box. If you sign up with LEXIS-NEXIS, you get documentation and training to help you figure out the most focused approach for a particular search.

✔ **Dow Jones Interactive:** In the Publications Library, click <u>Revise Publications</u>. Then, under Publications by Industry, select any or all of the broad industry categories shown.

The indirect approach

Competitive intelligence doesn't always come neatly packaged as *news*. You've heard of private investigators — some of them quite legitimate — who go through people's garbage or hire on as office workers or custodians to see what they can pick up. Don't worry; you won't be doing any dumpster-diving or undercover lurking here. But you can employ equally indirect methods to find out more about what the competition may be up to. For instance, you can

✔ **Monitor the patent databases (see Chapter 11) to see what new technologies they may be exploring or planning to exploit.** Search for the company as patent assignee, and include patent applications, for their early-warning value, as well as patents actually granted.

✔ **Check Web sites that *link to* the company you're investigating.** You may be surprised at who's saying what about your target company. Go to **Google** (`www.google.com`), type the company's Web site address in the format `link:www.kodak.com`, and click <u>Google Search</u>. Follow the links on the search results screen to see what other sites are saying about the company you're researching. Your target firm may not be talking about its joint venture with Company X, but Company X may be blabbing its little head off about the alliance.

✔ **Set up a current-awareness profile on the Web or a professional online service that you subscribe to.** New information on the company that you're investigating is delivered to your e-mail box, or waiting for you the next time you log on to the site or service, without your having to re-run the search yourself.

  • In Chapter 13, we show you how to set up a Web-based alerting service on general news and business information sites, such as **NewsPage** (`www.newspage.com`).

  • At **Northern Light** (`www.northernlight.com`), click <u>Alerts</u> to set up a free electronic clipping service. Northern Light alerts you via e-mail to new articles and Web mentions; you pay a fee to download certain articles from Northern Light's Special Collection.

Competitive intelligence is serious business for many companies — both start-ups and long-established organizations. If you've taken on the responsibility, either on your own or on behalf of your employer, consider joining the **Society of Competitive Intelligence Professionals** (www.scip.org). You can find out a lot more from SCIP than we can possibly show you in this chapter.

Doing Market Research

What's market research? Is it that woman with a clipboard in the mall, asking whether you prefer the blue package or the red one? Is it a focus group where some guy pays you $50 for your candid reaction to various scenarios and trial balloons? Is it the warranty card you fill out when you buy an electric toothbrush, or the questionnaire you have to wade through when you register for a gated site on the Web?

Market research encompasses all of those activities, and more. Yet such efforts to measure and quantify consumer response are only a small part of the picture. Market research also includes

- ✔ Industry overviews and background
- ✔ Surveys and descriptions of products and their manufacturers
- ✔ Product reviews
- ✔ Research and development
- ✔ New product introductions
- ✔ Competitive rankings and market share information
- ✔ Supply and demand indicators: production, shipments, imports and exports, and sales
- ✔ Overall market size in dollars or units sold
- ✔ Historical data, forecasts, and trends
- ✔ Market segments — how much to what kinds of customers
- ✔ Distribution channels
- ✔ Advertising and marketing strategies

What do the topics in the preceding list tell you? That you've changed your mind about tackling a market research project at all? Hang in there; we're going to give you some shortcuts to make it a lot easier than it may look right now.

One thing that the list indicates is that market research is concerned with *products and services* as much as, if not more than, individual *companies*. In that way, market research is a change from the kinds of business research covered earlier in this chapter.

Why do market research?

✔ Market research is a good first step in a competitive intelligence effort, helping identify the key and emerging players that you need to keep an eye on.

✔ Market research can overlap with CI, making sure that you keep a broad picture of the industry in focus at the same time that you're monitoring your main competition.

✔ Market research can help you decide whether there's room in the marketplace for a new product or service.

✔ Market research can help you identify new opportunities — and warning signs, too — as consumer tastes and market conditions change. Plow those tobacco farms into hemp fields, Mr. Marlboro Man.

✔ Market research provides quantitative information that you can plug into a business plan and use as the basis for revenue projections, mid-course corrections, and long-term strategic decisions.

✔ Market research is essential for convincing banks and other potential lenders that your business plan is sound and that they can expect to see a return on their investment.

Another thing the list suggests is that market research has a lot to do with numbers: quantitative information that takes time and money to compile. Your mission, if you choose to accept it, is to figure out how to get ahold of the figures you need without reinventing the wheel by going out and compiling it yourself. Hint: We can help.

Surveying sources for market research reports

Most of the market research information that you find online is based on in-depth studies conducted by corporations, consultants, trade associations, investment analysts, and (duh!) companies that specialize in producing market research studies.

These in-depth studies, some of which were prepared originally as customized reports for a particular corporate client, are typically based on interviews with scores of industry sources or thousands of individual consumers, supplemented with the analyst's own proprietary research contacts and deep professional insights.

For all that service, you won't be surprised to hear, you're going to pay big bucks.

But you can find ways around shelling out money in the three-, four-, or even five-figure U.S. dollar range (the going rate for many market research studies) for a report that may or may not tell you what you need to know. Here we introduce you, quickly, to some sources for packaged market studies online. Then we show you how to save money by using precise database search techniques to extract from secondary sources (trade journals, published report excerpts, newspapers, and industry newsletters) exactly the facts and figures you need.

Next to news and technology info, market research is one of the most abundant forms of information online. But except for data on the growth of the Internet itself, you won't find more than a handful of good, detailed, current market research reports on the open Web. Remember, somebody paid a lot of money to collect, compile, and analyze all that data. They've got to recoup their investment. And they're not going to give it away.

For high-quality market studies, look to the members-only sites and professional online services that we introduce you to in Chapter 9. They allow you to search for reports that deal with a particular industry, product line, or individual company; you can browse a table of contents before buying to judge whether the entire report, or just the most relevant sections, is worth purchasing. Read about some of the major market research report suppliers in the following subsections.

Northern Light

Northern Light (www.northernlight.com) is a hybrid research site — partly Web-wide search engine, partly gated online service with its own collection of documents. To find market research reports, click the <u>Business Research</u> link, and then scroll down the page to Limit Documents To and click the boxes next to <u>Investext (reports)</u>, <u>Investext (pages)</u>, and <u>Market Research (pages)</u>. (See the section, "Planning a Competitive Intelligence Operation," earlier in this chapter, for more about Investext.) Click an industry category that best describes your market, and then type a keyword or two, such as *semiconductors* or *exports,* in the Search For box to further focus your query. Finally, click <u>Search</u>. You see individual report pages pertinent to your search, as well as tables of contents for entire (read, *expensive*) market research reports.

Dialog

Dialog (www.dialogweb.com) features a database category called Market Research Reports Fulltext. As a Dialog subscriber, you log on and then type **b marketfull** in the Command search box at the bottom of the screen. Keep a hand on your wallet, though; remember that you can generally buy by the page instead of having to spring for the full report. You can also search the Investext database (see "Planning a Competitive Intelligence Operation," earlier in this chapter, for more about Investext). Type **b 545** in the Command search box to start your Investext search. The same price cautions apply here, too.

LEXIS-NEXIS

The LEXIS-NEXIS MKTRES library is available to users of the LEXIS-NEXIS proprietary software, though not through the Web-based LEXIS-NEXIS Universe. The MKTRES library (LEXIS-NEXIS is known for its elegant naming conventions) includes reports from major U.S. and international market research firms, such as Find/SVP, Freedonia, Frost & Sullivan, and Euromonitor. For details on setting up an account and getting the required software, check the **LEXIS-NEXIS** Web site (www.lexis-nexis.com).

Dow Jones Interactive

Dow Jones Interactive (djinteractive.com) provides access to the MarkIntel collection of market research reports from about 50 companies. After you've signed on, click <u>Company & Industry Center</u> and then click <u>Market Research Reports</u>. You can search by one of Dow Jones' industry categories, or type keywords in the Keywords search box. You can also limit the search by geographic region.

Before plunging into a market research spending spree, spend some time with the online Help files and database documentation on whatever service you've selected. Full-text market research is expensive, and you need to know the tricks that let you zero in on the sections that discuss market share — or whatever topics you're specifically interested in — and browse tables of contents before you buy.

Getting more for your money with secondary sources

We call ourselves general researchers — we can handle just about anything *except* chemical structure searching. (A person's gotta draw the line somewhere.) But, to tell you the truth, 75 percent of the projects we've done over the years have been market research–related.

A typical client research request goes like this:

> I need to know the market for fountain pens. I've heard that they're back, and people are even collecting them. How big is the market? How much has it grown in the last five years? What's the market like internationally? Who are the major manufacturers, and how much of the market does each of them control? What are the main retail outlets — stationery stores, department stores, gift shops, mail order, the Web? Why are people buying them? What particular features and styles do they like? What's the outlook for fountain pens in the future?

Now that we've introduced you to those grand and glorious sources for market research reports, we'll pull you up short by saying: We actually don't use them that much. Unless a client has specifically instructed us to find *one* good, comprehensive study — and is willing to pay for it — we start from an entirely different angle. We use those massive database collections of business and industry periodicals that we mention in the section on competitive intelligence (see "Planning a Competitive Intelligence Operation") earlier in this chapter.

Here's why: Market research firms release key findings — not necessarily all the details, but some good solid numbers — to writers and editors at those trade and general business publications. They do it to market *themselves,* to entice readers to buy the complete report, and because they're good guys and want to contribute to the store of knowledge on the planet. Yeah, right.

Trade and business databases are not only cheaper, but in many ways easier to search for specific market research information. Each one uses standardized indexing terms or codes that let you look for precisely the market data you need, for the exact product, service, or industry you're interested in. Because these databases include report excerpts from a wide range of sources, you can retrieve whatever's available, regardless of what market research firm produced it or what publication reprinted the tidbits that you're hoping to find.

Digging into Dialog

We usually start with Dialog, because it allows us to use all those specialized database features we mention in the section, in combination with Dialog's own powerful search language.

In PROMT (File 16), we can use Product and Event Codes to specify exactly what we're looking for. These codes are cascaded, which means that when you enter a short code like *395 (Pens, Pencils and Related Equipment),* it picks up all the more specific subcategories that begin with that number. We can enter *PC=395103* to search specifically for fountain pens. A broader category, *3951,* includes all kinds of pens and mechanical pencils. We may use both categories in this search, or even fold in the topmost *395* category. We can include the phrase *fountain pen(s)* to make sure that any general pen-market studies classified at the 395 or 3951 level do at least mention them.

Event Code 6 (which we search as *EC=6*) includes all kinds of market information — production, shipments, sales, orders received, and more. We can enter a more specific code like *EC=65* to focus on sales and consumption data only.

We can also use Dialog's Limit command (L/) to restrict our results to just the last couple of years. And, if we're only interested in the U.S. market, say, or western Europe or Japan, we can limit by using country and regional codes (like 4EUFR for France) to eliminate results from elsewhere in the world.

Our search on the fountain pen market in PROMT looks like this (*s* tells Dialog we're entering a search term; read more about Dialog search language in Chapter 9):

```
1. s pc=395103 or (pc=3951 and fountain()pen? ?)
2. s [combined results of step 1] and EC=6
3. s [combined results of step 2] and GC=4EUFR
4. L/[combined results of step 3] 1998:2000
```

Figure 12-4 shows some of the results, in brief form, for this search.

PROMT's sister file, Trade & Industry Database (File 148), is also an excellent source of market research information. Recent records in T&I are indexed with PROMT's product codes so that you can easily search both databases at the same time. We like to include T&I's own indexing terms as well: Phrases like *Pen Industry — Marketing* do the job just fine.

Another set of siblings, Business & Industry (File 9) and TableBase (File 93) provide equally precise searching, plus some unique sources and subject coverage. You search B&I much the same way that you do PROMT, by using product, concept or event, and geographic-type codes and terminology. The database includes a range of international business and industry publications, many of which PROMT doesn't cover.

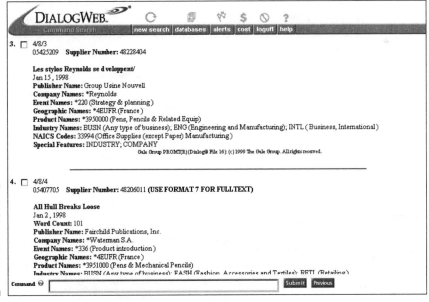

Figure 12-4:
Market research results in PROMT on Dialog.

TableBase is designed for hard-core number-junkies, people who want the cold, raw data without a lot of verbiage and explanation. You can search by industry, product, or service by using the same codes as in the Business & Industry database, and specify exactly the kind of quantitative information you want to see — time series, market size forecasts, price trends, sales, and so on. Figure 12-5 shows just the facts, ma'am, for duty-free sales of writing instruments worldwide.

Doing it with Dow Jones

We like Dow Jones Interactive for market research, because the publications are preselected for their value and organized into industry categories that make it easy to select the ones that are most relevant for a particular search. Because of this up-front effort on Dow Jones' part, we don't have to spend as much time constructing a search with codes and keywords as we do on Dialog. We go to the Publications Library, click <u>Revise Publications</u>, and, under Publications by Industry — assuming we're still on our quest for fountain pen market information — click to select the <u>Retail and Consumer Goods</u> category. We can go on to choose individual publications within that category, but this time we elect to search the entire group. We enter a simple search strategy (see Chapter 9 for more about the Dow Jones search language) and come up with a couple of promising-sounding items. We click the titles to read the full text, and find just about everything the client wants to know.

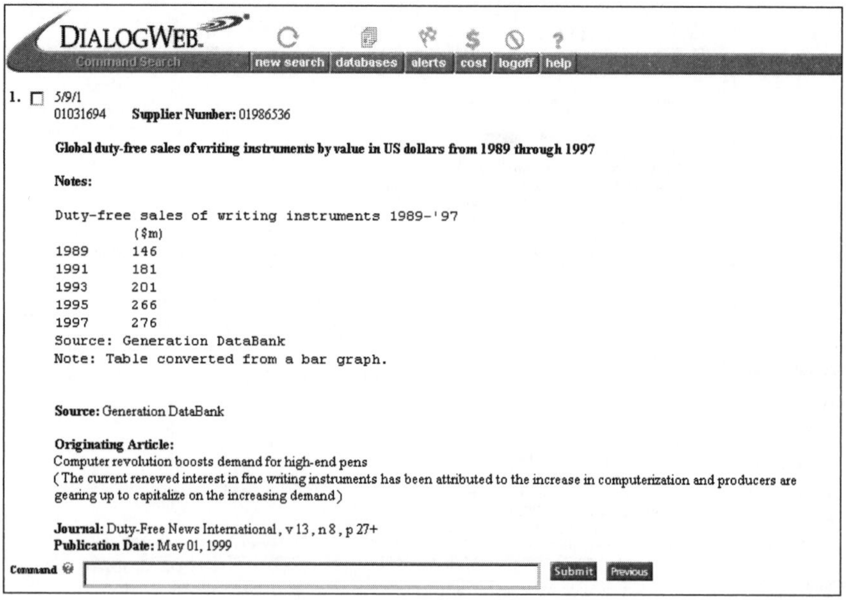

Figure 12-5:
Market data
from
TableBase.

DIALOGWEB.

Command Search | new search | databases | alerts | cost | logoff | help

1. ☐ 5/9/1
01031694   **Supplier Number:** 01986536

Global duty-free sales of writing instruments by value in US dollars from 1989 through 1997

Notes:

```
Duty-free sales of writing instruments 1989-'97
         ($m)
1989     146
1991     181
1993     201
1995     266
1997     276
Source: Generation DataBank
Note: Table converted from a bar graph.
```

Source: Generation DataBank

Originating Article:
Computer revolution boosts demand for high-end pens
(The current renewed interest in fine writing instruments has been attributed to the increase in computerization and producers are gearing up to capitalize on the increasing demand.)

Journal: Duty-Free News International, v 13 , n 8 , p 27+
Publication Date: May 01, 1999

Command ☺ [   ] Submit | Previous

Trademarking your new product

One important step in the market research process — after you've established that the idea is a "go" and before you've launched the big ad campaign — is to come up with a product name that's clever, memorable, and irresistible. Naming consultants charge big bucks to come up with winners like *Exxon, Telesis,* and *AirTouch.* Of course you can do better.

But creative naming is only part of it. You're not going to launch a multi-million-dollar advertising effort — or even a multi-dozen-dollar one — without first making sure that the name you want is *available,* that is, that it's not owned or in use by somebody else.

We're talking about *trademark searching.* You can do your own by using the Trademarkscan databases on Dialog. The producer of Trademarkscan, Thomson & Thomson, offers trademark searching to subscribers — plus a lot of useful information about trademarks and intellectual property — on its Web site (www.thomson-thomson.com). You can also do a quick, preliminary search for free at the U.S. Patent and Trademark Office site (www.uspto.gov/tmdb/index.html). Be sure to read the Important Notice at the site about the limitations of the database and how those limitations may affect your results.

Here are a few important concepts to keep in mind when trademark searching:

✔ **Degraded, phonetic, or cutesy spellings.** When it comes to trademark searching, *Quick = Qwik = Kwic.* The Trademarkscan database is smart enough to know this and builds at least the obvious equivalents in.

✔ **Embedded sounds or word-strings.** Trademarkscan allows you to search on a distinctive element that may appear anywhere in a word: RECOR, PRECOR, TRECOR, and so on.

✔ **Turning up an identical or oh-so-similar mark isn't necessarily the kiss of death.** Trademark law is based on the possibility of confusion in the consumer's mind. *Acme Scientific Instruments* is no threat to *Acme Candy Company,* and vice versa. (At least we hope not, but in this litigious society, who can be sure?) Use the Trademarkscan Goods and Services field to restrict the name you're researching to a category of relevant products and applications. Consult an intellectual property lawyer if you have any doubt.

✔ **No law says that names have to be trademarked.** It's stupid to gear up for production and actually get a product to market without first registering its name. But many businesses, especially small regional ones, operate without protection of trademark for their *company* names, if not for the products they manufacture. If you want to avoid possible conflict with someone who may sue to protect a business name they thought of first, run the name through business directory, professional magazine, and journal databases. A Web-wide search engine is great for picking up mentions of names that may not be trademarked but that could cause you problems because they were in use *first.*

✔ **If you do find a conflict with the name that you want, use the Trademarkscan Status field to discover whether the mark is active or abandoned.** Each database record includes contact information for the trademark holder, so if you really want to use a name that's registered to someone else, you can get in touch and negotiate. This works best when the trademark holder hasn't yet established a brand of his own. Don't try it with Budweiser, IBM, or Black & Decker.

Prospecting for Sales

People often talk about sales and marketing in the same breath: *salesandmarketing, marketingandsales.* They may go together like a horse and carriage, but they're really two different things. Marketing is strategic; you do *market research* to identify where and how you want to advertise and promote your product or service. Sales is tactical, hands-on. After you've identified a potential market — consumers at a particular income level, certain kinds of businesses — you focus more closely: Get a list of people, families, or firms that meet your criteria, and start calling, writing, or dropping by.

Obtaining and screening that list of potential customers is called *sales prospecting,* and you can do it online.

At the consumer level, your best bet is to deal with a reputable mailing list broker who can generate a list of prospects — usually on labels, for a direct mail campaign — at a reasonable cost. "Reasonable" varies with the size of the list, but often means no more than a few cents a listing. List brokers are also a good bet if you're contemplating a mass mailing to hundreds or thousands of businesses. You can find mailing list houses and direct mail firms in your local yellow pages or online. Check the Yahoo! <u>Business and Economy:Companies:Marketing and Advertising:Direct Marketing:Direct Mail:Mailing Lists</u> category, for starters. American Business Lists, Dunhill, and D&B — yes, *that* D&B — are a few that we know are reputable.

Yes, it *is* possible to harvest peoples' names and contact information directly from the Web, either from white pages listings, site directories, or public discussion groups. We don't recommend it unless you're looking for a particular individual or seeking to reach a highly-targeted group with an established interest in the type of product or service that you're selling. Why do we discourage searching for sales prospects on the Web? Partly because gathering such listings is time-consuming, and the information is often out of date. But mostly because bulk e-mail — the way most online marketers logically decide to reach their prospects — can be incredibly annoying. It's known as *spam,* and it deserves the bad reputation it's developed. Businesses are a different story, especially when you plan to contact a relatively small number individually, and your research has shown that they may actually be interested in what you have to offer.

Say you're a supplier of industrial shelving, and you want to sell to grocery and specialty food stores in your region. Or you manufacture a fine line of doggie chew-toys in your basement workshop, and you're looking for local pet stores to carry them. Perhaps you've developed a small business accounting software package that companies with 1 to 5 million dollars in annual sales would glom right onto, if only you could identify such firms. Maybe you're a management consultant, seeking to promote your fine services to companies with a thousand or more employees, anywhere in the western United States You get the picture. All are candidates for a targeted sales campaign.

In Chapter 4, we show you how to use online business directories like **BigBook** (www.bigbook.com) to locate certain kinds of businesses, such as banks, hardware stores, or pizza parlors, in a given geographic area. That approach works for sales prospecting, too, as long as you know the nature of the business you want to reach and can limit your prospects to certain cities, states, or regions. Business directories include street addresses and phone numbers, of course, and the maps and driving directions you sometimes get are a bonus if you're planning to call on your potential customers personally.

But what if you have broader or subtler customer-screening criteria, like the management consultant or software developer we mentioned a couple paragraphs back? You'd happily sell to anyone, regardless of their location or line of business, as long as they're a match — size, revenue, or otherwise — for your service or product.

Looking for prospects with CompaniesOnline

In the Company Backgrounder section at the beginning of this chapter, we mention **CompaniesOnline** (www.companiesonline.com). Instead of entering the name of a particular firm in the search form, we can look for prospects by using the following criteria:

- ✔ **Industry:** The pull-down menu gives us a choice of a dozen or so broad industry categories — Manufacturing, Food & Clothing, Computers & Software, Travel & Transportation, and more. We can select *ALL* if we don't want to restrict our search to a particular kind of business. For more precision, we can select the *Browse by Industry — Drill Down into Sub-Categories* option at the bottom of the page. That lets us refine our search from the too-general Food & Clothing category down to Retail Food Stores.

- ✔ **Location:** We can specify a city, a state, or neither.

The main drawback to using CompaniesOnline for sales prospecting is on the output end: The list you get gives you just the company name, city, and state. You have to click each company name to get its complete mailing address and phone number. If you're dealing with several-hundred prospects, this clicking-and-collecting can get tedious.

Have we got an alternative for you.

The Dun's-on-the-Web alternative

The same Dun & Bradstreet database used by CompaniesOnline is also available on **D&B Marketing Connection** (www.dnb.imarketinc.com). Its New Business Leads Online lets you do the following:

✔ Screen companies by criteria, such as size, location, type of business, years in business, or company name

✔ Select the type of list you want to display, such as mailing list, telemarketing list, or demographic list

✔ Generate a neat list of prospects in table form

As a bonus, D&B Marketing Connection offers you precise screening criteria:

✔ Instead of just Retail Food Stores, you can use SIC (Standard Industrial Classification) codes or standardized line-of-business descriptions to specify supermarkets, convenience stores, butcher shops, fish stores, produce markets, candy stores, bakeries, health food stores, and so on.

✔ You can screen for — or screen *out* — branch locations and sole proprietorships.

D&B Marketing Connection also offers a Market Profiles feature, that lets you drill down through industry categories to see an analysis of the market for a specific type of business. We look up sporting goods stores, for example, and see that half of the total sales are rung up by stores with fewer than ten employees, and that these stores average between $100,000 and $600,000 in annual sales. We can use this information to decide if this is an appropriate market for the product or service that we're selling.

Investigating Investments

We're timid when it comes to the stock market. We don't exactly keep our money under the mattress, but government-backed securities are about as risky as either of us wants to get. We do have a lot of foolhardy . . . uh, investment-savvy friends, though, and they use online resources for everything from preliminary research on a potential investment to actual trades, portfolio-tracking, and Monday-evening-quarterbacking with fellow investors.

Ask EDGAR

We'd like you to meet our friend EDGAR. We haven't introduced you until now because so many of the other business research resources in this chapter link to him — we should say *it* — or utilize its data. EDGAR, or Electronic Data Gathering Analysis and Retrieval, is the electronic publishing arm of the Securities and Exchange Commission (SEC), which regulates the affairs of publicly traded U.S. companies, the conduct of brokerage houses and other investment agents, and various other kinds of investment activity.

Public companies are required by law to disclose certain kinds of information to the SEC. This includes annual reports, proxy statements, and excruciatingly detailed financial reports of one sort or another, all of which the **SEC** site (www.sec.gov) describes. These forms and filings, eye-glazing as they may seem, are packed with information of interest to potential investors. If you don't find what you need at a company's own Web site or at one of the business research or investment mega-sites we describe in this chapter, EDGAR's your boy . . . er, site. He's a little fussy; it helps to know the exact name of the form that you need and the fund or company that you're researching. But he's thorough: EDGAR can help you retrieve any or all filings for a particular company, or run certain specialized searches by using pull-down menus.

EDGAR is a man . . . we mean, site, of many talents. For instance, a company filing an Initial Public Offering (IPO) with the SEC is required to disclose *risk factors,* which can provide valuable industry insights for competitive analysis and other kinds of research. EDGAR can supply you with a copy of that disclosure. Get to know him — okay, *it.* EDGAR can be a business researcher's best friend.

Taking stock

Investment information is easy to come by online. Dozens of Web sites purport to be your ideal pathway through the maze of stocks, securities, mutual funds, futures, IPOs, and dozens of other ways of losing your shirt — we mean, ensuring a comfortable retirement. Because we're neither committed investors nor very knowledgeable ones, we look for a site that (a) isn't too strongly associated with a particular brokerage firm or style of investing, and (b) gives us a lot of information in one place. We need a site that provides not just recent and historical stock and money market quotes, but business, investment, and economic news, screening and analytical tools, expert opinions, investment tips, and links to other useful sites.

Daily Stocks

Stephen Tondreault, a CPA with McNulty, Garcia and Ortiz in St. Petersburg, Florida, first pointed us to **Daily Stocks** (www.dailystocks.com), an utterly unglitzy site without a hint of a hidden agenda, that also happens to be way more comprehensive than its name implies.

Daily Stocks offers links to quotes, commentary and background on stocks, mutual funds, and futures, as well as info on IPOs, insider trading, and stock screening services. You also get news headlines, today's corporate filings direct from the Securities and Exchange Commission, information on the U.S. economy, and columns by well-known investment analysts and advisors.

Yahoo! Finance

We talk about Yahoo! in Chapter 5, but Yahoo! is more than just an organized index to the Web at large. A specialized financial version of Yahoo! provides links to U.S. and global stock markets, investment research sources, financial news and opinion, and even help with your taxes. Head to **Yahoo! Finance** (finance.yahoo.com), and browse through the categories or type a company's stock symbol in the search box to find current stock quotes and headlines. Yahoo! Finance also provides a stock portfolio service; click <u>Portfolios: Create</u> to set up a tracking file for the stocks you own or are considering buying. As for us, we'll stick to watching from the sidelines.

Dow Jones better-than-average

If you follow the stock market — or have read Chapter 9 — you know that Dow Jones is a major player in business information, especially when it comes to investments.

The **Dow Jones Interactive** Web site (djinteractive.com) is home to the <u>Historical Market Data Center</u>. Click that link when you first enter the site — remember: you have to sign up with Dow Jones in order to get access — or click the Market Data tab from anywhere after you're inside. Use the pull-down menus and boxes to select the kind of report you want (Pricing History, Dividend, or Capital Change), the type of security (U.S., Canadian, or international stocks or market indices; government debt, mutual funds, options, or unit trusts), pricing intervals and duration, currency units, adjustment for stock splits and other events, and finally — pant, pant — the format of the report itself.

We like Dow Jones because we're just a mouse click or two away from information that helps us make smarter investment decisions, including Investext company and industry reports, hundreds of business journals and news sources, and of course *The Wall Street Journal.*

Other investment research starting points

Daily Stocks may be *too* much information for the beginning investor — we know *we* feel a little woozy every time we visit. And you may not want to open an account with Dow Jones Interactive right away, especially if your interest in the stock market is as casual as ours. That's fine; besides Yahoo! Finance, the Web offers some easier entry-points:

TheStreet.com (www.thestreet.com) gives you a magazine-style format, stock quotes, and investment basics, plus a range of premium services for subscribers.

FinancialWeb (www.financialweb.com) is packed with investment news headlines, columns, analytical tools, and links to major indexes and quotations.

Wall Street Research Net (www.wsrn.com) offers links to company research, stock screening, market and economic news, publications, brokerage firms, and other investor resources. Subscribers can download full-text analyst reports on specific companies and industries.

InvestorGuide (www.investorguide.com) includes some excellent background information on personal finance and investing, along with the standard links to stock quotes, investment research, and news.

Digging deeper

Many of the sites that we mention in the preceding few sections lead you to sources of detailed information on individual companies and industries. Don't overlook the ones that we look at earlier in this chapter — Dow Jones Interactive, Investext, and the other full-text research reports available through the professional online services. In addition, **PR Newswire** (www.prnewswire.com) features an Investment Profiles section — complete with tables, graphs, and downloadable reports in PDF format — for several dozen of its client companies.

Getting personal

We just bet that you know somebody who's deeply into the stock market and can't wait to share (minor investment pun there) his or her hot tips. Your dentist, your brother-in-law, your neighbor down the block. . . . Sure, you may get rich. You may also get burned.

The online world is full of amateur investors, and some of them even know what they're talking about. The way we look at it, there's safety in numbers. When you tap into an online investment discussion group, you get the benefit of many people's opinions, not just one. They can't *all* be wrong, or *all* be trying to sell you something — can they?

misc.invest

You want opinions? Newsgroups give you opinions — both informed and off-the-wall. The `misc.invest` hierarchy (see Chapter 10 for more about newsgroups, how they work, and what they can do for you) is where you go to eavesdrop on people who are talking about investments. Subgroups include `misc.invest.financial-plan`, `misc.invest.futures`, `misc.invest. mutual-funds`, `misc.invest.options`, `misc.invest. real-estate`, and `misc.invest.stocks` — among others. The latest edition of the `misc. invest` FAQ, a veritable encyclopedia covering all aspects of personal finance and investment — and a surprisingly slick document for a FAQ — is at `invest-faq.com`. Before you plunge into a `misc.invest` discussion, invest some time in the FAQ.

The Motley Fool

The Motley Fool — despite its name — is probably the best-known online hangout for serious personal investors. It got its start on America Online, and is still accessible there (keyword: *fool*), but the Fool's now at home on the Web as well. The site (`www.fool.com`) looks like a magazine, and offers some links to prepackaged content, such as stock quotes, news, and financials. But its main claim to fame is the value that human insight brings to the investment game, and the give-and-take among participants in its various forums. Don't miss the Fool FAQ, which will answer many of your investment questions without making you look foolish.

If it weren't for the personal touch — the touch of *many* persons, not just the two guys who started Fooling around in the first place — which sets it apart from the investment mega-sites that we mention earlier in this section, we would have placed the Fool right up there as a starting point. Instead, we've saved the best for last. The Fool's motto is "to educate, amuse, and enrich," and that's almost enough to convince us to change our ultra-conservative investment ways. In fact, come to think of it, we *do* have a little extra this month. . . .

How Do You Manage?

We ask ourselves that every day. Seriously, effective company managers are constantly on the lookout for new techniques and best practices for improving their operations. Journals such as ***Harvard Business Review*** (`www.hbsp.harvard.edu/products/hbr/index.html`); the publications of the **American Marketing Association** (`www.ama.org/pubs`); traditional business magazines like ***Forbes*** (`www.forbes.com`), ***Fortune*** (`www.fortune.com`), and ***The Wall Street Journal*** (`www.wsj.com`); and new-wave periodicals like ***Fast Company*** (`www.fastcompany.com`), ***Upside*** (`www.upside.com`), and ***Red Herring*** (`www.redherring.com`) are full of ideas for innovation, change, and corporate fine-tuning.

If you're already in the habit of reading management periodicals that speak to your business and professional development needs — or feel like visiting publication Web sites like the ones we've mentioned, and browsing to see what bright ideas you can pick up — great. Well, not *great,* but okay.

But suppose you're grappling with a sticky accounting issue, or trying to implement a new benefits policy, or preparing for some major new initiative, like turning your company into a learning organization, or instituting a knowledge management program? You may pick up some insights in the course of your regular professional reading, but wouldn't it be useful to have just a few more data points — to know how other companies have faced similar challenges and dealt with them successfully? Sure it would.

One of our prime sources for business and management literature is **Dow Jones Interactive** (djinteractive.com). We can select a group of publications that focus on management issues, use the hlp qualifier to limit our search terms to the headline and first couple of paragraphs of the article — a quick way to improve relevancy — and sort our search results so that the most relevant articles appear at the top of the list. See Chapter 9 for more, much more, about the Dow Jones Interactive search language.

If we want to see how companies in the financial services industry deal with management compensation, we start by clicking <u>Revise Publications</u> and selecting the <u>Management and Business</u> and <u>Financial Services</u> publications groups. Then, at the main search screen, we enter:

```
executive compensation.hlp. and (bank$3 or financial service$1)
```

Dow Jones Interactive automatically restricts our search to the current and previous year, but we can expand or narrow the date range if we need to. We select Sort Headlines by Relevance and click <u>Run Search</u>. Bingo! We get a list of several dozen articles, with titles like "Bank performance should dictate directors' pay" and "Credit unions are getting more creative with executive compensation." To read the full text of the articles, we click the check boxes next to the titles and then click <u>View Articles</u>.

Chapter 13

Read All About It: News Media and Publications Online

In This Chapter

▶ Finding and using Web newspapers and magazines

▶ Tracking down articles in online databases

▶ Keeping up-to-date automatically

▶ Exploring the 'zine scene

*W*e're surrounded by news. It's on the doorstep when you go out for the morning paper, and on the radio as you drive to work or school. During the day, your friends and colleagues talk about the latest out of Washington, Detroit, Silicon Valley, the City Hall crowd downtown, and their own neighborhoods. You pick up weekly newsmagazines like *Time* and *Newsweek* at the corner newsstand or from a coworker's desk. At night, the evening news blares out of the TV. Maybe you go for one last recap before bedtime. Folks with satellite dishes or the right cable connection can watch the news 24 hours a day, from other cities and time zones around the country and the world. Fifty-seven channels, we hear you saying, and nothing on. Sometimes that's true, but you don't want to hear *our* rant about how the media's unflagging appetite can manufacture a big deal out of nothing; you probably have a similar rant of your own. But when something important *is* happening, nothing compares with broadcast news or the deeper coverage you get from a good daily newspaper. Nothing, that is — except online.

In this chapter, we start with the online equivalent of news the way you're accustomed to getting it — network news sites and the electronic editions of newspapers and news magazines. Then we lead you through some sources for finding a particular newspaper, tracking down stories from back issues, and digging into news archives to research people, stories, and events that may have made news months or years ago. We do the same for magazines. Finally, we wrap up with a glimpse at how the Net is changing the way we receive — and even think about — the news.

Chapter 12 shows you the value of online newspapers and magazines in business research — investigating companies, products, and industries. Our own files are full of examples of research projects that we could not have completed successfully without searching magazines or newspapers or both:

- The recreational maze craze of a few years back, for an entrepreneur trying to decide whether to construct one of his own
- Local tastes in fresh-baked bread and how it varies from city to city
- Accidents involving golf carts
- Coverage of a small, privately-held biotechnology company in Emeryville, California
- Background on a person who claimed to have no assets but who showed up in the society pages as a lavish spender
- How banks market a new consumer investment product
- Various cities' experiences with a certain shopping center developer
- Reviews of the same movie in different regions
- Identifying reporters and writers assigned to the alternative energy beat so the client could pitch a story idea of her own

Broadcast News

If you follow the news on TV, you probably prefer one network over the others. Your preference is probably based as much on style as on substance. Maybe you love Peter and hate Dan, or can't stand either of 'em but can tolerate watching Tom (feel free to substitute your own names and combinations). Perhaps you watch CBS because the ghost of Walter Cronkite (who?) still hovers over the set. Or maybe you just think ABC's graphics are cooler than NBC's.

Each TV news program has its own look and feel. Content-wise, one may occasionally scoop the others on a breaking story, but by the time you've rolled through a news cycle or two, they're all covering pretty much the same events.

On the Web, network news sites look a lot like newsmagazines — but with the added value of real-time headlines crawling across the screen, new features added throughout the day, and the ability to search previous issues and dig up background on the crisis *du jour*.

Check out the following network news sites, for starters, and bookmark the one (or, for you hard-core news freaks, the *ones*) that you prefer.

Tuning in to the Big Four: ABC, CBS, NBC, and CNN

ABC News (abcnews.go.com) offers breaking news headlines and in-depth stories in categories like Travel, World, Entertainment, and ESPN Sports. If the story you're looking for isn't right there at the top of the hour, you can search the ABC News multimedia archives by word, name, or phrase. Need to turn up a video clip of Al Gore to judge for yourself whether he's as wooden a speaker as they say? Want to look up the latest report on how much George W. Bush has spent on campaign advertising? Want to hear what Minnesota Governor Jesse Ventura has to say about politics — or wrestling? Just go to the ABC News site, click <u>Search</u>, and enter your terms in the search box.

For a more linear look at ABC's offerings, scroll down the main Web page to scan a listing of recent stories, organized by general category, such as U.S., Politics, World, Business, ABCNEWS on TV, Technology, Science, Health & Living, Travel, Sports, and Entertainment. You can browse the World listings, click a headline like "Clash in East Timor", and read a detailed background story, complete with pictures.

CBS (www.cbs.com) closely ties the content and organization of its site to CBS network programming. Click <u>CBS News</u>, then click <u>Programs</u>, and then select your program from the menu. CBS gives you background reporting and some multimedia options. You want the video from last week's *60 Minutes?* No problem — assuming you've got the right Web browser plug-in installed.

The NBC News site (www.nbc.com), called **MSNBC,** is a joint venture between NBC and Microsoft. Click <u>MSNBC News</u> to get headlines, and then scan Quick News — short blurbs on major stories — or select your choice of stories in clickable categories such as Business and Technology.

MSNBC's Local News feature enables you to choose a region from a map and tune in to the NBC affiliate in that area, which is especially cool if you want broadcast news from your own city or somewhere else in the United States. Start at www.msnbc.com and click <u>Local</u> to get to the map. If you're a Windows 95, 98, or NT user, you can get instant updates on topics of your choice by using MSNBC's specialized News Alert software. (In the section, "Staying Current," later in this chapter, we show you some other automatic news update options.)

CNN (www.cnn.com) gives you a choice of top news headlines and stories that you can scan by category, all on the same page. Coverage of individual issues is deep, with lots of hyperlinks to background and related stories. CNN is particularly strong in the area of personal finance, with a category covering the subject and a link to the CNNfn financial news network site. You can search the entire CNN site, as well as register at my.cnn.com to design your own customized page of news. (We describe My.CNN.com in more detail in the section, "Staying Current," later in this chapter.)

Viewing some other contendahs: Fox and C-SPAN

Fox News (`foxnews.com`) gives you a relatively small number of headlines, but supplements them with a scrolling list of newswire stories, plus background features arranged by category, a search function, and video for selected stories.

C-SPAN (`www.c-span.org`) is for obsessive newshounds and people who enjoy watching grass grow. The C-SPAN site mirrors its broadcast sibling, with coverage of congressional sessions and other stirring events. Watch House appropriation hearings in RealVideo, if that's your thing. C-SPAN's archives do include some interesting background documents and original source material on events currently in the news. When we last checked the site, it was featuring in-depth coverage of topics such as The Road to the White House, The Nuclear Test Ban Treaty, and the Managed-Care Debate, complete with vote tallies, news conferences, hearings, and floor debate. How can you resist?

Getting the story worldwide

Much like CBS, the **Canadian Broadcasting Corporation (CBC)** site (`www.cbc.ca`) is closely tied to its broadcast programming. You can click CBC News Online or go directly to its URL (`www.cbcnews.cbc.ca`) for current headlines, summaries of top national and international stories, and in-depth background reports on topics of ongoing interest, such as Northern Ireland, fishing disputes, hockey, and the Quebec separatist movement.

The **British Broadcasting Corporation,** or BBC (`news.bbc.co.uk`), has always been a sterling source for news from an international perspective. You can listen to the famed BBC World News — a special audio edition produced for BBC Online — while you pretend to work.

News AND weather and sports

If you're a serious sports fan, you almost certainly know about **ESPN.** If you're a serious sports fan who has traveled *anywhere* online, there's a very good chance you've already visited ESPN's online home (`espn.go.com`). If not, meet us back here in half an hour, okay?

ESPN is a one-stop gateway to real-time scores and other sports news as it happens, plus after-the-fact reports, analyses, breast-beatings, and lamentations. It covers *all* sports — women's college basketball, fantasy leagues (they're not the same thing, guys), soccer, golf, tennis, auto racing, sailing, skiing, and so on. Our sports consultant tells us they're weak on rugby and Australian Rules football — but so is most of the world.

To tell you the truth, the only reason Reva sits through the sports segment on TV — unless the Giants are in the playoffs — is to get to her favorite part of the news: the weather report. As far as the Web is concerned, **The Weather Channel** owns not only the domain — `www.weather.com` — but also the highs, the lows, and the entire range of meteorological forecasts and phenomena.

Weather is headline news, especially in an El Niño year, tornado season, or a winter marked by heavy snowstorms. You can program The Weather Channel site to show you your local weather whenever you log in. Or check the outlook for cities you're planning to visit, or to see what your friends in Montana or out on the coast are having to put up with. You can also get special reports, such as ski conditions, allergy season updates, and aviation weather for pilots. The Weather Channel covers international weather as well — click <u>World Weather</u>, and then choose a region from the pull-down menu and type your city name in the search box.

Newspapers Online

Newspapers online are even closer than your doorstep — assuming you have a computer at home and it's not in some obscure corner of your attic or sub-basement. You don't have to freeze delicate body parts or get rained on while retrieving the daily Web edition, and you won't have to scramble to get it out of the bushes or off the roof when the delivery person is having a bad arm day.

We don't think that reading the morning paper on the Net will ever replace the convenience of saving your favorite section, neatly folded, to peruse at your leisure on the bus or in some other, more-private venue. Besides, what would you use to line the cat box? But being able to scan the headlines and catch up with your favorite columnists online is handy, especially when you've been out of town or missed a day.

Online newspapers (and magazines, too) offer some features you don't get in print — bonuses like *The New York Times* CyberTimes section, forums where you can talk back to journalists and debate with your fellow readers, searchable archives of back issues, and links to background information and other content that didn't make it into print for space or other considerations, but for which the Web edition has plenty of room. Some of the major morning papers are putting out an afternoon Web edition, so you can get a peek at what's going to appear tomorrow a.m. in print.

Many of the online papers we've seen make an effort to emulate the graphics and section-by-section organization of the paper-and-ink original. **The New York Times on the Web** (www.nytimes.com) uses the same familiar typeface and Gothic nameplate as the Great Gray Lady herself. Other major papers, such as **USA Today** (www.usatoday.com), **The Washington Post** (www.washingtonpost.com), and the **Atlanta Journal-Constitution** (www.ajc.com), either look a lot like their print selves or have a <u>Print Version</u> link to take you to a familiar-looking page.

Appearances aren't supposed to matter, but the more the electronic version of a publication looks like what you're accustomed to, the easier it is to find your way around it. That's why we're not making a big deal about how to interact with newspapers on the Web. You scan headlines, browse through sections, and read what catches your eye, just as you would in print. If you want to look for particular topics in current or past issues, you enter search terms just as you do in a general Web search engine, and scan the results the same way. See Chapter 3 for the basics of search-engine searching.

City newspapers, large and small, are superb sources for in-depth information on events, companies, and people in that region. You may not live there, but you can visit — and research — remotely. Consider the *Los Angeles Times* for movie-industry coverage, for instance, and *The Washington Post* for inside-the-Beltway political news and gossip.

Finding your local paper online

If your daily newspaper is committed to a presence on the Web, you probably know about it already. If not, check the business section for promotional ads, or look for that telltale *www* on the masthead or in the tiny type that tells you how to get in touch with editors in various departments. Still nada? The newspaper mega-sites described in the next section can help you track down your local paper online.

Journalists' choice

AJR NewsLink (ajr.newslink.org) has the professionalism of the respected *American Journalism Review* behind it. It offers links to both print and broadcast news sources, including college newspapers; alternative papers such as the *San Francisco Bay Guardian* and New York's *Village Voice*; magazines of all kinds; and other regional, national, and international categories. You can just drill down through the appropriate category to find the news source you want by type or region.

AJR NewsLink offers several different search options, too:

✔ You can do a keyword search of the site itself to locate links to particular publications or broadcast outlets.

> ✔ You can search the actual content of publications at several specialized news mega-sites.
>
> ✔ You can search the entire Web with any of several leading search engines.

All the news, from everywhere

TotalNews (www.totalnews.com) specializes in collecting recent stories from major news sites all over the Web and making the content searchable on its site. The archive of recent stories includes content from many gated sites that wouldn't turn up in a Web-wide search-engine search. It's also a thorough catalog of news sites from around the world.

For a lead on your local news outlets — broadcast as well as print — go to TotalNews and click <u>US Local</u>, and then browse by state or click a state abbreviation. For international news, click <u>World News</u>, and then choose a region or click the first initial of a country for sources in that area. Often the source is in the local language.

Newspapers and more online

The name **Newspapers Online** (www.newspapers.com) may seem straight-forward, but it doesn't stop there. If you're a seeker-after-obscure-publications, you can appreciate this site's surprisingly broad scope. The streamlined, low-graphics pages offer links to classified ad papers (you may know them as shoppers' specials, penny savers, or classified flea markets), ethnic and minority publications, religious periodicals, plus some titles that are both esoteric and weird. If you can't find it anywhere else, you just may find it here. Newspapers Online doesn't offer either site-wide or cross-publication searching, but that's not really its purpose. It's a thorough, well-organized guide to both essential and elusive publications on the Web.

Searching newspapers on the Web

The sites we survey in the preceding section are *pointer* sites. Their main mission is to point you to the Web site of the individual newspaper you're hoping to find. Such sites are a good first stop when you're trying to track down your hometown paper or locate one in another region or in some spe-cialized field. Many of these sites are comprehensive catalogs of newspapers and other news resources worldwide.

A different breed of newspaper mega-site focuses on finding the news, regard-less of where it appeared originally. These *search* sites may not cover as many publications as the *pointer*-type sites in the preceding section, but if you care more about what's *in* the news than about a particular paper's per-spective *on* the news, try one of the following sites first:

✔ **HotBot News Channel** (`headlines.hotbot.com`) is part of the HotBot search engine. The News Channel is tailored to search general and international news, business, technology, and other specialized news sites. Coverage is pretty shallow — a week or so back — for most sources, but it includes more than two-dozen major newspapers, as well as wire services, trade publications, and broadcast news sites.

✔ **Moreover** (`www.moreover.com`) is in the business of selling news content to Web designers who want to include a customized feed of current news on their sites. Fortunately, everyone else can use Moreover's service for free. You select the kind of news you want from a list of 150 categories and then check back to read headlines from newspapers around the world. Click <u>Signup</u> to get started.

✔ **NewsHub** (`www.newshub.com`) is light on actual newspapers, but it does cover news sites all over the Web. With updates every 15 minutes, it may be the freshest news mega-site around.

✔ **NewsLibrary** (`www.newslibrary.com`) enables you to search any or all of about 75 newspapers, some going back as far as the early 1980s. All are listed by geographic region, along with the extent of their archives. NewsLibrary gets a research gold star for better-than-average documentation. Pull-down menus make it easy to search NewsLibrary for any or all of your terms, do a phrase search, or use advanced features, such as Boolean searching, searching in specific parts of the article, and wild cards (see Chapter 2 or click <u>Help</u> at the site for more about how to use these options). You can also limit the search by publication date, sort by date or relevance, and set a cap on the number of articles you want to see. Searching in NewsLibrary is free, but you need to get a "passport" and pay $2 to $3 each time you want to download the complete text of a story.

✔ Excite's **NewsTracker** (`nt.excite.com`) is a direct route into the Excite search engine site's News channel. NewsTracker features top news stories, headlines from Reuters and UPI, ongoing coverage of major stories, and links to newspapers and other news sites. NewsTracker's master list of searchable sources (click <u>Sources</u> to see it) includes not only newspapers worldwide, but also an assortment of popular, business, and special-interest magazines on the Web.

The Electric Library, described in the section "Search FOR and search OF," later in this chapter, offers yet another channel into Web-based newspaper searching.

Going deeper into the archives, part 1

Many, if not most, newspaper Web sites offer some sort of searchable archive. It may go back a few days, a week, a month, or as far as several years. You may have to register and/or pay a fee to search, or to search back beyond a certain point, or to retrieve the actual stories behind the headlines you've browsed.

Don't count on cover-to-cover completeness. Some archives include certain feature articles, bylines, or sections of the paper, and exclude others. Some index the Web version of the paper and ignore — or just occasionally pick up — stories that appeared only in print. And almost none of the archives include photographs or other graphics, or syndicated columns.

If you really need in-depth, comprehensive coverage, the only place you're guaranteed to get it is through a professional online service. Dow Jones Interactive, Dialog, and LEXIS-NEXIS all offer huge databases of full-text articles from hundreds of newspapers and other news sources, in the United States and worldwide. You can search them individually or as a group or regional subgroup, or handpick your own assortment.

Individual titles go back years — in the case of *The Washington Post* on LEXIS-NEXIS, for instance, as far back as 1977. (*The Post* is no slouch on the Web, either; its archives there go back to 1986, which is highly unusual for a Web publication.)

The content of these heavy-duty databases reflects what appeared in the actual printed newspaper, unlike the Web where you often get a mix of print and electronic-only stories, or only stories that appeared in the Web edition and not necessarily in print. Using sources equivalent to the printed publication is important for research projects with legal implications, or whenever you're trying to be as official and comprehensive as possible.

Professional online services let you restrict your search by date, byline, dateline, or words that appeared in the title or another element of the article. You can also search a group of newspapers by region without having to specify their individual names. And you can do all this, and cover multiple papers at once, much faster and more efficiently than you can on the Web.

These are our starting points for searching newspapers on the leading professional online services:

- On **Dow Jones Interactive** (djinteractive.com), click <u>Publications Library</u> and then select either Major News and Business Publications *or* Top 50 U.S. Newspapers. To customize your selection, click <u>revise publications</u>. Then choose Publications by Type, followed by All U.S. Newspapers. Or choose Publications by Region, followed by the national, international, or regional grouping you want. Click Add to include the entire category in your search, or click any category or subcategory name and pick individual publications from the resulting list.

- On **Dialog** (www.dialogweb.com), search the PAPERS or PAPERSNU file (the latter covers U.S. newspapers added to the service since March 1997), or PAPERSMJ for major U.S. papers. Or select a regional grouping such as PAPERSNE for the Northeastern United States or PAPERSCA for all California newspapers. Search individual newspapers, whether U.S. or international, by their Dialog file numbers. For a list of newspapers on Dialog, go to www.dialogweb.com, click <u>Databases</u>, then <u>News</u>, then

Americas, and finally a subcategory such as <u>Major United States Newspapers</u> or <u>United States Newspapers by Region</u>. Drill down another level for individual publication names and file numbers. They don't make it easy, do they?

✔ On **LEXIS-NEXIS** (`www.lexis-nexis.com/ln.universe`), click <u>Search</u> and then <u>News</u> to get to the search screen. Then, pull down the Source menu and select Major Newspapers, All Newspapers, or any regional group that's relevant for your research. For international news in the language of the country, click <u>World News</u> and then pull down the <u>Source</u> menu for All French Language News, All Italian Language News, or — if you're feeling particularly multilingual — All Non-English Language News. For a list of the publications that can be searched on their own or as part of a larger selection, go to the main LEXIS-NEXIS site (`www.lexis-nexis.com`), click <u>Customer Service</u>, and then click <u>Source Locator</u>. Pull down the <u>Type</u> menu and select Newspapers.

I Saw It in the Dentist's Office: Magazines Online

News comes in many guises — not always neatly packaged as a headline in today's or last week's newspaper or newsmagazine. What's news to *you* may have appeared anywhere — in a month-old magazine you meant to save but didn't, or a 2-year-old copy of a publication you don't even subscribe to.

In Chapter 8, we explain how professional *document delivery* services can track down an article from just about any publication, as long as you have some idea of when and where it appeared. Professional document delivery firms typically scour the earth, or at least the earth's libraries, for articles in obscure scholarly journals or ancient issues of popular magazines.

You can do your own document delivery — at least up to a point. Many mass-market magazines, like the kind you find at the supermarket or your corner newsstand, have set up a home on the Web. Typically, these Web magazines include feature articles from the current issue; perhaps some supplemental, cyber-edition-only copy; and a searchable archive of back issues going back a few months or, if you're lucky, years.

You want newsmagazines? Check out these sites for starters:
Newsweek (`www.newsweek.com`) **Time** (`www.time.com`) **U.S. News & World Report** (`www.usnews.com`),and **The Economist** (`www.economist.com`).

A word about wires

Wire service bureaus around the world specialize in reporting breaking news stories and following up as they develop, around the clock. Wire stories often appear in printed newspapers and on news media Web sites. You can find coverage from U.S. and international wire services such as the **Associated Press** (wire.ap.org), **United Press International** (www.upi.com), **Reuters** (www.reuters.com), **Agence France-Presse** (www.afp.com), the Russian news agency **TASS** (www.itar-tass.com), the Japanese wire service **Kyodo News** (home.kyodo.co.jp),

and mainland China's **Xinhua News Agency** (www.xinhua.org).

Some wire services provide stories and updates right at their sites. Others don't provide direct feeds to nonclients, or they require you to sign up for the service, or redirect you to a member newspaper or other subscriber site so that you can take your feed from there. Considering how easy wire service reports are to come by, we'd rather take them as we find them, at other news media sites — unless, of course, we have a reason to seek out coverage from a specific one.

Locating magazines online

How do you find a particular publication online or determine whether an electronic edition exists? We have a few suggestions.

Take a guess

You can always try guessing a publication's URL the same way you can guess at a company's Web site. If it's a multiword name such as *Business Week* or *Popular Science,* try running it together with a *.com* at the end: www.businessweek.com or www.popularscience.com (We're not guaranteeing that either of these addresses will work).

No go? Try hyphenating it — www.business-week.com or www.popular-science.com. Still no luck? Okay, think *abbreviations* and give it one more shot: www.busweek.com, www.popscience.com, www.popsci.com. Don't get carried away; be sure to stop while you can still see straight.

And don't be surprised if you don't come up with anything. (*Now* they tell me!) If you happen to hit it in the first couple of tries, using your intuition really is the fastest way. However, some magazines don't have their own separate addresses on the Web; instead, they're part of their publishers' domains. You'll find that especially true of some groups of trade publications, and journals published by professional associations.

Do a search

If the periodical's name is distinctive enough, or you can combine it with words from its *full* title such as *magazine* or *journal,* try running it through

GO, Excite, or another general search engine. *Online* alone isn't such a hot prospect for a search, but *Online Magazine* may get it.

Or try Yahoo!'s subject guide approach: Go to www.yahoo.com, click the News and Media category, and drill down through Magazines to the subject you want to cover. If you click the News subcategory, you find some of the usual suspects like *Time* and *U.S. News & World Report.* If you don't find the magazine you want right away, go to the main Yahoo! page and try typing in the periodical name in the search box.

Check a media mega-site

Several of the newspaper mega-sites we describe earlier in this chapter do a pretty decent job of tracking magazines online, too. If you have a particular publication in mind, check the Magazines link at **AJR NewsLink** (ajr.newslink.org) first.

Looking for a more obscure periodical? Try the **Electronic Journal Access Project** (www.coalliance.org/ejournal), produced by the Colorado Alliance of Research Libraries. This mega-site features several thousand electronic journals available only on the Web or via e-mail, as well as electronic versions of print publications. So you'll find listings for both *Dairy Today,* a print magazine that also posts articles on its Web page, and *DairyBiz,* a Web-only magazine for dairy professionals. (Got milk?) You can browse the E-Journal Access Project by title or by Library of Congress Subject Heading, or search the titles and descriptions of the journals by keyword.

Peer into print

One of the best sources we know for determining whether a publication is online *anywhere* is a print directory called *Fulltext Sources Online* (FSO). FSO covers not only magazines, but also newspapers, newsletters, wire services, and broadcast transcripts. Published twice a year, FSO tells you whether the publication is available on the Web or on a professional online service, such as Dialog, Dow Jones Interactive, or LEXIS-NEXIS. For professional services, it tells you the month and year of the earliest issue available. For Web editions, it indicates whether or not a free archive exists. FSO isn't cheap, but as a subscriber, you also get access to a private section of the publisher's Web site at www.infotoday.com where you can look up and link to publications that have free archives on the Web.

Search FOR and search OF

Say what? That's our succinct yet confusing way of introducing the **Electric Library** (www.elibrary.com), a hybrid site that allows you to locate publications and search them at the same time. The Electric Library collection includes newspapers, wire services, and hundreds of magazines, ranging from professional publications like *American Demographics* (a great example of how to make statistical data fun — we're not joking!), *China Business Review, Machine Design,* and *Training & Development,* to *Bicycling, Mother Jones,* and *Sports Illustrated.* Electric Library even has a collection of photographs, searchable by the words in the captions. For a complete listing, go to the Electric Library site (www.elibrary.com), click <u>Advanced Search</u> and then click <u>View Source Publications</u> for a complete list.

You can do a Boolean or natural language search of the Electric Library collection and sort the results by date or relevance. You can restrict your search by type of publication — magazines, books and reports, newspapers and newswires, and so on — and by date. You can search for specific elements or fields, such as author, title, or name of a particular publication. Click <u>More Info</u> and then <u>Detailed Help</u> to get more in-depth hints for effective searching.

Suppose you're interested in whether baby boomers are still influential in the marketplace. Type in that question verbatim — for example, **are baby boomers still influential in the marketplace** — and scroll down the screen to see the results. You'll get promising references from such sources as *Business Week, Futurist, Nightly Business Report,* and *Nation's Business.*

Electric Library is a subscription-based service — what we describe in Chapter 1 as a members-only site. You can try it out for free for a month. After that, the cost is $9.95 a month or $59.95 per year. This fee is a good value for the casual researcher, especially when you consider that you can easily spend $60 for a single search of a general periodical database on a professional online service. (We talk more about the professional online services in Chapter 9.)

Electric Library also offers a *business* edition (www.elibrary.com/ business) that includes company profiles, customized search screens to streamline your research on a particular industry, and market-share charts and graphs from major business news sources. (See Chapter 12 for more about business research.) Electric Library Business Edition is aimed at corporate customers and priced accordingly, so it's probably outside your budget if you're just a casual searcher.

Speaking of professional services, the Electric Library is a bridge — as both a directory and a searchable collection of periodicals — between the locator sites we've visited so far and the heavy-duty research databases we talk about in the very next section. Look out; here it comes.

Going deeper into the archives, part 2

So far, most of what we've described in this chapter is *information-gathering* — the kind you do every day when you leaf through the paper, catch the news on radio or TV, or burrow through the recycling pile looking for that article you meant to clip out last week. But none of those activities really qualifies as *research*. Random news-gathering and article lookups are very different from tracking down elusive or historical information in a vast collection of periodicals when you're not even sure of the source.

Go back and reread — assuming you read it in the first place — the section "Going deeper into the archives, part 1," about searching newspaper archives on professional online services, as opposed to searching them on the Web. If you haven't read it before, read it now. Everything we say there applies to magazines, journals, and other kinds of periodicals, too.

Professional online services enable you to

✔ Go way back in the archives — many years, instead of a few months.

✔ Cover dozens or even hundreds of publications at the same time — including many that you can't search elsewhere online.

✔ Use special system and database search features that you won't find on most Web sites.

✔ Search faster and more efficiently.

✔ Search publications that you not only don't subscribe to but may not even have *heard* of. Though you can do this through the Electric Library and some of the news-search mega-sites we've mentioned, services like Dialog, Dow Jones Interactive, and LEXIS-NEXIS provide a much broader and more complete selection.

In Chapters 11 and 12, we talk about tapping into databases of periodical literature in fields such as business, science, and engineering. If you're curious about the full range of publications available through any of these professional online services, visit their Web sites and browse through the database and source listings.

For general news, current events, and popular magazines, though, you can find the greatest concentration of hits in these databases:

✔ On **Dow Jones Interactive** (djinteractive.com) click Publications Library. Then click Major News and Business Publications on the following screen. To search periodicals in a particular industry, click revise publications. On the next screen, select Publications by Industry from the pull-down menu. Choose an industry grouping by clicking Add, or click the industry name to select individual titles within that group. To search more popular, mass-market or special-interest magazines, click revise publications, then click Type, and finally choose General Interest Publications from the pull-down menu. You can click Add to search the entire category, or scroll through the list of publications to select individual titles.

✔ On **Dialog** (www.dialogweb.com), search Magazine Database (File 47), Periodical Abstracts PlusText (File 484) or Readers' Guide Abstracts Full Text (File 141), individually or in combination. For broad coverage of companies, products, markets, and management issues, check Trade and Industry Database (File 148) and the other business databases we describe in Chapter 12. Dialog also offers a huge variety of magazines and journals in technical, scientific, and other specialized fields. You can scan the list of databases available on Dialog at no charge. Go to `library.dialog.com`, click <u>Bluesheets</u>, then click <u>Subjects</u>, and then select a general area you're interested in.

✔ On **LEXIS-NEXIS** (`www.lexis-nexis.com/ln.universe`), click <u>Search</u>, and then pull down the Source menu and select either All Magazines or All Newsletters.

Staying Current

In library-land, we used to call them SDIs. In Ronald Reagan's '80s (*1980s,* that is), those letters came to mean Strategic Defense Initiative. Imagine the confusion. But in a way, "strategic defense" is not that far off. The boring fact is that SDI originally stood for *Selective Dissemination of Information.* Ooo-eee; now *there's* a phrase you want to set to music and dance to. All it means is getting the right information to the right person at the right time — for defensive *or* preemptive use.

Today, we talk about *automatic updates, current awareness,* and the hyped-'til-it's-dead *push technology. Push* simply means that instead of having to seek out databases or Web sites and check them periodically for updated information, the information is automatically delivered — *pushed* — to you. As we said, *push* is not a new idea. Dialog's Alert feature, LEXIS-NEXIS' Eclipse, and Dow Jones' CustomClips have been providing push service for years.

E-mail is the easiest and most common form of push delivery. Hundreds of Web sites have jumped on the push bandwagon and now offer automatic delivery of new content — feature articles, columns, software, multimedia clips — filtered according to an interest profile that you set up in advance. You receive new pages, usually as HTML-coded documents, and you open and look at them — offline, if you prefer — in your browser's mail program or another HTML-compliant e-mail reader. For more information, you can connect and click through from the page that you've received to find additional content on the site.

Another delivery option involves logging onto a special area of the publisher's Web site where new information that matches your personalized profile is stored. Other options are even more sophisticated, notifying you through a window or other signal on your desktop when you have an update waiting — or even downloading new information automatically so that you don't have to go pick it up.

Sometimes the same site offers you a choice of delivery methods. Sites that provide push service — we still prefer SDI; it sounds so seriously geeky — usually advertise it prominently. They seldom use the word *push,* though; that sounds a little impolite, we guess. Instead, look for tip-off phrases such as *My Page, Personal Edition,* or *Custom News Alert.*

Newer versions of both Netscape Communicator and Internet Explorer let you define *channels* that automatically bring updated content from selected Web sites to your desktop for offline browsing.

The real trick to staying current is selecting a service that meets your needs — for both content and delivery method. In the next few sections, we outline just a few of the many options available to you.

The Daily Brief

The Daily Brief is nothing fancy. It's a plain ASCII text — no HTML — news page that shows up in e-mail every business day. Supported by sponsors and voluntary contributions, the Brief presents a concise summary of world, national, business, entertainment, and sports news. When we don't have time to read the paper, we rely on the Daily Brief. To subscribe, send a message to `subscribe-db@incinc.net`.

In-Box Direct

Netscape offers **In-Box Direct,** a one-stop subscription service for Web publications and other regularly updated sites. Each new issue comes to you in e-mail, as an HTML-encoded Web page, direct from the publisher's own site. You can get the following:

- ✔ Daily news summaries from ABC, CNN, and *The New York Times*
- ✔ Customized news from Excite and other services
- ✔ Sports and entertainment updates from CBS Sportsline, Disney.com, *People,* and *TV Guide*
- ✔ Travel discount bulletins
- ✔ Notices of sales and specials at Internet shopping sites
- ✔ Business and personal finance newsletters
- ✔ Computer news, reviews, and advice — including tips from Dummies Daily
- ✔ Reports from diverse online venues, such as parenting support groups, and gay and ethnic communities
- ✔ A selection of global content from Africa, Australia, Europe, Latin America, and Asia

To sign up for the service, go to `form.netscape.com/ibd`. Walk through the subscription process and select the sources and services that interest you. Within a few days — depending on their publication cycles — you'll start receiving your e-mail updates.

NewsPage

NewsEdge, a company formed by the merger of two pioneering Net-news delivery services, offers **NewsPage** (www.newspage.com), a subject-oriented approach to keeping current. You register at the site and then create your personalized edition by selecting from broad categories, such as Business, Internet, or General Interest. Within each category, you can add or delete specific topics, fine-tuning your profile to pick up mentions of particular industries and even individual companies. The information you receive is drawn from hundreds of sources, including local, national, and international newspapers and newswires; general business and specialized trade journals; and professional publications.

NewsHound

NewsHound (www.newshound.com) focuses on information from newspapers in the Knight Ridder chain, including the *San Jose Mercury News, Miami Herald, Philadelphia Inquirer,* and about ten others, plus wire service stories from AP, Reuters, Knight Ridder, and several business newswires. NewsHound is a sister of the NewsLibrary mega-site described earlier in this chapter. Neither one is a dog.

You can train your NewsHound to sniff out predefined topics or keywords. Unlike most other news update services, NewsHound actually lets you construct a detailed search strategy by using your own search terms, which produces more focused results than simply checking off categories and topics.

After you've created your Hound profile, NewsHound scours the Net on a regular basis and brings back stories for you to look at. You can do so by logging on to your own private area of the NewsHound site. Or you can take delivery in e-mail — either HTML or plain text. A sum of $7.95 a month or $59.95 a year buys you up to five separate Hounds, with no limit on the number of stories NewsHound can retrieve.

Northern Light Search Alert

The **Northern Light** (www.northernlight.com) search engine covers both the Web and a Special Collection of articles from magazines, newspapers, wire services, and other published material. Northern Light's Search Alert feature notifies you whenever items are added to the Special Collection or changes are made to Web sites that meet your search profile. To set up a Search Alert, click <u>Alerts</u> at the main Northern Light Web page and then click <u>Create New Alert</u>. Enter your search words, give the search a name, and click <u>Save Alert</u>. When new items are added to Northern Light, you'll receive an e-mail alerting you to a URL where you can browse and read the updated information. Search Alerts are free; you pay Northern Light's per-article charge if you want to view the full text of a Special Collection document. See Chapter 3 for more about Northern Light.

My Yahoo!

Okay, so we'll share — it's *your* Yahoo!, too. **My Yahoo!** is the personalized news page on Yahoo! (www.yahoo.com). Click the <u>My</u> button or click <u>Personalize</u> to set up what Yahoo! calls My Front Page. You can select the news sources or links you want; the choices range from Business News and New Movie Releases to Health Tips, the Ski Report, and a personalized calendar. News sources include Reuters, AP, National Public Radio, ABC News, and a number of daily newspapers from the United States and around the world. Some of these sources aren't obvious from the set-up page, but you can dig down and find them. Here's how:

1. **Click <u>Personalize Content</u>.**

2. **Click <u>Headline News</u> to select it as one of your modules.**

3. **When you're done making your selections, click <u>Finished</u>.**

   You return to the My Yahoo! menu.

4. **Click the <u>Edit</u> link next to the Front Page Headlines. You can then select categories and individual news sources to include in My Yahoo!**

You can even personalize the color scheme of the page and the greeting at the top of the My Yahoo! page; Mary Ellen's My Yahoo! now says *Welcome, alien,* but she changes it every few weeks.

Other news channels

Most of the major search engines (which we describe in more detail in Chapter 3) provide some kind of customized news service, usually labeled my.[whatever the site is] — for example, my.lycos.com, my.excite.com, my.netscape.com, and so on. Many of them offer similar sources in similar layouts: You have your stock quotes, you have your weather, you have your headline news. How to choose? Go with the personalized news service associated with the search engine you like the most, or one with a format you find agreeable, or one that lets you customize it the way you like.

CNN is the only major news source that offers its own personalized news page. And yes, you guessed it — the URL is my.cnn.com. After you've registered, you can select the kind of news you want to see. The choices extend to what baseball teams you care about, whether you want to read about disasters around the world, whether you want to track industries such as banking or aviation, and whether you want some comics along with your serious news. What's unusual about myCnn.com is that although it's produced by a news source, it includes news from other sources as well — Reuters, AP, and IDG Net.

The 'Zine Scene: New Sources for News and Information

Not all online publications are replicas or special editions of something that first appeared in print. The Net has given rise to thousands of new periodicals that have no counterparts in the ink-and-paper world. These online-only productions are often referred to as electronic magazines, e-zines, or just *'zines*.

Net publishing is cheap, especially compared with what it takes to reach a mass audience in print. Anyone with an opinion to express or a philosophy to further can rent server space and put a few Web pages out there for all the world to see. The Net is democratic that way, and much of its self-published content is refreshing, if not always reliable.

These three sites give you a taste of the alternative press, Net-style:

✔ **The Drudge Report** (www.drudgereport.com) is notorious for breaking hot political stories that may not always be firmly based in fact. Matt Drudge — that's his real name, apparently — does his own reporting, and also provides links to other popular columnists and commentators around the Web. He also links to an extensive list of wire services, major newspapers, and news-and-analysis magazines. Drudge is worth bookmarking for his outrageousness and occasionally valid scoops; his links to other top media sources are a bonus.

✔ **Salon** (www.salonmagazine.com) features solid background reporting by professional journalists on issues currently in the news, plus incisive analyses of the media itself and how it covers the issues. Regular columnists; feature articles; book, theater, and music reviews; and letters from readers all contribute to a substantial package that feels very much like a *real* magazine. We subscribe to Salon's e-mail updates so that we always know what's new on the site.

✔ **The Onion** (www.theonion.com) is one of our guilty pleasures. Okay, you *can* subscribe to it in print — and we do — but The Onion really made its reputation online. These sample news headlines give you a hint of what The Onion is like:

- "U.S. Ambassador To Bulungi Suspected Of Making Country Up"

- "Microsoft Patents Ones and Zeros"

- "Area Twenty-something Disillusioned With Disillusionment"

- "Just-Opened Factory To Create 250 New Jobs, 170 New Cancer Cases"

Help — we can't stop! It's just too . . . delicious. Yes, The Onion is outrageous, irreverent, and occasionally offensive. The Onion is our favorite antidote when *real* world news gets to be too much.

Breaking news on the Net

The Internet is a global network. People are online 24 hours a day, seven days a week, exchanging news and information. Although some national governments have made efforts to control the flow of information into and out of their countries, the Internet is essentially a borderless network; when something big develops anywhere in the world — a war, a mass rebellion, a natural disaster — word travels around the Net almost instantaneously. During the Chinese uprising in Tiananmen Square, the Persian Gulf War, and the bombings in Kosovo, the first news reports, and some of the best and most immediate continuing on-the-scene coverage, were carried over the Internet. Word spread, worldwide, in minutes. Newsgroups picked up early reports and promulgated them around the Internet. By the time conventional print and broadcast media got hold of the story, it was old news to many Net denizens.

Similar phenomena can happen locally, too. Northern California, where Reva lives, had a pretty rough time of it several years ago, with fires, earthquakes, and floods. She found that she could log on to The WELL, her regional online community, and get the equivalent of a standup reporter on the scene — *many* reporters, in fact, each with a unique perspective on what was going on.

No way can we anticipate what may happen or tell you where you should be standing — figuratively speaking — when disaster strikes. If a stock market crash is disastrous news for you, you can log on to the Motley Fool or one of the investment newsgroups we mention in Chapter 12. If a natural disaster occurs, a local online pub — The WELL is that kind of hangout for us — is the logical place for folks to gather. Wars and civic disturbances play out in political newsgroups and forums all over the world.

The message is: When big news happens, don't just turn on your radio or TV. Try logging on to the Net and get the full, chaotic, unedited story, as it's unfolding. And come to your own conclusion about what's really going on.

Chapter 14

Life Choices

*O*ne of the big plusses of the Net — and especially the Web — is the way that it empowers all of us to gather information that we need to make important decisions in our work, school, and personal lives. But there's a downside: You can burn up a lot of time, and sometimes money, too, by picking the wrong research tool, starting with a faulty assumption, or overlooking some obvious alternatives. You can avoid some of this online agony by *planning*.

If you haven't read Chapter 2, look at it now. Chapter 2 provides a mental map of the entire online world, the variety of tools available, and how to use those tools, whether solo or in combination. The chapter discusses how professional researchers analyze a research project before they even go online, how they move from one approach to another, and how they evaluate their results.

In this chapter, we walk you through some familiar information-seeking scenarios, such as investigating college opportunities, buying a new car, and planning a vacation. If our examples don't turn you on, feel free to substitute your own. We're giving you a sketch, not a detailed blueprint. This chapter is about getting the feel of an actual research project, and it will mean more to you if you're really *interested* in what you're hunting for online.

Choosing a College

Here's the premise: You're a high school junior looking for a college to attend. You don't want to be too far from home, and you're looking for a strong pre-med program. (Here's where you sub in your own choices — *you want it to be as far away from home as possible,* and you want to study *international relations* or *English lit* or *mechanical engineering* — whatever.)

Any good high school guidance counselor has printed directories and other resources that can help you. But you can get a jump on planning your future by searching for online directories and lists of colleges and universities, identifying schools that lie within your geographic range, and determining which of them offer good pre-med programs. You can also flip the equation on its head by starting with the profession that you want to enter, and searching for recommended schools and programs from that angle.

Unless your name is Trump or Gates, you may also want to find out about sources of financial aid. And you probably want to get a sense of campus culture — what the school is like, whether it's large or small, urban or rural, the mix of students, the activities, the clubs, and the facilities that are available.

Finding college and university directories

To locate college and university directories, you can

✔ Browse through a reference collection (see Chapter 7) like the **Internet Public Library** (www.ipl.org/ref) to find educational directories and mega-sites that link to a variety of schools and colleges.

✔ Start with a subject catalog like **Yahoo!** (www.yahoo.com) and a broad main-page category, such as Education: Colleges and Universities. You can use Yahoo!'s <u>College Search</u> feature (features.yahoo.com/college/search.html) to look for a school by name, or use the multipart search form to screen by criteria, such as location, major, size, and even how "wired" it is, computer-wise.

✔ Go directly to a site or database that you already know does the job, such as the online edition of **Peterson's Directory of Colleges and Universities** (www.petersons.com). Peterson's lets you search for specific programs or schools in a certain location, get detailed information on particular institutions, and perform side-by-side comparisons. You can request additional info from some schools, and even apply online, directly from the Peterson's Web site.

Following professional pointers

A trade group or professional association can be an excellent shortcut for collecting authoritative information about a particular occupation or professional pursuit. Although some organizations restrict their services to members only, many offer basic information — cheap or free for the asking — about the profession and how to prepare for it. You can find trade groups for everything from pickle packers to cosmetologists to — yes, indeedy — the medical profession. Not all organizations are online, so you may have to resort to phoning or writing a letter. You do remember how to do that, don't you?

✔ Take a vote among research pros, and you'll find that one of their most indispensable tools, both online and in print, is the *Encyclopedia of Associations,* also known as *Associations Unlimited.* The database version is on professional online services such as Dialog and LEXIS-NEXIS. Or you can call or visit your local library reference desk and ask them to check their listings in the print edition of the *Encyclopedia.*

✔ Another approach is to point your browser to the **Internet Public Library** (www.ipl.org/ref) and click the <u>Associations</u> link, or navigate directly to www.ipl.org/ref/AON. Figure 14-1 illustrates just a portion of the Associations on the Net subject category listing. You can also search the entire listing by keyword, or browse it alphabetically if you know the name of the group.

For pre-med, the American Medical Association seems a logical first choice. Click the name of the organization in the Internet Public Library listing, or go directly to www.ama-assn.org. (In case you're wondering, the American Marketing Association snapped up www.ama.org first. That figures.) After you reach the AMA site, point your cursor at <u>Ethics, Education, Science, Accreditation</u> and then choose <u>Medical Education</u> from the drop-down menu. Most of the information in the Medical Education section focuses on graduate-level medical schools (you can bookmark that for later). But the Medical Schools subsection includes a link to something called the **LCME** (www.lcme.org), which turns out to be the AMA's Liaison Committee on Medical Education. Again, the site is geared mostly toward graduate study, but click <u>Contacting the LCME</u> and *voilà:* Scrolling down the page, you see an Assistant Director for Undergraduate Medical Education, with a handy link to her e-mail address. Even if she can't help you, she may be able to tell you who can.

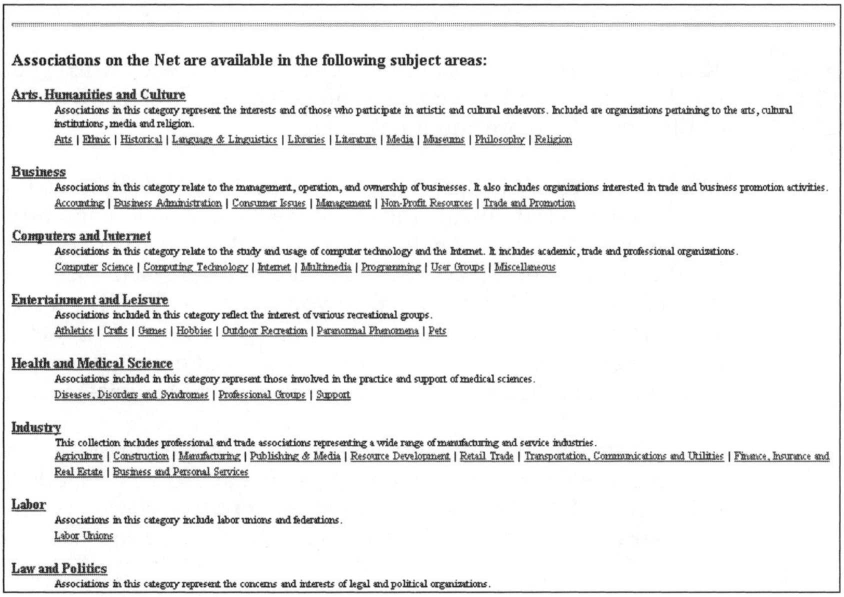

Figure 14-1:
Associations
on the Net.

Associations on the Net are available in the following subject areas:

Arts, Humanities and Culture
Associations in this category represent the interests and of those who participate in artistic and cultural endeavors. Included are organizations pertaining to the arts, cultural institutions, media and religion.
Arts | Ethnic | Historical | Language & Linguistics | Libraries | Literature | Media | Museums | Philosophy | Religion

Business
Associations in this category relate to the management, operation, and ownership of businesses. It also includes organizations interested in trade and business promotion activities.
Accounting | Business Administration | Consumer Issues | Management | Non-Profit Resources | Trade and Promotion

Computers and Internet
Associations in this category relate to the study and usage of computer technology and the Internet. It includes academic, trade and professional organizations.
Computer Science | Computing Technology | Internet | Multimedia | Programming | User Groups | Miscellaneous

Entertainment and Leisure
Associations included in this category reflect the interest of various recreational groups.
Athletics | Crafts | Games | Hobbies | Outdoor Recreation | Paranormal Phenomena | Pets

Health and Medical Science
Associations included in this category represent those involved in the practice and support of medical sciences.
Diseases, Disorders and Syndromes | Professional Groups | Support

Industry
This collection includes professional and trade associations representing a wide range of manufacturing and service industries.
Agriculture | Construction | Manufacturing | Publishing & Media | Resource Development | Retail Trade | Transportation, Communications and Utilities | Finance, Insurance and Real Estate | Business and Personal Services

Labor
Associations in this category include labor unions and federations.
Labor Unions

Law and Politics
Associations in this category represent the concerns and interests of legal and political organizations.

You may have to poke around to find the information you want — especially at Web sites that are set up for the benefit of a certain group and not the Net-public at large. Menu choices and links aren't always obvious. Don't give up too soon.

What's up, pre-doc?

Okay, we have some good leads on pre-med programs. But choosing a college — let alone a career — takes more than just a list of schools. What's the curriculum like? Can you get financial aid? Is there life after Organic Chemistry 101?

We started out with a very controlled and orderly approach, limiting our search to directories of higher education and the American Medical Association Web page. After we identify some institutions that we may consider favoring with our application — that's the way college admissions work, right? — we can go to their Web sites and get the details on enrollment, courses, and any special requirements. We can also find out about fun stuff, such as clubs, college traditions, special events, and what the off-campus environment has to offer.

To locate the Web site of a particular college or university, you can check the **American Universities** listing (www.clas.ufl.edu/CLAS/american-universities.html) or **College and University Home Pages** (www.mit.edu: 8001/people/cdemello/univ.html). The latter site hasn't been updated in a while, but colleges don't change their Web addresses — or their real-world ones — that often. Or try guesswork to short-circuit your quest: www.*nameofschool*.edu may take you directly to your goal.

Ask Jeeves (www.ask.com) provides some useful leads when you ask a question like "Where can I find college and university directories or Web sites?" See Chapter 3 for more about Ask Jeeves.

But our researcher's instincts tell us that useful information on the pre-med life is bound to exist outside the official realm of colleges and professional associations. Throw caution to the winds — it's time to fire up a search engine or two. Entering terms like *pre-med* or *pre-medical* (use whatever future career vision happens to float your boat) in Yahoo! or a search engine such as AltaVista, HotBot, or Excite, turns up a wealth of resources. Results include not only pointers to specific schools, but more general information, too, on curricula, scholarships, and medical school admissions.

We also discover dozens of pre-med information clearinghouses, tutoring ser-vices, and student support groups at particular schools, including the pre-med chapter of the **American Medical Student Association** (www.amsa.org) and other organizations at Hunter College (premed.edu/home.html), and

Emory University's Pre-Med Search & Rescue Page (www.emory.edu/CAREER/Premed). Search and *rescue?* That tells us something about our intended major — maybe more than we want to know.

Feeling listless?

Liszt (www.lizst.com), the finding aid for online mailing lists (see Chapter 10), shows several pre-med lists. But the lists are all restricted to students at particular institutions. Depending on your field of interest, you may have more luck with Liszt. It's worth a try.

We have better luck with newsgroups. We click Usenet newsgroups directory on the main Liszt Web page and then type *pre-medical* in the search box. We don't find any groups with *pre-medical* in their name, but the results page presents us with several alternative sites and ways to search. We try the Liszt/Deja News search form, which searches the content of newsgroup posts, not just the names of the groups themselves. We come up with several references to the misc.education.medical newsgroup. In a message headed "Re: Good colleges," someone mentions *The Gourman Report,* which reputedly publishes a list of the top 25 pre-med programs in the U.S. Sounds like exactly what we're looking for — not just a list, but some value judgment as well. Our next step is to plug the phrase *Gourman Report* into a search engine. Voilà: We find several references with titles such as Gourman Report Medical School Rankings — and one more click takes us directly to a list of outstanding schools. The prognosis looks pretty good.

Lessons learned

So maybe you can't picture yourself in a white lab coat, stethoscope at the ready. At this point, you may be thanking your stars that you're way past, or nowhere near, that mix of terror and anticipation that is the college admissions process. (Which envelope will it be — the thick, or the thin? We still break out into a cold sweat at the thought.)

You can make good grades, regardless of your intended major, by paying attention to what our brief excursion into higher education has taught us, research-wise:

✔ Start out focused.

✔ Try different approaches.

✔ Go beyond the obvious.

✔ Don't quit too soon; you can never tell when you may hit paydirt.

Finding a Job

The Net is stocked with resources for job hunters. We don't know what, if anything, this says about the employment status, or the work satisfaction level, of people who hang out online.

The old saying, "it's not *what* you know; it's *who* you know," is as true in cyberspace as it is in the real world. (If you want to get fussy, it's not *who* you know; it's *whom* you know.) Some of the best positions are never advertised; prospects emerge as you schmooze with your peers and potential colleagues in newsgroups, mailing lists, and other online forums. As these people get to know you, your background, and your skills, they sometimes approach you with offers — even if you're not marketing yourself directly. Over the years, we've gotten more writing, consulting, and research assignments than we can count through our participation in various online venues.

But the networking approach takes time. Suppose you're in a hurry? Perhaps you're just entering the job market, or hoping to change careers? The Net offers you a choice of career-advancing tactics:

✔ Visit job boards with the most listings and the greatest variety of occupations. Heavily-trafficked sites draw more job seekers and more prospective employers. Job boards like the ones we describe in the next section have sheer numbers on their side, plus some useful tips on career planning, resume writing, and job-hunting tactics.

✔ Go to job listing sites that specialize in specific careers or disciplines, or that cover your current or desired geographic area. These include newsgroups (see Chapter 10) as well as job boards on the Web.

✔ Go directly to the Web sites of companies that you might want to work for. Prospective employers often post hiring notices and specific job opportunities on their sites. Sometimes you can even apply, or request further information, right at the site.

Local newsgroups can be fine sources of employment listings, especially if you're looking for a high-tech position in a technology hotbed such as the San Francisco Bay area, Seattle, or Austin. See Chapter 10 for details on using **Lizst** (www.liszt.com) and **RemarQ** (www.remarq.com) to locate newsgroups in a particular area of interest. As Figure 14-2 shows, the key word here is *jobs*.

We're not going to take you through a hypothetical job hunt for a couple of reasons:

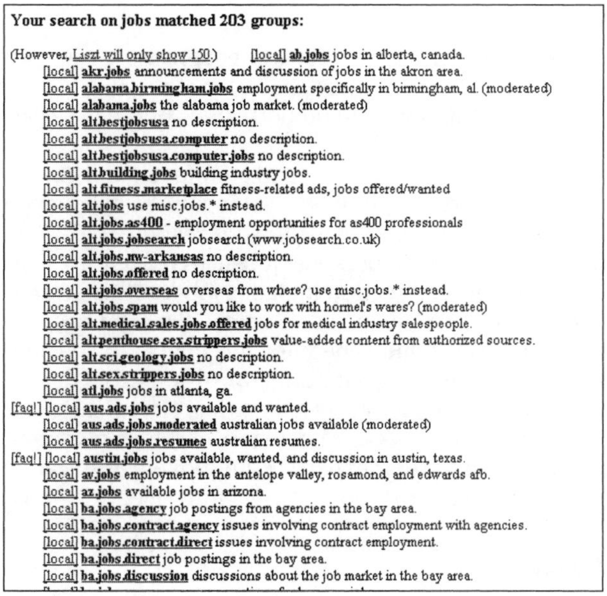
Your search on jobs matched 203 groups:

(However, Liszt will only show 150.) [local] **ab.jobs** jobs in alberta, canada.
[local] **akr.jobs** announcements and discussion of jobs in the akron area.
[local] **alabama.birmingham.jobs** employment specifically in birmingham, al. (moderated)
[local] **alabama.jobs** the alabama job market. (moderated)
[local] **alt.bestjobsusa** no description.
[local] **alt.bestjobsusa.computer** no description.
[local] **alt.bestjobsusa.computer.jobs** no description.
[local] **alt.building.jobs** building industry jobs.
[local] **alt.fitness.marketplace** fitness-related ads, jobs offered/wanted
[local] **alt.jobs** use misc.jobs.* instead.
[local] **alt.jobs.as400** - employment opportunities for as400 professionals
[local] **alt.jobs.jobsearch** jobsearch (www.jobsearch.co.uk)
[local] **alt.jobs.nw-arkansas** no description.
[local] **alt.jobs.offered** no description.
[local] **alt.jobs.overseas** overseas from where? use misc.jobs.* instead.
[local] **alt.jobs.spam** would you like to work with hormel's wares? (moderated)
[local] **alt.medical.sales.jobs.offered** jobs for medical industry salespeople.
[local] **alt.penthouse.sex.strippers.jobs** value-added content from authorized sources.
[local] **alt.sci.geology.jobs** no description.
[local] **alt.sex.strippers.jobs** no description.
[local] **atl.jobs** jobs in atlanta, ga.
[faq!] [local] **aus.ads.jobs** jobs available and wanted.
[local] **aus.ads.jobs.moderated** australian jobs available (moderated)
[local] **aus.ads.jobs.resumes** australian resumes.
[faq!] [local] **austin.jobs** jobs available, wanted, and discussion in austin, texas.
[local] **av.jobs** employment in the antelope valley, rosamond, and edwards afb.
[local] **az.jobs** available jobs in arizona.
[local] **ba.jobs.agency** job postings from agencies in the bay area.
[local] **ba.jobs.contract.agency** issues involving contract employment with agencies.
[local] **ba.jobs.contract.direct** issues involving contract employment.
[local] **ba.jobs.direct** job postings in the bay area.
[local] **ba.jobs.discussion** discussions about the job market in the bay area.

Figure 14-2: Job-related newsgroups found by Liszt.

- Job listings on the Net are like classified ads in the newspaper. Whether you're looking for an entry-level position at a local fast-food restaurant or a contract engineering job in Silicon Valley, the process is similar. You scan the Help Wanted category that matches your intended job most closely, you read the job descriptions, and you contact your potential employer or the agency that placed the ad. It's not that different online.
- Many professions have their own job placement centers or clearinghouses. Often, such services are limited to members only, or to certified or accredited practitioners. For some examples, check out the **Modern Language Association's Job Information List** at `www.mla.org`, the **Society of Competitive Intelligence Professionals' Job Marketplace** at `www.scip.org`, or the **American Marketing Association's Career Center** at `www.ama.org`. If you're looking for a high-level management or technical position, this approach — along with good old-fashioned networking and relationship building over time — may be your best bet.

Job boards

The name reminds us of the ads pinned to the bulletin board down by the local market or community center: You know — "Help wanted: Reliable teenager to mow lawn, walk dog, water houseplants. $2/hour." Thanks to the magic of the electronic medium, online job boards are a lot more sophisticated than that — but almost as easy to use. The Net boasts hundreds of help-wanted sites. Some sites are comprehensive while others focus on particular professions or parts of the world.

Monster.com

Figure 14-3 shows just the tip of the **Monster.com** iceberg (`www.monster. com`). Populated with cartoony critters that peer at us from every page, Monster.com offers job-hunting help on both sides of the interview desk.

You can find job openings by keyword, field, employer, and geographic location, worldwide. You can research potential employers by company name or location. As a registered user, you can add your resume to the Monster.com searchable database, or enlist a personal job-search agent to search on your behalf. The Career Resources section includes job-hunting strategies and tactics, pointers to hot occupations (we don't mean fire fighting), online talent auctions, discussion forums and scheduled live chats, advice on resume writing, interviewing, and — in case that perfect position turns out to be in Kansas, Kankakee, or Kuala Lumpur — relocating. Healthcare, high tech, and human resources professionals get a headstart in the employment race with special sections targeted to their expertise. Employers, too, can register, search resumes on file, and post job openings for the entire Web to see.

Other boardly resources

JobStar (`www.jobstar.org`) is a California-based job board that features solid advice, regardless of where you're located, about tapping into the *hidden* job market (remember — many of the best jobs never hit the want ads). The site offers resume tips and links to both general salary surveys and profession-specific surveys, like What Lawyers Earn. JobStar features a real-life information professional, code-named Electra, who provides personal guidance for specific job-hunting dilemmas.

Figure 14-3:
Searching for jobs on Monster. com.

Both **Career Mosaic** (www.careermosaic.com) and **Hotjobs.com** (www.hotjobs.com) let you channel your job search into broad subject areas, such as human resources, healthcare, and high-tech. You can also search for jobs by keyword, type of position, company name, and location.

The subject catalog approach (see Chapter 5) is great for unearthing other job boards, both general-purpose and specialized. Check Yahoo!'s <u>Business and Economy:Employment: Jobs</u> category for dozens of possible starting points. The **Excite** Careers channel (www.excite.com/careers) offers an excellent, though less comprehensive, list, plus its own job-classifieds search feature. Subject catalogs like Yahoo! and Excite, for example, can lead you to resources geared toward aviation and aerospace workers, human resources professionals, and folks who live or want to work in Australia, Thailand, or anywhere overseas. (You can find plenty of listings for North America, too, in case that happens to be overseas for you.)

Going to the source

Job boards are gaining in popularity among both employers and hopeful applicants, but not all companies subscribe to or are even aware of them. If you want to work for a particular firm, you have nothing to lose — and potentially, a lot to gain — by taking the direct approach. Aim your browser straight for that company's Web site — if they haven't nailed a no-brainer URL like www.ibm.com, you can usually locate them by running the company name through your favorite search engine — and look for a link labeled Job Opportunities, Employment, or the ever-so-promising Join Us!

Even Net-savvy firms may not consider it in their best interests to list their job openings worldwide; sometimes, as Chapter 12 points out, the nature and extent of a company's job postings can inadvertently provide competitors with valuable clues about its future plans.

Real-world placement services and employment recruiting firms are, like other profit-making ventures, well-represented on the Web. You can find them the same way you do job boards, by using the subject catalog approach. When you deal with a placement service or recruiting firm, you enter into a third-party contract with a company whose mission then becomes to find you a suitable position. Depending on the type of job and the employer, you may have to pay a fee, often a percentage of your salary for a given period.

Buying a Car

Both of us are old Bug-heads. Mary Ellen still drives a classic 1968 VW microbus, and Reva had a '66 Beetle, and a '72 with a rebuilt engine that . . . well, we'd better not get into the stories. But we were intrigued from the moment that we heard that Volkswagen was introducing a new model inspired by the old Beetles. Now that they've been out for a while, we're curious about the consumer response. Where can we go to gather more information?

Browsing car and consumer magazines

In the old days, we would start by going to the library and looking at magazines like *Consumer Reports, Motor Trend, Road & Track,* and *Car and Driver.* Today, we can search the electronic editions of all four magazines in a variety of online venues, including professional online services such as Dialog and LEXIS-NEXIS (see Chapter 9).

One of the best ways to determine what publications are online, on or off the Web, is a directory called *Fulltext Sources Online.* Chapter 13 describes this resource as well as some other ways to locate electronic editions of magazines and other periodicals.

Consumer Reports

The Web version of the familiar guide to sensible consumerism, **Consumer Reports** (www.consumerreports.org), reserves most of its detailed ratings and reviews for registered subscribers to the site. We can do a *model* search on the Beetle, which turns up several promising-sounding report titles, such as "VW Beetle: Then and Now." But we can't read the actual text of any of the reports unless we subscribe. Considering the size of the purchase we're contemplating, we figure that it's worth $3.95 to sign up for a month. After we sign up, we get a stack of reports and comparisons that, if we printed them all, would barely fit in the back seat of a Beetle (old or new). Well, we exaggerate, but still.

Consumer Reports is a gated site (see Chapter 9 for more on gated sites and why you should know about them). Most of its content is only available to people who register and agree to pay a fee. The reports we found would not have turned up in a general search of the Web.

Road & Track and its cruisin' cousins

We no longer have to drive to the library to check out three leading car magazines: **Road & Track, Motor Trend,** and **Car and Driver.** All have thoughtfully set up shop on the information superhighway. (Hey, give us a break; at least the metaphor is appropriate when we're doing automotive research.) We plug the keyword *beetle* into the search form at www.roadandtrack.com and pull up a couple of dozen stories, of which six or so focus heavily on the reincarnated Bug. We get similar results at *Car and Driver* (www.caranddriver.com) and *Motor Trend* (www.motortrend.com), including the information that the new Beetle was the latter magazine's pick for Import of the Year.

Life in the fast lane, yeaah. . . .

Searching the obvious sources described in the last two sections gives us what we need to satisfy our curiosity about the new VW Beetle. But if we really want to do a thorough job of collecting background articles and reviews, going from publication to publication on the Web might take all day.

Instead, we can plug a simple search statement like _Volkswagen near Beetle_ — in whatever form the specific online service requires — into Dialog's Magazine Database, the General News or Industry News search forms in LEXIS-NEXIS Universe, or Dow Jones Interactive's Major News and Business Publications. In fact, we _did_ just that — and in less than a minute, we had several dozen articles from newspapers and magazines. Some of these periodicals, such as _Time, The New York Times, AutoWeek,_ and _Automotive News,_ are sources that we may not have thought to search on the Web, and that a general Web search engine like AltaVista, HotBot, or Excite wouldn't have turned up. Some periodicals are only available through a subscription-based online service and not directly on the Web at all.

Chapter 9 tells you more than you ever thought you needed to know about professional online services, such as the aforementioned Dialog, Dow Jones, and LEXIS-NEXIS, including their ability to aggregate vast amounts of data that you can search with a single, precisely-targeted search statement. Our brief flirtation with the new Beetle illustrates the time-versus-money tradeoff that sometimes makes these heavy-duty database services worth the added effort and expense.

Northern Light's Special Collection (www.nlsearch.com) offers some of the same advantages of the professional online services, including the ability to search hundreds of periodicals at the same time. See Chapter 3 for more about Northern Light.

Getting serious

Suppose we really _were_ in the market for a new car? Two names very familiar to car buffs — _Edmund's_ and _Kelley Blue Book_ — have excellent Web sites packed with all the specs, road tests, ratings, and authoritative advice we may need.

> ✔ **Edmund's** (www.edmunds.com) publishes new and used vehicle price guides and reviews, complete with performance specs and other statistical data, and lists of standard and optional equipment. We click <u>New Cars</u>, then <u>Volkswagen</u> and <u>New Beetle</u>, and finally on the model(s) we're interested in.

✔ The **Kelley Blue Book** (www.kbb.com) site also features detailed pricing information for both new and used vehicles, plus an enlightening and occasionally amusing FAQ, or Frequently Asked Questions list. Kelley's price calculations account for regional variations (as in *Prices slightly higher west of Rockies*), optional equipment and, for used cars, overall condition.

On the Kelley site, we click <u>New Car Pricing</u> and then supply our zip codes (one at a time, of course). Next we click <u>Category</u> (All Cars, Luxury Cars, and Vans are some of the options). From the resulting list, we click <u>Volkswagen</u>, and then the current year's New Beetle, and finally the super-turbo model with the biggest engine. (Hey, why not? This is all fantasy, remember. We're joined at the seatbelt to our present cars.)

If either of us wanted to sell our faithful old vehicles — no chance of that, we repeat, *no* chance — we could check its dealer or private resale value by factoring in its condition, optional equipment, and market prices in our area.

We can also check to see if anyone's grown tired of their nouveau Bug, and what it may cost us used. We may save a few thousand bucks. Unless, of course, the New Beetle has become a collector's item, like the original Beetles are now.

Asking around

When it comes to cars, everybody's an expert, or thinks they are. We have a friend who's an encyclopedia of automotive lore — and she doesn't even drive. Before you buy, check out online discussion areas, such as

✔ Edmund's Town Hall, where drivers can ask questions or sound off about their favorite and least-favorite makes and models

✔ Newsgroups such as rec.autos and alt.autos (don't overlook subgroups in the hierarchy, such as rec.autos.marketplace and rec.autos.misc)

✔ CompuServe's Car Club Channel and Automotive Forum, America Online's Auto Center and Automotive Message Boards, and the Cars conference on The WELL

See Chapter 10 for more about participating in online discussion groups.

Doing the deal

If you're not the kind of car buyer who needs to kick the tires and sniff the upholstery before making a commitment — personally, we think *all* serious relationships require at least some hands-on investigation — you can actually negotiate the transaction online (at least up to the sign-on-the-dotted-line stage). Kelley's <u>Buy a Car</u> section leads you to dealers in your area and on the Web. Edmunds offers links to automobile locating and purchasing services, too.

You can also check one of the Web-based auto mega-sites (that's fun to say), such as **Autobytel.com** or **Autoweb.com** — you can probably guess the URLs — where you can research and spec out your purchase. Both give you a firm price quote and put you in touch with a dealer in your area.

As for our brief flirtation with the New Beetle, we blame . . . nostalgia. The car is awfully cute, especially if your taste runs to funky, bulbous little automobiles. But our research revealed — uh oh — plastic fenders. You can't just hammer the dings out of those, and we don't think we'd get away with painting a giant Band-Aid on 'em like we used to in the old days. Nah, we're going to stick with our old faithfuls. We were only taking a test drive, honest. The Vee-Dub is just a good friend. Really.

Lessons learned, continued

We find it amazing that we can actually buy a car online, not just research the possibilities. Our excursion into virtual-car-showroom-land also reminded us of some basic research truths:

- ✔ Focus on publications that you know have covered your subject in the past.
- ✔ For comprehensive, in-depth research, remember the professional online services and other *aggregator* sites.
- ✔ Tap into personal experience in online discussion forums.

Planning a Vacation

If you have any money left in your budget after buying a car, how about spending it on a major trip? Sure, that makes sense. Have we mentioned that *Indulgence* is our middle name?

Travel is big business on the Net, to the point where good travel agents are hurting because so many people have taken the planning and booking into their own hands. We like to do the research ourselves and then have our travel agent handle the details. That way, we know that we'll get the kind of experience we want, and she'll still get her commission.

It'll be so nice when it's finished: Remodeling a house online

The Web is full of home pages. No, wait. The Web is full of resources for people who want to buy, build, or remodel a home. We don't have the space to devote a full section to them here (and don't tell us to build a new wing for them, smart one). But we want to tell you a story about how, even before the Web began, a single small corner of the online world helped Reva and her sweetie remodel their house. This is the addition that The WELL built.

Reva and Jerry had decided that, because her home office had taken over the spare bedroom, they really needed more space. They started shopping around for a contractor to build a new master bedroom and bath. One of the places they looked was online, on The WELL, the virtual community (see Chapter 10) that they had joined a couple of years before.

The host of The WELL's Design conference heard about their quest — actually, he happened to be a contractor who submitted a bid on the job — and suggested that they start a topic, or discussion thread, in his conference. They did. They called the topic "Diary of a remodel: It'll be so nice when it's finished."

Reva and Jerry started posting to the conference even before they got their building permit. And one or both of them added at least one new message just about every day. Denizens of the Design conference responded, offering helpful suggestions, reality checks, and moral support throughout the process. Word spread in the rest of The WELL; people who didn't normally read Design but who had some interest or expertise in home construction joined the conference in order to contribute to the discussion.

Reva and Jerry got suggestions from architects, carpenters, and other homeowners who'd gone through it themselves — and lived. They heard from electricians, insulation gurus, and floor-finishing specialists. These folks offered alternatives, asked intelligent questions, and gave numerous assurances that the contractor knew what he was doing and that he wasn't trying to short-cut or rip them off. Nobody tried to sell their own services; nobody acted like a know-it-all. People were there to help.

The project took almost 5 months. Reva and Jerry lived on site, camping out in Reva's tiny office the entire time. But in the end, Reva and Jerry survived thanks to their highly-developed sense of the absurd and the support they had received from their unseen helpers on The WELL. And when it was all done, they had an addition-warming party and invited not only their real-world friends and neighbors, but everyone who'd participated in the Design conference discussion. Reva and Jerry met many of their online friends and supporters for the first time when these helpful people walked through the door of their newly remodeled house.

It *was* nice. But, best of all, it was *finished*.

Your idea of a dream vacation may be climbing in the Himalayas, an eco-tourist trek through a South American rain forest, or exploring the quaint cobbled streets of Paris, Amsterdam, or Rome. For us, a holiday destination has to meet one requirement — *warmth*. One traveler's lifetime goal may be another's ultimate nightmare — which is a good thing, or we'd all end up in the same place, and a lot of us would have trouble finding somewhere to sleep. But whether the idea of a Caribbean cruise appeals to you personally or not, we can probably get you to agree that it qualifies as the ultimate get-away-from-it-all vacation. So that's our starting point for exploring online resources for travel research. If the thought of cruising makes you seasick, you know what to do.

Caribbean cruise. To a researcher, that phrase immediately implies two things: *Caribbean* and *cruise.* See, you're beginning to think like a researcher, too. What we mean is, you've got two equally important concepts in a single search. You can start from either end. We've got a hunch that we may find less information on cruises than we will on the Caribbean, and that what we do find will probably be more focused. The Caribbean is loaded with islands, but the ones we're going to visit depends on the ship's itinerary. So we start with the cruise angle, and fill in the Caribbean side later.

How do *you* plan your vacations in real life? We're inspired by friends' accounts. We remember that Kay was in Paris last fall (she's there every couple of months, the *chienne*), that Rich and Dean just got back from Costa Rica, and that Anita and Steve seemed enthralled by Bali. But we can't think of anyone — in our generation, at least — who's traveled on a ship in the Caribbean, which is why we picked it as an example. So — surprise! — we have to turn to the Net.

Cruising through newsgroups

Our first stop is **Liszt** (www.liszt.com) to locate any newsgroups where cruising may be an ongoing conversational topic (see Chapter 10 for more about using Liszt and RemarQ to locate newsgroups in your area of interest). We click <u>Usenet newsgroups directory</u> and make sure the <u>Usenet newsgroups</u> button is selected. Then we type *cruise* in the search box. Up pop three possibilities, of which the most promising-sounding is the rec.travel.cruises newsgroup. One more click on the newsgroup name, and we see a list of message headers. rec.travel.cruises is a very active newsgroup, full of postings on particular cruise lines, ships, and ports of call. We spend a couple of hours following message threads with headers like "Which Cruise Line?," "Food/Meals on Cruise Ships," and "Sting Ray City, Grand Cayman" (why does that not sound like a laid-back place?), and generally soaking up the warm and friendly ambiance of the group. Mmmmm.

Check the rec.travel.cruises FAQ, or Frequently Asked Questions list, for a distillation of the newsgroup's wisdom on the hows and how-nots of cruising. Fittingly, the FAQ is titled "Everything You Ever Wanted To Know About Cruises But Were Afraid To Ask" (www.chesco.com/~hbtravel/faq.htm). See Chapter 10 for some pointers on how to locate FAQs in other subject areas.

Shipping out

A couple of cruise lines are beginning to emerge from our research as promising possibilities. Their ships seem more like, well, *ships,* than like floating hotels. The vessels carry far fewer passengers than the 1,200 or more that the gigundo party boats are capable of handling, and the staff and crew have a reputation for being efficient but not stiffly formal or overly familiar. We can run their names — the lines', not the crew members' — through **RemarQ** (www. remarq.com), as described in Chapter 4, and see what else the folks in rec. travel.cruises may have to say. From there, it's out to the Web to see what else we can pick up, and to gather some info from the cruise lines themselves.

Tom Raynor's List of Official Cruise Web Sites (members.aol.com/ tomraynor/cruises/index.html) is one of those guru pages (see Chapter 6) that every researcher hopes to find. The site includes all the cruise line links we need, plus pointers to online cruise publications and related sites, including goodies like — ooh — an official ship-by-ship summary of sanitation inspection results. How did we find this oceanic pearl? It turned up in Reva's search engine search. Just call her Ms. Lucky.

Most of the major cruise lines — and many smaller ones, too — have a presence on the Web, with detailed rundowns on their ships, the accommodations, and, of course, their upcoming itineraries. Some even feature their own FAQs and other interesting tidbits about the cruising life. We make some notes about the islands that our targeted prospects include among their ports of call. Now it's time to tackle the *Caribbean* end of our vacation-planning.

We be jammin'

The hard part here is filtering out all the ads for timeshares, local tour operators, dive shops (not *now,* mon!) and — because we've decided to do it the easy way — bare-boat charters. We want to concentrate on getting good general information about the region and the islands that can help us determine which cruise to take.

The subject catalogs described in Chapter 5 can give you a major assist in choosing a travel destination. In Yahoo!, we choose the <u>Recreation & Sports:Travel</u> subcategory, and then do a <u>Just this category</u> search on the keyword *Caribbean.* We get a manageable number of highly-focused sites to start exploring.

At **Excite** (www.excite.com), we click <u>Travel</u> and then <u>Caribbean</u> for our first-cut search. We find an abundance of links to specific islands, general travel and lodging guides, and weather reports for the Bahamas, Jamaica, and Cuba. Thanks a lot, fellas — like we really needed an incentive.

Obviously, you can substitute your own dream destination at any of these sites. It may even work for Cincinnati.

Travel is broadening

You can back up to the top level travel category in any of these subject catalogs to find general travel resources, such as message boards and discussion groups, information about frequent flyer programs, and links to sites like **Travelocity** (www.travelocity.com) and **Internet Travel Network** (www.itn.com). These sites enable you to book flights, hotels, rental cars, and sometimes even complete vacation packages.

A Yahoo! listing for Virtual Field Trips caught our eye. But unless it includes three meals a day and snorkeling off Cozumel, we don't think so.

Lessons learned, continued some more

We hope you had a pleasant virtual voyage to the Caribbean. Be sure to return your seat backs and tray tables to their full upright positions, and be careful when opening the overhead compartments . . . uh, sorry. Whether *your* next trip — and where were *we* just now? — is to Ocho Rios or oh-no-not-your-cousin's-again, keep these research tips in mind:

- ✔ People can be your best source of information online.
- ✔ Guru pages (collections of pointers to other excellent sites) can save you a lot of time and effort.
- ✔ Use a search engine's subject catalog or channels to get more filtered and focused results.

Chapter 15

Recreational Research: Hobbies and Interests

In This Chapter

▶ Pursuing your hobbies and personal interests online

▶ Exploring new pastimes and finding out more about them

▶ Getting into the research habit

"*G*lad you liked it. I found the recipe on the Net."

"There's this *great* kayaking URL. . . ."

"You like Phish, too? I've got pointers to a bunch of band pages on my Web site."

Research — it's not just for work anymore. We've heard comments like these at dinner parties, in the supermarket, and while waiting in line at the movies. Okay, we run with a particularly wired crowd, but it's not just *our* friends — our *moms'* friends are online. Folks that we knew in high school, and other previous incarnations, have found their way online. And everybody under the age of 12 seems to have a permanent, high-speed connection to the Net.

This chapter is about recreational research — using online resources in your everyday life to indulge your personal interests, assuage your curiosity, settle bar bets, whatever. There's no law against doing research just for fun, you know. In fact, we encourage it. The Internet is a fabulous resource for finding out more about nearly any subject you can imagine. Why restrict it to business, technology, and the other serious uses explored elsewhere in this book? The Net is part of our lives now — let's use it.

What's Cooking?

Reva let all her subscriptions to food magazines lapse after a fellow cook told her about **SOAR,** the Searchable Online Archive of Recipes (soar.berkeley.edu/recipes). SOAR is organized into general categories, such as Main Dishes, Ethnic Foods, Breads, Side Dishes, and, of course, Desserts. You can drill down through SOAR's main categories into more specific topics like the ones shown in Figure 15-1.

You can search the entire archive by ingredients, ethnicity, or specific recipe names. If you want to search by ingredient, click a topic like rice. A submenu appears offering an alphabetically arranged list of more than 500 recipes in that category. Browse the list, or enter a term like *Mexican* in the search form to narrow down your options.

If you prefer to search by ethnicity, click <u>Mexican</u> on the main page, and then run a search for rice in the 800-plus recipes listed there. Each recipe that you pull up includes an excerpt showing where in the recipe your search term appears, so that you can tell whether or not it's what you had in mind. Click a recipe name and get the full scoop. Print it out. Carry it into the kitchen. Cook.

Figure 15-1:
The Searchable Online Archive of Recipes (SOAR).

The SOAR search engine uses string searching, not Boolean AND/ORs. In other words, SOAR searches for the words that you enter as a literal phrase — *chicken or beef* doesn't retrieve both chicken and beef recipes; the search engine only picks up recipes that include phrases like "good with *chicken or beef.*" Entering the combination *Mexican and rice* turns up nothing — we can't imagine a phrase like that occurring in normal conversation *or* in a recipe — but *Mexican rice* is nice.

SOAR is part of the Recipe Ring, which is a Web ring like the ones we mention in Chapter 6. If you've searched SOAR's nearly 65,000 recipes and still haven't found what you're hungry for — or if you're just an inveterate foodie like Reva — you can click any of the navigation links at the bottom of SOAR's main page and see what's cooking elsewhere on the Web.

SOAR is our starting point for comprehensive recipe-hunting, but when we can't find what we're looking for there — amazingly, it sometimes happens — we check the following sites:

- ✔ **Epicurious** (`www.epicurious.com`) features recipes and feature articles from *Bon Appétit* and *Gourmet* magazines.

- ✔ **Internet Chef** (`www.ichef.com`) is a one-person venture that includes an extensive searchable recipe archive, columns, articles, and cooking tips.

- ✔ **The Gumbo Pages** (`www.gumbopages.com`) is the site to visit for total immersion in the Louisiana-New Orleans-Cajun cookin' ambience. Click The Creole and Cajun Recipe Page to get to the meat of the matter. And the crab. And the crawfish. And the cream, oh my.

Still not satiated? We find that hard to believe, but if you're still hungry for recipes, start with the Yahoo! (`www.yahoo.com`) Entertainment: Food and Drink: Recipes subcategory, and take it from there. Try to be back in time for dinner, okay?

Lights, Camera . . . Research

Both of us have friends who are walking encyclopedias of film lore. One specializes in Westerns; he can reel off — so to speak — the title of every movie that John Wayne ever appeared in, including the dates and the names of the characters that he played. Another friend can quote whole scenes of dialogue — he specializes in Monty Python — and tell you who said what, why they said it, and what happened next.

Visiting the **Internet Movie Database** (`www.imdb.com`) is like hanging out with those guys — and a roomful of people like them. Both blockbuster (and would-be blockbuster) movies and low-budget independent films are publicized on the Web. Major studios dedicate Web space to each of their productions, often well before the film is released. Popular stars have sites of their own, some created by avid fans.

Rooting your family tree

People ask us all the time about doing genealogical research online. Genealogy is a specialized art, and one that can fill an entire book. In fact, it does. *Genealogy Online For Dummies*, 2nd Edition, by Matthew and April Leigh Helm (IDG Books Worldwide, Inc.) tells you everything that you need to know. In the meantime, Reva asked her friend Janet Hubbard, who's a genealogy expert — although Janet denies that, because there's always more to find out — for some starting points. Here, in her own words, is what Janet had to say:

Genealogy sites can be broken down into a few large categories: super-sites with links to other sites, research sites based on surname databases, how-to sites, vital statistics sites, and sites containing background information, such as maps or history. Here are the ones that I return to most frequently: **RootsWeb** (www.rootsweb.com), a true super-site covering every conceivable subject, **Cyndi's List of Genealogy Links** (www.CyndisList.com), with more than 70 cross-referenced categories, and the **Genealogy SiteFinder** (sitefinder.tbox.com).

The Mormon (Latter Day Saints) Church's Family History Center (www.familysearch.org) has finally put its searchable records online. To take full advantage of this site, read the tips at www.firstct.com/fv/lds3.html. If the LDS site is busy, try this Canadian site: www.leth.net/fhc.

Search for a name at these sites (some charge a small monthly fee): **GenServ** (www.genserv.com), **Ancestry.com** (www.ancestry.com), **Family Tree Maker** (www.familytreemaker.com), **The Surname Web** (www.surnameweb.org), **GENDEX WWW Genealogical Index** (www.gendex.com/gendex), **Truly Searchable Genealogy Sites** (www.pclink.com/kg0ay/search.htm).

You can find genealogical search engines at **GenealogyPortal.com** (www.genealogyportal.com). Don't forget to use your favorite standard regular search engines and portal sites for maximum coverage.

You can search cemetery records (www.interment.net) and ship passenger lists (istg.rootsweb.com/index1.html). Many official census records are online (www.census.gov).

Learn more from the online edition of the classic genealogy reference book, **The Source**, (www.ancestry.com/home/source/srcindex.htm), and from **The Journal of Online Genealogy** (www.onlinegenealogy.com). Before buying genealogy software, read the reviews at the **GenealogySoftwareToolbox** (www.genealogysoftware.com) and subscribe to **ROOTS-L** (www.rootsweb.com/roots-l), one of many genealogy mailing lists.

The Internet Movie Database (IMDb) leads you to all those sites, and encourages you to wallow in its own mountainous collection of movie lore, too. Besides the searchable database of films, actors, production credits, movie quotes, and trivia (we'll get to all that in a minute), the site includes box-office rankings, daily movie and TV news, fun features like cinematic goofs, alternate versions, a daily movie quote, reader polls, discussion forums, trivia quizzes, and contests; and a movie recommendation service based on other films that you've seen and enjoyed. You can even find out what's currently playing in theaters in your neighborhood, or where to go to see the new releases. IMDb also links to movie photo, sound, and video sources Web-wide.

IMDb's powerful search capabilities, and the scope of the database itself, make it a terrific resource for tracking down motion picture trivia, researching an actor's or a director's career, and settling those late-night, late-show arguments. IMDb covers movies from around the world, from the dawn of the silent picture era through the current day, even films that are still in production. The site also covers TV programs, and includes the bit players and production crews as well as the big stars.

Suppose you want to search IMDb by movie name. In the Search the Database For box on the main page, select Titles from the drop-down menu. Then enter the title of the film in the text box (In this example, we'll choose *Toy Story 2* — IMDb ignores case, so *toy story 2* is okay, too), and before you can say *Cut!,* you get a tight synopsis that includes the studio and distributor names, cast and production credits, running time, genre, and numerous other factoids. You can click any cast member, or on links along the side of the page. These lead you to plot summaries, reviews and commentary from official media sources and the film cognoscenti who hang out in the `rec.arts.movies` newsgroups, and the official and unofficial Toy Story 2 Web sites.

To do a more complex search, click on <u>More Searches</u>. The multiple-part IMDb search form invites you to search by the following categories:

- ✔ **Movie/TV Title:** The drop-down menu lets you restrict your search to movie or TV titles only, or search both at once.

- ✔ **Cast/Crew Name:** The drop-down menu lets you restrict a name to one of three broad categories: actor, actress, or filmmaker/crew.

- ✔ **Character Name:** Here's where our memory usually fails. But you can search on a portion of the name if you don't remember it exactly, and restrict the results by gender. If we want to find out who played Fenster in *The Usual Suspects,* IMDb tells us immediately that Benicio Del Toro is our man. One more click and we get a complete working bio, including TV appearances, as well as other movie roles.

- ✔ **Word:** With this search box, you can look for a particular quote, shop for a soundtrack CD, or locate biographies, books, and articles about movie topics and personalities. You can find movie trivia by film or subject, and even turn up goofs in continuity, plot, or facts.

Don't overlook the <u>Popular Searches</u> and <u>Advanced Searches</u> options on the left side of the screen. The <u>Extended Search</u> option lets you screen for movies that meet multiple criteria, such as year, location, and production company. <u>Complex Name Search</u> allows you to look for people by very specific occupation, such as set decorators, special effects, and writers (yes!). <u>People Working Together</u> lets you enter multiple names to find movies in which both or all the people appeared.

Find IMDb Feature, the bottom box on the search form, allows you to search the IMDb site itself for special features, like reviews or a Frequently Asked Questions list. You can also click <u>Index</u> at the bottom of the screen for a neatly organized listing of IMDb content, or take a guided, annotated tour of the site. All those features are useful, because you can lose yourself — in a *good* way, of course — exploring the riches that IMDb offers.

Playing the Keyboard

Whether your taste in music runs toward a Midi keyboard or a Bösendorfer Grand, your melodic sensibilities can find a home on the Net. Music fans seem to split more decisively along genre lines than do cooks and movie buffs — unless, of course, you're a strict vegetarian or refuse to see anything but French films. We do know someone who's a fan of both Wagnerian opera and the Grateful Dead. And there's lots of crossover among folks who are into rock 'n' roll, traditional folk and country music, rockabilly, and the blues. But sites that cover the full range of musical expression are rare.

Music is a personal taste — as personal, for some of us anyway, as sex, religion, and politics (and you don't see any of *those* pastimes featured in this chapter, do you?). So we tread lightly here, and only impose our musical preferences on you a little bit. Feel free to call your own tune.

Yahoo!ing it

Because music research almost always depends on the genre, we recommend starting broadly, with a look at Yahoo!'s <u>Entertainment: Music</u> category. Click <u>Genres</u> for an idea of the amazing variety of musical forms and variations. The list (see Figure 15-2) runs from Alternative to World Fusion. The number in parentheses tells you how many sites Yahoo! has indexed on that topic. Wait a minute — *13* sites devoted to lounge music? We don't want to think about it.

For each separate type of music, Yahoo! lists individual sites devoted to the genre, and often, additional subcategories for particular singers, musicians, and bands or performing ensembles. Look for a <u>Web Directories</u> subcategory — this points you to guru pages, mega-sites (see Chapter 6 for more about guru pages and mega-sites), and other specialized catalogs of Web resources on that specific genre.

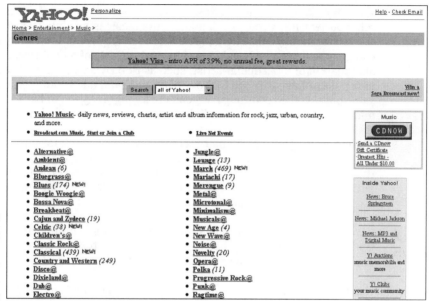

We don't know a whole lot about classical music, so we rely on Yahoo! to lead us to the **WWW Virtual Library's Classical Music Department** (`www.gprep.pvt.k12.md.us/classical`), which appears to be a comprehensive and ultra-current site. (The *last updated* notice at the bottom of the page was dated just a few days before the day we checked it. That's a good sign that the site's maintained and updated regularly.)

You can follow the same steps for jazz, country, progressive rock, or whatever makes you get up and shake your booty: Click a Yahoo! genre, and then check the Web Directories link, if there is one. Or just browse the listings and follow links until you find sites that are broad, deep, and timely enough to trust.

Shop 'til you bop

We haven't said much in this book about mining Web-based shopping sites for their information content. But some electronic commerce sites, such as **Amazon.com** (`www.amazon.com`), are far more than just a catalog of goods combined with a secure server for handling credit card transactions. Like any good retailer, the proprietors of these online stores realize that, to attract customers and keep them coming back, they have to add value to the experience of browsing through the merchandise. One way of doing this is to provide detailed information about the goods that they're selling in order to educate and intrigue you while they're relieving you of your hard-earned money.

When it comes to music, **CDNow** (www.cdnow.com) is one of our favorite retail outlets. It's wired for sound, and the music is much better than that mush-tone garbage that they pipe in at the mall. We can browse by musical category to find out who's hot and to read reviews of recent releases. We can also search for a particular artist, such as Bob Dylan, and get a list of recordings (all available through CDNow, of course) and audio samples. On the same page as the recordings, we can click Biography to get background information and photos, as well as links to related artists and recordings.

If we're looking for a particular recording, we can search for it by name and get a list of tracks and session musicians. This method is great for settling those arguments about who played with whom, who recorded a song first, and who did or did not do a cover version. You don't get into those kinds of arguments? Oh. You must have a *life*.

If we ask it nicely, CDNow offers recommendations of other artists that it thinks we'll like if we're Dylan fans. Let's see now. Neil Young, Eric Clapton, Joan Baez, and the Rolling Stones. Not bad, CDNow, not bad at all.

Hang around CDNow long enough and you can get quite a musical education. We're sure that CDNow — or any of the other electronic commerce sites where you spend time researching music, books, stocks, or whatever products they sell — want you to *spend* some money, too. That, of course, is entirely up to you. All that we can tell you is that CDNow keeps our UPS drivers busy.

Musical true confessions

What's in Reva's Music bookmarks file? She stands revealed:

- ✔ **IUMA, the Internet Underground Music Archive** (www.iuma.com) provides a window into cutting edge music and emerging bands, and features audio clips galore.

- ✔ **Cybergrass** (www.banjo.com) covers bluegrass music, one of our favorite genres, complete with a shades-of-*Deliverance* soundtrack. If you decide to check out this site at the office or while your roommate's asleep, you better turn your PC's volume control *way* down.

- ✔ **The International Lyrics Server** (www.lyrics.ch/index.htm) is known around Reva's house as the Argument Settler. This site serves up song titles, album tracks, and artists, as well as those elusive words that go with the music. If a fragment of a song is driving you nuts, click Full Text Search and key in the offending phrase. Whew. Steve Miller really did sing *pompitous of love*. We still have no idea what it means, but at least we know we heard it right.

- ✔ **Dead Net, the Official Home Page of the Grateful Dead** (www.dead.net). 'Nuff said, or *never* enough said. You had to be there, and, fortunately, we were.

Indoor Birding

Indoor birding sounds like a euphemism for what we used to call "watching the submarine races." Reva did not, er, *bird* until she moved to the country. She's still just a baby birder; she can't tell her Cedar Waxwings from her Bohemian Waxwings (yes, thanks; she *can* tell her elbow from a hole in the ground). In fact, the only birds that either of us are *sure* of are barn swallows, turkey vultures, blue jays, and robins.

Our first stop in finding out about birding was the **National Audubon Society** (www.audubon.org). After all, the National Audubon Society publishes those field guides that every birder seems to own. On the main page, under <u>Audubon & The Internet</u>, we find <u>Links to Other Relevant Web sites</u>. And in the <u>Ornithology</u> section of that list are links to promising-sounding sites, such as BIRDNET (www.nmnh.si.edu/BIRDNET).

The other big name in birding is Roger Tory Peterson. **Peterson Online** (www.petersononline.com) (don't confuse this site with the Peterson's college guides we discuss in Chapter 14) is definitely for the birds. The site includes articles from *Bird Watchers Digest,* calendars of birding events, a Q&A archive, and a massively deep categorized listing of birding links and resources.

Every hobby and occupation has at least one membership organization; for birding, it's the **American Birding Association** (www.americanbirding. org). The ABA site includes <u>Birders' Resources</u>, <u>Rare Bird Alerts</u>, and links to other organizations, bird counts and surveys, and local sources of information.

Birders are a sizable and sociable community. Birding relies heavily on reports of sightings, and sometimes birders travel hundreds of miles to add a new variety of feathered creature to their life lists. For that reason, birding mailing lists — where participants exchange news and information quickly — are quite plentiful. Some mailing lists are local, others are regional or national. Many are conducted in the language of their countries. Some focus on particular species and families of birds — seabirds, raptors, eagles, hummingbirds, or rare birds in general. Some deal with specialized topics like bird-banding. A mailing list even exists for teenage birders.

Reva's friends Rich and Dean are birders extraordinaire. They recommend BirdChat, an active, general-purpose mailing list that's a logical starting point for beginners. To subscribe, send e-mail to listserv@listserv.arizona. edu. In the body of the message, type *subscribe BIRDCHAT* followed by your first and last name.

Rich and Dean also recommend the following additional Web sites for fledgling as well as experienced birders:

✓ **Birding.com** (www.birding.com) features tips for beginning birding, bird identification, backyard birding, and other starting points.

✓ **Tina MacDonald's Where do you want to go birding today?** (www.camacdonald.com/birding/birding.htm) spotlights a collection of birding hot spots around the world, with links to relevant sites.

✓ **Bird Links to the World** (www.ntic.qc.ca/~nellus/links.html) is an international site with more than 3,500 links to museums and scientific institutions, newsgroups, FAQs, listservs, bird images and sounds, sources for binoculars and other birding gear, software and CD-ROMs, videos, magazines, books, travel guides, expeditions, and trip reports. Costa Rica, here we come. That is, as soon as we finish this book.

Doing It Yourself

No, we're not about to get into home improvement here, though that's certainly another possibility for do-it-yourself — and do-it-*for*-yourself — research. Suppose none of the examples in this chapter turns you on. Where can you find the best entry points for the kinds of recreational research that *you* want to do?

Well, you can go back and pick up some clues from other chapters where we talk about using search engines, subject catalogs, guru pages, and FAQs to zero in on the best starting points, or at least on sites that will get you through the door.

Or you can just *listen*. The Internet has developed to the point that practically every hobby, interest, or personal proclivity is represented online. If you know other people who share your interests, it's likely that some of them are already pursuing those interests on the Net. Ask them the same way we asked friends for tips on genealogy and birding.

You may be surprised. Even the most non-cyber-sounding pursuits — quilting, antique collecting, backpacking, and outdoor sports — have staked out significant territory on the Net. There's no substitute for getting together face-to-face with fellow enthusiasts and actually doing whatever it is you do. But between those opportunities, you can find plenty of company, and a lot of good information, online.

The Researching Online
For Dummies, 2nd Edition
Internet Directory

The 5th Wave   By Rich Tennant

"It's amazing how much more some people can get out of online researching than others."

In this directory . . .

This directory represents the best of the best — our selection of more than 100 Web sites, online services, publications, and other resources that you'll find useful, and in some cases essential, for researching online. Most of these resources play a starring role elsewhere in this book. Here, we've arranged them conveniently by broad category according to what they do or the subject areas they cover.

Use this directory for quick reference if you need to find a URL and don't feel like paging through the chapters or looking it up on the CD. Use it as a reminder so that you don't overlook any of the major research sites and services you want to factor in to your research project. Use it for inspiration when you want to try a new site or a different research approach. Use it to acquaint yourself with the amazing scope and depth of online research tools. We don't care what you use it for (actually, we can think of a couple of uses to which we'd rather not have you put it; we'll just say that anything that involves tearing out the pages is off limits). But *use* it.

The Researching Online For Dummies, 2nd Edition Internet Directory

- -

In This Directory

▶ Staying current in the online world

▶ Finding key resources in business, technology, government, and other research areas

▶ Locating search engines, subject catalogs, libraries, and Internet navigation aids

▶ Tapping into news, magazines, and other media

▶ Getting up-to-speed on information quality

▶ Connecting with research pros and other online experts

- -

This directory is a quick and handy guide to some key resources for online research. It includes both general search tools, such as search engines, subject catalogs, and online services, and some more specialized resources in areas such as government, business, news, science, and technology. You'll also find suggestions for keeping up with the ever-expanding online world and for assessing the quality of the information you find there.

We've divided all these resources into broad categories, and arranged the categories alphabetically. Some of the larger categories are subdivided further, to make it easier for you to find a particular type of resource. Here are the main categories in this directory:

About the Net/Staying Current

Art, Literature, and History

Business, Finance, and Economics

Document Delivery Services

Gated Sites

Government and Law

Libraries, Schools, and Universities

Magazines and Journals

Navigation Aids and Organizing Tools

News

Quality of Information

Reference Books

Research Groups

Science, Technology, and Medicine

Search Engines, Subject Catalogs, and Guides

Virtual Communities and Conferencing Systems

The sites and sources in this directory are just a small sampling of the hundreds of online resources we talk about in this book. Reading the rest of the book will give you more ideas about how to use these resources in your real-life research efforts.

The CD includes a list of just about all the Web sites referenced in this directory and elsewhere in this book. Each listing consists of the name of the site and an HTML link to its URL or location on the Web. When you read about a site that intrigues you, click on the corresponding category, and then browse the list, or use your browser's Find feature to look for its name (type in the most distinctive word from the site name for best results) and locate it quickly in the list on the CD. Then click the URL and — assuming you're online — connect directly to the site.

We've assigned mini-icons to many of these listings so you can tell at a glance what special features, restrictions, or claims to fame they possess:

🚂	This is a search engine site.
☰	This is a subject catalog, guide, or mega-site.
▦	This site (or the service it describes) features searchable databases.
📖	The resource described here is a book, magazine, or other print publication.
☛	Get in touch with experts here.
FAQs	The site is (or directs you to) a list of frequently asked questions.
🗐	The site offers interactive conversations, chat, or other people-to-people contact.
↘	The site offers files for downloading.
🎨	The site offers (or points you to) photos, illustrations, or other graphical materials.
🎬	The site features sound or video clips, or both.
🛡	You must register for access to some or all portions of the site.
$	You must pay for access to some or all of the information at the site.

About the Net/Staying Current

One of the biggest challenges for researchers is keeping on top of all the changes in the online world. This section includes both print and electronic publications that report on the online industry itself and the companies involved in it, evaluate new research tools and enhancements to older ones, and provide critical assessments of sites, search aids, and online services. See Chapter 16 for more about staying current on developments in the ever-changing online realm.

CyberSkeptic's Guide to Internet Research

www.bibliodata.com

The *CyberSkeptic's Guide* is a printed newsletter, published ten times a year, that evaluates Internet resources from a professional researcher's viewpoint. The publication compares information sources on the open Web with those found in gated sites and tells you in no uncertain terms when and why one is superior to the other for certain kinds of research. Check the Web site or e-mail ina@bibliodata.com for subscription details.

EContent and Online

www.onlineinc.com

EContent and *Online* are like bimonthly versions of *Time* and *Newsweek* for information professionals. Both are print journals published by Online, Inc. *EContent* focuses on content, whether it's on the Net and the Web, professional online services, or CD-ROM. *Online* takes more of a systems approach, dealing with online services, new features, and broader information issues. To tell you the absolute truth, we've subscribed to these two publications for more than 20 years now, and we still have a hard time telling them apart. Maybe that means we need both. Check the Web site for subscription details and selected articles from both magazines.

Information Today, Link-Up, and Searcher

www.infotoday.com

Information Today covers the online industry, with opinion columns, product announcements, and in-depth reviews of new and enhanced resources. *Link-Up,* its sister publication, is geared toward do-it-yourself information-hunters rather than professional researchers. Format-wise, both are newsprint tabloids. *Searcher,* the third publication in this trilogy, is a glossy print magazine, and the editorial home of Barbara Quint, online researcher and gadfly *extraordinaire. Searcher* is must reading for most info pros we know. Look at the Web site for sample articles and subscription information.

Net-happenings

**scout.cs.wisc.edu/caservices/
    net-hap/index.html**

Gleason Sackman, the man behind Net-happenings, has been keeping track of Internet-related resources and events since before the rise of the Web. Net-happenings' coverage of resources for school kids and teachers is particularly good, but Sackman's interests, and those of his contributors, range far beyond the K–12 set. You can subscribe to and get Net-happenings via e-mail (often several times a day — it *can* be a bit

overwhelming), follow it in the
`comp.internet.net-happenings` news-group, or check out the publication on the Web.

Netsurfer Digest

www.netsurf.com/nsd

Netsurfer Digest reviews Web sites both serious and not-so serious. Its well-written (and often tongue-in-cheek) blurbs highlight significant developments in the online industry, new and enhanced search tools, and destination sites for both research and recreation. Subscribe and get this extensive electronic newsletter (which includes HTML links to all the sites mentioned) weekly via e-mail, or browse to the aforementioned URL to read it on the Web.

Search Engine Report and Search Engine Watch

www.searchenginewatch.com

Search Engine Watch is the best way we know to stay up-to-date on the wonderful, and sometimes overwhelming, world of search engines. On the Web site, you can find current information about new search engines and changes to old favorites, as well as detailed, and often critical, performance comparisons. Search Engine Report is the e-mail supplement to the Search Engine Watch Web site. The Report provides periodic updates with HTML links to relevant sites, studies, and special reports. Check the Web site for the subscription how-to.

Search Engine Showdown

www.notess.com/search

Greg Notess monitors and compares the coverage and performance of all the major search engines, and spotlights interesting new ones. His site is like a *Consumer Reports* guide for search engine buffs.

Seidman's Online Insider

www.onlineinsider.com

When Seidman's newsletter lands in our e-mail boxes, it's as if a well-connected friend has pulled his chair alongside ours to share his weekly haul of online-industry gossip. Seidman schmoozes frankly about AOL, the Microsoft Network, CompuServe, and other online services, their brilliant or ill-conceived marketing and pricing tactics, their alliances and enmities, their triumphs and defeats. Best of all, he analyzes what's going on and tells you what it all means for you, the customer. Head over to the URL to read the Online Insider on the Web or to subscribe to the e-mail edition.

Art, Literature, and History

The Web is so full of varied treasures — artistic, graphical, literary, and historical, not to mention just plain weird — that it's difficult to choose just a few representative sites. You can find out more about online collections of literary works and digital archives in Chapter 8.

The American Memory Project

lcweb2.loc.gov/ammem

Put together by the U.S. Library of Congress, the American Memory Project is an electronic museum and exhibit hall featuring pictures, maps, and original manuscripts drawn from all stages of American history, from colonial times to the present. Add a multimedia dimension to your historical research by sampling the early-20th-century motion picture clips and sound recordings of historic speeches, interviews, performances, and folk music.

Berkeley Digital Library SunSITE

sunsite.berkeley.edu

The University of California's SunSITE is a clearinghouse for digital library projects around the world. These rich collections of what scholars call *source material* — documents, maps, illustrations, and other artifacts actually created and used by historic figures and others who lived during the era being studied — enable researchers to examine and analyze rare, often one-of-a-kind resources that may otherwise be locked away in some remote and practically inaccessible archive.

Project Gutenberg

www.gutenberg.net

Project Gutenberg started as a grass roots effort roughly 30 years ago, a labor of love by an army of dedicated volunteers. Its mission is to spread knowledge by digitizing classic works of literature, history, and science and getting them into the hands of online denizens everywhere. Check Project Gutenberg for electronic editions of writings by such well-known authors as William Shakespeare, Lewis Carroll, Jane Austen, and Joseph Conrad, as well as thousands of others, both ancient and modern.

Business, Finance, and Economics

Online has become an indispensable resource for business research. In Chapter 12, we talk about how to use both gated Web sites and the open Web for competitive intelligence, investing, market studies, sales prospecting, and other forms of business research.

American City Business Journals

www.amcity.com

American City Business Journals pulls together more than three dozen weekly (usually) business newspapers from cities all over the United States. You can search an individual publication or all publications at once. Local business periodicals, such as the ones clustered at this site, can give you deeper and more detailed information about companies and executives based in a particular location than you find in major national publications.

CEO Express

www.ceoexpress.com

CEO Express calls itself "the executive's toolbox." It's crammed with pointers to company directories, lists and rankings, general and business news sources, business and technology magazines, financial market data, stock quotes, analyst reports, economic indicators, small business resources, and online examples of new business models and technologies. Busy executives may appreciate the links to FedEx and other express delivery services.

Daily Stocks

www.dailystocks.com

We think of Daily Stocks as Everything You Wanted to Know About Investing But Were Afraid to Ask. This densely packed site is far more comprehensive than its name would lead you to believe. In addition to stock data, it includes hundreds of links to information on other investment markets, SEC filings, economic indicators, investment advice, and detailed company information, plus news headlines, magazine articles, and more.

D-8 Business, Finance, and Economics

Dun & Bradstreet

www.dnb.com

$

Dun & Bradstreet is one of the best-known names in business information and a source for financial and credit data on both publicly traded and privately held firms, worldwide. The main D&B Web site is your access point for purchasing several different kinds of detailed company reports. Don't overlook D&B's Companies Online (www.companiesonline.com) — which lets you search for companies that meet certain criteria, such as location, annual sales, or number of employees — and D&B Marketing Connection (www.dnb.imarketinc.com), which gives you access to information on industries and individual company offices.

Hoover's Online

www.hoovers.com

$

Hoover's is a searchable online directory site that provides basic company profiles for more than 12,000 public and private firms worldwide. A typical profile includes a link to the company Web site, lists of competitors, and links to financial information, news stories, and stock quotes. Subscribers to Hoover's get some additional features, such as detailed corporate backgrounds and financial data.

Investext

www.investext.com

$

Investext offers the complete text of in-depth reports on companies and industries, prepared by investment banking analysts and market research firms worldwide. Such reports can provide valuable insight into competitors' operations and business strategies, and can help you determine the potential demand for your company's products and services. You can tap into Investext through the Web, through its proprietary I/PLUS Direct, or through other online services such as Dialog and Dow Jones Interactive.

misc.invest FAQ

invest-faq.com

Investors are an opinionated and often quite knowledgeable bunch. One of the most thoughtful and comprehensive FAQs (Frequently Asked Questions lists) that we've seen represents the current collective wisdom of the misc.invest newsgroup hierarchy. Whether you're a novice investor or an old hand, you can search by keyword or browse by broad subject category and almost certainly come up with an answer.

Motley Fool

www.fool.com

For an investment site with an abundance of personality, look into The Motley Fool. You can find the Fool on the Web as well as via its original home, AOL (keyword: *fool*). The Fool's main draw is its lively online community, which is a collection of discussion forums devoted to every aspect of investing, including individual company stocks, industry outlooks, general advice, and personal financial management.

Statistical Resources on the Web

www.lib.umich.edu/libhome/
    Documents.center/stats.html

Statistics make you queasy? This site eases your hunt for numerical data by providing a detailed index, subdivided by topic and issuing agency, to statistical sources all over the Web. In addition to well-known statistics-generating agencies such as the U.S. Census Bureau, you can find statistics from trade associations; research institutes; worldwide educational, environmental, and economic groups; and more.

10-K Wizard

www.tenkwizard.com

A fast and easy search interface to 10-Ks and other financial filings from the Securities and Exchange Commission. This alternative to EDGAR (see Chapter 12 and a couple of entries down in this section) lets you view and download reports and tables in PDF (Portable Document Format) and Excel spreadsheet form.

Thomson & Thomson

www.thomson-thomson.com

$

Thomson & Thomson is about as synonymous with trademarks as Kleenex® is with disposable facial tissue. Trademarks are a way of protecting your intellectual property rights — and the revenue associated with them — by registering the names of products or services that you intend to market. Subscribe directly to T&T for trademark searching or search its Trademarkscan databases on Dialog.

U.S. Securities & Exchange Commission EDGAR Database

www.sec.gov/edgarhp.htm

EDGAR is your entree into SEC corporate filings and other forms of disclosure required of U.S. public companies. SEC documents such as 10-Ks and 10-Qs can provide detailed insight into a company's finances and operations. Such information is often valuable to competitors and potential partners, as well as investors. EDGAR lets you search for corporate filings by company name or type of filing.

The Wall Street Journal Interactive Edition

www.wsj.com

$

The online edition of *The Wall Street Journal* provides current business and economic news and feature articles, plus access to other Dow Jones publications and news stories and the thousands of periodicals in the Dow Jones Publications Library. (The Publications Library is described in Chapter 9 and in the "Professional Online Services" portion of this directory.) This subscription-only site also allows you to set up your own *Personal Journal* so that you can automatically receive your favorite WSJ columns and features, as well as custom-tailored information on the companies, products, and stocks you want to track.

Document Delivery Services

Document delivery companies specialize in locating articles, conference papers, and other items that you can't find online or at your local library. A document delivery firm can help when you're looking for something specific; know the name of the journal, book, proceedings volume, or other publication in which it appeared; and have a good idea of the author, title, and date. Chapter 8 mentions several such services; hundreds of others exist, all over the world.

UnCover

uncweb.carl.org

$ 📖

UnCover lets you search for a particular article by author, title, publication name, or subject; and order and pay for it with your credit card and take delivery via fax. UnCover's REVEAL service keeps you current by automatically delivering the tables of contents of your favorite publications via e-mail and alerting you to new articles on topics you've specified as they're added to the UnCover database.

Gated Sites

Gated sites require you to register and — usually — pay for the information you receive. In exchange, you often get access to unique research material, powerful search engines, and the ability to search hundreds, even thousands, of publications at once. Within the general category of gated sites, we classify the industrial-strength Dialog, Dow Jones Interactive, and LEXIS-NEXIS as *professional* online services. We call CompuServe and America Online *consumer* online services; they provide some research tools and sources, but aren't really geared toward serious research. We categorize Electric Library and Powerize (as well as Northern Light's Special Collection, listed under "General Search Engines" in this directory) as *hybrid* search services; they offer some of the advantages of the professional services, but a much more limited selection of information sources and search tools. Chapter 9 tells you a whole lot more about gated sites and how to use them.

Professional online services

Dialog

www.dialogweb.com

📖 $ 🗒

Dialog offers hundreds of databases covering subjects as diverse as art, language, religion, psychology, sociology, business, news, chemistry, medicine, engineering, and technology. You can search the system several different ways; start with the URL listed here, read the detailed database descriptions posted there, and sample the range and depth of the resources that Dialog can provide.

Dow Jones Interactive

djinteractive.com

📖 $ 🗒

Through its Publications Library, the subscription-based Dow Jones Interactive service offers many of the same magazines, newspapers, and other periodicals as Dialog. But Dow Jones's main claim to fame is as a business research service. The Dow Jones Interactive Web site offers *The Wall Street Journal,* in-depth company and market research reports, historical stock quotes, and CustomClips, an automatic update service for topics you want to follow. *Note:* Dow Jones Interactive and Reuters are part of a joint venture called *Factiva.*

LEXIS-NEXIS

www.lexis-nexis.com/ln.universe

 $ 🗒

LEXIS-NEXIS provides a broad range of business, news, trade, and international reports and publications, and the option of picking up case law and other specialized legal resources on the Lexis side. Various search options exist; LEXIS-NEXIS Universe provides Web-based access to much of the LEXIS-NEXIS service.

Consumer online services

America Online

www.aol.com

America Online, noted for its chat rooms and instant messaging, offers several areas of interest to researchers. Use that freebie AOL software disk to log in and check out areas such as the Business, Computing, and Research & Learn channels.

CompuServe

www.compuserve.com

CompuServe is the home of Iquest InfoCenter, a slimmed-down version (in price as well as content) of some of the same highly useful databases offered on the Dialog service. Iquest is also a gateway to Dow Jones Interactive's Publications Library, a great source for business information. Don't overlook CompuServe's traditionally excellent discussion forums, with their accompanying libraries of software and information in text form.

Hybrid search services

Electric Library

www.elibrary.com

Electric Library offers a deep collection of articles, book chapters, maps, photos, and broadcast transcripts. You pay a modest fee for monthly access, and no per-document or per-search fees. Electric Library also markets a powerful business version, priced for large corporate enterprises.

Powerize.com

www.powerize.com

Powerize.com provides access to the full text of articles and press releases, company directories, and stock quotes. Some items are available for free; others are pay-per-view.

Government and Law

Federal, legislative, regulatory, and legal information is abundant online and, increasingly, on the Web. Chapter 11 (isn't that bankruptcy?) goes into detail about government information sources, and Chapter 6 talks about locating mega-sites for legal and related kinds of research.

FedWorld

www.fedworld.gov

FedWorld is your gateway into a wide variety of U.S. government reports and other publications from executive-branch agencies such as NASA, the Department of Energy, the Environmental Protection Agency, and the Small Business Administration. FedWorld also leads you to individual agency Web sites where you can find even more information on your own.

FindLaw

www.findlaw.com

FindLaw is equivalent to Yahoo! for legal research — in other words, a highly organized catalog covering all aspects of the law, from Supreme Court decisions to law schools, consultants, and expert witnesses. FindLaw also offers discussion forums for attorneys and legal researchers.

LawCrawler

www.lawcrawler.com

Run by the folks who created FindLaw (see the preceding listing), LawCrawler is a search engine that covers only law-related sites. Legal researchers find LawCrawler extremely useful for targeted legal search queries.

Lexis

www.lexis.com

Lexis is the legal side of the two-headed online service known as LEXIS-NEXIS (see Chapter 9 and the "Professional Online Services" section of this directory for more about LEXIS-NEXIS). Lexis includes case law, statutory and administrative law, and special tools for citing, Shepardizing, and whatever else it is that legal researchers do. The Lexis Web site doesn't lead you directly into the full Lexis online service, but it gives you an idea of what Lexis offers and how you can get connected.

Social Law Library

www.socialaw.com

The Social Law Library is a legal mega-site offering links to Web resources for legal research of all kinds. From here, you can connect to the U.S. Supreme Court and a range of federal rules, regulations, and publications, or to state-by-state listings of codes, statutes, court opinions, and more.

The site also encompasses international law, as well as other lawyerly resources such as legal publications, library catalogs, online discussion groups, educational and employment resources, and professional associations.

Thomas

thomas.loc.gov

Thomas is to the legislative branch of government what FedWorld (see the entry earlier in this section) is to the executive branch: a gateway to information about the U.S. Congress, its various committees, and their doings. You can look up current and past legislation by bill number, subject, sponsor, or title; track pending legislation as it moves through the House and the Senate; and keep an eye on what your local Congress-critter is really up to in Washington, D.C.

TR's Legal Research Links

**www.netins.net/showcase/trhalvorson/
law/index.html**

Put together by a practicing attorney, this site is full of links to case law, law reviews and other legal periodicals, books, mailing lists and newsletters, sources for expert witnesses, and associations, organizations, publishers and courses of study relevant to lawyers and legal research specialists.

Libraries, Schools, and Universities

School and university Web sites can tell you more about courses, faculty members, extracurricular activities, and student life than old-fashioned printed college catalogs. This section includes sources for finding schools, and information about schools, online. University libraries — along with some public, government, and other specialized types of libraries — have their own distinct presences online as well, with searchable book catalogs and other research tools. This section gives you just a couple of examples. Chapter 8 tells you more about finding and using libraries online.

American Universities

**www.clas.ufl.edu/CLAS/
    american-universities.html**

College and University Home Pages

www.mit.edu/people/cdemello/univ.html

These two sites provide copious links to college and university Web sites and sometimes to specific university departments. The College and University Home Pages site includes international schools as well. Between the two, you should be able to locate the Web site of just about any bachelor's or advanced degree-granting institution in the world — assuming, of course, that the school you're looking for *has* one.

Peterson's Directory of Colleges and Universities

www.petersons.com

Peterson's is the mainstay of high school guidance counselors everywhere. The online edition — which we put to use in Chapter 14 — lets you search for schools by curriculum or location. The rundown for each institution includes a description of specific programs, tuition and other fees, admission requirements, and contacts. Some of the schools let you request additional information, and even apply online, directly from the Peterson's site.

U.S. Library of Congress

catalog.loc.gov

Of all the possibilities covered in Chapter 8, we've selected the Library of Congress (LC) as the very model of a modern major library. The collection includes millions of books published in the United States and elsewhere, as well as maps, sound recordings, original manuscripts, and much

more. LC's online catalog lets you search a great part of that collection by author, title, or subject, from the comfort of your own computer.

WebCATS

library.usask.ca/hywebcat

WebCATS is a research tool for locating library catalogs on the Web. You can search geographically, by continent and country, or by library type. It's a great way to locate library catalogs close to home that you may actually want to visit — or, if your research takes you there, library catalogs halfway around the world. You can also use WebCATS to identify special subject or regional collections to aid in a particular research project.

Magazines and Journals

Magazines — of all sorts — are one of the most common life forms on the Web. We talk about magazines generally in Chapter 13; about scientific, technical, and medical journals in Chapter 11; and about business periodicals in Chapter 12. Rather than fill up this section with our favorite online magazines (we're tempted, but it would be wrong), we give you three different ways to find the periodicals you want online.

Electronic Journal Access Project

www.coalliance.org/ejournal

The Electronic Journal Access Project leads you to magazines, newsletters, and scholarly journals on the Web. You can browse the listings by title or subject, or search for listings by keyword. Each listing includes a hypertext link directly to the electronic journal.

Electric Library

www.elibrary.com

$

The Electric Library allows you to locate publications and search them at the same time. Its collection includes newspapers and wire services as well as hundreds of magazines, both professional and popular. You can do a broad subject search or look for a particular article. Electric Library is a subscription-based site with a low monthly fee. You can try it out for free or sign up for a 30-day trial.

Fulltext Sources Online

www.infotoday.com/fso/default.htm

$ 📖

Our copies of *Fulltext Sources Online,* a print directory published twice a year and available by subscription, are among the most heavily used books in our research collections. *FSO* covers both the Web and professional online services, such as Dialog and the others discussed in Chapter 9. For professional online sources, it tells you how far back the archives go; for publications on the Web, it tells you whether a free archive exists. Subscribers get access to a private section of the publisher's Web site where you can look up and link to those publications that have free archives on the Web.

Navigation Aids and Organizing Tools

In the early days of the Internet, volunteers built and maintained their own resources for finding and organizing online information. Gophers were to the Net what search engines and subject catalogs such as AltaVista and Yahoo! are now — indispensable research aids. Many libraries put catalogs of their holdings online as well; even before the advent of the Web, researchers used a combination guide and navigation tool called Hytelnet to locate and connect to library catalogs. Both Hytelnet and much of gopherspace (the portion of the Net defined and mapped by Gophers) are now accessible through the Web. See Chapter 1 for more about Gophers, and Chapter 8 for more about library catalogs and Hytelnet. The sites in this section provide Web access to these resources. Type the address into your browser's Location or Address box just as you see it here.

Hytelnet

www.lights.com/hytelnet

Hytelnet is Peter Scott's contribution to cataloging and navigating through the rich resources of library catalogs online. Browse library listings by geographical area, or search the listings by name or subject. Click a particular institution's telnet address to connect directly to its online catalog.

Internet Wiretap Gopher

gopher://wiretap.spies.com

The Internet Wiretap Gopher provides a good compilation of some of the gopher sites still maintained on the Net. Click the Electronic Books on Wiretap link for a miscellaneous collection of books and other publications in the public domain (see Chapter 17 for more about copyright and public domain material). The Wiretap Online Library link leads to additional e-texts. Be cautious about relying on information in the Government Docs link; many of these documents are outdated or superceded.

News

News online comes in several different forms: broadcast media Web sites, individual newspapers, newsmagazines, and wire services. The news arena also features mega-sites that direct you to various news and current events resources, and services that automatically keep you up-to-date. We have divided this section of the directory into broad categories and give you some leading examples of each kind. See Chapter 13 for more about finding and using news sources online.

Broadcast news

Most of the major broadcast networks, both North American and international, have a substantial presence on the Web. Typically, you can find real-time news headlines, feature stories, and tie-ins to the network's regular programs. If you're researching a topic that's currently in the news, broadcast media sites can provide the latest scoop, as well as background information and analysis of the news behind the news.

ABC News

abcnews.go.com

Of the major U.S. networks, ABC's Web presence is one of the most substantial. The site offers current news and background on ABC program content, a collection of recent stories arranged by topic, and a searchable multimedia archive with video and sound clips of people and events in the news. Check out the competition, too: CBS News (www.cbs.com), NBC News (www.nbc.com), Fox News (foxnews.com), and CNN (www.cnn.com).

BBC News

news.bbc.co.uk

For Americans, the British Broadcasting Corporation is a sometimes-necessary reminder that the world does not always revolve around the United States. For the rest of the world, the BBC provides authoritative, thoughtful coverage of people, events, issues, and trends. The BBC Web site features not only news stories, features, and commentary, but also a special audio edition of its BBC World News program.

CBC News

www.cbc.ca

The Canadian Broadcasting Corporation site covers breaking news in Canada and internationally. It provides an interesting perspective on events in the United States, too. The site features links to detailed background information and commentary on issues in the news, plus audio newscasts and interactive discussion forums and polls.

C-SPAN

www.c-span.org

C-SPAN rates a mention here because it's so darned thorough, especially where the workings of the U.S. government are concerned. You want continuing coverage of Congressional committee hearings? C-SPAN is your network. Click top news stories for background and new developments throughout the day. C-SPAN offers sound and video clips, too.

The Weather Channel

www.weather.com

Weather can be major news, not just a conversation starter. The Weather Channel Web site is a weather fan's delight, with major national and international weather-related stories, city-by-city forecasts, maps, skiing and air-travel reports, special weather briefings for pilots, and background on weather phenomena, such as El Niño, La Niña, hurricanes, and tornadoes.

Newspapers

Newspapers are a prime resource for many kinds of research. In addition to daily coverage of the news, newspaper sites frequently maintain searchable archives (in the old days, they were called *morgues*) of back issues. Local papers can provide deep insight into companies, industries, and individuals based in the region, and offer a different perspective on environmental, political, and social issues that particularly affect communities in their area. Besides the sites listed in this section, you can find hundreds of city newspapers on the Web. Even more extensive backfiles are available on professional online services like Dialog, LEXIS-NEXIS, and Dow Jones Interactive, which allow you to search dozens of publications at once.

Los Angeles Times

www.latimes.com

The *LA Times* is your window into the Southern California economy, Hollywood culture, and, of course, the film and entertainment industry. On the Web, you can read daily news headlines and hourly updates, browse particular sections of the paper such as business or regional news, do keyword searches for articles, or register to participate in online discussion forums.

Mercury Center

www.sjmercury.com

 $

Backed by the San Jose, California *Mercury News,* Mercury Center is your doorway to Silicon Valley and the *Mercury News*'s coverage of high-tech happenings, issues, and personalities. Mercury Center also provides access to the NewsLibrary searchable archives, which cover the *Mercury News* as well as two dozen other newspapers and the NewsHound personalized news-alerting service. We describe both of these resources in Chapter 13.

The New York Times on the Web

www.nytimes.com

 $

The New York Times is a national newspaper as well as a local one. The Web edition preserves some of the feeling of the printed *New York Times,* including the Gothic-script logotype. The CyberTimes section, a Web-only exclusive, provides in-depth, ongoing coverage of computers, online culture, business technology, and the high-tech industry. You can search an archive of past articles and read summaries for free, and then pay a small fee for each story that you want to see in full.

USA Today

www.usatoday.com

The familiar graphics and editorial style of "the nation's newspaper" come through loud and clear on the *USA Today* site. We look forward to the U.S.-wide weather graphic whenever we travel to another city. Now we can get it on the Web.

The Washington Post

www.washingtonpost.com

$

The online home of *The Washington Post* gives you the inside scoop on goings-on in D.C. Read today's front-page stories online or browse the paper by section. You can search the *Post*'s archives as far back as January 1977, and retrieve the full text of stories from the last two weeks, for free. For older stories, you must set up an account and pay $1.50 to $3 (depending on the time of day) to get the complete text.

Newsmagazines

Weekly newsmagazines obviously aren't as timely as daily newspapers, but they often provide more detailed analysis and background.

The Economist

www.economist.com

  $

For an international perspective on the news, check out the U.K.-based *Economist*. The online home of *The Economist* offers stories from the current issue and selected highlights — often cover stories — from some past issues. Register to search the *Economist* archive and get business and political updates via e-mail, too. Or subscribe to the Web edition and get additional content such as surveys, reviews, and reference material.

U.S. News Online

www.usnews.com

The *U.S. News & World Report* site provides stories from this week's print issue plus a searchable and browsable archive of back issues. The site also features additional content and analysis that you won't find in the print edition. Want to talk back to the journalists? You can register to participate in the *U.S. News* online discussion forums. Prefer a different newsweekly? Never fear; your beloved *Time* (www.time.com) and *Newsweek* (www.newsweek.com) are readily available on the Web.

Wired News

www.wired.com

For news with a technology twist, put www.wired.com on your online reading list. The site, originally a *Wired* magazine venture, also covers world and national news, general business news, politics, and culture. We get our minimum daily adult requirement of *Wired News* by subscribing to the daily e-mail edition.

Wire services

Wire services are responsible for getting the story fast, distributing it to subscribing media outlets around the world, keeping on top of new developments, and filing continuous updates on rapidly changing events. TV and radio stations, news-oriented Web sites, and newspapers large and small all make use of wire service copy. You can benefit from their on-the-spot reporting even without visiting their sites. But you can also check out wire service sites directly when you want to monitor developments worldwide from the perspective of a local correspondent.

Agence France Presse (France)

www.afp.com

The Associated Press (U.S.)

wire.ap.org

Kyodo (Japan)

home.kyodo.co.jp

Reuters (UK and international)

www.reuters.com

TASS (Russia)

www.itar-tass.com

United Press International (U.S.)

www.upi.com

Xinhua (China)

www.xinhua.org

News media mega-sites

How do you locate a particular newspaper or other news source on the Web? You start with a mega-site like one of those listed in this section or described in Chapter 13. These sites all provide more-or-less comprehensive listings of news media Web sites, along with links to each one.

AJR NewsLink

ajr.newslink.org

NewsLink is a production of the prestigious *American Journalism Review*. The site features links to both print and broadcast news sources, including not only the usual suspects, but also college newspapers and alternative papers such as the *San Francisco Bay Guardian* and New York's *Village Voice*. NewsLink covers magazines, too, and a variety of regional, national, and international periodicals that focus on news and current affairs.

Newspapers Online

www.newspapers.com

Newspapers Online isn't much to look at, but don't let that stop you. Instead of flashy graphics, you get lots of content at this site. The name Newspapers Online doesn't begin to describe its scope — classified ad *shoppers,* religious periodicals,

various ethnic and minority publications, and some downright strange stuff. If you're looking for an outside-the-mainstream periodical, you may well find it here.

News updates

Want to keep up with the news without having to drive all over the Web? You can get automatic updates via e-mail, or by logging in to your private, personalized portion of a news provider's site. Chapter 13 talks about a variety of update options. Here are two:

In-Box Direct

form.netscape.com/ibd

In-Box Direct is really a one-stop subscription service for Web publications and other regularly updated sites. You register at the Netscape In-Box Direct site, pick the periodicals and services you want, and get each new issue via e-mail — direct from the publisher — as an HTML-coded page. Click a link that interests you and go right to the site for the full story.

Individual.com

www.individual.com

 $

Register at Individual.com (formerly known as NewsPage) and then create your own personalized news edition by selecting specific topics, including companies and industries that you want to follow. Whenever you return to the site, you can click My NewsPage to see updates that match your interest profile. The new information is drawn from newspapers, wire services, business and specialized trade journals, and other publications. For a small monthly fee, you can receive your daily customized news bulletins via e-mail, too.

Quality of Information

Librarians, educators, and other interested parties have created some excellent Web sites to help encourage students, and information-users in general, to think critically about the information they find online. Some of these sites contain bibliographies of readings on the subject; some suggest questions to ask and criteria to apply when assessing documents and other material you locate online; some take the form of essays and presentations with embedded links to examples and additional information on the topic; still others are practical tutorials on how to determine the quality of information in electronic form. Read Chapter 17 for more on information quality, and check the sidebar in that chapter for some additional sites on the subject.

Evaluating Quality on the Net

www.tiac.net/users/hope/findqual.html

Hope Tillman, library director at Babson College, has posted her extensive presentation on assessing the quality of information on the Net. She covers the issues involved in judging information quality, suggests some criteria, points out existing Net-based tools that can be used in the evaluation process, identifies key indicators of quality, and makes some suggestions about how to proceed on your own.

Evaluating Web Resources

www2.widener.edu/Wolfgram-Memorial-Library/webeval.htm

Evaluating Web Resources is a tutorial developed by reference librarians at Widener University. It includes lists of specific questions to ask and criteria to apply. The tutorial uses actual Web pages as examples in showing how to assess the authority and accuracy, objectivity, currency, and completeness of a site. Other sample pages illustrate some of the challenges that Web information presents — for instance, pages that mix information with advertising or entertainment. Still other samples show the characteristics of certain kinds of sites: advocacy, business and marketing, information, news, and personal home pages. The site also includes a bibliography for further reading on information quality, and links to additional sites.

Reference Books

Some kinds of research involve just a quick lookup in what librarians call a *reference book* — a dictionary, an encyclopedia, an almanac, or a directory of some kind. Chapter 7 tells you how to locate reference books online. Here are some sites designed to help you find the reference book you need, and a few examples of the many reference volumes available to you online.

Encyclopedia Britannica

britannica.com

Britannica.com is the virtual version of the world-class *Encyclopedia Britannica.* You can search by keyword or phrase and read the entire article from this classic research source. Just be forewarned; we find it so compelling that we can spend hours clicking from one article to the next.

Research-It!

**www.iTools.com/research-it/
   research-it.html**

Research-It! provides links to what librarians call *ready reference* sources — places to find answers to those frequently asked questions that reference-desk librarians hear all the time. Use Research-It! to find online acronym dictionaries, books of quotations, maps, phone books, currency converters, stock quotes, and zip codes.

The Virtual Reference Desk

thorplus.lib.purdue.edu/reference

Purdue University's Virtual Reference Desk leads you to reference books all over the Web. You can find dictionaries; phone books; maps and travel information; resources in government, science, and technology; and a fascinating collection of miscellaneous tools for looking up the answers you need. Click a general category for a list of specific publications, as well as a brief and helpful description for each. Click the title of the virtual volume to connect to it.

World Factbook

**www.odci.gov/cia/publications/
   factbook/index.html**

Despite the CIA's reputation for secrecy, its *World Factbook* was one of the first reference books made available on the Net. The Factbook provides concise yet detailed profiles of just about every country in the world, complete with a color map and depiction of the country's flag. The information for each country includes geography, demographic and economic statistics, trade and commerce, form of government, communications and transportation networks, military strength, and any ongoing wars, border disputes, or other transnational issues.

Research Groups

Members of professional associations frequently trade tips with each other, participate in educational conferences, and create and distribute newsletters and other informative publications. Here are two such groups that cater to researchers who work on the kinds of projects described in this book.

Association of Independent Information Professionals

www.aiip.org

The Association of Independent Information Professionals (AIIP) is an organization of professional researchers — not just online, but library, telephone, and document retrieval specialists as well. Members charge for their services, provide estimates of what a project may cost, and usually work on a not-to-exceed basis. The AIIP Web site includes a directory of members with descriptions of their research specialties and subject expertise. Interested in joining? You can sign up as an associate member, and upgrade to regular membership when you've gained some experience — and some clients — of your own.

Society of Competitive Intelligence Professionals

www.scip.org

Members of the Society of Competitive Intelligence Professionals (SCIP) work either independently or as part of a company's strategic planning or competitive intelligence operation. If you're intrigued by the kind of business-information gathering we describe in Chapter 12, you can find out a lot more by visiting SCIP's Web site, checking out its publications, and possibly even joining the organization.

Science, Technology, and Medicine

Originally, much of the online information needed by scientists, engineers, and medical researchers was available only in specialized databases on professional online services such as Dialog. But many of these sources are now up on the Web as well. The Web has also proved to be a popular platform for science education and for getting a basic understanding of particular scientific disciplines and issues. See Chapter 11 for the full range of scientific, medical, and technology-related research sources online.

Galaxy: Medicine

galaxy.tradewave.com/galaxy/
  Medicine.html

Galaxy: Medicine is a dense and detailed subject catalog of medical resources on the Net. You can search by keyword, or drill down from very broad categories — sometimes through several levels of increasingly specific subcategories — to find the exact topic you want. For each topic, the site lists articles from medical journals that you can read directly. Galaxy: Medicine also links to medical schools and centers, organizations, periodicals, newsgroups, and other medical resources, both on and off the Web.

How Stuff Works

www.howstuffworks.com

How Things Work

Landau1.phys.virginia.edu/Education/
  Teaching/HowThingsWork/qsearch.
  html

These sites answer virtually any question you have about, well, how the world works. How Things Work focuses on devices — internal combustion engines, airplanes, and cameras, for example. How Stuff Works takes a broader view and looks at everything from cell phones to bird houses and even how *time* works. Be careful when reading: If you knew how coffee actually works, for instance, you'd pour the cup you're drinking down the drain.

IBM Intellectual Property Network

www.patents.ibm.com

IBM's Intellectual Property Network covers patents back to 1971. You get a choice of simple or advanced search forms, with pull-down menus to make your results more precise. The IBM site also covers European patents and patent applications, Japanese patents, and publications from the World Intellectual Property Office (see the WIPO entry in this section).

National Library of Medicine

www.nlm.nih.gov

The National Library of Medicine is the home of Medline, a comprehensive database of article summaries from the international medical literature. Through the NLM Web site, you can search Medline in three ways: Grateful Med uses pull-down menus and a step-by-step search form. PubMed is for more advanced users. Medline*plus* is a selective collection of authoritative articles; you can browse by subject or broad topic, or do a simple keyword or phrase search. Grateful Med also provides access to several supplementary NLM databases, including AIDS-related ones. You can order copies of relevant articles through NLM's document delivery service, Loansome Doc.

SciCentral

www.scicentral.com

SciCentral is a catalog of more than 50,000 online resources in the biological and health sciences, and in earth and space science, engineering, chemistry, and physics. You can also find science-related news stories, information on issues such as women and minorities in science, and links to government agencies, universities, and research institutes.

U.S. Patent and Trademark Office

www.uspto.gov

Think you've invented something? The U.S. Patent and Trademark Office is your starting point for background information on how the patent process works. The PTO can also be your gateway into *trademark searching,* described in Chapter 12, and into *patent searching,* a necessary step for making sure that nobody else had the same bright idea first. The PTO Web site offers free searching of patents from 1976 to the present, including the images of the patents. That's a start, but to do a complete job, you may have to use a commercial patent database like those mentioned in Chapter 11.

World Intellectual Property Office

www.wipo.org

For European and international patents, the recognized authority is the World Intellectual Property Office in Geneva, Switzerland. Its Web site can educate you in the intricacies of cross-border patent-granting, as well as copyrights and other forms of intellectual property. The WIPO site also lets you do keyword searches or browse current and back issues of the *PCT* (Patent Cooperation Treaty) *Gazette,* a weekly publication highlighting new patent applications.

Search Engines, Subject Catalogs, and Guides

Search engines, subject catalogs, and other guides to Net resources are as essential for online research as hammers, saws, and drills are for building a house. Chapters 3 through 6 cover these basic search tools in detail. This section highlights a few of the resources available to you in such categories as general and specialized search engines, meta–search engines, collections of pointers to search sites, subject catalogs, lists of FAQs (Frequently Asked Questions), guru pages, and mega-sites.

General search engines

General search engines enable you to do a keyword search over a broad range of sites, Web-wide. Each one works differently; each has its own special features and strengths. But no single search engine covers the entire Web. For best results, check out Chapter 3 for details about each one. Then check the search tips and other documentation at individual search engine sites, and do some sample searches to see how each search engine performs for you.

AltaVista

www.altavista.com

AltaVista has a reputation for going deep, and pulling out references in Web pages that are buried well below the top level of a site. Besides straightforward keyword searching, AltaVista lets you look for your search terms in specific portions of a document, such as the title or URL, or restrict your results to items in a certain language. You can also identify Web pages that link to a particular site or to a page within a site. AltaVista's translation feature is interesting, too, though sometimes the results are more amusing than enlightening.

Excite

www.excite.com

Excite is smart enough to look for terms and concepts closely related to the keywords you supply. That means you don't have to wrack your brain to come up with all possible synonyms for your search term. When you find a document that seems to be on target, click Search for more documents like this one. Excite uses the terminology in that document to further refine — you hope — your search, and to bring back even more relevant results.

GO Network

infoseek.go.com

GO lets you refine your first-round search results without running an entirely new search. Select the Search Within Results option and add one or more terms to make your search more specific. If you're looking for news stories or company profiles in particular, you can confine your GO search to wire services, industry journals, national newspapers, and other Web-based news sources.

HotBot

www.hotbot.com

HotBot allows you to search the Web at large or to restrict your search terms to certain kinds of sites, such as current news, business directories, people-finders, stock quotes, or newsgroups and other discussion forums. You can also target your search by geographic region, or look specifically for images or other kinds of multimedia files.

Northern Light

www.northernlight.com

 $

The Northern Light search engine covers not only the Web, but also a Special Collection of articles from thousands of sources not readily available outside professional online services, such as the ones described in Chapter 9. Northern Light organizes your search results into Custom Search Folders, based on the Web sites and the types of information the search turns up. You can look at your results arranged by folder or browse a standard relevance-ranked list. Northern Light offers a reasonably-priced pay-as-you-go option for items from its Special Collection.

Specialized search engines

When you're looking for certain kinds of information — such as people, business listings, maps, software, mailing lists, and newsgroup postings — we suggest starting with a search engine designed for that purpose. See Chapter 4 for more information on putting these specialized search sites to work in your research projects.

BigBook

www.bigbook.com

BigBook is a company directory that lets you search by business name or by category. You can use BigBook to do market research, or investigate potential competition by locating all businesses of a particular type in a certain city, zip code, or telephone area code.

infoUSA

www.infousa.com

infoUSA lets you look up telephone directory white pages listings for both business and residential listings. You can also do a Reverse Lookup in which you type in a phone number, and infoUSA retrieves the listing associated with that phone number (nope, you can't use this to look up unlisted numbers).

Liszt

www.liszt.com

The Liszt search engine specializes in finding online mailing lists that deal with a specific subject such as accounting, physical therapy, travel, or library science. You can search by keyword or browse through broad subject categories to find the list you want. After you've subscribed to a mailing list, you can stay up-to-date, and sometimes participate in discussions, via e-mail. Liszt also allows you to search Usenet newsgroups; just go to
`www.liszt.com/news`.

MapQuest

www.mapquest.com

MapQuest is all about maps. The site features an interactive world atlas that lets you zoom in and out from a country-wide view down to street level. You can pinpoint a specific address, get driving directions from point A to point B, and locate places of interest such as restaurants, hotels, museums, theaters, and even ATMs. MapQuest also lets you create personalized maps, with your own landmarks and destinations, that you can print out or download.

RemarQ

www.remarq.com

RemarQ allows you to search Usenet newsgroups by keyword or browse them by general subject category. You can search not only for words in newsgroup names but also for any messages within the newsgroups in which your keywords appear. You can monitor newsgroups of interest by setting up a *MyRemarQ* profile.

Shareware.com

www.shareware.com

Download.com

www.download.com

Shareware.com and Download.com help you locate publicly available software in archives and other distribution sites around the world. You can use Shareware.com to look for a specific program name, or search by type of application, hardware platform, operating system, and other criteria. Download.com also includes trial versions of commercially available software. After you've located what you want, another click or two downloads it to your computer. Unless you're absolutely sure of the source, it's a good idea to run a virus-checking program before installing shareware on your hard drive.

Tile.Net

www.tile.net

Tile.Net lets you search for e-mail discussion groups, newsgroups, and FTP sites by topic. You can also find a relevant group by browsing Tile.Net's lists. Mailing lists are organized by name, by description, or by the Internet address of the mailing list. You can browse newsgroups by general subject or by description.

WorldPages

www.worldpages.com

WorldPages offers an assortment of specialized searches, including attorneys, automobiles, restaurants, entertainment, and travel. Research-wise, one of its most valuable assets is its <u>International</u> search link, which leads you to business directory listings in countries around the world.

Yahoo!'s People Search

people.yahoo.com

Switchboard

www.switchboard.com

Yahoo!'s PeopleSearch and SwitchBoard are two of the leading people-finding aids online. Both sites let you look up e-mail addresses and phone numbers. Both sites offer business lookups as well. If you don't find the listing you want in one of these directories, try the other.

Meta–search engines

Meta–search engines run your search request through several search engines at once. You can cover a lot of ground quickly, though you don't get to take advantage of all the specialized search features that individual engines offer. Experiment with meta–search engines like the ones described here (and in Chapter 3) by using simple keyword searches.

Ask Jeeves

www.ask.com

Ask Jeeves is an unusual meta–search engine. To begin with, it encourages plain-English search queries; just type in your question as if you were asking another person. Before going out and submitting your request to other search engines on the Web, Jeeves checks its own *knowledge base,* or in-house Q&A collection, and attempts to match your question to the answers it already knows. Sometimes the attempt succeeds, sometimes not. If not, Jeeves offers a set of results from other search engines. When you find something good, click it and go check it out in more detail.

Dogpile

www.dogpile.com

Dogpile runs your search through as many as 18 search engines at once, including newsgroup and newswire search sites. You can select and prioritize the search engines you want to put to work. The more engines you select, though, the greater the odds of getting strange and unexpected results. For best results, keep your search query as simple as possible.

Inference Find

www.infind.com

Inference Find is one of the easiest search interfaces we've found: Enter your keywords and click the search button.

Inference Find submits your search request to half a dozen of the top search engines, merges the results, removes duplicates, and groups the remaining items according to their main topic or the type of site they came from.

Invisible Web

www.invisibleweb.com

Invisible Web is a directory to searchable information contained within gated Web sites, material generally invisible to most Web-wide search engines. You can browse by category, or search by broad keywords to find the specialized site you need.

Query Server

queryserver.dataware.com/general.html

Dataware's Query Server, a favorite of search engine guru Sue Feldman, covers ten or so leading search engines and categorizes the results by content and by site.

Search engine mega-sites

Unlike meta–search engines, the sites in this section don't actually run your search in several engines at once. Instead, they point you to a vast number of search engines, both general and specialized. You can explore, individually, the ones that interest you.

All-in-One Search Page

www.allonesearch.com

The All-in-One Search Page provides a simple search form for most of the roughly 50

engines it lists, so you can submit your search from the All-in-One page. For the results, you're transported to the actual search engine site. All-in-One encompasses a dozen or so broad categories of search engine types, including Web and General Internet, Specialized Interest, Software and Images, Publications, People, News/Sports/Weather, Technical Reports, Documentation, and Desk Reference.

Beaucoup Search Engines

beaucoup.com

Beaucoup lists more than 2,000 search engines, directories, and indexes in more than a dozen different categories. These categories include Geographical, Health, Society, Sciences, and Media. Click a category and then click a site listing to go directly to the search engine you want.

Search.Com

search.com

CNET's Search.Com provides a directory of specialized search engines in categories ranging from Automotive to Travel. The site also includes an A–Z List of links to hundreds of individual search engine sites.

General subject catalogs

Web-wide subject catalogs lead you to selected resources by allowing you to drill down from a general category, sometimes through several levels of progressively more specific subcategories, until you find the site or sites you want. Chapter 5 tells you more about researching with subject catalogs.

About.com

about.com

About.com hires real-life experts to identify and point you to worthwhile resources in their areas of expertise. Those areas run the gamut from Chinese culture to business management to geology, and beyond. About.com guides also answer questions and keep you up-to-date through newsletters, e-mail, bulletin-board discussions, and scheduled online chats. Search the site by keyword or browse for your area of interest.

Argus Clearinghouse

clearinghouse.net

The Argus Clearinghouse is a catalog of *other* subject catalogs — and indexes, bibliographies, and guides — all over the Net. The categories often go two or three levels deep. Each resource is rated for content, design, organization, and overall usefulness. The Clearinghouse began as a joint project of students at the University of Michigan's library school.

Internet Public Library

www.ipl.org

The Internet Public Library leads you to resources much as a real-world public library would. You can find a reference collection, special exhibits, resources for kids and young adults, and departments devoted to magazines and serials (arranged by subject category), newspapers (arranged by geographic region), and online texts. In the online texts department, you can do a keyword search, select an author or title from an alphabetical list, or browse the collection by Dewey subject classification.

World Wide Web Virtual Library

vlib.org

The WWW Virtual Library was one of the first Web organizing tools. It covers topics from Agriculture and Education to Information Management, International Affairs, Regional Studies, Science, and Society. The catalog pages for individual topics reside on computers all over the world. Each page is different, but they're all maintained by certified experts in the field.

Yahoo!

www.yahoo.com

Yahoo! is the best-known online research tool. A fine starting point, especially when you don't know where else to begin, Yahoo!'s broad subject categories and selective listings make it easy to find useful sites for most kinds of research.

FAQ finder

FAQs, or Frequently Asked Questions lists, are an Internet tradition. A FAQ is generally a collective effort by participants in a newsgroup or other online discussion area, intended to provide the answers to . . . you guessed it. The right FAQ can sometimes tell you everything you need to know about a subject. Chapter 10 explains more about FAQs and how to use them.

Internet FAQ Archives

www.faqs.org

The Internet FAQ Archives lets you do an exhaustive, full-text search of actual FAQ contents. You can confine your search to newsgroup names, authors, subject headers, and keywords for greater precision. Or browse the FAQ listings by newsgroup name, hierarchy, or category.

Guru pages and mega-sites

Information on the Internet is organized in different ways, including a great many volunteer efforts. Individuals, agencies, and professional organizations often post collections of links to useful sites that they've discovered. *Guru page* is our term for these personal labors of love; *mega-site* is the more formal, and all-encompassing, term. Chapter 6 talks about and gives you more examples of both kinds.

Awesome Lists

209.8.151.142/awesome.html

John Makulowich's Awesome Lists began as an answer to questions like "What's so interesting about the Internet? Can you really find anything useful there?" It consists of links — divided into two lists, *A* (the truly awesome) and *B* (the merely awesome) — that show the incredible diversity of cool sites on the Web.

Direct Search

gwis2.circ.gwu.edu/~gprice/direct.htm

Gary Price has compiled a massive collection of links to directories, lists, and other resources invisible to most Web search engines, and organized the links into subject areas such as Business/Economics, Government, and Humanities.

Librarian's Index to the Internet

sunsite.berkeley.edu/InternetIndex

The Librarian's Index to the Internet isn't just for librarians — it's for anyone who wants a well-organized catalog of the best sites, directories, and databases on a wide range of topics.

New York Times CyberTimes Navigator

www.nytimes.com/navigator

Built for journalists at *The New York Times,* the CyberTimes Navigator, compiled and maintained by Rich Meislin, is a great starting point for anyone who needs quick access to the best Net sources for who, what, when, where, and why.

Sources and Experts

sunsite.unc.edu/slanews/internet/ experts.html

Sources and Experts is a guide to online directories of experts in various fields, assembled by news researcher Kitty Bennett. The list is arranged by site, with a brief description of the areas of expertise covered by each one. Many of the sites let you search or browse by topic, and examine individual expert credentials in detail.

WebRing

www.webring.com

Web rings are linked collections of individual Web sites on the same or similar topics — snowboarding, Grateful Dead music, iMac computers, and medieval studies, to name a few. You can move around a ring from one site to the next. WebRing and its

Ringworld Directory are your keys to locating rings in your area of interest. Search by keyword or phrase, or drill down through subject categories to find the ring of your dreams.

Offline meta-alternatives

One of the limitations of the meta–search engines (described in an earlier section and in Chapter 3) is that you have to keep the searches very simple — meta-search sites use very few of the *power search* tools available in individual search engines. Offline meta-engines are smart enough to use the special features of each search engine, enabling you to construct a more sophisticated search than you can with a Web-based meta-engine.

BullsEye

www.intelliseek.com/prod/bullseye.htm

BullsEye lets you specify words that you want searched as a phrase, limit your search to Web sites added or changed since a specific day, and — a feature most search engines don't offer — search for your terms in near proximity to each other. The CD packaged with this book includes a copy of the BullsEye software.

Copernic

www.copernic.com

Copernic offers a free version of its software (included on the CD that comes with this book) and two added-value commercial editions. You can build fairly complex searches, indicating whether you are searching an exact phrase or words that must be capitalized (*Bond* but not *bond*, for example).

SSSpider

www.kryltech.com/spider.htm

Subject Search Spider submits your search to multiple search engines and delivers results to your computer. Read more about it, and download a trial version, from the URL here.

Virtual Communities and Conferencing Systems

Virtual communities and online conferencing systems are gathering places for Net denizens. Some of these cyber-hangouts feature ongoing conversations on just about any subject you can imagine. Others are more specialized, dealing with particular issues or catering to the needs of doctors, lawyers, and other professional and special-interest groups. Chapter 10 explains how participating in one of these online communities can deepen and enrich your research results.

Forum One

www.ForumOne.com

Forum One is a guide to the variety of virtual communities and discussion groups or forums that exist online. You can browse the "Mega" Forums category to find forums that talk about a variety of subjects. Or you can search by category or keyword to find discussion groups dedicated to a particular subject. Forum One's main categories include Current Events, Society and Culture, Business and Finance, Health, Computers, Science, and Education, plus a listing of regional forums, both U.S. and international. Forum One isn't totally comprehensive, but it's a very good start.

Parent Soup

www.parentsoup.com

As a member of Parent Soup, you can participate in real-time chats and ongoing discussions about all phases of parenthood and all aspects of being a parent. Non-members can still read discussion forums (or message boards) and search them by keyword for postings on a particular topic. Parent Soup's main discussion areas are arranged by age of child, from pregnancy into the teens. Discussions deal with topics ranging from what to expect at various stages of pregnancy, to how to survive middle school. The Parent Soup site features such extras as a baby-name finder, a guide on fertility options, a library of readings arranged by topics and subtopics, child-rearing-related news stories, and other resources.

SF Gate

www.sfgate.com

SF Gate is a mix of publishing and community. The site offers news stories, feature articles, and columns from its two newspaper sponsors, the *San Francisco Chronicle* and the *San Francisco Examiner*. Click the Conferences link to enter the discussion area of the site. Gate conferences cover business, books, current events, movies, food, music, travel, health, technology, and more. Newspaper writers and staffers participate in, and sometimes host, many of these discussions.

Third Age

www.thirdage.com

The Third Age site describes itself as *The Web for Us*. Translate that to mean mature adults and our generation of aging baby boomers. Third Age features ongoing conversations in broad subject areas like money, technology, news and politics, health, and relationships and other personal concerns. As a non-member, you can read forum messages and search archived postings by keyword, but you can't post your own responses until you register. After you do join (it's free), you can participate in forums as well as both scheduled and impromptu real-time chat.

The WELL

www.well.com

   $

The WELL is our favorite online community, with conferences covering books, music, movies, politics, media, computers and technology, spirituality, and hundreds of other subjects. As one of the oldest communities in cyberspace (founded in 1985 or so), The WELL has had time to develop a distinctive culture of its own. You can sign up, choose from a variety of pricing plans, and explore The WELL for yourself, either through the Web or — our preference — a text-based interface called Picospan.

Part IV
The Broader Picture

The 5th Wave   By Rich Tennant

IF BOB DYLAN HAD PURSUED A CAREER IN RESEARCH

"He's a whiz at researching online, but thank goodness for e-mail because I can't understand a word he says when he talks."

In this part . . .

Maybe you've gotten hooked on finding information online. Or maybe you're resisting even trying — not because it's hard, but because you figure you'll never be able to keep up with all the new Web sites, databases, and other research tools that keep popping up out there.

Not only that — you say to yourself — what about actually *using* all that information? Can I just go ahead and quote or make copies of what I find online, or incorporate it into a paper or presentation of my own? How can I be sure that I'm not breaking the law? And how do I know that the information I've located is worth using at all — that it's accurate, reliable, complete, and up-to-date?

No kidding — when it comes to electronic information, plenty of hard and complex issues are still unresolved. This part sketches out some of the questions and challenges you'll run into, and gives you some pointers to help you cope.

Chapter 16

Keeping Up with the Online Jones(es)

•••

In This Chapter

▶ Subscribing to electronic updates

▶ Taking advantage of newsletters in print

▶ Getting by with a little help from your friends

•••

*J*ust in case you're not up on 1950s underground slang, a *jones* is an addiction. Not to make light of people struggling with real-world substance abuse problems, but the online habit can become addictive in its own way. This problem has been clinically documented and reported, sometimes over-sensationally, in the media. We know folks who are online far into the night and again first thing in the morning. It's not a pretty sight. Given the attractions of the Net, we understand and sympathize. But we can quit anytime. Right.

One of the first things you notice after you've been online for a while is that this thing is moving awfully fast. You can try saying, "Slow down, honey," and threaten to fling yourself out the passenger door, but that probably wouldn't be too productive. We've often said that trying to keep up with the cyber-information scene is like changing a tire on a moving car. These days, it's like trying to change that tire while the car is moving *and* the road is still under construction beneath you.

Hardcore Net-addicts aren't the only ones who feel overwhelmed. Unless you're a member of a cloistered religious order, or you've resolved to live off the grid and away from civilization (in either case, we doubt you'd be reading this book right now), chances are you suffer from information overload as much as we do. Fortunately, you don't have to turn your back on the outside world in order to get some relief. The solution lies in letting others do some of the filtering for you.

Help Is in the Mail: Electronic Resources

Electronic newsletters and other online subscription services are a convenient way to stay current on new developments online. You don't have to do anything. Just sit back, check your e-mail, and read the easily digestible summaries of changes that other intrepid cyber-scouts have discovered. Some of these publications appear weekly, some just monthly, and others several times a week. All the ones we're about to describe are free.

Prefer to get your information on the Web? Many of these services offer a Web edition, too. All you have to do is bookmark the URL and remember to check in once a week or so.

Don't overlook the *push* option, described in Chapter 13, for getting timely notices and actual fresh content from some of the Web sites you visit — or wish you *remembered* to visit — regularly. It's like the difference between subscribing to a magazine and having to go out and buy it at the newsstand.

We try to set aside one day every couple of weeks to follow up on the new sites and other developments that our *e-subscriptions* (shorthand for electronic subscriptions) have brought to our attention. We mark the date on our calendars just as we would a meeting, a deadline, or any other obligation.

Netsurfer Digest

Netsurfer Digest tracks new and interesting Web sites regardless of their research value. Think of it this way: Even the hardest-working information hunter needs a break now and then. The issue that landed in our mailboxes a couple of days ago featured sites for the newest dinosaur fossil discovery, updates on urban legends, a celebration of the 30th anniversary of both the Internet and Monty Python's Flying Circus (coincidence? we don't think so), a parody of Ernest Hemingway's writing style, and Scottish slang — plus several dozen others.

Netsurfer Digest's short blurbs are witty and informative. You need to use an HTML-compliant e-mail program — such as the ones that come with newer versions of Netscape Communicator and Internet Explorer — so you can click right through from Netsurfer's live links to the sites that they're describing. If you prefer, you can read the current issue or browse the archives on the Web (www.netsurf.com/nsd). To subscribe to the e-mail edition, click—you guessed it—Subscribe.

Net-happenings

Net-happenings makes a valiant effort to keep up with everything new on the Net. It does a particularly good job of tracking serious research sites as well as resources for kids and educators. Notices from *Net-happenings* cover the following topics:

- ✔ General reference sites
- ✔ State, federal, foreign government, and political resources
- ✔ K-12 (kindergarten through 12th grade) resources
- ✔ New mailing lists
- ✔ Electronic magazines, newsletters, and journals
- ✔ Software
- ✔ Internet-related books
- ✔ Conferences, workshops, training, and seminars
- ✔ General information

Net-happenings subscribers can contribute their own pointers to the list. As you can imagine, that makes for a very active list. To avoid terminal overload, we subscribe to the *digest* version of Net-happenings. Instead of receiving dozens of individual messages each day, we only get three or four, each containing anywhere from a handful to a couple of dozen postings. See Chapter 10 for more about using digest mode for your mailing lists.

To subscribe to Net-happenings, e-mail listserv@hypatia.cs.wisc.edu with the message **subscribe net-happenings**, followed by your first and last name. When we signed up, we started receiving the digest version automatically. If you find dozens of messages cluttering up your inbox the first day, send a message back to that same listserv address saying **set net-happenings digest**. If you prefer the newsgroup environment (see Chapter 10 for more about newsgroups), you can follow Net-happenings in comp.internet.net-happenings.

You can also sign up via the Web, or stick around and catch up with Net-happenings there. Go to scout.cs.wisc.edu/caservices/net-hap/index.html and click <u>Today's Postings</u>, <u>This Month's Postings</u>, or <u>Net-happenings Archive</u>. The archive is keyword-searchable, too.

NEW-LIST

You've got it — a mailing list about mailing lists. **NEW-LIST** is for announcements of new e-mail lists and significant changes in old ones. Much of the news in NEW-LIST does eventually make its way into other current awareness services like Net-happenings. But if you want to sample the range of what people are talking about online, or you just want to be among the first to know, you can subscribe to NEW-LIST by sending e-mail to `listserv@cs.wisc.edu`. Leave the subject line blank, and in the body of the message, type **sub new-list**, followed by your first and last name. To get a weekly digest instead, send an e-mail to the same address to which you subscribed, saying **set new-list digest**.

Getting really obsessed with listservs? Listing to port *and* to starboard? You can make sure that you haven't missed anything by browsing the NEW-LIST archives on the Web (`scout.cs.wisc.edu/caservices/new-list/index.html`). You can sign up for NEW-LIST via that Web address, as well.

Seidman's Online Insider

If you're interested in the companies, the personalities, and the wheeling-and-dealing behind the scenes of America Online and other consumer online services, Robert Seidman is your man. He's opinionated, well-connected, and a cat person — which gives him instant credibility in Reva's eyes. Typical issues of **Seidman's Online Insider** cover topics such as Netscape's plans to market itself as an online service; why the free Internet service provider business model will never work; and an analysis of the ratings of the most-currently-visited sites and what that means in the infinite scheme of things.

We read Seidman for the same reason that we read the business section of the local newspaper. The strategizing and maneuvering he describes have a direct effect on the online resources we use now, and the ones we'll be using in the not-so-distant future. For a text version of the newsletter, send a blank e-mail message (nothing in the subject line or in the body of the message) to `insider-text-on@seidman.infobeat.com`. For an HTML version of the newsletter, send a blank e-mail message to `insider-html-on@seidman.infobeat.com`. If you prefer, you can read the current issue or browse through back issues at his Web site at `www.onlineinsider.com`. And don't miss the pictures of Seidman's cat, Brady, under the <u>About Me</u> link.

Edupage and NewsScan

Edupage bills itself as "a summary of news about information technology." That may sound kind of ho-hum, but reading it is one of the best ways we know to keep up on some of the larger issues that affect the online realm. Three times a week, we get eight to ten well-written one-paragraph summaries on current topics — current at the time, anyway — such as Internet domain registration fees, proposals to tax the Net, and the development of electronic wallet services to make spending money online even easier.

To subscribe to Edupage, send an e-mail to `listserv@listserv.educause.edu`, typing **subscribe edupage** and your first and last name in the body of the message. For more information about Edupage, to read the publication on the Web, or to search back issues, check it out on the Web (`www.educause.edu/pub/edupage/edupage.html`).

NewsScan isn't a source for current events in Scandinavia but rather a daily summary of technology-related news. Each news item, about a paragraph long, includes a link to the full text of the article. A recent issue covered standards for wireless Internet access, a suit by Priceline.com against Microsoft, and AOL's plan to deliver e-mail to handheld wireless devices.

You can start your free subscription or read the current day's NewsScan by going to its Web site (`www.newsscan.com`).

The Rapidly Changing Face of Computing

That's a mouthful for a journal title — **The Rapidly Changing Face of Computing** — but RCFoC is a great way to stay two steps ahead. The publication started out as an internal newsletter for employees of Digital Equipment Corp. but is now available to everyone else as well. This more-or-less weekly includes lengthy, well-written news and opinion pieces by Jeff Harrow, a long-time Digital employee.

Articles focus on trends and future developments in the information technology arena. Recent issues covered topics such as the likely convergence of the Internet and television, cool new data storage devices such as transparent CDs using holography, and five-year forecasts of the electronic-commerce marketplace.

In keeping with its goal of tracking new developments, every issue is available as a radio "broadcast" from the RCFoC Web site (`www.digital.com/rcfoc`), as well as in HTML. The archives are fully searchable with AltaVista's search engine. You can read the current issue on the Web or start an e-mail subscription by sending a message to `majordomo@mail-lists.compaq.com`; type **subscribe rapidly-changing-face-of-computing** and your e-mail address in the message field.

Search Engine Report

The **Search Engine Report** is a monthly e-mail newsletter about new search engines, enhancements, and performance, as well as search techniques and sneaky trends, such as spamming keywords (loading a Web site with hidden words to increase its chances of being retrieved), that may affect your search results. We mention the Report and say more about Search Engine Watch, its Web-based home, in Chapter 3.

You can subscribe to the Search Engine Report by sending a blank e-mail message — nothing at all on the subject line or in the body of the message — to `search-engine-report-text-on@list4.internet.com`. Or use the sign-up form at the Web site (`searchenginewatch.com/sereport`).

This advice may seem woefully obvious, but it's all too easy to overlook those "What's New" announcements, updates, and warnings that greet you when you log on to a Web site or an online service such as Dialog or AOL. Even if you're a frequent visitor and already know where you're headed after you connect, take a moment to check such notices — even if you have to stop and click a link to find out what's new.

Remember Paper? — Print Resources

Your best resource for keeping up with online may be *offline* — a print publication that specializes in pointing out what's new on a particular online service or on the Net at large. One advantage of print is that it's always around, even when you're logged off, reminding you by its very existence that the online world is moving on and you've got some catching up to do.

Talk about pressure. But we refuse to give in until that pile of professional periodicals on our coffee table or nightstand has toppled onto the floor at least four times. As long as the pile remains stable, we figure the situation hasn't yet reached the critical point.

System-specific newsletters

If you have an account with one of the professional online services, such as Dialog, LEXIS-NEXIS, or Dow Jones Interactive (Chapter 9 talks more about these services), you periodically receive mailings from them — *snailmailings*. Dialog, for instance, publishes the *Chronolog,* where you can read about new databases and system features, tips for more effective searching, and upcoming changes in pricing, policy, and content. You can also read it on Dialog's Web site at `library.dialog.com/chron`. Dow Jones Interactive also maintains a Web site of newsletters, White Papers, documentation, and FAQs (Frequently Asked Questions). Subscribers receive mailings of most of this material, but you can also go to `askdj.dowjones.com` and see recent updates. Most of the material is right on that front page; click <u>For Information Professionals</u> for the InfoPro newsletter.

The problem with Web-based newsletters and updates is that you have to *remember* to go to the sites and read them there. And in fact, some services are not only mounting the latest edition of their newsletter on the Web, but are also moving in the direction of providing e-mail editions, with your choice of plain text or an HTML summary with links back to the full text on the Web.

Independent publications

For staying up-to-date on online developments, one of our colleagues swears by the publications he's always read — periodicals like *The Wall Street Journal, Business Week,* and even his local newspaper. His reasoning is that, by the time the news hits those general-interest outlets, it has to be of major importance, and therefore worthy of attention. He has a heavy-duty information filter in place, and it works for him. Personally, we're glad we heard about and had the opportunity to use Netscape and Yahoo! before the companies went public.

Print magazines such as *Internet World* and *Wired* are closer to the center of what's happening online. So are the popular PC and Mac publications that occasionally run good feature stories and comparative surveys on online search tools and other resources. Even if you don't subscribe, scan them at the newsstand to see what they're covering, and buy an issue now and then to stay — or *get* — in the loop.

Information professionals rely on several publications to help them stay on top of changes in professional online services, research databases, and the Net. For a taste of what these periodicals have to offer, check the **Information Today** Web site (www.infotoday.com) for selected articles from *Searcher* and *Information Today,* and the Online, Inc. sites for selections from **Online** (www.onlineinc.com/onlinemag) and **EContent** (www.ecmag.net) magazines.

Our vote for MVP in the paper-based update world is an eight-page monthly newsletter called *The CyberSkeptic's Guide to Internet Research,* published by **BiblioData** (www.bibliodata.com). *CyberSkeptic* is written and edited by information professionals who understand the relative strengths, weaknesses, and tradeoffs between professional research databases like those on LEXIS-NEXIS, Dow Jones Interactive, and Dialog, and equivalent (or maybe-equivalent) information on the open Web.

A typical *CyberSkeptic* issue may provide an in-depth profile of a valuable research Web site, such as: the Library of Congress, DialogWeb, Hoover's, or Business Week Online; a comparison of Medline on the Web versus the same database on Dialog; brief sketches of useful Net resources in specific fields like Business/Finance, News, Legal/Government, Technical Industries, International, and the Information Industry itself; an article on a new or recently enhanced search engine or some other research tool; plus editorial picks, tips, and techniques for effective searching. You can see why we like *CyberSkeptic* so much; it thinks the same way we do.

Human Resources

Reva will never forget her first glimpse of the multimedia Web. She had viewed it in text-only mode, using Lynx, a rudimentary text-only browser. But one day, her friend Howard Rheingold brought over a videotape from a friend of his in Japan. Joichi Ito had gotten hold of an early version of Mosaic, one of the first graphical Web browsers. They popped the tape into her VCR and she watched, rapt, as Joichi pointed and clicked and moved from page to image-bedecked page.

Kind of weird, huh, watching the Web on TV? Or maybe not — the people behind WebTV apparently think it's a natural. The point is, she found out about the Web from a friend, someone in the know, somebody who knew somebody who was a very early adopter of this new and enthralling technology.

Personal contacts are the best way we know to stay current on what's really happening online — and to distinguish the truly significant new developments from all the marketing hype, wishful thinking, and vaporware that's out there.

We belong to a private professional e-mail discussion list run by and for members of the **Association of Independent Information Professionals** (www.aiip.org). When a colleague speaks up on the list about a new search engine, database, or resource on the Web, we listen. The technical forums on CompuServe have long had the reputation for informative, helpful discussions. WELL conferences — especially those devoted to Web technology telecommunications, virtual communities, and libraries and information services—have been incredible sources of leads on cutting-edge developments in the online research field.

The trick is to hang out with people who are actually working with the new products and services they're discussing. Newsgroups are fertile ground for unfettered firsthand reports. If you're interested in search engines, hang out in comp.infosystems.search. Browsers? Try the comp.infosystems.www.browsers hierarchy. (For more about reading and participating in newsgroups, take a look at Chapter 10.) Remember — if you're reluctant to speak up in the public forum, you can always follow up in e-mail.

Whether you're a tax accountant or a graphic artist, a college student or a retiree, listen to your Net-knowledgeable friends. And if they don't volunteer the information, *ask* them. It's amazing what you can find out from a simple "What's new?"

Chapter 17

The Big Issues: Copyright, Information Use, and Quality

In This Chapter

▶ Understanding copyright

▶ Ethics, professionalism, and Netiquette

▶ Verifying information quality and reliability

"*I* found it on the Net." Well, put it *back*. No, that's not the extent of the advice you'll receive in this chapter. But too many people think, just because they "found it on the Net" — apparently free for the taking — that they're entitled to use it in any way they want. It just ain't so. Copyright law and other legal and ethical considerations govern what you can and can't do with information — and, for that matter, graphics, video, sound, and other multimedia files — that you find online.

You wouldn't appropriate someone else's term paper, or a hot idea that someone came up with in a meeting, and claim it as your own. (If you *would,* go to your room; we don't want to hear about it.) The same standards apply to using information that comes from the Web or an online database. You must act responsibly with regard to information that someone else has created, and respect their rights as owners of that intellectual property. Besides, it's just plain good manners — another aspect of the *netiquette* we talked about in Chapter 10.

We'll get off our soapbox now. In this chapter, we look at copyright and some of the other factors that affect how you make use of information that you find online. We have something to say about information quality, too, and some pointers on how to judge whether what you've retrieved is even worth using at all.

Getting Right with Copyright

What is *copyright,* exactly? When you create an original work — an article, a poem, a book, or a painting, published or unpublished — you own it. With ownership comes the right to license others to use, copy, sell, or distribute it. That right is called copyright.

You may assign copyright to someone else, as writers do when they undertake a work for hire. *Work for hire* indicates that the publisher, or whoever has commissioned the work, owns the rights to it. You may grant someone else the rights to your work in one medium, like print, while retaining the rights in a different medium, such as electronic.

But the bottom line is that copyright belongs to the creator of a work automatically, whether or not the work is marked with a © symbol, unless that person has explicitly assigned the right to that work to someone else.

Fair use

Copyright seems pretty clear-cut, right? Wrong. Copyright law also includes the concept of *fair use,* which means that other people can make limited use of your work — as long as they're not profiting from it, plagiarizing it, or distributing it *en masse* to others — without asking your permission. Without fair use — and the brief quotes and non-profit uses that it generally allows — it would be well-nigh impossible to hold a scholarly conference, bolster an argument with evidence, or even write that term paper.

We're not lawyers, nor do we play lawyers in this book. But we can tell you this: You're usually on safe ground if you

- ✔ Quote brief portions of a work, as long as you credit the source.

- ✔ Quote longer sections of a work or incorporate them in your own work, as long as you both credit and *obtain permission from* the source.

- ✔ Point someone else to a URL or database citation so that they can make use of the information directly.

You're stepping into dangerous territory if you

- ✔ Quote someone else's words without crediting the author.

- ✔ Incorporate someone else's words — or images, or multimedia creations — into your own work without obtaining permission (sometimes you have to pay a fee; sometimes a simple acknowledgment will do).

- ✔ Distribute someone else's work to others without obtaining permission.

Confusion, copyright, and the Net

Between the extremes of permissible and questionable conduct outlined in the preceding section lies a huge gray area filled with confusion. Copyright law came into being long before electronic publishing. Most experts hold that the law as it stands adequately covers this new medium. Even so, the issues and ambiguities that have arisen regarding copyright since the advent of the Net have created a Guaranteed Full Employment Act for attorneys that'll probably last for the next 20 years.

Even if the same legal principles apply online that apply to print — or to art-works created in paint or any other medium — the law, and our understanding of it, has to stretch to encompass realities such as these:

- On the Net, everyone's an author. But sometimes you can't even tell who created or holds the right to the information on a site.

- Computers and the Net have made it vastly easier to copy and distribute information. In the print world, you're limited by practical factors such as the number of copies your photocopier can crank out, and the time and effort involved in distributing them to your 500 closest friends.

- On the Net, a copy is indistinguishable from the original document, with no telltale second-generation fade. You can't detect whether you're looking at an original, a first-generation copy, or something that's been around the world and back. (Maybe if someone *did* invent an electronic document fading effect, we'd finally get rid of the Good Times Virus scare and all those other "oh no, not *that* again" mailbox-stuffers that never seem to die.)

- Electronic documents can be altered invisibly in ways that affect the author's meaning by omitting or changing critical information.

- Text from one document can be cut and pasted seamlessly into another document, as if it were part of the original.

- Electronic documents can be distributed around the world easily and instantaneously, or posted in online venues where thousands of people can read them.

Factor in other legal questions, such as what constitutes an original work, or whether a work is too short or otherwise uncopyrightable, and you've got enough loose ends to keep the intellectual property lawyers — not to mention their plaintiffs and defendants — preoccupied for decades.

In the public domain

What does it mean when a work is said to be *in the public domain?* Public domain has nothing to do with Internet domains — except that if the domain ends with *.gov,* it may be in the public domain. Huh? Okay, back up: You can use and disseminate freely a work that's in the public domain, such as most publications of the U.S. government, without having to worry about copyright. Our tax dollars at work.

Historic documents such as the Declaration of Independence, the *Bible,* and works of classical literature are usually — though not always — in

the public domain as well. You don't have to ask Shakespeare's estate for permission to quote him. Most of the works in Project Gutenberg (www.gutenberg.net), a full-text collection of literary and historic writings, are there because they're in the public domain — no fees, no contracts, no legal wrangles involved in distributing them more widely on the Net.

Public domain is the exception, though, rather than the rule. Chances are that most of the information you want to use *is* covered by copyright. Sorry.

Copyright and the professional online services

Users of professional online services such as Dialog (see Chapter 9 for more about them) dealt with the copyright issue ages ago. The information climate in these online services is more controlled than on the Web. Dialog, for example, licenses the databases it carries from individual producers, who in turn negotiate contracts with the publishers whose content they use. The publishers, in turn, negotiate with authors — or should, in the best of all possible worlds — for the use of their material in electronic form.

When you pay — and pay you do — to download or print items from Dialog or another proprietary service, a portion of that fee goes back to the entity, usually the publisher, that holds the copyright on each item. In other words, you're covered for one-time, non-commercial, use of the information. But suppose you want to distribute it to your co-workers or publish it in an in-house newsletter? Dialog has a system in place for tracking and paying for multiple copies. These guys think of everything.

Copyright and the Web

Copyright works differently on the open Web. The rules aren't as clear, and the procedures aren't built in the way they are on a closed system such as Dialog. As a starting point, you can usually assume that downloading or printing a single copy of something you find on the Web (as long as it's for your own personal, non-commercial use) or quoting brief excerpts, and giving credit where due, is okay.

Some sites, especially those run by publishers and other commercial organizations, spell out their copyright policies for you. If you click the copyright notice at the **New York Times on the Web** (www.nytimes.com), you see:

> *All materials contained on this site are protected by United States copyright law and may not be reproduced, distributed, transmitted, displayed, published or broadcast without the prior written permission of The New York Times Company. You may not alter or remove any trademark, copyright or other notice from copies of the content.*
>
> *However, you may download material from The New York Times on the Web (one machine readable copy and one print copy per page) for your personal, noncommercial use only.*
>
> *For further information, see Section Two of the Subscriber Agreement.*

Section Two spells out the copyright terms in even more explicit, excruciatingly legalese terms.

The **Wired News** copyright policy (www.wired.com) is a shade more liberal than that of the *New York Times on the Web*. See whether you can spot the differences:

> *Wired Digital materials may be copied and distributed on a limited basis for noncommercial purposes only, provided that any material copied remains intact and that all copies include the following notice in a clearly visible position: "Copyright © 1994-99 Wired Digital Inc. All rights reserved." These materials may not be copied or redistributed for commercial purposes or for compensation of any kind without prior written permission from Wired Digital Inc.*

Even when you don't see a copyright notice or the telltale © symbol, don't assume that what you find online is there for the grabbing. Remember, an original published work is automatically protected by copyright — it don't need no steenkin' symbol. If you don't find the terms and conditions of use spelled out somewhere on the site, and you'd like to use the material in a more extensive manner, such as distributing copies within your organization, you can e-mail the Webmaster, the site administrator, or the person responsible for the content. Ask permission. Sometimes that's all it takes.

You may occasionally encounter Web sites and other online distribution points that invite you to take what you want and distribute it freely. The site's owner wants to get the word out, promote her cause, or market her product, service, or professional expertise. What better way to spread the word than through an army of Net volunteers? We take explicit permission like this at face value.

For more information on copyright law, check out Brad Templeton's **A Brief Intro to Copyright** (www.templetons.com/brad/copyright.html).

Using Information Responsibly

Your responsibility doesn't end when you clear the copyright hurdle. Even if you receive blanket permission to use material that you find online, or pay a fee, or determine that you're covered by fair use or that the material is in the public domain — you should still give credit where it's due.

When using or quoting online sources in a paper, talk, handout, or PowerPoint presentation, *attribute* the source. Attribution simply means that you supply the URL for a Web site, or the author, title, journal name, and date for a work that first appeared in print. Don't attempt to pass the work off as your own. Even if that's not your intention, not citing your sources is tacky and unprofessional.

If you got your information from a newsgroup, say so. If the author sent you a copy of a document, let you pick his brain (ugh; we hate that expression), or shared his random thoughts with you in e-mail, say that, too. Notes in printed books and articles sometimes reference a source by giving the person's name and adding the phrase *private correspondence with the author,* followed by the applicable date. You don't have to be that formal, unless you're writing for publication, too. But *do* share your sources. It's not just polite; it's the professional thing to do.

Hopping along the audit trail

Documenting your information sources isn't just good manners. When Reva worked at a research company called Information on Demand, some of her projects involved gathering information on the phone from dozens of industry experts and analysts, and then synthesizing what they told her into a narrative report. Along the way, she kept a complete list of everyone she talked to, their title, affiliation, and the date she spoke to them, as well as a record of what they said and whom they may have referred her to. She gave the client a copy of this contact list along with the finished report.

If a client questioned an assertion she'd made, she pointed them to the original source. If someone had doubts about the thoroughness of her work, she referred them to the complete list of everyone she'd spoken with — and also pointed out, where appropriate, that she could have done more with a bigger budget.

Keeping track of where you got your information not only increases your credibility with your audience, be it a client, a teacher, a trial judge, a graduate seminar, or a professional meeting, but covers your tail as well. That list of contacts and sources creates an *audit trail:* a route for you, and whoever else may be interested, to re-create your information-gathering process and validate what you found at each step of the way.

YOYOW: You own your own words

Folks on The WELL, the online community where we both spend too much time, have a saying: *You own your own words.* The exact meaning of that statement is open to debate, and is debated so frequently, in fact, that the community came to abbreviate it YOYOW.

One interpretation of YOYOW is that you're responsible for what you say online. We can't argue with that. An alternative explanation — and they're not mutually exclusive — is that you, and only you, should determine how your online utterances may be used. They're not to be removed from The WELL and published or reposted in other venues without your permission. Some WELL-beings hold that what you say in one WELL conference shouldn't even be ported over to another without your explicit approval.

Putting aside the hair-splitting that always seems to accompany YOYOW discussions on The WELL, in practice it seems to boil down to good manners. Online conversation isn't fixed like a copyrightable work, and quoting someone probably won't run afoul of the law. Paraphrasing is safer than quoting directly. But it's still good form to ask. That goes even more strongly for private e-mail than for utterances in public conferences.

Thinking about Linking

One of the concerns behind the "you own your own words" philosophy described in the preceding section is that your words may be taken out of context. Web page owners have a similar concern. Anyone can link to somebody else's site just by including a simple bit of HTML code that points to the referenced site. Linking is what makes guru pages and mega-sites, like the ones we talk about in Chapter 6, such rich and robust resources.

In general, it's considered polite to ask permission before linking to someone else's site, especially if the potential linkee is an individual or small operation. Asking permission is less important if you're using a Web-wide resource such as Yahoo!, or a well-known site like the Library of Congress, which already gets thousands of hits a day.

Usually, the intention behind linking is helpful — to point you to other useful resources on a topic. But sometimes the motivation is not so benign. Consider the implications if a company's multimillion-dollar Web site were linked to an environmental group's list of corporate polluters, or a professional woman's management consulting page were linked to Babes on the Web, or the Boy Scouts of America home page were linked to a pedophile site. You get the idea — linking can subvert an author's original intentions, hold them up to ridicule, or completely change the way their message is perceived.

Inappropriate linking can work the other way around, as well. A site can gain credibility, or attempt to, by linking to other, more prestigious locations. We *do* judge people by the company they keep, and a marginal, shoddy, or unreliable operation can prop itself up with links to A-list, blue-ribbon companions.

What does this mean for you, the researcher? It means that you must think about *context* — maintaining an awareness of where you are as you move around the Web. Are you still under the IBM.com corporate umbrella? Or has your point-and-click meandering led you to a site that *parodies* IBM? Are you going to accept the content of the Drudge Report (see Chapter 13) as true on the strength of its prominent links to AP, UPI, Reuters, and other well-known news sources? Or are you going to examine Matt Drudge's allegations with the critical eye that they require?

Linking has ties to the intellectual property issues raised by copyright and the you-own-your-own-words philosophy described in the preceding section, and to the *quality* issues we talk about in the next section.

Assessing Information Quality

At Information on Demand, the research firm where Reva worked for several years, the staff used the library, the telephone, and computer databases, in various combinations, to locate whatever their clients were paying them to find. Back then, business magazines were just beginning to run articles on companies like IOD and the astounding feats that they could accomplish with just a computer, a modem, and a connection to an online service.

As a result, IOD would get a flurry of calls from prospective clients who wanted them to "pull something out of the computer." But not every project was a candidate for what the staff formally referred to as an *online literature search,* and when callers heard that their project might involve a trip to the library instead, or some phone calls to industry experts, they were sometimes horribly disappointed.

Even today, information that comes "from the computer" has a reputation for being cleaner and more reliable, somehow, than the equivalent material pulled together from dusty old books or an assortment of human experts. If you've ever had to deal with a screwed-up bank statement, you know that's not necessarily the case.

Garbage in, garbage out is an old saying from the early days of computers. It's true: The information that you get from databases and other online resources is no more accurate than the information that went in. Professional searchers have struggled for years with typos, missing paragraphs, incorrect indexing, and countless other manifestations of *dirty data.* If we had to boil down our many years of experience with online information quality into one rule of thumb, we'd say: *Never take anything at face value.*

We were luckier than we realized back when proprietary services like Dialog were our main online research tools. The information in those databases went through several stages of editorial review — first when an article appeared in print, and then again when it was converted to electronic form for inclusion in a database like Trade and Industry or Medline. Publishers took responsibility for fact checking, verifying author credentials, and making sure that none of the statements or assertions made in the article raised a red flag, legally speaking. Still more editorial massaging and overall quality assurance happened later, when the document was added to the online database.

Judging quality and reliability on the Net

You can still find a high level of reliability at some locations on the Internet. Well-known, reputable publications like *The New York Times, Forbes,* or *Consumer Reports* generally reflect the same first-rate standards of editing and quality control online that they do in print. Professional associations, such as the American Bar Association, major universities, and government agencies, tend to put as much thought and care into their Web presence as they do into their real-world transactions. Such attention to quality isn't always the case. We've seen some egregious lapses. But a recognizable brand name, whether it's a corporation, trade group, educational institution, or other official agency, is a good rough indication of quality and reliability.

A URL ending in *.gov, .edu,* or *.mil* usually indicates reliable information, as long as it represents the official presence on the Net of an institution such as the Library of Congress, Harvard University, or the U.S. Army. But remember that the online accounts of students, enlistees, and government employees end with the same set of letters; they, as a group, are no more reliable than us *.net*-heads and *.com*-mon folk.

What about the vast number of unbranded sites on the Net? How can you tell whether the information that these sites offer is worth a second glance, let alone good enough to factor into an important personal decision, present at a business meeting, or offer as evidence in court?

Some things to look out for are:

> ✔ **Accountability:** Who's responsible for the site? Is he who he purports to be? What are his credentials and his qualifications for presenting the information he presents? In the **WWW Virtual Library** (`vlib.org`), for instance (we describe that institution in Chapter 5), an individual subject site typically identifies both the institution and the individual responsible for maintaining it. The Virtual Library banner is a brand name of sorts; it provides some credibility to begin with. But if you need more specifics, or have questions about the content of the site, the responsible party's e-mail box is just a click away.

✔ **Bias:** Even reputable publications have a slant. *The Wall Street Journal* is pro-business. *Mother Jones* leans to the left. It's a lot easier to judge the bias of a Web site, and to adjust for it accordingly, when you're familiar with, or can readily determine, its underlying philosophy. But it's easy to *conceal* agendas on the Web. When laser printers first came out, every document seemed professional-looking and official. A document may not have been worth the paper it was printed on, but it looked so *good.*

Anyone can put up a substantial, handsome-looking Web site that purports to offer definitive, unprejudiced information. But unless you know the person or group and the motivation behind the site, you have to dig deeper, and read between the lines, to figure out whether to trust them.

✔ **Currency:** Information floats around the Net in a random and unpredictable way. Documents still in circulation may be outdated or superceded by more recent versions. The further you get from the source, the greater the possibility that what you're looking at is not the latest and greatest. Check to see when the Web site was last updated. Check back with the original author or issuing body to verify whether you've got the definitive edition.

Okay, that's easy enough. Now think about this one: Many Web sites are updated dynamically — often several times a day — on a continuous, rolling basis. The document you downloaded yesterday may already have been replaced by a later version, and by fresh, and perhaps even contradictory, information. If you're going to rely on a Web site to bolster your position, be sure you know what's on the site *now.*

Gopher sites (we describe these pre-Web information resources back in Chapter 1) present even more of a problem, currency-wise, than the Web. Although some people still rely on such sites, most have been neglected or even abandoned entirely in favor of the more user-friendly Web. When you land at a gopher site, poke around to see how current, in general, its files and documents appear to be. If they seem stale, be especially wary about getting outdated information.

✔ **Integrity:** The issue of document integrity ties in to our earlier discussion about copyright and how easy it is to alter electronic information, whether intentionally or unintentionally. Kids used to play a game called "Whispering Down The Lane." The point was to see how distorted a saying could become after it had passed through a dozen sets of lips and ears. Documents on the Net may be incomplete, or altered from the original in some gross or imperceptible way. Text gets scrambled, sections get lost, and new and sometimes incorrect information gets pasted in.

Widely circulated items often lose all trace of their origin. Sometimes they even get credited to another source, with a totally bogus explanation. A perfect example of this was a speech supposedly delivered by the author Kurt Vonnegut at an MIT graduation ceremony. It was a great speech; we got dozens of copies of it, ourselves, before the darned thing finally went away. But it turned out that Kurt Vonnegut had never addressed an MIT graduating class; the speech was a piece written by Mary Schmich, a columnist for the *Chicago Tribune.* Things are not always as they seem online.

Establishing expertise

The Net is full of self-appointed experts. Newsgroups are particularly fertile breeding grounds for people who claim to know what they're talking about because the newsgroup population is often transient, and anyone can post. Before taking someone's assertions at face value, click the Deja.com Member Profile link (see Chapter 10 for more about Deja.com and other newsgroup search tools) for a bio. Or click Posting History to see where else the "expert" has posted, what she's said, and how deep and accurate her knowledge appears to be.

Apply the same standards to online information that you do when deciding whether to believe something you read in the newspaper or overhear on the street:

✔ Who's saying it?

✔ What are his credentials?

✔ Does he have proof for his assertion?

✔ How current and how valid are the facts or research on which the information is supposedly based?

You can use the search engines, people-finders, and other research tools described in earlier chapters of this book to check out experts and verify that they are who they purport to be. The guy's posting from a columbia.edu address? Can you find him in the faculty directory at www.columbia.edu? Is his home page linked off the Columbia server? Is he a graduate student or tenured professor? Or an undergrad or lower-echelon staff person just out to see what he can stir up?

Or maybe you've run into a purported medical researcher who's touting a radical new treatment. What's her track record? Run her name through **Medline** (on Dialog, or at www.nlm.nih.gov) and see if anyone salutes.

Don't overlook e-mail as an investigative tool. If you're skeptical or need more documentation, get in touch with the person responsible for the statement or the site. Ask politely (of *course* you will), and chances are the individual will be happy to help you. If he's defensive, or you don't hear back from him at all, well, that may tell you something, too.

Evaluating quality: Some online resources

Librarians and information specialists have put together dozens of Web sites devoted to measuring and evaluating the quality of online information. To find out more about this crucial issue, visit any or all of these sites:

Evaluating Quality on the Net

```
www.tiac.net/users/hope/
     findqual.html
```

Evaluating World Wide Web Information

```
crab.rutgers.edu/~scholzcr/eval.
     html
```

Evaluating Web Resources

```
www2.widener.edu/Wolfgram-
     Memorial-Library/webeval.
     htm
```

Evaluating Internet Research Sources

```
www.sccu.edu/faculty/R_Harris/
     evalu8it.htm
```

Evaluating Information Found on the Internet

```
milton.mse.jhu.edu:8001/
     research/education/net.html
```

Practical Steps in Evaluating Internet Resources

```
milton.mse.jhu.edu/research/
     education/practical.html
```

How to Critically Analyze Information Sources

```
www.lib.sfu.ca/kiosk/corse/
     libguide5.htm
```

Information Quality WWW Virtual Library

```
www.ciolek.com/WWWVL-
     InfoQuality.html
```

Surveyors, geologists, and other field research types use the principle of *triangulation* to verify the location of an object in the landscape. As an online researcher, you should triangulate, too, by verifying the information you find in at least a couple of other sources. Check it in a book. Follow through on an article cited by the author. Find independent corroboration elsewhere on the Net. Ask a *different* expert.

Thinking critically

Want to know our single best tip for judging the quality of online information? Here it is in a nutshell: *Trust but verify.* Leave yourself open to the possibility of knowledge coming from unexpected, and previously undiscovered, sources. But don't accept any of it at face value. Apply the critical filters that we give you in this chapter:

- ✔ Is it backed by a brand name or trustworthy reputation? If you're looking at a Web site, what can you find out from the URL?

- ✔ Can you verify an expert's credentials, or determine who's really responsible for a site, and what she's trying to accomplish?

✔ Can you determine whether the document in front of you is complete, unaltered, and current?

✔ Did a credible source point you to the site or information source in the first place? If not, can you verify the information in at least two other independent sources?

You may not want — or need — to go through the full interrogation every time you read and decide to use something you find online. But keep these questions in mind. Retain that skeptical edge. Don't believe it just because it "came out of the computer."

Part V

The Part of Tens

The 5th Wave   By Rich Tennant

"From now on, let's confine our exploration of ancient Egypt to the Internet."

In this part . . .

So what's this Part of Tens business? It sounds vaguely medieval — *This kingdom shall henceforth be known as The Part of Tens* — or like the next card in line after the King of Hearts, the Jack of Diamonds, and the Queen of Spades. Maybe it's actually The Port of Tines — you know, the old forks' home. Or an unpleasant look on someone's face — the Pout of Tense. Or cookware — the Pots of Tin.

How much will you pay us to stop?

All right, already — this part is about lists. Lists that consist — astoundingly enough — of exactly ten items apiece. You'd almost think we planned it this way.

We enjoy making lists. We're world-class list-makers. We make lists of things we've already done for the sheer satisfaction of crossing them out. We make lists of lists. If it weren't for lists, we wouldn't remember where we put our car keys. In fact, where *are* the car keys? Oh, here they are, under the cat. We hope he wasn't out joyriding again. We worry about him.

Speaking of joyriding, this part is fast, fun, and easy to take. It's the thrill ride of the century. You must be *this* tall to read these chapters. Perhaps we exaggerate slightly. But we hope you hop in when the mood strikes you, and read a pointer here and there. You're sure to pick up some tips that, one way or another, will make your researching more interesting, effective, and rewarding.

Chapter 18

Ten Clarifying Questions for Better Research Results

In This Chapter

▶ Determining what you're really looking for

▶ Monitoring your research as you go

▶ Evaluating and fine-tuning your results

*R*esearch pros must deal with more questions than just the one they set out to answer. The pros ask questions at the beginning of a project, even before going online. They ask questions in the midst of the project and still more at the end.

Why? Glad you asked that question. The first round of questions, which librarians call the *reference interview* (see Chapter 2 for more about reference interviews), is designed to sharpen your understanding of what you're hoping to accomplish, set your goals for the research session, and suggest some opening tactics. If you're working on behalf of a client, friend, or colleague, ask that person those reference interview questions, too.

You continue asking questions as you get underway with your search, to keep on track, and to adjust and regroup if necessary. That series of questions is more like a continuous feedback loop that plays throughout your search. If things are under control, they're like a low murmur in the background; if your research quest is getting out of hand, you may crank up the volume a little. Or a lot. If you find yourself getting in too deep, you may want to stop and ask yourself these questions out loud.

The final phase of self-questioning helps you evaluate the results you're getting, figure out whether you need to do more work, and decide when you've had — we mean *gathered* — enough.

Ask the right questions and you get the right answers. Uh-uh; we wish it were as simple as that. It's not. But by continuing to ask the right questions throughout your search, you can home in on the right answers and come up with the high-quality research results that you need.

What Am I Trying to Accomplish?

A research query involves more than a list of keywords. Although keywords help define the subject, they don't say anything about *why* you need the information. For example, if you're searching on *road rage,* are you interested in news stories about drivers going berserk, or do you need information about the psychological aspects of that behavior? For news stories about aggressive drivers, you can check some of the newspaper Web sites mentioned in Chapter 13. But for psychological studies on what triggers over-the-top aggression on the highway, you'd probably go to a professional online service like Dialog to search a scholarly database such as Psychological Abstracts. Or suppose you're searching on *tomatoes.* What is it about tomatoes that interests you — growing them, throwing them, genetically engineering them, or cooking with them? Your purpose in asking the question determines where — and sometimes how — to look for the answer.

What Is This Really Worth?

You could spend days, theoretically, on even the simplest search. But most research projects aren't worth that great an investment of your time. Are you looking for the name of the 1983 American League Most Valuable Player to settle a bet? You probably don't want to spend more than 15 minutes searching for the answer. Or do you need to prepare a comprehensive report on electronic commerce in the financial services industry? In that case, several hours of research may be justified.

Researchers have their own jargon for the wide variety of searches they encounter. Each kind requires a different level of effort:

- ✔ **Quick-and-dirty:** This type of search is fast, limited, and by no means definitive. A quick-and-dirty search gives you an idea of how much information is out there and how much time, money, and effort you can expect to spend on getting it.

- ✔ **No-stone-unturned:** Also known as a *scorched-earth search,* this type covers as many sources as you can manage, in as much depth as possible. The no-stone-unturned search is a common approach when preparing for lawsuits, resolving questions of liability, and researching business takeovers or other situations that involve large amounts of money.

- ✔ **Just-a-few-good-articles:** You conduct this type of search if you need a half dozen (or so) full-text stories from authoritative publications in the field. The ideal articles will provide background on a subject and an overview of current issues, trends, and problems. Busy people like to read someone else's analysis, rather than having to go through hundreds of articles and prepare their own.

✔ **A fishing expedition:** This type of search is an open-ended quest, under-taken when you're not sure what you're looking for and are hoping to stumble across some ideas you can use to further refine your search. Fishing-expedition searches can be time-consuming and frustrating. Try to do some of that refining offline by reference-interviewing yourself (see Chapter 2 for more about reference interviewing).

✔ **Document delivery:** Conduct this type of search if you have a pretty good idea of when and where a particular article or document was published.

Answering a simple *curiosity question* requires a different level of effort than researching a high school term paper. That term paper, in turn, calls for less effort than preparing for a business deal, challenging a patent, or researching a doctoral dissertation (which is a good thing, especially if you're in high school). Know ahead of time what level of effort is appropriate for your project, and proceed accordingly.

What Else Should I Consider?

"What else should I consider?" is a catchall question intended to make you think about any special circumstances or unquestioned assumptions that you should factor into, or out of, your search query. Examples include:

✔ **Whether the topic can be expressed in terms of trade jargon or other specialized terminology.** If so, adding such terms to your search query may help broaden, deepen, or focus your results.

✔ **Whether the definitive research on the subject may come from a non-English-speaking country.** If that's a possibility, you may have to search databases that cover international sources, or journals and Web sites based outside North America and the U.K. You may even have to engage a translator or someone fluent in that language to help you out.

✔ **Whether the event is recent or historical.** If your research depends on sources that are more than a couple of years old, you may have to search the archives in a professional online service rather than on the Web.

✔ **Whether the technology is cutting-edge or well-established.** You may find more on a new technology because it's hot, or less because few people know about it yet. You may find more on an older technology because so many people have paid attention to it, or less because it's so accepted now that nobody has anything left to say. The same applies to events and people in the news. Knowing whether your subject is "old" or "new" helps you determine where to look first, and whether it makes sense to search further back in time.

✔ **Whether the person or company is high-profile or publicity-shy.** A high-profile subject practically guarantees that you'll find a lot of infor-mation; one that shuns the limelight takes more effort to research.

If you're conducting research for somebody else, ask them where they've already looked, what they found, and how much information — if any — they expect you to find. For certain kinds of projects, like determining whether you have a patentable invention, zero hits can be the best possible result.

You may be aware of some of these factors going in. Others you may glean as you examine your preliminary search results, and adjust your approach accordingly. The important thing is not to assume that you've thought of all the angles: Ask, analyze, and adjust.

Am I Likely to Find My Answers Online?

Some types of information generally aren't available on the Web. For example, you probably won't find this kind of information online:

- **Studies and surveys that cost a bundle for someone to produce and market:** Professional online services like the ones we talk about in Chapter 9 do offer some such reports, but you can expect to pay a share of that bundle.

- **Older material, such as magazine articles from the '80s or before:** Again, you may find some of this material in the professional online services, but very little on the open Web.

- **Data that's highly labor-intensive to collect:** This type of information is especially problematic if it's ultra-specific. For example, you may be able to find sales statistics online for flannel bed sheets sold in North America, but statistics for flannel bed sheets sold annually for the last ten years in Moose Jaw, Saskatchewan, broken down by king, queen, or twin-sized sheets? Dream on. Or commission your own study.

- **Confidential documents and privileged information:** Yes, top-secret, hush-hush material is sometimes leaked to the Internet, but not so routinely that you can count on finding it there. If you don't have a "need to know," face it, you may never find out.

Is Online the Best Place to Look?

Don't discount the obvious. When planning your research, check your bookshelves for basic reference volumes, such as almanacs, phone books, dictionaries, and encyclopedias. Just because you *can* look up information online doesn't mean that you should. Picking up a book is often faster and more effective than going online and searching for the same information.

Remember that your local library is one of the best resources going, whether it's a neighborhood branch or a major university library. Although you *may* be able to find a 1950s magazine article on vintage aircraft somewhere on the Net (some aviation buff may have scanned it in), why not check with your library, too? As a bonus, libraries generally come equipped with *librarians,* who can point you to useful indexes and other reference tools — not to mention particular books and journals that you can't get access to online.

What's My Plan?

Where do you begin? We're talking research strategy here. Some questions fall naturally into the search engine domain — and then you have to decide on the best engine for the job. Other research questions are candidates for the broader, more filtered *subject catalog* approach. Still other searches may benefit from the collective expertise that you get in a newsgroup FAQ. Some answers reside only in fee-based databases. Some just require a quick lookup in a particular online reference book.

Knowing the form in which you expect your information to appear — a newspaper or news wire story, or the name of an expert on a topic — will often help determine your starting point.

Chapter 2 goes into much more detail about strategizing your search. The point is to stay aware of the dazzling array of research options available to you, and to deploy them in a way that makes sense for the project at hand.

Who's Likely to Know the Answer?

If you're wondering why your rose leaves are turning yellow, you don't search every book in your house for the answer — you go right to your gardening manual, or you ask Mrs. Green-Thumb next door. The same principle applies online: Draw on your own intuition and accumulated knowledge to go right to the source — or what you hope is the source — of the information you're looking for.

For example, if you need to find information on the housing industry, your thought process may go something like this:

> "Statistics on housing construction? The government publishes a lot of statistics. . . . I read about something called FedWorld in Chapter 11. . . . Before I slog through a search-engine search on the open Web, let's see what I can find at the FedWorld site."

Or perhaps your thoughts follow this course:

"Who would know about housing construction? Builders! Maybe I can find a trade association. . . . Didn't I see a link to Associations on the Web last time I visited the **Internet Public Library** (`www.ipl.org/ref`)? Yahoo! probably has a category for home builders' associations, too. . ."

The point is to see if you can save time by taking a wild, intuitive leap (doesn't that sound like fun?) and landing right on, or near, the answer. Easy for us to say? When you get into the habit of thinking like a researcher, leaping to good conclusions should be easy for you, too.

What Have I Gathered So Far?

Answers come in many forms. Sometimes your goal is clear-cut — a phone number, a name, a statistic, a business directory listing. Often, however, you must piece together facts, comments, observations, and analyses from many different sources to come up with the complete picture.

If you think you're getting close to the finish line of your research session, pause to evaluate the information that you've collected so far. Where are the holes in your answer? What data do you still need? For example, if the only gap remaining is a single fact, a quote from the CEO, or a product description from one of the companies you're researching, you know that it's time to refine, refocus, and go after those missing pieces specifically.

Complex searches go through several iterations, from the general to the more specific, from one angle to another. Check your results periodically against your ultimate goal, and change your approach to pick up the parts you're missing.

What Have I Overlooked?

Are you not finding what you need? Or do you just want to be sure you've covered all the bases? In either case, it's probably time to step back and double-check your search strategy, your starting assumptions, and the search tactics that you've tried thus far:

✔ **Are you sure that you've entered your search terms correctly?** Have you accounted for spelling variations, other forms of the word, synonyms, and related terms and concepts? Don't overlook British and American variations in spelling (labour/labor, aluminium/aluminum) and usage (lorry/truck, aubergine/eggplant). What about human error — are you certain that you've spelled your search words correctly? Inconceivable as it may seem, could you have made a typo?

✔ **Have you imposed false assumptions or limitations on your search?** For example, a search engine may default to information published in just the last week or so, unless you tell it differently.

✔ **Are you checking the correct database?** Perhaps you're looking for an article that appeared in a magazine, but you've been searching in a newspaper article database. Or perhaps that once-reliable mega-site has gone stale since you last used it. You're not likely to pick up current pointers from a page that was last updated in 1996.

✔ **Have you utilized all the resources that you meant to?** What about that other search engine you intended to try? (See Chapters 3 and 4.) How about a Boolean search — you'll get different results than with relevance-ranking. (See Chapter 2 for more on Boolean searching.) Have you taken advantage of the special search-engine features that let you focus your search more precisely? (See Chapters 3 and 4 again.) What about those links that you intended to follow before you went off in another direction? How about venturing into new territory, such as newsgroups or guru sites (see Chapters 4 and 10 for newsgroups, and Chapter 6 for guru sites) if you haven't explored those sources before?

✔ **Can you locate broader data, or information from an allied field, that may shed some light on your search?** If you're not finding exactly what you need, try the indirect approach. What tangential indicators (such as sales of a related product, or statistics for a similar commodity) can help you develop a picture, however impressionistic, of the information landscape surrounding your topic?

How Do I Know the Information Is Good?

You can expect your research project (if it's typical) to pull up data, descriptions, and factoids from a wide variety of sources. Some of those sources will agree with each other. If the information matches from source to source, you have a built-in measure of reliability right there (either that, or you've put your finger on a widespread hoax).

However, some of the information you find is likely to be contradictory, or just not in sync. How do you weigh your catch and decide what's worth keeping and what you should throw back?

Chapter 17 has a lot more to say about judging the quality of the data you find online. Here are a few simple guidelines to get you up to speed:

✔ Scan for names that you recognize. Look for acknowledged experts, reputable publications, institutions, such as government agencies and university departments, that have a vested interest in getting it right.

✔ Look for the most current version available. A title that matches the article of your dreams is worthless if it's obsolete.

✔ Dig below the surface, if necessary, to discover the individual or organization responsible for the site, their agenda, and whether they really are who and what they claim to be.

The Web can be a masquerade ball. Some folks delight in spoofing reputable sources and pretending to be what they're not. Develop your analytical skills, and learn to trust your intuition. An investigative reporter we know always talks about the *JDLR factor* — if it Just Doesn't Look Right, it's probably not.

Chapter 19

Ten Simple Tune-Ups for Streamlined Searching

. . . .

In This Chapter

▶ Getting the most out of your browser

▶ Overcoming Web glitches

▶ Maximizing your time online

▶ Searching smarter, not harder

. . . .

*R*esearching online is like driving a car. No matter how skilled you are, you're always at the mercy of your equipment, the road, and the traffic around you. Web browsers aren't the only vehicles on the Net, but it's a good bet that you'll be racking up quite a few miles on Netscape Navigator or Microsoft Internet Explorer.

This chapter gives you some hints for keeping your browser tuned up and running smoothly, and some ideas for coping with congestion on the (cliché alert!) information highway, dealing with detours and apparent dead ends, and otherwise ensuring yourself a smooth and successful ride along the research road.

Change Your Start Page

Both Netscape and Microsoft ship their browsers with the *start page* (also known as the *default home page* — the one your browser seeks out as soon as you connect to the Web) programmed to take you automatically to their own Web sites. Our guess is that 90 percent of Web browsers still head for either home.netscape.com or home.microsoft.com as soon as they're fired up. If these companies built TV sets, they'd probably rig them to switch to the Netscape or the Microsoft channel every time you turned on the TV.

We find nothing wrong with a preprogrammed start page, as long as you can change it at will. Your browser has to start *somewhere* — and you may want to know about product upgrades, enhancements, or potential problems each time you log on. Going directly to the manufacturer's home page is one way of ensuring that you get all that information, along with other pertinent news, tips, and handy connections to Web-searching tools and other resources.

But you may have other priorities when you go online. If so, you can easily change the start page to any Web site that you choose. For example, if your first stop is usually your local newspaper's site, a search engine like AltaVista, a research gateway like the Library of Congress, or a special-interest site like The Astronomy Net, then why not retune your browser to head directly for that site each time you go online?

To change your start page in Internet Explorer 5.0, follow these steps:

1. **Go to the Web site that you want to use as your new start page (for example, www.astronomy.net).**

2. **Choose Tools⇨Internet Options.**

   The Internet Options dialog box appears.

3. **Click the General tab.**

4. **Click the Use Current button.**

   This action makes the currently displayed Web page your new starting point. (You can just as easily type the URL of your new start page directly in the Address text box.)

5. **Click OK.**

   Now, each time you start your browser (or click the Home button), you go directly to the Astronomy Net site.

To change your start page in Internet Explorer 4.0, follow these steps:

1. **Go to the Web site that you want to use as your start page.**

2. **Choose View⇨Options.**

3. **Click the General tab.**

4. **Click the Use Current button.**

5. **Click OK.**

To change your start page in Netscape Communicator 4.*x*, follow these steps:

1. **Choose Edit⇨Preferences.**

   The Preferences dialog box appears.

2. **Click Navigator.**

   The Navigator dialog box appears.

3. **Click the Navigator Starts with Home Page button.**

4. **Under Home Page — where it says** Clicking the Home Button Will Take You to This Page **— click Use Current Page.**

   The currently displayed Web page — www.astronomy.net, or wherever you happen to be — is now your new starting point. (You can also type the URL of your new start page directly in the Location box.)

5. **Click OK.**

You can now be sure that you'll see stars — or whatever — every time you log on. Or at least until you change your start page again.

Bookmark Your Favorite Web Pages

Did you forget the address of that awesome-sounding site that you heard some guy talking about on the bus? Have you misplaced the scrap of paper where you scribbled down that great URL? If you have (and we have), you know that losing track of Web sites not only is frustrating, but can also be a huge waste of time.

A bookmark file can be a Web searcher's best friend. If you discover a great site, bookmark it — right then and there, while you're thinking about it. Or add it to your Favorites folder, if you're speaking Internet-Explorer-ese. Same thing.

To bookmark a site with Internet Explorer 5.0, follow these steps:

1. **Choose Favorites⇨Add to Favorites.**

   The Add Favorite dialog box appears.

2. **Click OK, or click the Create In button to file in a particular subfolder within the Favorites list.**

3. **If you click the Create In button, click the subfolder in which you want to file the bookmark.**

4. **Click OK.**

To bookmark a site by using Internet Explorer 4.0, follow these steps:

1. **Choose Favorites⇨Add to Favorites.**

   The Add Favorite dialog box appears.

2. **Click OK.**

To bookmark a site by using Netscape Communicator 4.*x*, follow these steps.

1. **Drag the Location icon on the Location Toolbar to the Bookmark file.**

2. **Drop it in the folder where you want to store it.**

3. **Click the <u>Bookmarks</u> link along the top bar.**

4. **Click the <u>Add Bookmark</u> link.**

   The URL of the site you're looking at will be added to your bookmark file.

Bookmarking saves time in a couple of ways:

- ✔ Bookmarking a Web site helps you easily find the site again.
- ✔ Bookmarking the site eliminates the need to type — and possibly typo — the URL each time.

You can shave a few more seconds off your Web searching by bookmarking the exact page that you want — as opposed to the general "Welcome to Our Grand and Glorious Site" top-level page. Bookmarking a specific page is especially helpful if the site is complex and you're only interested in a particular portion.

For example, suppose you've explored **Thomas: U.S. Congress on the Internet** by coming in the front door (`thomas.loc.gov`). You decide that all you really need is the directory of government Web sites that you discovered there. Bookmark that specific page at `lcweb.loc.gov/global/executive/fed.html` instead of the main site at `thomas.loc.gov`.

Don't be stingy with your bookmarks. Bookmarks don't cost anything and you don't have to dust them or feed them. Besides, you can always delete unwanted bookmarks later during one of those mad frenzies of housecleaning that we're sure you, too, perform every two or three years whether your browser needs it or not.

Speaking of housekeeping, you can also save time by getting into the habit of organizing your bookmarks by general type and subject. The left side of Figure 19-1 shows Mary Ellen's bookmark list, the names of some of her folders, and the contents of her Miscellaneous folder. Well, she still has some filing to do; she's been meaning to get around to it.

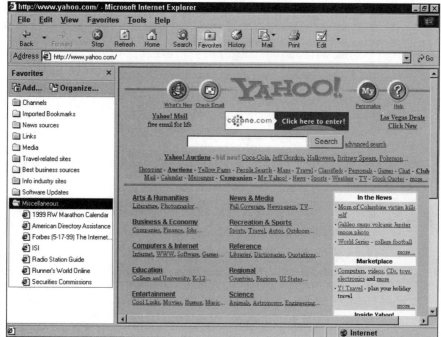

Figure 19-1:
A semi-
organized
bookmark
list.

Fight Link Rot

Link rot is one of the online researcher's biggest disappointments: You click a promising-sounding link — often the best one in a long list of search results — and it leads you nowhere. The dreaded 404: File not found message, or equivalent messages saying "we can't find this on our server," are symptoms of a condition known as *link rot.* Link rot occurs when Web pages or other referenced files move to a different host computer, change their names, join the Federal Witness Protection Program, or leave this mortal sphere.

Don't give up when the link you follow leads you smack into a dead end. Sometimes the material you want is truly dead and gone. But maybe the page merely got a makeover, or moved and left a forwarding address. Try these tactics to be sure:

- **Look for a pointer to a new URL.** Some Webmasters are thoughtful enough to provide a *pointer,* an intervening page that tells you where your desired page has gone. Sometimes they even include a link to its new location.

- **Type the complete URL into your browser.** Don't rely on what may be a broken link from the referring page.

✔ **Back up a level.** If `www.completelyclueness.com/1999/duh.htm` has gone 404 on you, try `www.completelyclueless.com/1999`. You may find a note on that page, telling you that all the 1999 files have been moved to `www.completelyclueless.com/archives`.

✔ **Back up one more level (or to the top of the Web site).** Perhaps `www.completelyclueless.com` provides a pointer to `www.totallyoblivious.com`, where all the `duh` reports now live. Or the main page may display a notice saying that the `duh` series was too controversial for the public eye, and has been withdrawn. Or that `www.completelyclueless.com` itself, and all its mighty works, has vanished into dust. We'd be sad if that happened, but at least we'd know.

Turn Images Off

Appealing as they are, GIFs, JPEGs, and other image files can create a gargantuan traffic snarl on the information speedway. Image files are much larger than text files — in fact, a moderate-sized GIF file can take up more space in digital form than a chapter of this book. Graphics-heavy Web pages are slow to load, and can bog down your research efforts big-time.

The solution? Don't look at the pretty pictures unless you're sure that you need them. A picture isn't always worth a thousand words — and sometimes the words are all you're after.

When we say don't look, we don't mean avert your eyes or browse with a blindfold on. Both of those tactics are counterproductive. Instead, exercise your browser's ability to turn images off, which speeds up the rate at which Web pages appear in your browser.

To turn images off in Netscape Communicator 4.*x*, follow these steps:

1. **Choose Edit⇨Preferences.**

   The Preferences dialog box appears.

2. **Click Advanced.**

3. **Make sure that the Automatically Load Images check box is deselected (or unchecked).**

4. **Click OK.**

To turn images off in Internet Explorer 5.0, follow these steps:

1. **Choose Tools⇨Internet Options.**

2. **Click the Advanced tab.**

   Scroll down the list of options to the Multimedia section.

  3. Deselect the Show Pictures check box.

  4. Click OK.

To turn images off in Internet Explorer 4.0, follow these steps:

  1. Choose View⊏⊃Internet Options.

  2. Click the Advanced tab.

  3. Deselect the Show Pictures check box.

  4. Click OK.

With your browser now set on STUN (for *Stop The UNnecessary*), you're on your way to faster Web maneuvering.

Some people think that turning images off is the equivalent of spending time in a sensory deprivation tank. If you're one of those people, you can still save time online by resisting the urge to zone out like you may in front of the TV. Be proactive. Anticipate what comes next: If you're familiar with the Web site, you don't have to wait for the entire page to appear before you start on your way. Click the link or label you want as soon as you see it. It's not like you're being impolite — though the Web site designers and advertisers may think otherwise. Why wait for them to draw you a picture if you already know where you're going?

Have a Cookie

Cookies are small text files stored on your computer. They contain data about you that some Web sites collect for various reasons. You voluntarily supply such information — for example, your name, age, gender, and occupation — when you register at a gated Web site like The New York Times on the Web. For more info about cookies, see the first sidebar in Chapter 9.

When a Web site asks you to register, issues you an ID and password, and then gives you the option of recognizing you automatically (and maybe even remembering your preferences) when you return, chances are that it's preparing to hand you a cookie.

Sometimes cookie information is collected in a more subtle way. For example, a cookie may contain a record of the links that you clicked recently, or the items that you chose to look at, find out more about, or purchase from other Web sites.

If this idea sounds a little creepy to you, you're not alone. Lots of people are wary of Web sites that gather personal information. Site owners use the information that they glean from cookies to tailor advertising and product content to your personal interests and tastes. We're not saying that this information-gathering is benign, but it's not necessarily ill-intentioned, either. Your attitude toward cookies may be the same as your attitude toward having a personal shopper: Would it appeal to you, or would it weird you out, to shop with a near-stranger who knows your birthday, the names of your family members, and whether you prefer boxers, briefs, or bikinis?

Personally, we're not that concerned about cookies. You can set your browser to notify you whenever a site attempts to write a cookie to your hard drive.

In Netscape Communicator 4.*x,* follow these steps:

1. **Choose Edit⇨Preferences.**

2. **Click the Advanced menu option.**

   You see a list of preferences, including a section devoted to cookies.

3. **Select one of the following check boxes:**

   - Accept All Cookies (the cookie-passing process will be invisible to you)

   - Accept Only Cookies That Get Sent Back to the Originating Server (you don't get cookies from a site — such as an advertiser — other than the one that you are actually visiting)

   - Disable Cookies (accept no cookies at all)

   - Warn Me before Accepting a Cookie (you can decide whether or not to accept a cookie)

4. **Click OK.**

In Internet Explorer 5.0, follow these steps:

1. **Choose Tools⇨Internet Options.**

2. **Click the Security tab, and then click the Internet icon.**

3. **Click the Custom Level button.**

   A dialog box appears.

4. **Scroll down to the Cookies section and click to select the Disable radio button in both cookies subsections.**

5. **Click OK, and then click Yes at the next prompt. Click OK one more time to exit the dialog box.**

In Internet Explorer 4.0, follow these steps:

1. **Choose View⇨Internet Options.**

2. **Click the Advanced tab and scroll down to find your options for cookies.**

3. **Select one of the following check boxes:**

    • Always Accept Cookies (you accept all cookies without warning)

    • Prompt before Accepting Cookies (an alert dialog box appears when a cookie is being sent to you)

    • Disable All Cookie Use (you reject all cookies)

Cookies are now so widely used that you may find the warning notices more annoying than anything else. We appreciate the convenience of having our IDs and passwords stored in our computers so that we don't have to remember them and type them in every time we visit a members-only site. That's where the streamlining comes in. Cookies are useful to us — but we still don't want to share our underwear preferences with a personal shopper.

Don't Just Sit There

Whoever first referred to the World Wide Web as the *World Wide Wait* surely spoke from experience. Images, which we tackle in an earlier section, aren't the only speed bumps in the road. Try the following suggestions to minimize your browsing time:

✔ If your browser stalls out while waiting for a page to finish loading, click the Stop button and then click the Reload or Refresh button. Sometimes that action can get you past the hump.

✔ Is the server not responding? Don't raise your blood pressure and risk repetitive stress injury by clicking like a lab rat at an empty treat-dispenser. The site may be down for maintenance, too busy to handle more traffic, or offline for an hour or so while someone edits a page. Try again a little later.

✔ Look for a mirror site somewhere else in the world. A *mirror site* is a site that's authorized to carry an exact, up-to-date replica of what's posted on the originating site. Mirror sites are specifically intended to ease congestion on the Net. Popular software-download sites, in particular, frequently include links to mirror sites. You generally find them listed right on the main site. If Cupertino is too congested, Copenhagen may be ideal.

✔ If at all possible, avoid rush hour completely. Anything that draws attention to a particular Web site is bound to result in a massive jam, whether it's a rock concert simul-Webcast, a solar eclipse video from the path of totality, or real-time election night returns. In general, traffic is lighter during off-peak hours. For example, America Online is much quicker to navigate on weekdays than during evenings and weekends.

✔ Play the time-zone game. For example, searching the Dialog system from Washington, D.C., where Mary Ellen lives, seems faster in the early morning, her time, before most of Dialog's west coast users have started work.

✔ When all else fails, multitask. Work in another window while your browser continues to churn away in search of enlightenment. Word-process that report. Open your e-mail program and catch up on correspondence. Balance your checkbook in Quicken. Plan your next research project. Do what you'd do while waiting on the phone for Microsoft tech support. In extreme cases, we've been known to go for a run, weed the file cabinet, and catch up on a pile of magazines. If it makes you nuts to wait while that little symbol at the top right of your browser twinkles and pulses and twirls . . . don't wait. Turn your attention elsewhere for a while. At least you can accomplish something — and the time will pass (or seem to pass) more quickly.

Pay Attention

Driving can be fun, relaxing, even energizing. So can researching online. But both activities require that you pay attention. A good driver sees things out of the corner of his or her eye and reacts to them instinctively, almost without thinking. So does a good researcher. Use your instinct. Stay aware. Don't be hypnotized by the rhythm of the road.

Leverage what you find. Read between the lines. When Reva used to interview industry experts, she never got off the phone without asking, "Who else should I be talking to?" Like Detective Columbo, she'd pick up on offhand comments and throwaway lines, backing up and getting people to clarify what they meant. Online, that technique translates to scanning sites with a critical eye, looking for contact names and helpful links that may be disguised under not-so-obvious labels. Burrowing deeper into a site can uncover additional resources that may not turn up in a search engine or other conventional research tool.

Paying attention online also means keeping track of where you've been and where you're going — and not forgetting about those promising-sounding pointers, six or seven sites back, that branch off in a different direction entirely. Your browser's Back button can help you recall the sites you meant to revisit.

You can also apply your browser's History function, which provides a more detailed record of the sites you've visited. To view your History file in Netscape, choose Communicator⇨Tools⇨History. In Internet Explorer 5.0, click the History button. In earlier versions, choose Go⇨Open History Folder. You didn't know that your browser kept such records? Heh heh. Don't worry; you can delete items by right-clicking on them and choosing Delete. In IE 4.0, you can clear the entire list at once by choosing Tools⇨Internet Options⇨ Clear History.

Resist Temptation

Searching isn't surfing. Although it's tempting to leap from one interesting-sounding site to another, before you know it, it's next Tuesday, your project's due, and you *still* haven't found what you were looking for.

The Net is made for pleasure as well as business. But when you're online for a specific purpose like research, the word of the day is *focus*. Don't let yourself be distracted. Take a look at Chapter 2 for more about how a researcher thinks. And use these quick tips to make the most of your online research session:

- **Plan ahead:** Think about what you want to accomplish. Jot down some terms and concepts that describe what you're looking for.

- **Map out your strategy:** Plan what subject catalogs, search engines, and other starting points you want to use.

- **Anticipate:** If your current tactic is unproductive, what can you try next?

- **Set limits:** Decide how long you're going to stay online, and how much effort you're going to devote to the current phase of your search.

- **Keep your budget in mind:** If you're using an online service that charges by the item, be selective about what you download or print.

- **Use your bookmarks:** Bookmark that fascinating but irrelevant page you landed on and file it under Playtime. It'll give you something to look forward to after your work is done.

Aggregation, Not Aggravation

Aggregated sources, like the kind you find at some of the gated sites and services described in Chapter 9, can save you time and aggravation online. You encounter two kinds of costs for information on the Web — the apparent cost and the true cost. The apparent cost is what you pay at the turnstile to search a professional online service, what you're charged to download an article from a gated service such as Northern Light, or what you're *not* charged when you gather information from free sites on the Web. The true cost is what you pay out of pocket *plus* the time you spend looking for the information. You may not be billing anyone for your time, but it's still a valuable commodity.

Say you need to search major newspapers and general newsmagazines. You can go from one publisher's Web site to another, searching each one individually. The apparent cost is probably zero, but you'll spend a lot of time figuring out how each site is organized, where to find its archive, how to search for a phrase or alternate terms, and so on. The true cost, after you factor in your time to navigate through each site, can be quite high. If, on the other hand, you take your wallet in hand and head to a gated site that aggregates content, you can search hundreds of sources at once, in a single search. Sure, you'll probably pay for access to the site, or for each article you download, but you'll finish your search in a fraction of the time it would take you to search those individual publication sites. Aggregated sources really do help prevent aggravation, particularly if you need to cover a number of publications.

Share Your Toys

We don't agree with the sentiment "everything I need to know I learned in kindergarten." If that were true, we must have been a lot more precocious — dangerous, even — than anyone realized at the time.

However, one of the lessons we were all taught back then was to share our toys. That's a lesson that has enduring value. Online, it plays out as the universal rule of the Net, which we mention in Chapter 6: Give something back.

When you find a definitive site for biotechnology, beer brewing, or whatever, or an undocumented search-engine trick, or a new electronic newsletter that cuts through the hype, let other people know about it. Share your discoveries.

If you compile a list of pointers for your own use, offer a copy to the people who helped you put it together. Mention your tips in the newsgroups, e-mail discussion groups, or other online venues where your friends and colleagues hang out. Post your discoveries on your Web site, if you have one, or send copies on request via e-mail. Give something back.

What does being thoughtful have to do with streamlining your searching? You gain karma points, the same way you do when you let a car merge in front of you on the highway. Your fellow Netizens will remember you, and they'll be much more willing to lend a hand, volunteer, or do *you* a favor the next time around. Maybe, by the time you inch up to the tollbooth, you'll discover that the guy ahead of you has already paid your toll.

Chapter 20

Ten Trends to Keep an Eye On

In This Chapter

▶ Intelligent software at your service

▶ Truly personal computing

▶ The next-generation Net

▶ Back to the future?

*P*redicting the future is a risky business. If you've ever read one of those old magazine articles with a title like, "Here's how we'll be living in . . . 1988!" then you know what we mean. Where are our self-cleaning homes? Where are our personal jetpack transportation machines? And if we're supposed to be getting all our nourishment from yummy food-like substances packaged in tubes, how come we still have to cook?

No matter how visionary we try to be, nobody has issued us a pair of magic goggles that enable us to peer far, far into the future. All we have to go on is the present and the past. Extrapolation is the name of the game: Futurists make predictions based on the current scene, and on new and possibly significant trends that have already begun to emerge.

Welcome to the edge. Read now about some emerging trends that may give you a preview of your future.

Smarter Search Engines

The next generation of search engines will be smarter and more specialized than what we have today. You won't have to exert as much effort to come up with synonyms or to ensure that your terms appear in the context that you intend. These search engines may employ a *cognitive net,* a matrix of alternative terminology and related concepts, plus an understanding of syntax, word usage, and other forms of linguistic analysis, to determine your meaning — much as a person who's listening to you knows what you mean without your having to spell it out in a literal, explicit way.

Intelligent Info-Bots

A *bot,* short for robot (the computer scientists call it an intelligent agent), is a clever piece of software that roams around the Net, bringing you the information you need even before you know you need it. Bots examine your selections and rejections, analyze your choices, and use that data to refine their own searching skills.

Shopping bots exist today, sniffing out best buys at e-commerce sites around the Web, and bringing them to your attention. The bot of the future may be your indispensable research assistant, with a personality you design to get along with your own.

Online Everywhere

Early adopters — those clued-in folks whose noses are always in the air, sniffing out the latest trends — already brag that they no longer own desktop computers; they just use their laptop — or their palmtop — machines. Wireless telecommunication will free us from modems, phone jacks, and power cords.

Embedded computers are already starting to appear in common household appliances. Expect to see Net access blossoming everywhere, including devices as familiar and easy to use as telephones and TVs. Can you live with a refrigerator that knows how to check its own inventory and order groceries from the Net?

Personal Programming

Whether it comes in over your TV, through a window on your PC monitor, or to your personal digital device, tomorrow's version of the customized news services described in Chapter 13 will be highly tailored to your needs. The Net — and the information you need right now — will live on your desktop, on flat-screen displays throughout your tastefully furnished mansion, or wherever you've parked your palmtop appliance.

Ultra-Personal Programming

Imagine a pair of eyeglasses fitted with a tiny video camera and pattern-recognition software that matches the person you're looking at against a database of acquaintances and friends. The device would whisper in your ear, or scroll text on a transparent heads-up display: "That's Bob from Accounting. Ask him about his grandkids."

How about bandages that detect how well an injury is healing and dispense antibiotics in precisely the right quantities? Can we interest you in a bio-monitoring and feedback device built into your wristwatch? How about a pair of . . . smart socks? Wearable computers like these haven't yet left the labs in large numbers, but they're under development. And after they make it out of the experimental stage, holiday gift-giving will never be the same.

Virtual Environments

Online has moved from text to pictures, and from static images to dynamic multimedia, in a very short time. The next step? Three-dimensional worlds that you can step into and move around in, or that create that illusion for you. Instead of typing on your keyboard, you'll manipulate data structures by picking them up and putting them over . . . there. You'll be able to visualize complex ideas by walking around and through them.

You'll scan your measurements, digitize a full-size, 3-D image of yourself, and upload it to the Web. Then, when you go clothes shopping online, you'll see how those pants really fit and how they look on *you.* And of course, you — or, strictly speaking, your personal *avatar* or cyber-projection — can leave the store and meet, in the virtual flesh, all those other people you've been talking to online. Hey, nice outfit.

Fatter Pipes

The popularity of the Web has bogged down the flow of information through electronic pipelines that were never designed to carry that much traffic. Better connectivity, more bandwidth, and increased speed are essential for the future of the Net. Alphabet-soup solutions like DSL (Digital Subscriber Line, or something like that) and hardware alternatives like satellite and cable modems, are already replacing slow dial-up connections in many parts of North America.

Meanwhile, a consortium of universities and other research institutions is experimenting with an entire fast-track network — much speedier than the current Internet — called (are you ready for this?) Internet 2.

Looking Forward to the Past

In the headlong rush to embrace the next big techno-thing, is anyone thinking about preserving the past? Every society needs a sense of its history in order to grow and thrive. That goes for cyberculture, too. Who are the custodians and historians of the Net?

One venture, **Alexa** (`www.alexa.com`), has made a small start on archiving the Web and has even deposited a "copy" of it with the U.S. Library of Congress. But in this new age of electronic books, Web-zines, and dynamic, constantly changing online content, we should be paying more attention to documenting the Web, present and past, so that we can learn from it in the future.

Internet Backlash?

Constant change can be tiring. You burn out on novelty after a while. The world is moving so much faster than it used to. Overnight delivery services take too long. You drum your fingertips on your desk while waiting for a fax in progress to finish. E-mail is convenient, but it speeds up communications even more — your correspondents know you're online, and they expect a response almost as immediately as if you were speaking with them face to face. What's next — telepathy? Answering *before* you get their message?

We predict an online backlash, a reaction to all this rapid change and sudden acceleration in the pace of our work, school, and even social lives. Not a total withdrawal, but what stock market watchers call a *correction*. Watch for the terminally wired to become the terminally tired. Taking time off and being out of touch will be stylish. So pry those fingers off the keyboard, unplug yourself from the Net, and get away. At least for a few hours.

A Hiccup in the Continuum

Real change comes from totally unexpected directions — a skipped beat, an extra measure, a hiccup in the continuum. Think back, if you can, to 1992 or so, before the Web burst on the scene. Would you have imagined that banks, movies, and manufacturers of sporting goods and fancy chocolates would all feature Web addresses prominently in their ads? Could you have conceived of the Internet — assuming you'd heard of it at all — being relevant in any way to your life? The Web changed everything. Even those of us who were already living and working online didn't see it coming. We were blindsided. And it's going to happen again.

Appendix

About the CD

The CD packaged with this book contains a variety of useful software tools for researching online and managing your search results more effectively. The CD also includes click-and-go hyperlinks to just about all the Web sites and sources mentioned in *Researching Online For Dummies,* 2nd Edition. This appendix tells you what's on the CD and how to install and use its contents.

System Requirements

Make sure that your computer meets the minimum system requirements listed in this section. If your computer doesn't meet most of these requirements, you may have problems using the contents of the CD-ROM:

- A PC with a 486 or faster processor, or a Mac OS computer with a 68030 or faster processor
- Microsoft Windows 95 or higher, or Mac OS system software 7.5 or higher
- At least 16MB of total RAM
- A CD-ROM drive — double-speed (2x) or faster
- A monitor capable of displaying at least 256 colors or grayscale
- A modem with a speed of at least 14,400 bps and an Internet connection

If you need more information on the basics, check out *PCs For Dummies,* 5th Edition, by Dan Gookin; *Macs For Dummies,* 5th Edition, by David Pogue; *Windows 95 For Dummies,* 2nd Edition, by Andy Rathbone (all published by IDG Books Worldwide, Inc.).

Using the CD with Microsoft Windows

To install the items from the CD to your hard drive, follow these steps:

1. Insert the CD into your computer's CD-ROM drive.

2. **Choose Start⇨Run.**

3. **In the dialog box that appears, type** D:\.

4. **Double-click the file called License.txt.**

    This file contains the end-user license that you agree to by using the CD. When you are done reading the license, close the program, most likely Notepad, that displayed the file.

5. **Double-click the file called Readme.txt.**

    This file contains instructions about installing the software from this CD. It might be helpful to leave this text file open while you are using the CD.

6. **Double-click the folder for the software you are interested in.**

    Be sure to read the descriptions of the programs in the next section of this appendix (much of this information also shows up in the Readme file). These descriptions give you more precise information about the programs' folder names, and about finding and running the installer program.

7. **Find the file called Setup.exe, or Install.exe, or something similar, and double-click that file.**

    The program's installer walks you through the process of setting up your new software.

Using the CD with a Mac OS

To install the items from the CD to your hard drive, follow these steps:

1. **Insert the CD into your computer's CD-ROM drive.**

    In a moment, an icon representing the CD you just inserted appears on your Mac desktop. Chances are the icon looks like a CD-ROM.

2. **Double-click the CD icon to show the CD's contents.**

3. **Double-click the Read Me First icon.**

    The Read Me First text file contains information about the programs and other contents of the CD, and gives you any last-minute instructions that you may need in order to correctly install the files from the CD.

4. **To install most items, just drag the folder from the CD window and drop it on your hard drive icon.**

5. **Some programs come with installer programs. With these programs, you simply open the program's folder on the CD, and then double-click the icon with the words "Install" or "Installer."**

Sometimes the installers are actually *self-extracting archives,* which means that the program files have been compressed and bundled up into an archive with the software tool needed to un-compress and install them on your hard drive. This kind of program is often called a .sea. Double-click any file with .sea in the name, and it will run just like an installer.

After you have installed the programs you want, you can eject the CD. Carefully place it back in the plastic jacket of the book for safekeeping.

What You Get on the CD

Here's a summary of the contents of this CD, arranged by category. If you use Windows, the CD interface helps you install software easily. (If you have no idea what we're talking about when we say "CD interface," flip back a page or two to find the section, "Using the CD with Microsoft Windows.")

If you use a Mac OS computer, you can take advantage of the easy Mac interface to quickly install the programs.

Research help

Lycos search engine tips

Lycos (www.lycos.com) offers both a Web search engine and a directory of selected resources, organized by category. The Help files explain how to get the most out of your search, how Lycos organizes its database, and how to interpret search results. To read these files, open the LYCOS.HTML file as described in the following steps. Then click <u>Click Here to Begin</u>.

© 1999 Lycos, Inc. Lycos® is a registered trademark of Carnegie Mellon University. All rights reserved.

To read this HTML file, follow these steps:

1. **With the CD-ROM in your CD drive, launch your Web browser.**

   See the "Internet tools" section of this appendix to find more about the Web browsers included on this CD-ROM.

2. **Choose File⇨Open (Open File or Open Page, depending on your browser) and then type** D:\LYCOS\LYCOS.HTML.

   If your CD-ROM drive is not the D: drive, enter the corresponding drive letter instead.

3. **Click OK.**

   Your browser opens the HTML file that contains the helpful search tips.

Norther Light search engine tips

For a look at the often-hidden extra features that can make your research more precise and productive, open the NORTH.HTML file as described in the following steps. Then click Click Here to Begin. A collection of tips and handy information appears, telling you how to get the most from the Northern Light search engine (www.northernlight.com). For search tips, click Search. And remember that useful, in-depth help for most search engines, not just Northern Light, is just a click away when you're online. Get into the habit of looking for help.

To read this HTML file, follow these steps:

1. **With the CD-ROM in your CD drive, launch your Web browser.**

   See the "Internet tools" section of this appendix to find more about the Web browsers included on this CD-ROM.

2. **Choose File➪Open (Open File or Open Page, depending on your browser) and then type** D:\NORTHERN\NORTH.HTML.

   If your CD-ROM drive is not the D: drive, enter the corresponding drive letter instead.

3. **Click OK.**

   Your browser opens the HTML file containing the helpful search tips.

Research tools

BullsEye (Windows 95/98/NT)

BullsEye (www.intelliseek.com/prod/bullseye.htm), from IntelliSeek, Inc., is a demo version of a desktop meta-search tool that lets you construct your query offline, then run it through multiple search engines at once. You can limit the search to Web sites added or changed since a certain day, create reports and summaries of your research results, and much more.

Copernic (Version 2000 for Windows and Version 99 for Mac)

Copernic (www.copernic.com) is a demo version of a desktop meta-search tool that lets you construct your query offline, then run it through multiple search engines and return the results to you. If you like it, you can buy an added-value version that offers additional features.

SurfSaver 1.5 (Windows 95/98/NT)

SurfSaver, from askSam Systems, is a trial version that lets you store and search Web pages from your browser. You can quickly search and browse your saved pages, even when you're not connected to the Internet. SurfSaver gives you a permanent archive of your research results and a way of organizing them. The current version runs on Internet Explorer 4.0 or higher, and Netscape 4.0 or higher. For more information about SurfSaver, check www.surfsaver.com.

Webforia (Windows 95/98/NT)

Webforia (www.webforia.com) provides tools for saving and browsing Web pages offline, adding notes and other information, and compiling them into reports. The CD includes trial software for Webforia Organizer, which saves Web pages for later reference, and Webforia Reporter, which lets you create an annotated report.

WebWhacker 2000 (Windows 95/98/NT)

WebWhacker is a freeware version that enables you to save Web pages directly to your hard disk so you can open them with your browser and read them when you're offline. The software on this CD is a demo copy that expires after a certain period of time. If you like WebWhacker after trying it, you can download and purchase the software from the Web site, www.bluesquirrel.com/products/whacker/whacker.html.

Internet tools

Anarchie 3.7 (Mac)

Anarchie 3.7 (from Stairways Software) is a Macintosh shareware File Transfer Protocol (FTP) program. You can use Anarchie to find files on the Net and to copy files between your Mac and a computer on the Net. FTP programs were more useful before the World Wide Web took hold and made finding and downloading files a snap. However, FTP programs are still handy for activities not directly supported by the Web, such as uploading your own files and Web pages. To register the software, or just to find out more about the product, check out its Web site at www.stairways.com.

FreeAgent 1.21 (Windows 95/NT)

Free Agent (from Forté, Inc.) is a Windows-based freeware program that lets you read and participate in ongoing newsgroup discussions like those described in Chapter 10. Tens of thousands of newsgroups exist, devoted to virtually every topic under the sun. Free Agent lets you read newsgroup articles offline, which can save you money and free up your phone line. For more information about how to use Free Agent, visit its Web site at www.forteinc.com.

WS_FTP Pro Windows 95/98/NT)

WS_FTP is a File Transfer Protocol (FTP) program for Windows-based computers. This program lets you transfer files and Web pages between your computer and a computer on the Net. The CD contains a trial version of the software; you can purchase a full copy from www.ipswitch.com.

Netscape Communicator 4.5 (Windows 95/98/NT and Mac)

One of the two leading Web browsers, Communicator is a basic tool for navigating the World Wide Web. To find out about the latest updates, visit the Netscape Web site at www.netscape.com.

Internet Explorer (Version 5.0 for Windows 95/98/NT and Version 4.5 for Mac)

Internet Explorer, the other leading Web browser, has essentially the same basic functionality as Netscape. Try them both and see which one you prefer. To find out about the latest updates, see the Microsoft Web site at www.microsoft.com/ie.

Utilities

Acrobat Reader 4.05 (Windows 95/98/NT and Mac)

Acrobat Reader, from Adobe Systems, is an evaluation version that lets you view and print *Portable Document Format* (or PDF) files. Many Web sites on the Internet use the PDF format for storing and presenting certain kinds of information. PDF supports the use of assorted fonts, graphics, and elegant layouts that the HTML coding used in Web pages does not. You can get more information about the Acrobat Reader from the Adobe Systems Web site at www.adobe.com.

Eudora Light 3.1.3 (Windows 95/NT and Mac)

Eudora Light is a freeware version of QualComm's popular Eudora Pro e-mail program. The Pro version includes additional features. Try out Eudora Light, and get more information about Eudora Pro at www.eudora.com.

StuffIt Expander (Mac)

StuffIt Expander from Aladdin Systems, Inc., is a file-decompression shareware utility for the Macintosh. Many files that you find on the Internet or receive as e-mail attachments are compressed, both to save storage space and to cut down on the amount of time required to download them. StuffIt Expander can decompress many types of compressed files. Visit www.aladdinsys.com for more information about StuffIt Expander.

StuffIt Lite 3.6 (Mac)

StuffIt Lite is a trial version of a file-compression program from Aladdin Systems, Inc. This Mac program lets you squeeze large files (and small ones, too, for that matter) into a fraction of the space they normally take up, so you can store and transfer them more quickly and efficiently. For information about StuffIt Deluxe, the commercial version of the program, visit www.aladdinsys.com.

DropStuff with Expander Enhancer (Mac)

DropStuff with Expander Enhancer from Aladdin Systems, Inc. is a shareware program that lets you compress files by simply dragging and dropping them on the DropStuff icon. Expander Enhancer allows you to expand a wide variety of Windows, Mac, and Internet file formats. You can use this program, if you prefer, in place of StuffIt Lite and StuffIt Expander. For more information about DropStuff with Expander Enhancer, visit www.aladdinsys.com.

WinZip 7.0 (Windows 95/98/NT)

WinZip 7.0, from Nico Mak Computing, is a shareware version of a Windows-based file compression and decompression utility. Many files you find on the Internet or receive as e-mail attachments are compressed or "zipped" to save storage space and cut down on the amount of time it takes to download them. Once you have a compressed file on your hard disk, you can use WinZip to decompress it and make it useable again. To find out more about WinZip, visit www.winzip.com.

Knowing the Difference between Freeware and Shareware

Freeware is a program that the developer makes available for public use, free-of-charge. You can download freeware from the Internet or get it on CDs like the one packaged with this book. You don't have to register your copy of the program, and you can use freeware for as long as you'd like with no obligations.

Shareware is another story. Shareware is not free — it's commercial software that you are allowed to use on a trial basis for no charge. After the trial period is over, you must decide whether to keep, and pay for, the shareware. If you decide *not* to pay for the shareware, you're expected to delete it from your computer. (Sometimes the copy you download becomes unusable upon expiration of your trial period.) If you decide to buy the shareware, follow the registration instructions that come with it.

Demo versions of commercial software products may not include all features available on the full commercial product.

Using the Internet Directory Links

The *Researching Online For Dummies* Internet Directory provides URLs and descriptions for most of the research-related sites that we mention in this book — plus a few extras that we thought might interest you. A picture (or a Web site) is worth a thousand words, so we recommend that you visit the sites we describe to get a better idea of what they can do for you.

Rather than make you flip page by page through the Internet Directory to find these URLs and then type them into your Web browser navigation window, we figured we'd save you some time and typing. So we've created a list of links to all the sites in the Internet Directory, plus the others mentioned throughout this book, arranged by category. Here's what you do to use these links:

1. **Insert the CD into your computer's CD-ROM drive.**

   Give your computer a moment to take a look at the CD.

2. **Open your browser.**

   If you don't have a browser, follow the easy steps as described in the "Using the CD" (with Windows or Mac) sections to install one. For your convenience, we have included Microsoft Internet Explorer as well as Netscape Communicator.

3. **Choose File⇨Open (Internet Explorer) or File⇨Open Page (Netscape).**

4. **In the dialog box that appears, type** D:\LINKS.HTM **and click OK.**

   Replace the letter D with the correct letter for your CD-ROM drive, if it is not "D."

5. **A file displays that will walk you through the contents of the CD.**

6. **To navigate within the interface, simply click any topic of interest to take you to an explanation of the files on the CD and how to use or install them.**

   You'll see Install buttons that will install the software for you. When you select that option, instead of installing directly from the CD, select Open This File when the Download File dialog box pops up. After you're done with the interface, simply close your browser as usual.

Use your browser's Find in This Page feature to locate a particular site or resource whose name you know.

If You've Got Problems (Of the CD Kind)

We tried our best to select programs for the CD that work on most computers with the minimum system requirements outlined earlier in this appendix. Alas, your computer may differ in some subtle and maddening aspect, and — for whatever reason — some programs may not work properly for you.

The two likeliest problems are not enough memory (RAM) for the programs you want to use, or other programs that conflict with installing or running them. If you get error messages like `Not enough memory or Setup cannot continue`, try one or more of these tips and then try using the software again:

- ✔ **Turn off any anti-virus software that you have on your computer.** Installers sometimes mimic virus activity and may make your computer incorrectly believe that it is being infected by a virus.

- ✔ **Close all running programs.** The more programs you're running, the less memory is available to other programs. Installers also typically update files and programs; if you keep other programs running, installation may not work properly.

- ✔ **In Windows, close the CD interface and run demos or installations directly from Windows Explorer.** The interface itself can tie up system memory, or even conflict with certain kinds of interactive demos. Use Windows Explorer to browse the files on the CD and launch installers or demos.

- ✔ **Have your local computer store add more RAM to your computer.** This is, admittedly, a drastic and somewhat expensive step. However, adding more memory can really help the speed of your computer and enable more programs to run at the same time.

If you still have trouble installing the items from the CD, please call the IDG Books Worldwide Customer Service phone number: 800-762-2974 (outside the U.S.: 317-572-4998).

Index

• A •

ABC News site, 229, D15
About.com, 79–80, D27
Acrobat Reader, 330
advice on streamlining searches
  bookmarking sites, 311–313, 319
  changing browser start page, 309–311
  fighting link rot, 313–314
  having a cookie, 315–317
  minimizing browsing time, 317–318
  paying attention online, 318–319
  resisting distractions, 319
  sharing your discoveries, 320
  turning images off, 314–315
  using aggregated sources, 319–320
aggregated sources, 319–320. *See also*
    gated sites or services; professional
    online services
Agriculture Online discussion groups, 164
AJR Newslink, 232–233, D18
Alexa software, 52
Alexa Web site, 324
All-in-One Search Page, 57–58
AltaVista search engine
  description of, 46–47, D22–D23
  subject catalog, 75
America Online, 121–124, D11
American City Business Journals, 200,
    201, D7
American Medical Association Web
    page, 249
American Medical Student Association, 250
American Memory Project, 112–113, D6
American Museum of Natural History, 190
Anagram Server, Internet, 93
Anarchie 3.7 (Macintosh shareware), 329
archiving of Web material, 323–324
area codes, looking up, 97
Argus Clearinghouse, 78, D27
art, literature, and history, D6–D7
article photocopies, 108–109
article wholesalers, 143–144

Ask Jeeves meta-engine, 54, 55, 250, D25
Associated Press site, 237, D17
Association of Independent Information
    Professionals, 189, 284, D20
associations, professional, 248–249
attribution, 290
audit trails, 290
Austen, Jane, D7
automatic updates
  CNN's personalized news page, 244–245
  Daily Brief, The, 242
  defined, 241
  In-Box Direct, 242, D18
  My Yahoo!, 244
  NewsHound, 243
  NewsPage, 243
  Northern Light Search Alert, 243–244
automobiles
  dealers and purchasing services, 258–259
  discussion areas on, 258
  Edmund's Web site, 257
  Kelley Blue Book site, 257, 258
  magazines on, 256–257
Awesome Lists, 86, D28

• B •

Baseball Links site, 86
basic research techniques
  Boolean searching, 29–33
  case-sensitivity tips, 38–39
  field searching, 35–36
  knowing when you're done, 39–40
  mental-mapping of online resources,
    20–23
  pluralization, truncation, and wild cards,
    36–37
  problem-solving when bad things happen,
    25–29
  proximity operators, 33–35
  reality-checking, 24–25
  reference interview, 18–19, 301
BBC (British Broadcasting Corporation)
    site, 230, D15

Beatles Album site, Internet, 86
Beaucoup search engines, 58, D26
Bennett, Kitty, D28
Berners-Lee, Tim, 77
Bibliomania site, 98
BigBook, 64–65, D24
BigHub.com meta-engine, 53
birding, 273–274
Blake, William, 98
Blue Book site, Kelley, 257, 258
bookmarking a site
  with Internet Explorer 4.0, 311–312
  with Internet Explorer 5.0, 311
  with Netscape Communicator 4.*x*, 312
  organizing bookmark list, 312–313
  resisting distractions by, 319
books online, full-text, 98
Boole, George, 29
Boolean searches
  AND, 29–30
  defined, 26
  NOT, 32
  OR, 30–31
  parentheses and, 33
Brain, Marshall, 97
broadcast news
  ABC News site, 229, D15
  BBC (British Broadcasting Corporation)
    site, 230, D15
  CBC (Canadian Broadcasting
    Corporation) site, 230, D15
  CBS News, 229
  CNN site, 229
  C-SPAN site, 230, D15
  directory listing, D15–D16
  ESPN's online home, 230–231
  Fox News site, 230
  NBC News site, 229
  real-time headlines, 228
  Weather Channel site, 231, D16
browsers
  cookies and, 316–317
  History function of, 319
  Internet Explorer (on CD), 330
  Netscape Communicator 4.5 (on CD), 330
  stalled, 317
  start page of, 309–311
Bulfinch's Mythology, 98

BullsEye offline meta-engine
  demo on CD, 328
  description of, 56, D29
business periodicals, 202
business research
  company background, 194–202
  competitive intelligence, 194, 202–210
  management theory and practice, 194,
    224–225
  market studies, 194, 210–216
  resources, D7–D9
  sales prospecting, 194, 218–220
  stocks and investment research, 194,
    220–224
Business Wire press release distribution
    service, 200
businesses, locating
  BigBook for, 64–65, D24
  infoUSA for, 65, D24
  trickiness of, 63
  WorldPages for, 66, D25

• C •

Career Mosaic job board, 255
Caribbean cruises, 261–263
Carroll, Lewis, D7
cars
  dealers and purchasing services, 258–259
  discussion areas on, 258
  Edmund's Web site, 257
  Kelley Blue Book site, 257, 258
  magazines on, 256–257
case-sensitivity, 38–39
CBC (Canadian Broadcasting Corporation)
    site, 230, D15
CBS Healthwatch, 179–180
CBS News, 229
CD packaged with this book
  Internet Directory links and, 332
  Internet tools on, 329–330
  problems with, 333
  research help on, 327–328
  research tools on, 328–329
  system requirements, 325
  using CD with Mac OS, 326–327
  using CD with Microsoft Windows,
    325–326
  utilities on, 330–331

Census Bureau, U.S., 176
CEO Express, D7
charting your future
  buying a car, 255–259
  choosing a college, 247–251
  finding a job, 252–255
  planning a vacation, 259–263
Chaucer, 98
China's Xinhua News Agency, 237
Christian Science Monitor, 202
CIA World Factbook site, 95
civil engineering, 183. *See also* sci-tech
    information
clarifying questions for better research
    results
  Am I likely to find my answers online?, 304
  How do I know the information is good?,
    307–308
  Is online the best place to look?, 304–305
  reference interview, 18–19, 301
  What am I trying to accomplish?, 302
  What else should I consider?, 303–304
  What have I gathered so far?, 306
  What have I overlooked?, 306–307
  What is this really worth?, 302–303
  What's my plan?, 305
  Who's likely to know the answer?,
    305–306
CNN site, 229
colleges and universities
  American Universities listing, 250
  College and University Home Pages,
    250, D13
  directories of, 248
  pre-med programs, 249, 250–251
communities, virtual
  defined, 161–162
  Forum One as guide to, D29–D30
  Parent Soup, 162, D30
  SF Gate, 162, D30
  surveying range of, 163
  Third Age, 162, D30
  The Well, 162, 163, 246, D30
CompaniesOnline, 198
company background research
  business periodicals for, 202
  company and industry news
    sources on, 200
  company directories and packaged
    reports on, 196–199
  company Web site and, 195–196
  defined, 194
  national newspapers for, 202
  public versus private companies, 199
  types of information included in, 195
competitive intelligence
  Business Background Reports (BBR),
    198–199, 205
  defined, 194, 202–203
  indirect approach for gathering, 209–210
  informed analysis as source of, 205–207
  local newspapers as source of, 207–208
  trade and industry databases as sources
    of, 208–209
  Web site of company you're researching
    and, 203–204
Competitive Intelligence Professionals,
    Society of, 210, D20
CompuServe, 23, 121–122, 124–125, D11
concept searching, 47
Congressional Record, 175
Conrad, Joseph, D7
consumer online services
  America Online, 121–124, D11
  CompuServe, 121–122, 124–125, D11
  defined, 116
  directory listing of, D11
conversation, information as, 16
cookies
  defined, 118, 315
  pros and cons of, 118
  warning notices for, 316–317
Copernic offline meta-engine
  demo on CD, 328
  description of, 55–56, D29
Copyright, A Brief Intro to, 289
copyright, defined, 286
copyright issues
  confusion over, 287
  fair use, 286
  professional online services and, 288
  Web copyright policies, 288–289
  works in the public domain, 288
countries, researching, 95
Cronkite, Walter, 228
C-SPAN site, 230, D15
curiosity, 3

CyberSkeptic's Guide to Internet Research, The, 283, D5

• D •

Daily Brief, The, 242
Daily Stocks site, 222, 223, D7
databases, defined, 15
databases, professional online
  advantages of using, 126–127
  choosing a service, 146–148
  cost of, 126, 129
  defined, 15
  Dialog, 132–140, 147, D10
  directory listing of, D10–D11
  Dow Jones Interactive, 129–132, 147, D10
  hints on when to use, 22–23
  information pyramids in, 127–128
  LEXIS-NEXIS, 141–143, 144, 147–148, D10–11
  newsletters of professional online services, 282–283
  quirks of, 125
  three-step process for searching, 129
Deja.com newsgroup search engine, 151
Detwiler, Susan, 86
Dialog information service
  AND operator for, 30
  as authors' favorite, 147
  case insensitivity of, 38
  database structure, 133–134
  directory description of, D10
  as gated information service, 132
  for market research, 212, 214–216
  output options, 137–139
  pricing, 140
  sci-tech information, 183–185
  Select Steps command, 135
  special search features on, 136–137
  standard way for searching, 135–136
  wild card, 37
Dictionary, Webster's, 96
digital libraries
  American Memory Project, 112–113, D6
  defined, 110
  Images from the History of Medicine, 113
  SunSITE, 111, D7
Direct Hit search engine, 52
Directory, Internet

  about the Net/staying current, D5–D6
  art, literature, and history, D6–D7
  business, finance, and economics, D7–D9
  document delivery services, D9–D10
  gated sites, D10–D11
  government and law, D11–D12
  icons in, D4
  libraries, schools, and universities, D12–D13
  magazines and journals, D13–D14
  navigation aids and organizing tools, D14
  news, D15–D18
  quality of information, D19
  reference books, D19–D20
  research groups, D20
  science, technology, and medicine, D21–D22
  search engines, subject catalogs, and guides, D22–D29
  virtual communities and conferencing systems, D29–D30
Discovery.com, 191
discussion groups (newsgroups)
  basic newsgroup hierarchy, 152–153
  defined, 58, 150
  etiquette for posting, 156–157
  FAQs (Frequently Asked Questions), 155–156, D27–D28
  for financial research, 223–224
  job hunting with, 252, 253
  Liszt search engine for browsing, 151, 152, D24
  misc.invest, 224, D8
  of professional communities, 164
  reading newsgroup posts, 154
  RemarQ search engine for finding, 59–60, 153–154
  taking temperature of a newsgroup, 155
  thrilling true life scenario about, 158
  vacation planning with, 261
document delivery services, 108–109, D9–D10
Dogpile meta-engine, 54, D25
Dow Jones Interactive
  AND operator for, 30
  as business research service, 209, 213, 216
  case insensitivity of, 38
  directory description of, D10
  field searching on, 35

as gated information service, 129–132
Historical Market Data Center, 222
Investext through, 206
management literature, 225
OR operator for, 31
pricing model, 147
wild card, 37
Download.com, 70, D24
drilling down, 71–72
DrKoop.com, 181
DropStuff with Expander Enhancer
    (Mac), 331
Drudge Report, The, 245
Dun & Bradstreet
    Business Background Reports (BBR),
        198–199, 205
    directory description of, D8
    Marketing Connection, 220

• E •

Earthquake Bulletin guru page, 86
Econtent magazine, 283, D5
EDGAR (Electronic Data Gathering
    Analysis and Retrieval), 221, D9
Edmund's Web site, 257
educational institutions
    American Universities listing, 250
    College and Universities Home Pages,
        250, D13
    directories of, 248
    pre-med programs at, 249, 250–251
Edupage newsletter, 280–281
Ei Village, 117, 120–121
Electric Library, 146, 201, D11
Electronic Journal Access Project, D13
electronic newsletter subscriptions
    as answer to information overload, 277
    Edupage, 280–281
    Net-happenings, 279, D5–D6
    Netsurfer Digest, 278, D6
    NEW-LIST, 279–280
    NewsScan, 281
    Rapidly Changing Face of Computing,
        The, 281
    Search Engine Report, 281–282, D6
    Seidman's Online Insider, 280, D6
e-mail, 163

e-mail filtering, 166
embedded computers, 322
Encyclopedia Britannica, 95–96, D19
engineering disciplines, 183. *See also*
    sci-tech information
Engineering Information Village, 16
ESPN's online home, 230–231
ethics, professionalism, and Netiquette
    assessment of information quality,
        292–297, D19
    attribution, 290
    audit trails, 290
    copyright issues, 286–289
    YOYOW (you own your own words), 291
Eudora Light, 330
Eudora Pro program, 166
EurekAlert!, 191
evaluating quality of information
    accountability for Web site, 293
    bias of Web site, 294
    critical thinking for, 296–297
    currency, 294
    editorial review of databases, 293
    experts' backgrounds and credentials, 295
    integrity of online documents, 294–295
    reputation of online literature and, 292
    resources for, 296, D19
Excite search engine
    description of, 47–48, D23
    subject catalog, 75–76
Experts listing, Kitty Bennett's Sources
    and, 150, D28
Exploratorium site, 190

• F •

fair use, 286
false hits, defined, 26
family trees, 268
FAQs (Frequently Asked Questions),
    155–156, D27–D28
Fast Company (periodical), 224
favorite Web pages, bookmarking
    with Internet Explorer 4.0, 311–312
    with Internet Explorer 5.0, 311
    with Netscape Communicator 4.*x*, 312
    organizing bookmark list, 312–313
    resisting distractions by, 319

Federal Paperwork Reduction Act, 170
FedWorld, 171–173, D11
fee-based services
  consumer online services, 116,
    121–125, D11
  defined, 14, 115–116
  directory listing of, D10–D11
  Electric Library, 146, 201, D11
  members-only Web sites, 15–16, 116,
    117–121
  Northern Light, 145, D23
  Powerize, 146, D11
  professional online services, 15, 117,
    125–144, D10–D11
  tips on choosing, 146–148
  when to use, 22–23
Feldman, Sue, D26
field searching
  on open Web, 36
  on professional online services, 35–36
financial research (stocks and
    investments)
  Daily Stocks site for, 222, 223, D7
  defined, 194, 220
  discussion groups for, 223–224
  Dow Jones Interactive site for, 222, 223
  EDGAR (Electronic Data Gathering
    Analysis and Retrieval), 221, D9
  FinancialWeb for, 223
  InvestorGuide for, 223
  misc.invest FAQ, 224, D8
  Motley Fool site for, 224, D8
  PR Newswire Investment Profiles
    section for, 223
  TheStreet.com for, 223
  Wall Street Research Net for, 223
  Yahoo! Finance for, 222
FindLaw site, 85, D12
flame wars, 165
Forbes magazine, 224
Fortune magazine, 224
Fox News site, 230
Franklin, Ben, 102
Free Agent 1.21 (Windows-based freeware
    program), 329
free electronic subscriptions
  as answer to information overload, 277
  Edupage, 280–281
  Net-happenings, 279, D5–D6

Netsurfer Digest, 278, D6
NEW-LIST, 279–280
NewsScan, 281
Rapidly Changing Face of Computing,
    The, 281
Search Engine Report, 281–282, D6
Seidman's Online Insider, 280, D6
free software
  from Download.com, 70, D24
  from Shareware.com, 69–70, D24
freeware versus shareware, 331
Fulltext Sources Online, D14
fun, research as, 7
future developments
  archiving of Web material, 323–324
  change from unexpected directions, 324
  embedded computers, 322
  fatter electronic pipelines, 323
  intelligent info-bots, 322
  Internet backlash, 324
  personal programming, 322
  smarter search engines, 321
  ultra-personal programming, 322–323
  virtual environments, 323

• *G* •

Galaxy subject catalog, 180, D21
gated sites or services
  consumer online services, 116,
    121–125, D11
  defined, 14, 115–116
  directory listing of, D10–D11
  Electric Library, 146, 201, D11
  members-only Web sites, 15–16, 116,
    117–121
  Northern Light, 145, D23
  Powerize, 146, D11
  professional online services, 15, 117,
    125–144, D10–D11
  tips on choosing, 146–148
  when to use, 22–23
genealogy, 268
general search engines
  AltaVista, 46–47, D22–D23
  defined, 44
  directory listing of, D22–D23
  Excite, 47–48, D23
  GO Network, 48–49, D23

HotBot, 49–50, D23
Northern Light, 16, 39, 50–51, D23
GO Network
directory description of, D23
as general search engine, 48–49
as subject catalog, 76
Google search engine, 52, 209
Gophers, 13–14, D14
government information
depth and variety of, 170
directory listing for sources of, D11–D12
Economic Statistics Briefing Room,
175–176
FedWorld search options for, 171–173, D11
IRS site, 171–172
Thomas site on legislation, 174–175, D12
U.S. Census Bureau, 176
USGovsearch from Northern Light, 175
guru pages
bookmarking, 83
defined, 12, 21, 83
directory listing of, D28
examples of, 86
links on, 82

● *H* ●

Haber, Dave, 86
Halvorson, T.R., 85
Harrow, Jeff, 281
Harvard Business Review, 224
healthcare industry resources, 86
healthcare information sources
CBS Healthwatch, 179–180
DrKoop.com, 181
Galaxy Medicine section, 180, D21
Health A to Z, 181
HealthGate, 181
InteliHealth, 181
Medline, 177–179, D21
Pharmaceutical Information Network, 181
StayHealthy.com, 181
support groups, 181
history
American Memory Project, 112–113, D6
History Channel, The, 97
History of Medicine, Images from, 113
Project Gutenberg, 98, D7
University of California's SunSITE, D7

hit, defined, 26
hobbies and interests
birding, 273–274
genealogy, 268
movies, 267–270
music, 270–272
recipes and cooking tips, 266–267
home remodeling, 260
Hoover's Online, 197, 205, D8
HotBot search engine, 49–50, D23
Hotjobs.com, 255
How Stuff Works, 190, D21
How Things Work, 97, 190, D21
human side of the Net
caveats and cautions on, 164–166
conversation as information, 16
e-mail, 163
for firsthand reports and personal
accounts, 149
mailing lists, 157–161
newsgroups, 150–157, 158
online experts as, 23, 150, 295
professional communities, 164
venues for, 150
virtual villages and conferencing systems,
161–163
hybrid subject catalogs
AltaVista, 75
Excite, 75–76
GO Network, 76
Yahoo!, 73–75
hypertext links in this book, 5

● *I* ●

IBM Intellectual Property Network, 188, D21
icons used in this book, 6
image map, defined, 91
In-Box Direct, 242, D18
Inference Find meta-engine, 53, D25–D26
Information Professionals, Association of
Independent, 189, 284, D20
information quality issues
accountability for Web site, 293
bias of Web site, 294
critical filters for information, 296–297
currency, 294
editorial review of databases, 293
experts' backgrounds and credentials, 295

information quality issues *(continued)*
  integrity of online documents, 294–295
  reputation of online literature, 292
  resources for evaluating quality, 296, D19
information services, gated
  consumer online services, 116,
    121–125, D11
  defined, 14, 115–116
  directory listing of, D10–D11
  Electric Library, 146, 201, D11
  members-only Web sites, 15–16, 116,
    117–121
  Northern Light, 145, D23
  Powerize, 146, D11
  professional online services, 15, 117,
    125–144, D10–D11
  tips on choosing, 146–148
  when to use, 22–23
Information Today Web site, 283, D5
information use
  attribution, 290
  audit trails, 290
  copyright issues, 286–289
  YOYOW (you own your own words), 291
Infoseek. *See* GO Network
infoUSA, 65
Insite 2, 144
InteliHealth Web site, 181
interlibrary loan (ILL), 107
Internet Directory
  about the Net/staying current, D5–D6
  art, literature, and history, D6–D7
  business, finance, and economics, D7–D9
  document delivery services, D9–D10
  gated sites, D10–D11
  government and law, D11–D12
  libraries, schools, and universities,
    D12–D13
  magazines and journals, D13–D14
  micons in, D4
  navigation aids and organizing tools, D14
  news, D15–D18
  quality of information, D19
  reference books, D19–D20
  research groups, D20
  science, technology, and medicine,
    D21–D22
  search engines, subject catalogs, and
    guides, D22–D29

  virtual communities and conferencing
    systems, D29–D30
Internet Explorer (on CD), 330
Internet Movie Database, 24, 267–270
Internet Public Library, 91, D27
Internet tools on CD packaged with this
    book, 329–330
Internet Wiretap Gopher, 13, D14
Investext, 205–206, D8
investment research
  Daily Stocks site for, 222, 223, D7
  defined, 194, 220
  discussion groups for, 223–224
  Dow Jones Interactive site for, 222, 223
  EDGAR (Electronic Data Gathering
    Analysis and Retrieval), 221, D9
  FinancialWeb for, 223
  InvestorGuide for, 223
  misc.invest FAQ, 224, D8
  Motley Fool site for, 224, D8
  PR Newswire Investment Profiles
    section for, 223
  TheStreet.com for, 223
  Wall Street Research Net for, 223
  Yahoo! Finance for, 222
InvestorGuide, 223
Invisible Web meta-engine, 54, D26
IRS site, 171–172
italicized words in this book, 5

• J •

Japanese wire service, 237
JDLR factor, 308
Jefferson, Thomas, 174
job hunting resources
  company Web sites, 252
  job boards, 252, 253–255
  local newsgroups, 252, 253
JobStar job board, 254
Joichi Ito, 284

• K •

keeping up with the online Jones(es)
  electronic newsletters for, 278–282
  information overload and, 277
  newsletters in print for, 282–283
  personal contacts for, 284

Kelley Blue Book site, 257, 258
Kyodo News site, 237, D17

● *L* ●

Law News Network, 164
legal resources
  directory listing of, D11–D12
  FindLaw, 85, D12
  LawCrawler, D12
  Lexis, D12
  Social Law Library, 85, D12
  TR's Legal Research Links, D12
legislation, 174–175
leisure-time pursuits
  birding, 273–274
  cooking, 266–267
  genealogy, 268
  movies, 267–270
  music, 270–272
LEXIS-NEXIS service
  case-sensitivity, 38
  defined, 141
  directory description of, D10–D11
  payment options, 141, 143, 147–148
  special searching features, 142–143
  wholesaler databases instead of, 143–144
  wild card, 37
librarians, expertise of, 1, 100
Librarians' Index to the Internet, 85, D28
libraries, digital
  American Memory Project, 112–113, D6
  defined, 110
  Images from the History of Medicine, 113
  SunSITE, 111, D7
Library, Internet Public, 91
library catalogs and archives
  advantages of, 99–100
  finding, 100–103
  getting ahold of items you've located, 106–109
  hints on when to use, 21–22
  telnetting to OPACs (Online Public Access Catalogs), 104–106
Library of Congress
  catalog on the Web, 103–104, D13
  site, 12
life choices
  buying a car, 255–259
  choosing a college, 247–251
  finding a job, 252–255
  planning a vacation, 259–263
life sciences, 183. *See also* medical information sources; sci-tech information
limiting results of searches, 27
link rot, 313–314
linking, inappropriate, 291–292
links on guru pages, 82
listservs. *See* mailing lists
Liszt search engine, 151, 152, D24
literary sites, 98, D7
Los Angeles Times, 232, D16
Lycos search engine tips (on CD), 327

● *M* ●

magazines, online
  archives of, 239–241
  business periodicals, 202
  car, 256–257
  Economist site, 236
  locating, 237–239
  Newsweek site, 236
  on online developments, 283
  Time site, 236
  U.S. News & World Report site, 236
mailing lists
  dealing with info- and subscription-bots, 160–161
  locating, 158–160
  netiquette for, 160
  types of, 157–158
Makulowich, John, 86, D28
management theory and practice, 194, 224–225
mandatory terms, 27
MapQuest, 67–68, D24
market research
  defined, 194, 210
  Dialog online service for, 212, 214–216
  Dow Jones Interactive for, 213, 216
  LEXIS-NEXIS for, 213, D10–D11
  Northern Light hybrid research site for, 212
  reasons for doing, 211
  sources for market research reports, 211–213

materials science, 183. *See also* sci-tech information
maximizing your time online
  bookmarking sites, 311–313, 319
  changing browser start page, 309–311
  fighting link rot, 313–314
  having a cookie, 315–317
  minimizing browsing time, 317–318
  paying attention online, 318–319
  resisting distractions, 319
  sharing your discoveries, 320
  turning images off, 314–315
  using aggregated sources, 319–320
mechanical engineering, 183. *See also* sci-tech information
medical information sources
  CBS Healthwatch, 179–180
  DrKoop.com, 181
  Galaxy Medicine section, 180
  Health A to Z, 181
  HealthGate, 181
  Images from History of Medicine, 113
  InteliHealth, 181
  Medline, 177–179, D21
  Pharmaceutical Information Network, 181
  StayHealthy.com, 181
  support groups, 181
Medieval & Classical Library, The Online, 98
Medline
  defined, 177, D21
  Grateful Med search forms, 178–179
  Medlineplus, 179
  PubMed approach to, 178
mega-sites
  defined, 12, 21, 82
  directory listing of, D28
  examples of, 84–85
  links on, 82
Meislin, Rich, D28
members-only Web sites
  defined, 15–16, 116
  Ei Village, 117, 120–121
  hints on when to use, 23
  New York Times on the Web, 117, 118–119, 289
  Wall Street Journal Interactive Edition, 117, 119–120, D9
Merck Manual of Medical Information — Home Edition, 180

Mercury Center, D16
meta-engines
  Ask Jeeves, 54, 55, 250, D25
  BigHub.com, 53
  defined, 44, 52
  Dogpile, 54, D25
  Inference Find, 53, D25–D26
  Invisible Web, 54, D26
  offline, 55–56
  pros and cons of using, 52
  SavvySearch, 53
mirror sites, 317
misconceptions about online research, 14
Monster.com, 254
Motley Fool, The, 224, D8
movies, 267–270
museums, 190–191
music, 270–272
My Yahoo!, 244
myths of online research, 2

• *N* •

National Library of Medicine Web site, 177, D21
navigation aids and organizing tools, D14
NBC News site, 229
Net beneath the Web
  defined, 12
  Gophers, 13–14
  telnet, 14
Net-happenings newsletter, 279, D5–D6
Netiquette
  attribution as, 290
  linking and, 291–292
  mailing list, 160
  newsgroup, 156–157
Netscape Communicator 4.5 (on CD), 330
Netsurfer Digest, 278, D6
network news sites
  ABC News site, 229, D15
  BBC (British Broadcasting Corporation) site, 230, D15
  CBC (Canadian Broadcasting Corporation) site, 230, D15
  CBS News, 229
  CNN site, 229

C-SPAN site, 230, D15
ESPN's online home, 230–231
Fox News site, 230
NBC News site, 229
real-time headlines, 228
Weather Channel site, 231, D16
New York Times' Cybertimes Navigator,
    85, D28
New York Times on the Web
    copyright policy, 289
    as members-only Web site, 117, 118–119
    as online newspaper, 232
newsgroups
    basic newsgroup hierarchy, 152–153
    defined, 58, 150
    etiquette for posting, 156–157
    FAQs (Frequently Asked Questions),
        155–156, D27–D28
    job hunting with, 252, 253
    Liszt search engine for browsing, 151,
        152, D24
    misc.invest, 224, D8
    reading newsgroup posts, 154
    RemarQ search engine for finding, 59–60,
        153–154
    taking temperature of a newsgroup, 155
    thrilling true life scenario about, 158
    vacation planning with, 261
NewsHound, 243
newsletters, electronic
    as answer to information overload, 277
    Edupage, 280–281
    Net-happenings, 279, D5–D6
    Netsurfer Digest, 278, D6
    NEW-LIST, 279–280
    NewsScan, 281
    Rapidly Changing Face of Computing,
        The, 281
    Search Engine Report, 281–282, D6
    Seidman's Online Insider, 280, D6
newsletters, print, 282–283
NewsPage, 243
newspapers, online
    advantages of, 231
    archives of, 234–235
    directory listing of, D16–D17
    finding your local paper, 232–233
    Los Angeles Times, 232, D16
    New York Times on the Web, 232, D16

professional online services and, 235–236
    searching, 233–234, 235–236
    USA Today, 202, 232, D16
    Washington Post, 232, D17
NewsScan newsletter, 281
Northern Light search engine
    Alert feature, 51, 243–244
    case-sensitivity, 39
    directory description of, D23
    as general search engine, 50–51
    market research reports, 212
    as members-only Web site, 16
    tips (on CD), 328
    USGovsearch, 175
Notess, Greg, D6
Nova Online, 191

• O •

offline meta-engines
    BullsEye, 56, 328, D29
    on CD with this book, 55, 328
    Copernic, 55–56, 328, D29
    Sherlock, 56
On the CD icon, 6
Onion, The, 245–246
online conferencing systems
    defined, 161–162
    Parent Soup, 162, D30
    SF Gate, 162, D30
    surveying range of, 163
    Third Age, 162, D30
    The Well, 162, 163, 246, D30
online magazines
    archives of, 239–241
    business periodicals, 202
    about cars, 256–257
    Economist site, 236
    locating, 237–239
    Newsweek site, 236
    about online trends, 283
    Time site, 236
    U.S. News & World Report site, 236
online network news
    ABC News site, 229
    BBC (British Broadcasting Corporation)
        site, 230
    CBC (Canadian Broadcasting
        Corporation) site, 230

online network news *(continued)*
CBS News, 229
CNN site, 229
C-SPAN site, 230
ESPN's online home, 230–231
Fox News site, 230
NBC News site, 229
real-time headlines on, 228
Weather Channel site, 231
online newspapers
advantages of, 231
archives of, 234–235
directory listing of, D16–D17
finding your local paper, 232–233
Los Angeles Times, 232
New York Times on the Web, 232
professional online services and, 235–236
searching, 233–234, 235–236
USA Today, 202, 232, D16
The Washington Post, 232
online research
copyright and, 286–289
as fun, 7
Internet Directory for, D1–D30
misconceptions about, 14
quality of information from, 292–297, D19
questions for better results from, 301–308
reference interview, 18–19, 301
responsible use of information from, 290–291
tips for streamlined searching, 309–320
open Web
defined, 20
field searching on, 36
overload, online world, 166

• P •

Parent Soup site, 162, D30
parentheses, 33
parts of this book, 4–5
Patent and Trademark Office (PTO) Web site, 186–188, D22
patent searching
IBM Intellectual Property Network for, 188, D21
Patent and Trademark Office (PTO) Web site for, 186–188
professional patent searchers for, 188–189
synonyms and, 186
patents
defined, 183, 185
international, 186
Penn Library Web site, 102
people finders
Switchboard, 60, 62, D25
Yahoo! People Search, 60–61, D25
people resources (human side of the Net)
caveats and cautions on, 164–166
conversation as information, 16
credentials and background of, 295
e-mail, 163
for firsthand reports and personal accounts, 149
mailing lists, 157–161
newsgroups, 150–157, 158
online experts, 23, 150, 295
professional communities, 164
venues for, 150
virtual villages and conferencing systems, 161–163
people-finding, tips on, 62–63
personal interests and hobbies
birding, 273–274
cooking, 266–267
genealogy, 268
movies, 267–270
music, 270–272
personal programming, 322–323
Peterson, Roger Tory, 273
Peterson's Directory of Colleges and Universities, 248, D13
Pharmaceutical Information Network, 181
Physicians Online, 164
pluralization, 36–37
plus sign, 44
pointer sites, defined, 233
Powell's bookstore, 107
Powerize, 146
PR Newswire press release distribution service, 200
predictions for the future
archiving of Web material, 323–324
change from unexpected directions, 324
embedded computers, 322
fatter electronic pipelines, 323

intelligent info-bots, 322
Internet backlash, 324
personal programming, 322
smarter search engines, 321
ultra-personal programming, 322–323
virtual environments, 323
Price, Gary, 84, D28
prior art search, 185
private companies, 199, 205
professional online services
advantages of using, 126–127
choosing a service, 146–148
cost of, 126, 129
databases in, 127–128, 130
defined, 15
Dialog, 132–140, 147, D10
directory listing of, D10–D11
Dow Jones Interactive, 129–132, 147, D10
hints on when to use, 22–23
information pyramids in, 127–128
LEXIS-NEXIS, 141–143, 144, 147–148, D10–11
newsletters of, 282–283
quirks of, 125
three-step process for searching, 129
professionalism and information use
assessment of information quality, 292–297, D19
attribution, 290
audit trails, 290
copyright issues, 286–289
YOYOW (you own your own words), 291
Project Gutenberg, 98, D7
proprietary resources, 14. See also gated sites or services
ProQuest Direct, 144
prospecting, sales
business directories for, 219
CompaniesOnline for, 219
defined, 194, 218
Dun & Bradstreet Marketing Connection, 220
mailing list brokers and, 218
proximity operators, 33–35
public companies, 199, 205
public domain, works in the, 288
Public Library, Internet, 91, D27

publications, online
magazines, 236–241, 256–257, 283
newsletters, 277–282
newspapers, 231–236
pure subject catalogs
About.com, 79–80, D27
Argus Clearinghouse, 78, D27
World Wide Web Virtual Library, 77–78, 79, 271, D27
push services
CNN's personalized news page, 244–245
Daily Brief, The, 242
defined, 241
In-Box Direct, 242, D18
My Yahoo!, 244
NewsHound, 243
NewsPage, 243
Northern Light Search Alert, 243–244

• Q •

quality of information
accountability for Web site, 293
bias of Web site, 294
critical filters for judging, 296–297
currency, 294
editorial review of databases, 293
experts' backgrounds and credentials, 295
integrity of online documents, 294–295
reputation of online literature, 292
resources for evaluating, 296, D19
Query Server, D26
questions for better research results
Am I likely to find my answers online?, 304
How do I know the information is good?, 307–308
Is online the best place to look?, 304–305
reference interview, 18–19, 301
What am I trying to accomplish?, 302
What else should I consider?, 303–304
What have I gathered so far?, 306
What have I overlooked?, 306–307
What is this really worth?, 302–303
What's my plan?, 305
Who's likely to know the answer?, 305–306
Quint, Barbara, D5

• R •

Rapidly Changing Face of Computing, The, 281
Raynor, Tom, 262
ready references, 22, 89
recipes and cooking tips, 266–267
recreational research
  birding, 273–274
  genealogy, 268
  movies, 267–270
  music, 270–272
  recipes and cooking tips, 266–267
Red Herring (periodical), 224
reference ace, becoming a, 94
reference books on the Net
  directory listing on, D19–D20
  Encyclopedia Britannica, 95–96, D19
  Roget's Thesaurus, 96
  Webster's Dictionary, 96
  World Factbook, The, 95, D20
reference collections, virtual
  Internet Public Library, 91, D27
  ready reference collection and, 89, 90
  Research-It!, 92–93, D19
  Virtual Reference Desk, 92, D20
  Yahoo! reference collection, 94
reference goodies on the Net
  area code lookup, 97
  History Channel, The, 97
  How Things Work search form, 97, D21
reference interview, 18–19, 301
reference questions, 90
relevance ranking, defined, 26
RemarQ search engine, 59–60, 153–154, D24
Remember icon, 6
remodeling a house, 260
research, online
  copyright and, 286–289
  as fun, 7
  Internet Directory for, D1–D30
  misconceptions about, 14
  quality of information from, 292–297, D19
  questions for better results from, 301–308
  reference interview, 18–19, 301
  responsible use of information from, 290–291
  tips for streamlined searching, 309–320
research groups, D20

Research Lingo icon, 6
research tools on CD packaged with this book, 328–329
researcher
  Boolean searching by, 29–33
  case-sensitivity tips for, 38–39
  characteristics of good, 2–3
  common problems facing, 25–29
  field searching done by, 35–36
  mental-mapping of online resources by, 20–23
  pluralization, truncation, and wild cards used by, 36–37
  preparation done by, 17
  project completion by, 39–40
  proximity operators used by, 33–35
  reality-checking done by, 24–25
  reference interview done by, 18–19, 301
Researching Online For Dummies, 2nd Edition
  conventions and icons used in, 5–6
  new stuff in this edition, 6–7
  parts of, 4–5
Researching Online For Dummies CD
  Internet Directory links and, 332
  Internet tools on, 329–330
  Mac OS and, 326–327
  Microsoft Windows and, 325–326
  problems with, 333
  research help on, 327–328
  research tools on, 328–329
  system requirements, 325
  utilities on, 330–331
Researching Online For Dummies Internet Directory
  about the Net/staying current, D5–D6
  art, literature, and history, D6–D7
  business, finance, and economics, D7–D9
  document delivery services, D9–D10
  gated sites, D10–D11
  government and law, D11–D12
  libraries, schools, and universities, D12–D13
  magazines and journals, D13–D14
  micons in, D4
  navigation aids and organizing tools, D14
  news, D15–D18
  quality of information, D19

reference books, D19–D20

research groups, D20

science, technology, and medicine, D21–D22

search engines, subject catalogs, and guides, D22–D29

virtual communities and conferencing systems, D29–D30

Research-It! reference collection, 92–93

responsible use of information

attribution, 290

audit trails, 290

copyright issues, 286–289

YOYOW (you own your own words), 291

Responsive Database Services, 144

results list, defined, 26

Reuters Web site, 237, D18

Rheingold, Howard, 161, 284

Roget's Thesaurus, 96

• *S* •

Sackman, Gleason, D5

sales prospecting

business directories for, 219

CompaniesOnline for, 219

defined, 194, 218

Dun & Bradstreet Marketing Connection, 220

mailing list brokers for, 218

Salon online magazine, 245

San Francisco's Exploratorium, 190

SavvySearch meta-engine, 53

Schmich, Mary, 295

SciCentral site, 190, D22

Science News Web site, 191

sci-tech information

average person's need for, 182

Dialog database service for, 183–185

patents, 183, 185–189

sites for satisfying scientific curiosity, 189–192

Virtual Frog Dissection Kit, 86

World Wide Web's origin and, 181–182

Scott, Peter, D14

Scout Report for Science & Engineering, The, 190

Search Engine Report, 281–282, D6

Search Engine Showdown site, 56

Search Engine Watch site, 56

search engines

choosing a search engine, 45–46

general, 44, 46–51, D22–D23

meta-engines, 44, 52–54, D25–D26

offline meta alternatives, 55–56

pros and cons of, 20

smarter, 321

specialty, 57–58, D23–D25

tips for using, 44

types of, 44

Web rings and, 87

Web sites that compare and monitor, 56

Search.com, 58, D26

searching versus surfing, 2

Seidman, Robert, 280, D6

Seidman's Online Insider, 280, D6

self-questioning for better research results

Am I likely to find my answers online?, 304

How do I know the information is good?, 307–308

Is online the best place to look?, 304–305

reference interview, 18–19, 301

What am I trying to accomplish?, 302

What else should I consider?, 303–304

What have I gathered so far?, 306

What have I overlooked?, 306–307

What is this really worth?, 302–303

What's my plan?, 305

Who's likely to know the answer?, 305–306

Shakespeare, William, D7

shareware versus freeware, 331

Shareware.com, 69–70, D24

Sherlock offline meta-engine, 56

Skilton, John, 86

Smithsonian Institute, 191

SOAR (Searchable Online Archive of Recipes), 266–267

Social Law Library, 85, D12

Society of Competitive Intelligence Professionals, 210, D20

soft news, defined, 23

software shopping

Download.com for, 70, D24

Shareware.com for, 69–70, D24

spam filters, 166

spamming, invisible, 28
specialized search engines, defined, 44
specialty search engines, Web sites on
  All-in-One Search Page, 57–58, D26
  Beaucoup, 58, D26
  Search.com, 58, D26
Spider, Subject Search, D29
spiders, defined, 14
sports information
  Baseball Links site, 86
  ESPN, 230–231
start page, browser, 309–311
starting on the right track
  assumptions about, 19
  summary of resources, 20–23
Statistical Abstracts of the United States, 176
statistical resources on the Web, D8–D9
statistics, government
  Economic Statistics Briefing Room,
    175–176
  U.S. Census Bureau, 176
staying current
  CNN's personalized news page, 244–245
  Daily Brief, The, 242
  In-Box Direct, 242, D18
  Individual.com, D18
  My Yahoo!, 244
  NewsHound, 243
  NewsPage, 243
  Northern Light Search Alert, 243–244
  push technology for, 241
Stevenson, Robert Louis, 98
stocks and investment research
  Daily Stocks site for, 222, 223, D7
  defined, 194, 220
  discussion groups for, 223–224
  Dow Jones Interactive site for, 222, 223
  EDGAR (Electronic Data Gathering
    Analysis and Retrieval), 221, D9
  FinancialWeb for, 223
  InvestorGuide for, 223
  misc.invest FAQ, 224, D8
  Motley Fool site for, 224, D8
  PR Newswire Investment Profiles section
    for, 223
  TheStreet.com for, 223
  Wall Street Research Net for, 223
  Yahoo! Finance for, 222

streamlining your searches by
  bookmarking sites, 311–313, 319
  changing browser start page, 309–311
  fighting link rot, 313–314
  having a cookie, 315–317
  minimizing browsing time, 317–318
  paying attention online, 318–319
  resisting distractions, 319
  sharing your discoveries, 320
  turning images off, 314–315
  using aggregated sources, 319–320
StuffIt Expander, 330
StuffIt Lite (Mac program), 331
subject catalogs
  hints on when to use, 21, 73
  hybrid, 73–76
  narrowing your search with, 71–72
  pure, 77–80
  versus search engines, 72–73
  for vacation planning, 262–263
subscribing to electronic updates
  as answer to information overload, 277
  Edupage, 280–281
  Net-happenings, 279, D5–D6
  Netsurfer Digest, 278, D6
  NEW-LIST, 279–280
  NewsScan, 281
  Rapidly Changing Face of Computing,
    The, 281
  Search Engine Report, 281–282, D6
  Seidman's Online Insider, 280, D6
SunSITE, 111, D7
surfing, 2
SurfSaver (on CD), 328–329
Switchboard, 60, 62, D25
synonyms, finding, 96

• T •

Technical Stuff icon, 6
telnet, 14
Templeton, Brad, 289
thinking like a researcher
  with Boolean searching, 29–33
  case-sensitivity tips, 38–39
  characteristics of good researchers, 2–3
  field searching, 35–36
  knowing when you're done, 39–40
  mental-mapping of online resources, 20–23

pluralization, truncation, and wild cards, 36–37

problem-solving when bad things happen, 25–29

proximity operators for, 33–35

reality-checking, 24–25

reference interview for, 18–19, 301

Third Age site, 162, D30

Thomas site on legislation, 174–175, D12

Thomson & Thomson, D9

Tillman, Hope, D19

Time Web site, 236

time-saving tips
  bookmarking sites, 311–313, 319
  changing browser start page, 309–311
  fighting link rot, 313–314
  having a cookie, 315–317
  minimizing browsing time, 317–318
  paying attention online, 318–319
  resisting distractions, 319
  sharing your discoveries, 320
  turning images off, 314–315
  using aggregated sources, 319–320

Tip icon, 6

Tondreault, Stephen, 222

trademark searching, 217, D9

travel
  cruise lines, 262
  newsgroups on, 261
  RemarQ for, 262
  subject catalogs on, 262–263
  travel agents and, 259

trends
  archiving of Web material, 323–324
  change from unexpected directions, 324
  embedded computers, 322
  fatter electronic pipelines, 323
  intelligent info-bots, 322
  Internet backlash, 324
  personal programming, 322
  smarter search engines, 321
  ultra-personal programming, 322–323
  virtual environments, 323

tricks of the trade
  Boolean searching, 29–33
  case-sensitivity tips, 38–39
  for common problems, 25–29
  field searching, 35–36
  mental-mapping of online resources, 20–23

pluralization, truncation, and wild cards, 36–37

project completion questions, 39–40

proximity operators, 33–35

reality-checking, 24–25

reference interview, 18–19, 301

truncation, defined, 29, 37

• *U* •

UnCover document delivery service, D10

United Press International Web site, 237, D18

updates, automatic
  CNN's personalized news page, 244–245
  Daily Brief, The, 242
  defined, 241
  In-Box Direct, 242, D18
  My Yahoo!, 244
  NewsHound, 243
  NewsPage, 243
  Northern Light Search Alert, 243–244

updates on online developments
  Cyberskeptic's Guide to Internet Research, The, 283, D5
  Edupage, 280–281
  Internet World, 283
  Net-happenings, 279, D5–D6
  Netsurfer Digest, 278, D6
  NEW-LIST, 279–280
  NewsScan, 281
  from personal contacts, 284
  Rapidly Changing Face of Computing, The, 281
  Search Engine Report, 281–282, D6
  Seidman's Online Insider, 280, D6
  system-specific newsletters, 282–283

Upside (periodical), 224

URLs in this book, 5

U.S. Census Bureau, 176

U.S. government information
  Census Bureau site, 176
  depth and variety of, 170
  Economic Statistics Briefing Room, 175–176
  FedWorld search options for, 171–173, D11
  IRS site, 171–172
  Thomas site on legislation, 174–175
  USGovsearch from Northern Light, 175

U.S. Library of Congress
  catalog on the Web, 103–104
  directory description of, D13
  site, 12
U.S. News & World Report site, 236
U.S. Patent and Trademark Office (PTO)
    Web site, 186–188, D22
USA Today site, 232, D16
use of information
  attribution, 290
  audit trails, 290
  copyright issues, 286–289
  YOYOW (you own your own words), 291
Usenet. *See* newsgroups

• *V* •

vacation planning
  cruise lines, 262
  newsgroups for, 261
  RemarQ for, 262
  subject catalogs for, 262–263
  travel agents and, 259
Vault.com, 198
virtual communities
  defined, 161–162
  Forum One as guide to, D29–D30
  Parent Soup, 162, D30
  SF Gate, 162, D30
  surveying range of, 163
  Third Age, 162, D30
  The Well, 162, 163, 246, D30
virtual environments, 323
Virtual Frog Dissection Kit, 86
Virtual Library, World Wide Web, 77–78, 79,
  271, D27
Virtual Reference Desk, 92, D20
Vonnegut, Kurt, 294, 295

• *W* •

Wall Street Journal Interactive Edition
  directory description of, D9
  as gated information service, 117,
    119–120
  as members-only Web site, 16, 23
Wall Street Research Net, 223
Warning icon, 6
Washington Post site, 232, D17

Weather Channel site, 231, D16
Web rings, 87, D28–D29
Web spiders, defined, 14
WebCATS, 101–102, D13
Webforia software (on CD), 329
Webster's Dictionary, 96
WebWhacker 2000 (on CD), 329
wild card, defined, 37
Wilde, Oscar, 98
WinZip 7.0 (shareware version), 331
wire services, 237, D17–D18
Wired magazine, 49, 283
Wired News
  copyright policy, 289
  directory description of, D17
Wiretap Gopher, Internet, 13, D14
Wodehouse, P.G., 98
work for hire, 286
World Factbook, 95, D20
World Intellectual Property Office (WIPO),
  186, D22
World Wide Web Virtual Library, 77–78,
  79, D27
WorldPages, 66, D25

• *X* •

Xinhua News Agency, 237, D18

• *Y* •

Yahoo!, directory description of, D27
Yahoo!, My, 244
Yahoo! Finance, 222
Yahoo! People Search, 60–61, D25
Yahoo! reference collection, 94
Yahoo! subject catalog, 73–75
Yahoo! web rings, 87
YOYOW (you own your own words), 291

• *Z* •

zero-hits scenario, problem-solving for, 27

IDG Books Worldwide, Inc., End-User License Agreement

READ THIS. You should carefully read these terms and conditions before opening the software packet(s) included with this book ("Book"). This is a license agreement ("Agreement") between you and IDG Books Worldwide, Inc. ("IDGB"). By opening the accompanying software packet(s), you acknowledge that you have read and accept the following terms and conditions. If you do not agree and do not want to be bound by such terms and conditions, promptly return the Book and the unopened software packet(s) to the place you obtained them for a full refund.

1. **License Grant.** IDGB grants to you (either an individual or entity) a nonexclusive license to use one copy of the enclosed software program(s) (collectively, the "Software") solely for your own personal or business purposes on a single computer (whether a standard computer or a workstation component of a multiuser network). The Software is in use on a computer when it is loaded into temporary memory (RAM) or installed into permanent memory (hard disk, CD-ROM, or other storage device). IDGB reserves all rights not expressly granted herein.

2. **Ownership.** IDGB is the owner of all right, title, and interest, including copyright, in and to the compilation of the Software recorded on the disk(s) or CD-ROM ("Software Media"). Copyright to the individual programs recorded on the Software Media is owned by the author or other authorized copyright owner of each program. Ownership of the Software and all proprietary rights relating thereto remain with IDGB and its licensers.

3. **Restrictions on Use and Transfer.**

   (a) You may only (i) make one copy of the Software for backup or archival purposes, or (ii) transfer the Software to a single hard disk, provided that you keep the original for backup or archival purposes. You may not (i) rent or lease the Software, (ii) copy or reproduce the Software through a LAN or other network system or through any computer subscriber system or bulletin-board system, or (iii) modify, adapt, or create derivative works based on the Software.

   (b) You may not reverse engineer, decompile, or disassemble the Software. You may transfer the Software and user documentation on a permanent basis, provided that the transferee agrees to accept the terms and conditions of this Agreement and you retain no copies. If the Software is an update or has been updated, any transfer must include the most recent update and all prior versions.

4. **Restrictions on Use of Individual Programs.** You must follow the individual requirements and restrictions detailed for each individual program in the "About the CD" appendix of this Book. These limitations are also contained in the individual license agreements recorded on the Software Media. These limitations may include a requirement that after using the program for a specified period of time, the user must pay a registration fee or discontinue use. By opening the Software packet(s), you will be agreeing to abide by the licenses and restrictions for these individual programs that are detailed in the "About the CD" appendix and on the Software Media. None of the material on this Software Media or listed in this Book may ever be redistributed, in original or modified form, for commercial purposes.

5. Limited Warranty.

(a) IDGB warrants that the Software and Software Media are free from defects in materials and workmanship under normal use for a period of sixty (60) days from the date of purchase of this Book. If IDGB receives notification within the warranty period of defects in materials or workmanship, IDGB will replace the defective Software Media.

(b) IDGB AND THE AUTHOR OF THE BOOK DISCLAIM ALL OTHER WARRANTIES, EXPRESS OR IMPLIED, INCLUDING WITHOUT LIMITATION IMPLIED WARRANTIES OF MERCHANTABILITY AND FITNESS FOR A PARTICULAR PURPOSE, WITH RESPECT TO THE SOFTWARE, THE PROGRAMS, THE SOURCE CODE CONTAINED THEREIN, AND/OR THE TECHNIQUES DESCRIBED IN THIS BOOK. IDGB DOES NOT WARRANT THAT THE FUNCTIONS CONTAINED IN THE SOFTWARE WILL MEET YOUR REQUIRE-MENTS OR THAT THE OPERATION OF THE SOFTWARE WILL BE ERROR FREE.

(c) This limited warranty gives you specific legal rights, and you may have other rights that vary from jurisdiction to jurisdiction.

6. Remedies.

(a) IDGB's entire liability and your exclusive remedy for defects in materials and workmanship shall be limited to replacement of the Software Media, which may be returned to IDGB with a copy of your receipt at the following address: Software Media Fulfillment Department, Attn.: *Researching Online For Dummies,* 2nd Edition, IDG Books Worldwide, Inc., 10475 Crosspoint Boulevard, Indianapolis, IN 46256, or call 800-762-2974. Please allow three to four weeks for delivery. This Limited Warranty is void if failure of the Software Media has resulted from accident, abuse, or misapplication. Any replacement Software Media will be warranted for the remainder of the original warranty period or thirty (30) days, whichever is longer.

(b) In no event shall IDGB or the author be liable for any damages whatsoever (including without limitation damages for loss of business profits, business interruption, loss of business information, or any other pecuniary loss) arising from the use of or inability to use the Book or the Software, even if IDGB has been advised of the possibility of such damages.

(c) Because some jurisdictions do not allow the exclusion or limitation of liability for consequential or incidental damages, the above limitation or exclusion may not apply to you.

7. U.S. Government Restricted Rights. Use, duplication, or disclosure of the Software by the U.S. Government is subject to restrictions stated in paragraph (c)(1)(ii) of the Rights in Technical Data and Computer Software clause of DFARS 252.227-7013, and in subparagraphs (a) through (d) of the Commercial Computer–Restricted Rights clause at FAR 52.227-19, and in similar clauses in the NASA FAR supplement, when applicable.

8. General. This Agreement constitutes the entire understanding of the parties and revokes and supersedes all prior agreements, oral or written, between them and may not be modified or amended except in a writing signed by both parties hereto that specifically refers to this Agreement. This Agreement shall take precedence over any other documents that may be in conflict herewith. If any one or more provisions contained in this Agreement are held by any court or tribunal to be invalid, illegal, or otherwise unenforceable, each and every other provision shall remain in full force and effect.

IDG BOOKS WORLDWIDE BOOK REGISTRATION

We want to hear from you!

Visit **http://my2cents.dummies.com** to register this book and tell us how you liked it!

- ✔ Get entered in our monthly prize giveaway.
- ✔ Give us feedback about this book — tell us what you like best, what you like least, or maybe what you'd like to ask the author and us to change!
- ✔ Let us know any other *...For Dummies*® topics that interest you.

Your feedback helps us determine what books to publish, tells us what coverage to add as we revise our books, and lets us know whether we're meeting your needs as a *...For Dummies* reader. You're our most valuable resource, and what you have to say is important to us!

Not on the Web yet? It's easy to get started with *Dummies 101*®: *The Internet For Windows*® 98 or *The Internet For Dummies*®, 6th Edition, at local retailers everywhere.

Or let us know what you think by sending us a letter at the following address:

...For Dummies Book Registration
Dummies Press
10475 Crosspoint Blvd.
Indianapolis, IN 46256

BESTSELLING
BOOK SERIES

Installation Instructions

Please see the Appendix for full details on the CD and its contents.

Using the CD with Microsoft Windows

1. **Insert the CD into your computer's CD-ROM drive.**

2. **Click Start⇨Run.**

3. **In the dialog box that appears, type** D:\

4. **Double-click the file called License.txt.**

   This file contains the end-user license that you agree to by using the CD. When you are done reading the license, close the program, most likely NotePad, that displayed the file.

5. **Double-click the file called Readme.txt.**

   This file contains instructions about installing the software from this CD. It might be helpful to leave this text file open while you are using the CD.

6. **Double-click the folder for the software you are interested in.**

   Be sure to read the descriptions of the programs in the appendix (much of this information also shows up in the Readme file). These descriptions give you more precise information about the programs' folder names and about finding and running the installer program.

7. **Find the file called Setup.exe, or Install.exe, or something similar, and double-click that file.**

   The program's installer walks you through the process of setting up your new software.

Using the CD with a Mac OS

1. **Insert the CD into your computer's CD-ROM drive.**

2. **Double-click the CD icon to show the CD's contents.**

3. **Double-click the Read Me First icon. (The Read Me First text file contains information about the CD's programs and other contents.)**

4. **To install most items, just drag the folder from the CD window and drop it on your hard drive icon.**

5. **Some programs come with installer programs. With these programs, you simply open the program's folder on the CD, and then double-click the icon with the words "Install" or "Installer."**

   Just double-click any file with .sea in the name, and it will run just like an installer.